The Black Book of Warwick. Transcribed and edited by Thomas Kemp.

Anonymous, Thomas Kemp

The Black Book of Warwick. Transcribed and edited by Thomas Kemp.
Anonymous
British Library, Historical Print Editions
British Library
Kemp, Thomas
1898
xxx. 465 p. ; 4°.
10360.dd.24.

The BiblioLife Network

This project was made possible in part by the BiblioLife Network (BLN), a project aimed at addressing some of the huge challenges facing book preservationists around the world. The BLN includes libraries, library networks, archives, subject matter experts, online communities and library service providers. We believe every book ever published should be available as a high-quality print reproduction; printed on- demand anywhere in the world. This insures the ongoing accessibility of the content and helps generate sustainable revenue for the libraries and organizations that work to preserve these important materials.

The following book is in the "public domain" and represents an authentic reproduction of the text as printed by the original publisher. While we have attempted to accurately maintain the integrity of the original work, there are sometimes problems with the original book or micro-film from which the books were digitized. This can result in minor errors in reproduction. Possible imperfections include missing and blurred pages, poor pictures, markings and other reproduction issues beyond our control. Because this work is culturally important, we have made it available as part of our commitment to protecting, preserving, and promoting the world's literature.

GUIDE TO FOLD-OUTS, MAPS and OVERSIZED IMAGES

In an online database, page images do not need to conform to the size restrictions found in a printed book. When converting these images back into a printed bound book, the page sizes are standardized in ways that maintain the detail of the original. For large images, such as fold-out maps, the original page image is split into two or more pages.

Guidelines used to determine the split of oversize pages:

- Some images are split vertically; large images require vertical and horizontal splits.
- For horizontal splits, the content is split left to right.
- For vertical splits, the content is split from top to bottom.
- For both vertical and horizontal splits, the image is processed from top left to bottom right.

The Black Book of Warwick.

The Black Book of Warwick

Transcribed and Edited by

Thomas Kemp,

Deputy-Mayor of Warwick.

Henry T. Cooke and Son.
Publishers.
High Street. Warwick.

PREFACE.

During the term of my Mayoralty I had the opportunity of perusing the old volume preserved among the archives of the Borough, known as the "Black Book of Warwick," and was so much interested in tracing the doings of those, who more than 300 years ago trod our streets, conducted their public business in buildings still existing, and worshipped in the same beautiful edificies in which congregations now assemble, that from time to time I made extracts, which were published in the Warwick Advertiser: these extracts appear to have been read with interest by my fellow-townsmen, and so I have been induced to make a transcript of the book, with the few exceptions of copies of leases and wills entered in the book. The various elections of Bailiffs and principal burgesses are in many cases not given in full, as they are merely repetitions. A great many pages of the Black Book are taken up with copies of Corporation leases and the wills and deeds of gifts of donors of local charities. As these can scarcely be called original portions of the book, and as the charities are known and administered in the town, and as the wills and deeds are already published, they have not been copied. An exception has been made in giving some extracts from the Will of Thomas Oken, because he occupies a prominent place in the

PREFACE.

Book. The rules and ordinances of the different Guilds are set out in full; they are for the most part identical, but differ in some particulars: they show that the members of the Guilds were rigid protectionists. Some years ago the earlier portion of the Black Book was, as far as the visit of Queen Elizabeth, published in the Warwickshire Antiquarian Magazine, and it is to be regretted that the learned Editor did not complete his work. I can only add that as I went on reading and copying the Book, I began to feel almost a personal interest in the sayings and doings and careers of the people, who play their part in the events narrated in its pages, and I felt a further interest in following some of them in the Registers and Churchwardens' Accounts of St. Nicholas Parish, as published from the careful transcripts of Mr. R. Savage, of Stratford-on-Avon, (St. Mary's earlier ones having been lost), and there they are found acting as Churchwardens, paying their pew rents, &c., until the item of "bell money" tells us when they ceased to have any thing to do with the affairs of the Borough. I have supplied a few notes for the most part explanatory of matters relating to local circumstances, which would otherwise be unintelligible to readers not acquainted with the locality, or with local matters; otherwise I have not attempted any commentary on the Book, as it, for the most part, speaks for itself. I believe that I have made a careful and correct copy of the manuscript, and even in cases where the writer has manifestly made an error, I have not made an alteration, as I wished to give an exact transcript of the original. Wherever there is a blank space between brackets, this indicates that there is a blank in the original; where there is a blank unbracketed, the word in the original has not been deciphered. The marginal notes have been printed, some in old English type, and some in Roman type, to represent respectively the legal text hand and ordinary hand-writing of the original. A few of the marginal notes were evidently made subsequently to the writing of the narrative and by another person. To the Mayor and my other colleagues in the Corporation I tender my thanks for an extended loan of our literary treasure. In conclusion I should like to add that I have ventured to issue this edition of the Black Book, as it seemed to me to be a pity that so interesting a manuscript should longer remain unpublished.

WARWICK.
1898.
                                                                                  THOMAS KEMP.

INTRODUCTION.

WARWICK AS IT WAS DURING THE EARLIER PERIODS DEALT WITH IN THE

BLACK BOOK.

Although the Black Book is a history of Warwick, particularly during the reign of Queen Elizabeth, yet it contains no description of the town, and therefore I ventured to think that it would be of interest and an assistance to readers to have presented to them from such other sources as are available, a sketch of Elizabethan Warwick, the home of the people mentioned in the Black Book during its earlier period. I have therefore endeavoured, so far as I am able, to give a description of the Warwick in which the various events narrated in the Black Book took place. The materials for the Sketch are derived from Leland, Dugdale's Warwickshire, the Book of John Fisher, which is an interesting manuscript written by Mr. Fisher, (1580 to 1588), for the most part devoted to records of magisterial proceedings, and another old minute book, both of which hitherto unnoticed volumes I was so fortunate as to discover among the Corporation archives, old plans of the town, a drawing and ground plan of old St. Mary's, in All Souls College Library, Oxford, and references to the town in the Black Book.

INTRODUCTION.

THE STREETS AND BUILDINGS.

The main thoroughfares and chief features of Warwick in the 16th century were much the same as they are now. Although the great fire of 1694 destroyed a large portion of the town, as well as the nave of St. Mary's Church, there are still enough of the old houses remaining to shew us what the Warwick of that day was like. Near to the present Court House in Jury Street, which probably occupies the site of the old one (see p. 225) there stood a cross, which is often referred to as the High Cross or simply the Cross. If any one will stand at this spot with his back to the Court House he will have Church Street and St. Mary's Church facing him; on his right down Jury Street he will see one of the old gates of the town, viz. the East Gate, with St. Peter's Chapel above it, on his left up High Street, called in Elizabeth's days High Pavement, he will see another gate, the West Gate, with St. James's Chapel above it. Both these gateways at the time of the commencement of the Black Book were in a ruinous condition, and most of the town walls were down. The North Gate, which stood in Northgate Street, had even at that time disappeared.[1] The Castle stood for the South Gate. The beautiful Chancel of St. Mary's, the Vestry and Chapter House, and the Beauchamp Chapel were much the same as at present. Opposite to the Chapter House a door, now filled up by a cupboard, led into the Chancel, and the screen dividing the lobby from the Vestry was not then pierced for a doorway. In the south-east angle of the South Transept there was a circular staircase leading to an organ loft at the west end of the Beauchamp Chapel.[2] The body of the Church which covered nearly the same area as the existing one consisted of nave,

(1) Leland.
(2) Ground plan of the Church in Library of All Souls College, Oxford.

INTRODUCTION.

aisles and transepts, of shallower projection than the present ones, the nave having four bays, and being lighted by six clerestory windows, and in the walls of each aisle were three windows. The transept windows were large and handsome, and somewhat similar to the Chancel east window.[3] At the east end of the South Aisle stood the large altar tomb, with canopy over, of Thomas Beauchamp Earl of Warwick, who built the nave in the latter half of the 14th century, and of his Countess,[4] but this was destroyed in the great fire. The brass effigies which were on the tomb however survived, and are now placed against the east wall of the south transept. St. Mary's was then, as now, sometimes called the High Church, either from its position on the top of the hill, or from its being the principal Church in the town.[4a] The Tower was lower than the present one, and over the South Porch there was a room, which had been once occupied by John Rous the Warwickshire Antiquary, who died in 1491, and was buried in St. Mary's.[5] The tower appears to have contained a peal of eight bells.[6] St. Nicholas Church, possibly as old as St. Mary's, was pulled down and re-built in 1779. Our information with regard to old St. Nicholas is very meagre, as there are no plans or drawings extant, except the distant view in Hollar's view of Warwick, in Dugdale, and in some other old engravings. It consisted, in Elizabeth's reign, of nave, chancel, and west-end

(3) South Elevation of Church in All Souls Library.

(4) Dugdale's Warwickshire, p. 324.

(4a) Among the letters published by the Camden Society there is a begging letter from a Mr. Leach, Master of Arts, to Sir Robert Throckmorton, in which he says, "you mynistred unto mee in the highe Church of Warwike, in the latter dayes of our late souerayn Queen Marie."

(5) Bloxam's Churches of Warwickshire, Vol. 1, p. 12.

(6) Oken's Will, "I will that the viij ringers shall have for their paynes viij"

INTRODUCTION.

tower and spire, and had a north porch. In the churchyard there was a cross. The Tower contained a clock and bells, which were continually being repaired. A bell was rung at 5 o'clock in the morning, and at 8 o'clock at night. The Church roof was of shingles, i. e. thin pieces of wood instead of tiles, which were frequently renewed.(5a) The Chancel was also roofed with shingles.(5b) The Priory, on the north side of the town, now the residence of S. S. Lloyd, Jun., Esq., was then a modern building, occupying the site however of a very old ecclesiastical establishment. In a westerly direction from the Northgate ran a street called Walldyke. In the Saltisford, in a decayed condition, stood St. Michael's Church. The remains of this building, consisting of the east and west gables, the walls and a portion of the roof, now form part of a blacksmith's forge. Going westwards from St. Mary's, we pass through the Old Square, and reach the Market Place. In Elizabeth's time the Old Square was called Pibble Lane, and in it were Oken's almshouses: these were destroyed by the great fire, and were re-built adjoining Eyffler's houses on the Castle Hill. In the Market Place there stood a Booth Hall, in which were shops let to tenants for terms as long as 21 years, and somewhere near to the spot which the Market Hall and Museum now occupy, there were the remains of St. John the Baptist's Church, even then a ruin, of which no vestige now remains.(7) In the Market

---

(5a) Churchwarden's Accounts. In the account of 1572, "It'm payde to John Woode for wasshynge off the churche & clansynge the crosse in the church yarde vj· viij^d." In 1582, "Item payde for mendynge off porche vj^d." In 1589 the porch is spoken of as on the north side. In 1597, "p^d to Thomas peyne his wholl yeares wages for over seinge the clocke & to Ringe five a clocke in the morning & eight at night xx·."

(5b) The book of John Fisher, Bailiff's Accounts, "Item for CCC Shingles bought & occupied in the Roof of the chancell of St Nicholas Church in Warwick x·."

(7) Dugdale's Warwickshire, p. 362.

INTRODUCTION.

Place also, stood the pillory,(8) and the stocks. Towards the north side there was a Market Cross, which was afterwards pulled down by Col. Purefoy during the Civil War between Charles 1st and the Parliament.(9) Close by here was Horse Chipping or the Horse Market. Turning down Brook Street, then called Cow Lane at the lower end of which was the Rother Chipping or Beast Market, we come to the Leycester Hospital, which presents the same appearance now as it did in Elizabeth's reign, although even at that time it was of respectable age, having been built in the latter half of the 14th century.(10) Close to this is the West Gate. Somewhere near to West Street stood St. Lawrence's tithe barn. From the South side of the West Gate ran a lane called Britten Lane in which were several barns and gardens.(11) From the West Gate the street runs straight to the East Gate. Beyond this gate is Smith Street, in which stood another tithe barn. Turning southward from the East Gate, and going down Castle Hill, we come to Mill Street, which is full of ancient half-timbered houses; at the bottom of this street, which runs down to the Avon, the river was spanned by a bridge of many arches, spoken of as the great bridge, and now a picturesque ruin. Over this bridge we come to Bridge End, which was once a more populous suburb of Warwick than at present, and turning to the left the road leads to Myton; it was over this bridge that Queen Elizabeth rode when she

---

(8) Old Minute Book, p 107. 18th of May, 1632, "It is agreed that a survey be presently made and a computacon what the charges will amount unto to paue the markett place about the pillorie."

(9) Bloxam's Churches of Warwickshire, Vol. 1., p. 63.

(10) Rous' Roll "In hys tyme he (i. e. Thomas Beauchamp Earl of Warwick) be gan the gold (guild) of the trinite and seynt Georg of Warwick."

(11) The Book of John Fisher.

INTRODUCTION.

entered Warwick; it was over this bridge also that the Bailiff and his company passed, when they went to Myton to vindicate the law, as described in the account of the Myton riots. As the road over this bridge was the highway to London, it must have been a place of some traffic, and the noble owner of the Castle in Elizabeth's days would see from the Castle windows the pack-horses bringing goods to the houses of Thomas Oken and other tradesmen in the town, and altogether gaze upon a busier scene than that presented to the view of the present Earl and Countess. From the bottom of Mill Street another Street, Castle Street, led up by the Castle walls to the High Cross before mentioned. In no part of Warwick have there been so many changes as about the old bridge, consequent on the building of the present bridge, the enlarging of the Castle grounds, and the diversion of the road to the Asps, which took place about 100 years ago. The Castle in Elizabeth's days was more open to the town, and nearer to the boundary than at the present time, as the wall enclosing the grounds was then almost close to the moat. By this wall ran a road which joined Castle Street near to Guy's Tower, and at this point a gate opened into the grounds, from which there was an approach to the Castle gateway. Part of Castle Street, and other ground within the town, were added to the Castle grounds, as before mentioned, by George, Earl of Warwick, at the end of the last century. The gateway between the Bear Tower and Clarence Tower appears to have been opened since Elizabeth's time. The Castle Park then consisted of fields, which were enclosed by George, Earl of Warwick, at the same time that he built the present Castle Bridge, or contributed the greater part of the cost of its erection, and formed the lake, known as the "New Waters," and diverted part of the Banbury and London Road. This road ran across part of the present

INTRODUCTION.

park, and crossed ground now covered by the New Waters. Along this road came Queen Elizabeth, when she visited Warwick in 1572, and on the side of the New Waters, farthest from the town, is Ford Mill Hill, where she was met by the Bailiff, as described in the Black Book, (see page 86). Turning northwards from the East gate we are in the Butts, where stood the Butts for the practice of Archery.

ARCHERY BUTTS. Firearms had not yet superseded the bow and crossbow, and the government felt it necessary to keep an eye on the proficiency of the citizens in archery, and so we find by an entry in the "Book of John Fisher," that there was given in the reign of Elizabeth " xx^s to such persones as came wth the comission to trye how Archery was mayntened w'thin this borough," also £2 14s. 10d. was paid to Mr. Dyche "for the newe making of Saint Marye Buttes this yere and for newe Rales & postes set up about the said butts and for the hire of the workemen laboring there as by his bill pticulerly appereth." In the Butts also stood the Deanery and College; the Deanery is now St. Mary's Vicarage, but the College has been pulled down.

POPULATION. I calculate that the population of Warwick at this period was in round numbers about 2,600. In "John Fisher's Book" the number of households in the six wards in St. Mary's Parish is stated to have been 371: allowing 5 persons to each household, this would give for St. Mary's parish a population of 1855. There were in St. Nicholas Parish two wards, the Smith

INTRODUCTION.

Street ward, and the Bridge end ward; in estimating the population of St. Nicholas, it would hardly be correct to take an average of the wards in St. Mary's, as some of them contained but few houses, and it is probable that in the streets forming the two wards in St. Nicholas parish there were as many households as at the present day, so I have calculated their population on the numbers in the Saltisford ward, which I think would be more on a par with them in population. The Saltisford ward contained 75 houses or 375 people; this number multiplied by two gives 750 as the population of St. Nicholas; add this to 1855 and we have 2,605 as the population of the borough. This estimate is supported by a statement in a petition for an increase of stipend, presented by Mr. Roe, Vicar of St. Nicholas, in 1636, in which he states the number of Communicants in St. Nicholas Parish to be 500; and thus if we calculate in the same proportion as St. Mary's communicants bore to the households, we have about 750 as the population of St. Nicholas Parish in 1636.(12) The above particulars, as regards St. Mary's parish, are derived from a memorandum giving not only the wards and the householders in each ward, but also the number of communicants in the parish of St. Mary's at Easter, 1581: the memorandum, which states that the details were derived from an examination of the book of Communicants at the Festival of Easter is as follows: M^d qd per scrutineum librorū coicantiū ad festū pasch anno xxiij^{cio} R^e Elizabeth inveni numerū coicantū predict. Et sunt in parochia bee Marie Warwic infra wardas subnotas scilt

(12) Old Minute Book, p. 115.

INTRODUCTION.

howseholds

In the mket place warde	Domestici	97	
	comunicantes	393	
In the high pavement	Domestic	40	
	comunicantes	191	Domestic 371
In le castelstrete	Domestic	36	Comunicant 1247 Inde
	coicantes	122	
In le Jury	Domestic	30	femini generis 705
	coicantes	98	masculini 542
In le West strete	Domest	93	
	comunicant	226	
In le saltesford	Domestic	75	
	Comunicant	217	

And then there is this further memorandum, which shows that the population had increased in four years.

per scrutiniū libri coicantiū ad festum pasche 1585 infra parochiam beate Marie Warwic

totalis numerus comunicantiu infra parochiam predict—1321

Inde

masculini generis—609
feminini generis—712

xvii.

INTRODUCTION.

For the year 1586 a full list of communicants is written out, each household being given separately. One household in the High pavement, on account of its being headed by the name of Thos. Cartwright, is evidently a list of the Master and brethren of the Leycester Hospital. Mr. Cartwright was a celebrated Puritan divine, and had only just then recently been appointed Master. I may here remark that the most common christian names among men were Thomas, John, Robert and Richard, and among women, Elizabeth, Isabel, Alice and Marjory or Margaret.

CONDITION OF TRADE. The condition of the trade of Warwick at this period is described by Mr. John Fisher in an interview which he had with the Earl of Leycester, an account of which will be found at p. 45, so that I need not speak of it here. As both the men and women of Elizabeth's time were very extravagant in their dress, we are not surprised to find that the mercers and drapers were the most prosperous tradesmen in the town. The rate of wages to be paid by an employer was settled by the Justices of the peace, and a minimum time of service fixed, and from time to time the Bailiff held his sessions, at which the Jury enquired whether these rules were carried out, and presented any one who paid more than the regulation wage, or engaged a labourer for a shorter time than one year.(13)

SHOPS. From the presentations made by the Jury with regard to the different trades, and by comparing the names of those presented with the list of householders already referred to, it is to some extent possible to judge how

(13) The Book of John Fisher.

INTRODUCTION.

the shops were distributed throughout the town. Some trades seem to have been attached to no particular locality, but the butchers appear to have been located principally in High Pavement and Jury Street; the Mercers, Grocers and Haberdashers in High Pavement, Church Street and Castle Street, and the Tanners, who were numerous, in West Street, Saltisford, Smith Street and Bridge End. Thomas Shakespeare, Butcher, lived in West Street.(14)

MARKET DAY. By the Charter of Philip and Mary, Tuesday and Saturday were appointed Market days; and so on these days buyers and sellers came from all the villages round about to Warwick Market; they came even from villages and places some distance away, as among the licenses to people to sell and buy wheat, rye, barley, &c., in the market, and to badgers, i.e. men who bought corn or grain to sell again for profit, licenses were given to people from Tanworth, Coleshill, Meriden, Minworth, Northfield and King's Norton, and it is curious and interesting to notice that licenses were granted to people from Birmingham and our neighbour borough of Leamington, then the little village of Priors Lemington. On these Market days proclamations, if any, were made from the High Cross, and criminals were publicly whipped about the Market Place.(15) The market tolls were collected, as they are at the present day, by the Sergeant at Mace, who was an officer appointed each year by the bailiff on his entering upon his term of office.(16) There appears to have been a considerable fair on St. Bartholomew's day, when a nag could have been bought for 16s. or 17s., and an ox for £3.(16a) There was also a fair on St. Simon's & St. Jude's day.

(14) The Book of John Fisher.   (15) Ibid.
(16) Ibid, and Old Minute Book, p. 2. and 82.
(16a) The Book of John Fisher.

INTRODUCTION.

INNS AND ALE-HOUSES. For the refreshment of the market folk, there were various hostels and alehouses, the keepers of which were under certain restrictions, such as not to have "dressed or eaten any fleshe in their houses in the time of lent or uppon daies forbidden as fridaies saturdaies or other fishdaies;" vintners were also forbidden to retail "any french or gascoiyn wine above xij^d the gallon or any swete wine or spainesh wine above xvj^d the gallon or to retail wine to be droonke in their owne howses by gallon pottall quarte or pint."[17] In whatever part of the town these houses of refreshment were situated, in all probability there was a good hostelry on or near to the site of the present Warwick Arms Hotel, in High Street, as in the list of householders before mentioned there is entered John Grene and his wife, and eleven others as belonging to one household; this indicates a large house, and as the position of this entry on the list of the householders in the High Pavement corresponds closely with the position of the present hotel in this street, it is highly probable that an hostelry stood on this spot, or at any rate very near to it: moreover Mr. John Grene, who was bailiff at the time of the Myton riots, is spoken of in the Black Book as John Grene of the Crown; so that we may fairly come to the conclusion that in all probability a large Inn called the Crown occupied the site of the present "Warwick Arms." Of course during the Commonwealth the sign of the Crown would be removed, and a new one substituted. There was a Cross Tavern near to the High Cross, and somewhere in the town an Inn with the sign of the Unicorn.[18] There is no further record of the names of any other Inns at this period, but in 1657 there was an Inn called the Bell in the High Pavement,

(17) The Book of John Fisher.
(18) Ibid.

INTRODUCTION.

and another called the King's Head, in Castle Street.(19)   There was a large household in Northgate Street, which rather points to the presence of a large Inn there.

HOUSEHOLDERS.   Thomas Powell had a Draper's shop in the High Pavement, and Richard Roo, a Butcher's shop, and in this street also lived Robert Philips and Thomas Cawdrey, the Executors of Thomas Oken, Thomas Cawdrey being a Butcher, and having a considerable establishment.   Here also lived Richard Griffin, the founder of Griffin's Charity.   In this street one Richard Blick carried on the trade of a Vintner, as in the Churchwarden's accounts for St. Nicholas Parish, there are entries of payments to him for wine for communicants. Richard Fisher, who was six times Bailiff of Warwick, lived in Church Street, and had a household of seven people, communicants, besides Isabell his wife. In this street also was the dwelling of John Fisher.   In Canon Row lived Mr. Martin Deleyn, Vicar of St. Mary's.(20)   Nicholas Eyfler, a well-known benefactor, lived in Jury Street.

SUBSIDIES.   In John Fisher's Book there is a list of the inhabitants taxed and assessed for the payment of subsidies granted by Parliament in 1581 and 1582, and also the amount which the constables of the wards were directed to collect from each person assessed: and in 1584 there was a taxation of inhabitants "towards the furnyture of viij horsemen to be sent unto Irelond out of this county of Warr. in the moneth of September 1584."   In these lists, Nicholas Eyfler is described as a stranger, although he had received a patent of denizenship dated the 29th of March, 1562.

(19) Old Minute Book, p. 154.   (20) The Book of John Fisher.

INTRODUCTION.

RENTS. A list called the task book in John Fisher's book, gives some particulars as to the rents paid for houses, barns and gardens in the town. This list was made up from returns furnished by the constables of the various wards, for the purposes of taxation. The rents vary from 2s. a year for a cottage to 30s. a year for a good-sized house. The cottages were chiefly in the Market Place ward, the Saltisford and West Street, and were let at from 2s. to 5s. The rents of houses in Jury Street and the High Pavement ranged from 4s. to 30s., which latter is written against the name of John Grene, who would be mine host of the Crown before mentioned. A lease of a house in High Pavement was granted to Thomas Powell at an annual rent of 16s. Barns and gardens let at from 2s. to 4s. In some cases there was a condition that the tenant should bring a fat goose, or two fat capons, or two fat hens, or a pig, or a rabbit, or some ribs of beef, or something else in kind in addition to the rent.(21)

VAGRANTS. There seem to have been a good many men and women tramping about in search of work, as people from all parts of the County, as well as from Yorkshire, Lancashire, Lincolnshire, and other Counties were brought up before the magistrates and examined as to their means of support. These examinates included the scholar who made his moan to the Vicar, the travelling doctor, the man who journeyed from place to place with a false passport, and the common vagrant, who was sent to the stocks for a day and a night as a rogue. The ruffian also, the drunkard, the common thief, the Sabbath breaker, and the recusant, who absolutely refused to go to the Church, were all features in Elizabethan Warwick. There were also a considerable number of beggars, both men and women and children about the town.

(21) Old Minute Book passim.

INTRODUCTION.

RELIEF OF THE POOR. For the relief of the poor the Bailiff and principall burgesses assessed the amount which each person considered capable of contributing, was ordered to give weekly, the amount ranging from 1s. to ½d., those giving ½d. being chiefly in St. Nicholas' Parish, and they also appointed the sum which the poor were to receive weekly, the sums given varying from 1s. to 1d.(22)

SCHOOLS There was a free Grammar School, which is supposed to have existed since Edward the Confessor's time, and which, in the earlier part of Elizabeth's reign, appears to have been located at the Burgh Hall, now the Leycester Hospital, until this building passed into the hands of the Earl of Leycester. The School would then seem to have been transferred to the East gate, for evidence of which see the grant to the Corporation of the East gate at p. 224. It at length found a home in the College on the Butts, or in a building adjoining until it was transferred about 20 years ago to the present large and handsome buildings at Myton. The Schoolmaster seems to have been either the Vicar of St. Mary or St. Nicholas. There was also another School in the town, conducted in a building in the Market Place, the lower part of which was let for shops, as to which see page 399; and there may have been other Schools, for Mr. T. Hall complained to the Corporation about the multiplicity of Schoolmasters. Moreover Thomas Oken besides leaving £2 a year for the Master of the Grammar School, also left £2 a year " to the use of a skolemaister to be founde & kept in the said towne of Warwik for ever to teache pettyes & pooremens chieldern." Thus Education seems to have been fairly well looked after.

(22) The Book of John Fisher.

INTRODUCTION.

HIGHWAYS. The duty of seeing that the roads were kept in proper order seems to have been entrusted to four men called highwaymen, and they appear to have made use of oxen, as means of carrying about materials for the filling up of ruts, and for other repairs, as there is a record in an old minute book of "a loan to buye sixe oxen to maynteyne the higheways," and a close called the Highway Close at Wedgnock Park was set apart for these oxen to graze in. These oxen appear to have been used principally, if not entirely, for carrying stone and gravel for the repair of Wedgnock Lane.[23]

PARLIAMENTARY The Borough returned two Burgesses to Parliament, one of whom appears to have been a nominee of the Earl of Warwick. Several elections are mentioned in the Black Book. It is an interesting fact that Warwick was represented in the year 1260 by Peter de Montfort, who was the first Speaker of the House of Commons, and that the last member, whom it returned as a single Borough, before being joined with Leamington to form a Parliamentary Borough, was The Rt. Hon. Arthur Wellesley Peel, (now Viscount Peel), Speaker of the House of Commons.

THE CORPORATION The town was governed by a Bailiff and 12 principal burgesses and 12 assistants, who held their meetings sometimes in their Burgh Hall, sometimes in the Shire Hall, and sometimes at St. Mary's Church, either in the long room over the Vestry, or in the Chapter House, and once at least in the Lady Chapel. In this sketch of Elizabethan Warwick, I have, with a few exceptions, only touched upon the history and topography of

[23] Old Minute Book, p. 40

INTRODUCTION.

the town so far as they illustrate the Black Book. Having given this outline of the town I will not further refer to the inhabitants but will leave it to the Black Book to tell of the sayings and doings of those who lived and moved and had their being in Warwick in the years gone by.

THE BLACK BOOK AND ITS WRITERS.

The Black Book of Warwick is a large and ancient volume, covered with brown calf skin, in which are entered minutes of the meetings of the Corporation, records of the elections of the Bailiffs and principal burgesses, copies of corporation leases and agreements, the elections of Members of Parliament, accounts of public ceremonials, in which the Bailiff and Burgesses took part, records of Corporation law suits, and other matters for the most part relating to municipal life. There are various books which are called Black Books, and among them there is the class in which are recorded rules and ordinances of guilds, minutes of proceedings, and penalties, and fines for breaches of regulations: to this class the Black Book of Warwick belongs. It is 16 inches long, 11 inches wide, and 4 inches thick, and contains 890 pages, numbered by folios: there are 4 pages before the numbering commences, and then it is folioed up to 363, many pages being unused, and beyond that there are 164 pages neither folioed, nor written upon. The first 15 folios have a margin on each side of the page, lined off in red ink, as are also the top and bottom of the page. The events are not always entered in chronological order, and sometimes an account is broken off

INTRODUCTION.

and continued some pages further on, while the intermediate leaves are used for recording something else. Most of the entries were made during 27 years of the reign of Queen Elizabeth, and they were frequent; after that time they were only occasional, and were continued to the beginning of last century. In perusing the Book it will be seen that the Corporation made presentations to livings, and granted leases of tithes, and were in possession of church furniture, such as crucifixes and patens. To explain this it is necessary to state that when Henry VIIIth dissolved the collegiate establishment of St. Mary, he gave by his Charter of Incorporation of 37 Henry VIIIth, 15th May, 1545, to the burgesses inter alia "All that our Rectory and Church of the Blessed Mary and all that our Rectory and Church of St. Nicholas with the privileges &c. to the late College of which Blessed Mary belonging. And also all that our Rectory and Church of Chadesley in our County of Worcester &c. And all that our Rectory of Budbrook &c. And the advowsons gifts rights of patronage belonging to the Dean and Chapter &c. And all houses &c" subject to the payment of stipends to the Vicars of St. Mary, St. Nicholas, and Budbrook, and to the Master of the Grammar School, and to other payments. On the passing of the Municipal Corporations Act of 1835, these properties and trusts passed to and became vested in a body of Trustees called "The Trustees of King Henry VIIIth's Charity Estate," by whom they are now administered. A large portion of the Black Book is taken up with an account of the death of Thomas Oken, and of the law suits arising upon the carrying out of his will, and with the troubles consequent upon the actions of a restless burgess named Richard Brooks, who appears to have lived in Bridge End, and who seemed determined that matters should not go on too quietly in the town, and who is described as one "qui interturbat omnia." We

INTRODUCTION.

are also introduced to several County gentlemen, whose descendants still live in Warwickshire, and whose names are familiar to us, such as Greville, Leigh, Throckmorton, Boughton, Staunton; and particularly I may mention the Sir Thomas Lucy of Shakespeare fame, who seems to have settled a law-suit in connection with Thomas Oken's affairs, which the Court of Arches and the Court of Chancery had failed to put to rights. The writer of the earlier and greater part of the Black Book was Mr. John Fisher, Deputy Recorder and Town Clerk of Warwick, and to him we owe a debt of gratitude for the circumstantial accounts of the meetings of the Corporation, which he has recorded, as well as of their law-suits and quarrels, and for the elaborate details of the royal visits and ceremonials which happened in his time; to him we are indebted for the preservation of much that is curious and interesting in connection with municipal life, with an occasional glimpse at domestic and social life in a provincial town more than 300 years ago. We read here of the ways and manners of the burgesses, of their early morning meetings, of their Sunday meetings at the Church, and of their jealousies, and bickerings and open violence. In the fight at Myton it is curious to read of the use of crossbows side by side with firearms. They do not appear to have been altogether a happy family, and the bailiff often had rather a hard time of it in trying to rule the turbulent spirits in the Corporation and out of it. At many meetings personal remarks were made, and one meeting was so hot, that the Town Clerk deemed it better not to record it at all. Mr. John Fisher was a man of some importance in Warwick, for besides being Town Clerk, he was Bailiff in 1564-5, and again in 1580-1, and also for many years M.P. for the Borough. He sat in the Parliament which assembled in March, 1571, and remained at Westminster until the dissolution, and

INTRODUCTION.

consequently he was in his place when the "Bill for Licence unto the Earl of Leicester to found a Hospital" was passed. The Bill was read the first and second time on Monday, May 21st, 1571, and the third time on Tuesday, May 22nd. He was brother of Mr. Thomas Fisher, who built the present Priory, and therefore, on the authority of Dugdale, a son of one Hawkins, who sold fish in the Market Place, and who was usually known by the name of Fisher. We first meet with him on the 29th of September, 1563, when he appended his signature to a minute of the election of Richard Roo, and we part with him on the 26th of April, 1590, on which day he was present at a meeting of the Corporation, at which Serjeant Puckering was appointed to the Recordership. His signature corresponds with the writing in the book, besides that on folio 209, the writer speaks of himself as "Mr. Fisher the writer of this book." His abode was at one time at the sign of the Swan. He seems to have been rather a self-important man, often suffering from ill-health, (one conference in fact was held in his bedroom) afraid of not being sufficiently appreciated, and anxious to appear in everything going on, as is shown by his returning himself in the list of wounded during the assault on the tithe barn at Myton, as wounded on the thumb, and yet withal a most useful man. His remarks on the characters of his fellow-burgesses, and on the motives which actuated them, particularly his bursts of indignation with regard to Richard Brookes are very amusing, and the way in which he addressed members of the Corporation was on more than one occasion abusive. One unpleasant experience happened to him when he was bailiff, which he relates in the old volume already mentioned. An outrageous fellow named Dongon alias Donghill had been brought before him for assault, but was released on the intercession of the party assaulted. Two days afterwards he presented

INTRODUCTION.

himself at the bailiff's house very drunk, and was sent away, Mr. Fisher being at that time ill in bed. Some days after this he came again, and secretly made his way to the bed-chamber, where the bailiff, sick and ill, lay asleep, and made such a noise by the bed-side that the bailiff "fell sodenly into a great feare, and skreched being in doubt of his lief." His cries brought on to the scene one of his servants, who promptly put Donghill out of the room. After Mr. Fisher's death, or after he ceased to be Town Clerk, the entries in the book are not numerous, and are not of the same interest as the earlier ones. Mr. Edmund Gregory, who was appointed Town Clerk by Mr. Serjeant Puckering the Recorder, would be responsible for the entries made during the next ten or twelve years. The few entries during the first 4 or 5 years of the 17th century were made by Mr. William Spicer, who was the second Deputy-Recorder and Town Clerk after Mr. Fisher. This is ascertained by a comparison of the hand-writing of these entries, with a memorandum signed "W. Spicer," which records some of the last words of John Fisher. The writing is closer, and more difficult to read than that of Mr. Fisher. Mr. Spicer represented Warwick in Parliament: he died on the 3rd of August, 1611, and was buried in St. Nicholas' Church, in Warwick.[1] William Spicer may have been the son of, as it is scarcely likely that he was the same individual as, the Mr. Spicer, whom the Earl of Leicester sent to report upon the burgh hall and buildings adjoining, when he was proposing to found an hospital. This Mr. Spicer appears to have been an engineer of some ability, for when the Earl of Leicester was engaged in getting up associations for the defence of Queen Elizabeth's person, he wrote a letter, which is published in the Egerton papers at p. 101, dated the 9th of April, 1584, from his house at

(1) Old Minute Book, p. 14.

INTRODUCTION.

Wanstede to Mr. Egerton, Solicitor General, stating that the Queen had appointed his servant, William Spicer, surveyor of the works and fortifications at Berwick, and asking for a "bill to be drawen to that end" for the Queen to sign. After Mr. Spicer's time the minutes of meetings, and records of the Corporation's transactions were almost entirely entered in another minute book, which I have referred to as the old minute book. The few remaining entries were presumably made during their respective Deputy-Recorderships and Town Clerkships by Mr. Spicer's successor, Mr. John Norton,[2] who died on the 14th of September, 1635, and was buried in St. Mary's Church, and whose monument is in the South Transept, by Mr. Edward Raynsford,[3] who died on the 10th of December, 1652, by Mr. Matthew Holbeche[4] who followed Mr. Raynsford, by Mr. Jacob Prescott, who was appointed Deputy-Recorder by the Charter of Charles II., of 13th October, 1665, and again in the Charter of Charles II., of the 18th December, 1684, and by Mr. Thomas Newsham, who was appointed by the Charter of William and Mary of the 18th of March, 1694. The account of the noisy meeting of the Corporation in December, 1564, (see page 9), is by an unknown writer.

(2) Old Minute Book. p. 16.
(3) Ibid p. 148.
(4) Ibid p. 152.

The Black Book of Warwick.

The Othe of the Principall Burgesses.

"Ye shall faithfull and true bee to the Quenes ma^tie and her heires and Successours Kinges & Quenes of this Realme of Englond And the ffraunchises Liberties privelegies customes & order of this Borough of Warwik ye shall observe kepe maynteyne and Susteyne to the best and uttermost of yor knowleig & power Ye shall not doo or consent to be doone any thing to the hinderaunce hurt or preiudice of the said borough or of the ffranchies libties or comodoties of the same Ye shallbe obedient assisting aydyng comforting counsailing & helping to the Balief of the said Borough as one of the twelve principall Burgesses from tyme to tyme and at all tymes Such things as youe are and shallbe callid to counsaill of towching the said Borough ye shall kepe secrete And not revele to any person out of the counsaill house or place where the same shalbe by youe and others of the principall burgesses spoken of resolued and determyned And therin ye shall give yor best counsaill consent & advisement to the best of yor understanding & power Ye shall not have conferrens aprement or consent w^t any p^rson whatsoever to the hurt hinderaunce or overthrowing of any graunt priviliege charter or libtie graunted to this borough or corporacion But the same pryvileges ffraunchises & libties ye shall contynewe defend susteyne & maynteyne to the uttermost of yor power And all good orders which bee have bene or shalbe devised made & agreid uppon by the

Bailief and principall burgesses for & towching the good goverment of this borough ye shall pforrme maynteyn & defend to the uttermost & best of yo{r} hability and power   As god yo{u} helpe the holy Evang{l} and the contents of this book"

The following on folio 1 is a note of the creation and election of Humfrey Heath as first Bailiff of Warwick under letters patent or charter of Philip & Mary.

(folio 1) "Humfridus Heith prim{s} et modernus balliv{s} Burgi Warwici electus et creatus p. lras patentes Dni Regis et Dne Regine Phillipi et Marie Dei gra reg{s} et regine anglie hispanii aq francie utriusq   Cicilie Jerusalem et hibni fidei defensq   Archducis Austrie Ducum burgundie mediolani et Brabanae comit hapsburgi flaundre et Tyrolis ——— die ——— anno Regnor suor primo et Sed̄o ut plenius patet p p'dicas lras patentes

In whose yere the Twesday mkett was ordenyd and appoyntid to be kepte at the highe crosse That is to say the whete mkett in the Castell strete and the barley mkett in the Churche stret

Also in his yere the beyffe mkett upon the faire days was remowyd out of the Jury strete unto the baksid of the Deanry and colledge extending up to the Saltisford strett

Also the mkett of butter and chese was removid from the crosse unto the churche Strett and the barley mkett upon the feire days into the Jure strete

(folio 8)   AN ORDINANCE FOR BAKERS.

The following is written in engrossing hand.

An ordynance made & sett forth the viii{th} day of Marche in the second and thyrde yeres of the reign of Kyng Philipp and Quene mary tochyng caryeng of bred by the Bakers of Warwyk out of the Burrough

"Where long before this tyme by the old auncyent hedds and grave witts of the Inhabytaunts of the said Burrough of Warwyk itt hath been thought that the caryeng of bred by the Bakers of Warwyk out of the Burrough to divers & sundry marketts and other place in the Countye as well in Warwykshyer as other shyers hath been mythe preiudycyall & hurtfull to the Inhabytunts of the seyd Burrough as by sondry good and pbable reasons they of heretofore made hath obydently appered   And upon that before this tyme att a leete holden in the seyd Burrough about the iiird yere of the reign of Edward late Kyng of England the syxt itt was ordeyred that no Baker shuld carye eny bred by horses or otherwyse out of the same Burrough to any markett pound or other place to be sold which ordynaunce was put in execucyon and took effect unto suche tyme as upon ernest suyt made by the same Bakers to the Gouernours of the toune for that tyme beyng the seyd Gouvernours took upon them to make frustrate the same ordynaunce and sett the same Bakers att there lybertye agen to the grete hurt of the seyd Burrough as by the sequele thereof manyfestly itt dyd appere *Where* uppon now the Baylyff and pryncypall Burgesses of the seyd Burrough tenderyng the welth pfett & comodytye of the same Burrough well weyeng & confyderyng the wayght of the pmysses and Consultyng as well with the xxiiii of the chyfest of the comeners of the seyd Burrough and others the wyse men theye havyng also the adwyse councell and consent of the Kyng and Quenys ma^{tyes} Justice of assise of the seyd countie of Warr have ordeyned and establyshed that after the feest of Easter next comyng no Baker Dwellyng in the same Burrough or Suburbes of the same shall in any wyse Cary eny maner of bred out of the seyd Burrough to eny markett pound or other place to be sold uppon payne to forfett to the use of the seyd Burrough for eny tyme that eny of them shall carye owt eny bred contrary to this ordynauce ten shellyngs to be levyed furthwith of his goods & catalls by the offycers of the Burrough to the use beforeseyd

Provided always that yf itt shall appere att eny tyme hereafter that this ordynance shallbe prudiciall and hurtfull to the seyd (folio 9) Burrough or Countys adjoynyng that then the seyd ordynance to be broken by the Baylyf &

pryncypall Burgesses and that the seyd Bakers shall be sett att lybertye agen to cary there bred in to the Countye & markett Tounes as they dyd before the makynge of this ordynance eny thyng to the contrayry made not withstondyng"

The Account of Daniel Haylye, Bailiff questioned

xxj^{mo} die Decemb^r Anno Regin. Dne Regine Elizabeth quarto

"At whiche daie thole Companye aswell the Bailief as the more pte of the xij princiapll Burgesses being assembled in their comon hall to receyve thaccompt of Danyel haylye Bailief for the yere passed of the said Borough and pasing the same found that he demandid for his twoo dyners the some of v^{li} xiiij^s ij^d whiche the said Companye thought to moche And therefore at this pn. it is ordered by thole assent of the presents of the company whose hands be hereunto that from hensforth whosoer shall happen to be the Baylief shall not Aske allowaunce for his twoo Dyners above the some of xl^s for a Dyner thole s. iiij^{li}

  by me Wyllm huddyson balyffe
  by me Roger Byworth burges
  by me John Butler   Willm hyll
  by me Rychard ffisher   Wyllym Edmonds
    thomas Oken   Thomas Barrett
    Richard townsend John Nason
    John dyche

The signature of Thomas Oken is in a plain firm hand: that of William Hill is followed by a most remarkable flourish

(folio 11) Burgus Warr.

Vicesimo nono die Septembris 1563. Anno regni Regine Elizabethe Quinto

The Burgesses assembled in their coen (common) hall choose Richerd Roo, Boocher, to be Bailiff.

Facsimile of folio 9a, printed on page 4.

Many of the Signatures here have some very curious marks and signs. After this the reports of Meetings are not signed

(folio 12)   BAILIFF'S ACCOUNTS.

(folio 13) THE CORPORATION PRESENT TO A LIVING AND GRANT LEASES

Anno dni 1565 et R^e Elizabethe vii. John ffisher tunc ballivo.

p'sentaccion to Tho. Lawley

"Memorand: that the xxii daie of May 1565 the bailief and burgesses of the towne of Warwick by the name of the Burgesses of the same Towne have at the special desire and request of Thomas Blount of Kidderminster Esq named one Thomas Lawleye clerk to be Viker of Chadesley And to him so named have given and delivered their presentacion under the seale of the said towne of Warwik The graunt was made by John ffisher Bailief John Butler Richerd ffisher Thomas Oken Richard Townsend Willm Hudson Willm Edmonds Richerd Roo and others And the same was sealed by the said John ffisher John Butler Thomas Oken & Richerd Townsend w^h the consent of the rest leaving their keys The date of the pntacion is xxij^o may a^o vij^o Rⁿpred"

a leace granted to Th. Sheldon

"The same daie and tyme John ffisher surrendered a leace of the dovehouse in the guild hall gardens and in considern thereof the said Bailief & Burgesses graunted a new leace of the same dovehouse and half the garden & the walk thereby and the Storeyard and house thereto belonging to Thomas Sheldon for xxj yeres The date of the leace is xxij of may aforesaid The rent p ann. xx^s

a leace granted to Jo. ffisher

"Memorand that the last day of September anno pred. the Bailif and principall Burgesses aforesaid in their comon hall having conferrens of the state of their borough considered of the ruyn of the chapell nere to their hall wch then began to dekay and had been spoiled by dyvers unknowen so as the same chapell if present remedy were not provided was like to come in further ruyn to the g^{rt} defacing of the towne wheruppon it was thought very mete & convenyent to graunt the same by leace to some man for reasonable rent and to maynteine the reparacion and theruppon offred and graunted to John ffisher that he should have the same by leace for xxj yeres paing yerely rent v^s and mayntaining the repacions and then he to put the same to what use he best liked

A Difficulty in Electing a Bailiff.

Vicessimo nono die Septembris 1565 viz. ffm Sci Michi Archi anno vij^o R^e Elizabeth

(folio 14)

Election of Willm hylle to be Balif

"At wch daie John ffisher then bailief w^t the rest of the company that is to saie John Butler Richard ffisher Thomas Oken Richerd Townesend William hudson Richerd Roo Roger Egeworth John Diche John Nason and Thomas Barryt assemblid together w^t a good nombre of the comoners betwene the houres of nyne & eleven of the clock after long consultacion had named electid and appointid Willm hill gentleman then absent to be the bailief for the yere to come who being callid and given to understand therof refuzed to take the said office uppon alledging that neither for want of habilitye nor of good will he so did, but desired that his cause might be thoroughly considered of and w^t all declared that the want of a wief to governe his house and famylie was such a mayme unto him as thereby not hable to take the charge in hand least he might rather hinder the good reaport of that office wch his allegacions thoroughly considered it was thought to the company reasonable excuse and thereuppon apointid a newe meting on the morrow being the last day of Sept. aforesaid

Displacing of John Dyche John Nason Thomas Barret from their place of principall burgesses

At wch daye the said bailief & chief or principall burgesses and other comoners mett in their burges hall and their the said bailief & principall burgesses having conferens for a newe election and apointing the said office to John Diche he refused then to Thomas Barret he refused and lastly to John Nason he refused who all showed cause both of infirmyty and lack of hability bothe to that office of bailief and also of chief burges and wold in no wise further deale therin And desired that they might be displaced and others chosen in their places of wch request the said bailief & his company having due consideracion and consultacion weing at length the aptnes or unaptnes of the said three to that place fynding in them desire of quyetnes and ympotence to serve graunted concluded & agreid to displace them and in their places & romes to chose others and than considering of enery mans wisdome discrecion hability & metenes to that office they determyned to take and associat unto them Richerd Brokes humfrey Crane Thomas Powell and Willm ffrekleton to be in places & romes of Willm Edmonds and of the said John Diche John Nason and Thomas Barret

Richerd Brookes humfrey crane Thomas Powell electid Willm ffrekulton in place of Willm Edmonds

Richard ffisher chosen bailief the second tyme

And at the said day the said bailief and chief burgesses associated elected determyned named and apointed twoo viz. Richerd ffisher and Thomas Oken to be and delyuered their names to the comoners to choice of them wch they thought mete Wheruppon the said comoners electid & named Richerd ffisher to be bailief for the yeare to come

And theruppon the said Richerd Brokes and Willm ffrekleton being callid before the said bailief and principall Burgesses the second day of october following were before the said Bailief & Burgesses sworne in their comon hall as principall burgesses of the said towne and the said humfrey crane being also callid and psuaded w^t hall wold in no wise take uppon him any such office and so obstynately depted And on the vj^th of the said october the said bailief and burgesses having chosen Symon Yong in the place of the said humfrey crane associatid themselves together and sent for the said Symon yong and Thomas Powell and recevid them into their Company as burgesses wheruppon the said Symon Yong & Thomas Powell were sworne as burgesses before the said bailief & the rest of the principall burgesses

Richard Brook Willm ffrekulton electid principall Burgesses

humfrey crane refusith

Symon yong & Thomas Powell sworn

And on the x^d day Sr Robert Throkmorton cam to Warwik to treate as well w^h the said Bailief & his company as also w^h Mr Kynyat & Mr Blount officers to my L of Warwik for the cancelling of an oblegacion wherein the said Sr Robert stood bound to the Bailief and his company for the paym^t to the Bailief yerely of one yerely fee of lx^s wch the said bailief & bgesses had bought of the said Sr Robert wch being behind for four yeres the said Bailief and burgesses required of the said S^r Ro. to pay unto them according to his bonde (folio 15) wch the said Sr Robert refuzed not but affirmed that by covenat betweene my L. of Leicester & him my L therle of Leicester had promissed that my L therle of Warwick should see yerely answerid and paid And therefore the said Sr Robert peured therle of Leir l^re to the said Bailief & burgesses requiring thereby that the said bond might be delyved to the said Sr Robert and that Mr Kynyatt Audito^r to therle of Warwik had pmissed to give allowance of the said fee and also that my said L. of Warwik wold see the same answrid accordingly from tyme to tyme nevertheles Mr Kynyatt nowe being at Warwik semed at the first to stick in the matter but in thend pmissed that paym^t of arrearages should be made this tyme of Audite & that from thenceforth my L of Warwike's pleaso^r was to pay the same accordingly Wheruppon it was pmissed by the said bailief and his company that uppon the receipt of the said arrearages the bonde should be delived to Mr Kyniat to be cancelled and likewise was it promissed by Sr Robert that the bonde wherein the bailief & burgesses stonden bounden to him for the pricking of the bailief should be delivered to them to be cancelled But for the Indenture of Covenant betweene the said Bailief & burgesses and the said St Robert remayn uncancellid wch was consented unto the rather to satisfy the unreasonable request of Mt Kyniatt and others The same day the said Sr Robert pricked Ric. ffisher to be bailief for the yere to come"

—(A STORMY MEETING OF THE CORPORATION.

The fine block of buildings, now known as The Leycester Hospital, situated in High Street close to the West Gate, was the scene of the noisy proceedings narrated in the following extract. Originally belonging to the Guilds of the

Holy Trinity and St. George, it passed from them to the Corporation, by whom a few years after the aforesaid noisy proceedings, it was granted to Robert Dudley, Earl of Leicester, for the purposes of a Hospital. About this grant there will be more further on in this book. Through a gateway you enter the Courtyard, which is surrounded on three sides by buildings; on the right is a covered staircase leading to a gallery, open to the Courtyard. At the head of the staircase is a hall, now divided into rooms for the Brethren; it was in this hall, that without doubt the altercation took place, which is hereinafter described. Having the building before our eyes, as it was in the days of Elizabeth, we can picture the scene. We can imagine the Sergeant coming down the stairs with his prisoners, and then beating a retreat; the bailiff coming into the gallery, and addressing the noisy burgesses in the Courtyard, and then these latter going to the West Gate close by and being joined by a lot of idlers ready to promote a row. It may be noted that four of the men engaged in the disturbance, became, in after years, representatives of law and order, filling each in his turn the office of bailiff. The account of the meeting was not written by John Fisher, as the writing is closer and more cramped. The account is as follows :—)—

Anno vij Reg^e Eliz

"Be yt remembred that the third day of December 1564 and in the seventh yere of Q. Elizabeth John ffisher being than Balief of the Borough of Warwik offred in the ther Burges hall an accompt for the Burges offyce for the yere then past before the xij pryncypall Burgesses and dyvers other comoners of the said Borough uppon which accompt declared there remaned due to the towne xxx^{li} viii^s ix^d ob. which money was there tendered to be paid and was told by Mr Willm Edmondes than one of the pryncipall Burgesses wherupon the said ffisher then Balief desyred the company present to procede to ellection of one to be Burges for the yere to come as before had bene used That is to saye from the Sonday next after St Andrewes day untill that tyme twelve moneth uppon which mocyon some of the pryncipall burgesses desired the said ffisher to contynewe the said oyffyce that yere, which he refused and therefore agayne desired them to procede to the elecion wheruppon one of the company stood upp and sayd That as he understood the meanyng of Mr Balief and his bretherne was to have an other company to the number of xxiiij honest men wch shoulde be the Assistants to Mr Balief and the pryncipall burgesses whereof election had bene made and part of them were sworne and some not yet sworne & some be dead and not many lyving and therfore wished that that nomber of xxiiij might be full and that yt woolde please Mr Balief & the xij principall burgesses to choose & name such for that purpose as they shoulde please to place for that nomber to the end they might the better procede in such cawses as shoold happen   This mocyon was well acceptid and theruppon it was agreyd That on that day fortenight after the Balief and pryncipall burgesses shoulde mete agayn in the same place to take further order for the election of a burgesse and also for chosing and namyng of the xxiiij   In the meane tyme the mony should remayne in the said Baliefs hand   And theruppon for that tyme they departid

On Sonday the xviith of Decembr being the day prefixed the Balief and the gretest nombr of the pryncipall burgesses assemblid in the same place consulted of the election and agreed that the psones whose names doo followe should be the xxiiij.   Vide^{lt} Richard Brooks Thomas Beawfoo Thomas powell Thomas Jenks Thomas Staunton Thomas Burges Nycolas Purfloo Ry^d Trykitt John Bykar Willm ffrekleton Olyver Brookes Robart Sheldon John Gryffin humfrey Crane Rychard heynes John Rey Symon Yong John Ridgeley Thomas Cawdrey Roger hurlebutt John Grene Thomas Dych William Hicks and William Townesend who all having bene named were present   To whom yt was said That Mr Balief & his bretherne had named them and Electid thes xxiiij to bee theyr assistants for dyvers causes & respects   And therefore requyred them to take such Othe as should be there redd agreing to good order and the lawes of the land   And to the end that they might the better consider thereof before they did swear M Roger Egeworth redd openly the othe   The tenore wherof ensuyth youe shalbe faithfull & true to the quenes ma^{ty} & her heyres Kyngs and Quenes of that Realme of England and to that borough of Warwik The francheses lybertyes pryveleges customes & orders of the same youe shall keape maynteyne & susteyne to the best & uttermost of your knolege & power youe shall not doo or consent to be done anythyng to the hynderance hurte or preiudyce of the said Borough (folio 16) or any francheses lyberties or comodytyes of the same ye shall be obedyent assisting aydyng comforting counsiling & helping to the Balief and twelve pryncypall Burgesses of the said borough from tyme to tyme & at all tymes when ye shallbe callid Such thynges as ye are or shallbe callid to counsell of within the same borough ye shall kepe secret and not reveale the same unto any person out of the counsell house or place where the same shall bee by youe & yor fellowes of yor company specyally chosen & apoyntid spoken of reasoned & determyned and therof yo shall gyve your best counsayle consent & advisement to the best of your power & understonding youe shall not have Conferens agreement or consent wth any pson whotsoever to the hurt hynderance or overthrowyng of any graunt pryvelege charter or lyberty graunted to this borough but the same graunts & charters & lybtyes ye shall contynewe susteyne & maynteyne to the uttermost of yor power All such disorders as you shall knowe to bee done or suffered within this borough ye shall declare & give knolege of the same to the Balief of this borough for the tyme being, or in his absence to his deputye & your best advyse for the reformacyon thereof And generally ye shall doo all that to a good subiect & assistant of the comen weale shall apteyne & belong to the best of yor knowlege conyng & power So help you God and the holy Evangelyst Which othe being red & by them heard was allowed of And Richerd Brooke and Thomas Beawfoo layng there handes on a book ready to sweare Nycolas Purfloo begynneth with many wordes to fynde himself grevid for that dyvers things had bene leaced & sett without his & his fellowes consent therto first had And as he was babling Thomas Powell mysliking not a litle that Richard Brooks & Thomas Beawfoo should bee placed befre him burst out & began to saye that he had bene ones before that tyme sworne & therefore thought it not requisit or nedefull that either hee or any other which had bene sworne to bee sworne agayne ffor saith hee yf I shoulde sweare agayne I should be forsworne as a nomber of youe that sytt at the boorde bee, whereuppon Richard Roo stood up and askid whom he knewe to have bene forsworne and what he could charge him with to whome Powell made answere that hee and three or fowre more was not of the company which he spake of but the rest were And so the said Powell waxing very whote sware by Gods blood & other grait othes That the Balief and twelve had spent & consumed bothe the stock & lond of the towne and never made reconyng or accompt for yt   And said further that whan any payment is to be made the poore comoners beare yt And the they twelve pay nothing   As saith he for example whan my Lord of Warwik had mony geven to hym It was gathered of the poore comons And never one of the masters that payd one grote And further swering a great othe said that if any of them woold say that he had payd any thing I wooll (said Powell) say to his face that hee lyeth—yea by Gods b. he lyeth Wheruppon Mr Hyll sittyng very nere him and layng his hand very gently uppon Powell his arme said unto him Mr Powell I myself payd towards that money and so dyd other men to   To whom Powell answered very hotely and sayd 'youe lye'   Then said Mr Hille 'I lye not you lye'   Wheruppon the Balief desirous to stop any further Brawle said to Powell These woords beeseme not this place or company   And therefore willid hym to speak as became hym or ells to holde his peace but that notwithstanding the man growing more hote left not of his purpose against Mr Hill & dyvers others but affymed still saying to M^r hill 'thowe lyest'   And withall spattered or w^t fervent speaking spytt in M^r hill his face   And whiles this was yn doyng Jenks & Purfloo stepp fourth & dyvers other of theyr faccyon put & shewed their mysdemano^r so whotely that the Balief thought it hye tyme to put them to sylence And therfore comandid the Serjaunt to take Powell and to bring him home to the Baliefs house And willid Powell to goo with the S^{r}jant which he pmysed to doo & so did awhile Then stept forth Tho. Jenks Tho. Burges Nicolas Purfloo William ffrekulton and others to the nomber of xvij and said that if Powell went to warde they wolde goo w^t him wherewith the Balief being content comandid the Sarjant to take them with him Wheruppon they went downe the stayres together And being come downe Powell & Jenks saye to the Sarjaunt 'gett thee away or ells thowe shalt have thy pate broken and thy master his handes full' Whereuppon the S^rjant cam up agayn and told the words to the Balief and his company And then the Balief arose & went into the galery to see the demeano^r of those deptd & spying them in twoo Companyes spake unto them & said 'fellowes as many as Entend to be of o^r company come upp agayn to us & the rest depart' Wheruppon Powell Jenks Purflo Burges Frekulton Olvere Brooks and some others went towards the gate Then the said Balief said to Powell & Jenks 'ye say youe will not obey me wooll ye not bee at my commandement' 'no' say Jenks & Powell & therewith went away Then with them at the gate dyvers others yet unknowen to the Balief and said 'stick to yt fellowes for youe shall want no helpe ffor youe are for the comon wealth But yet it so happenyd that they went away to the Church And the Balief and his Company tarryeng a while in the halle considered what was to be done And upon consultacion thought it good to forbere their ponishment at that tyme lest worse might happen And then the Balief and principall burgesses calling for Richard Brook Symon Yong humfrey Crane Richard Tuskott Robert Sheldon Robt Phillippes Willm Thownders Thomas Dyche & Baldwyn Bewford they all came and showed themselves very ready & willing to doo any thing resonably requested and to bee of that felowship And so they weere offred the book & they all every of them did take the othe & were sworne And that being done the Bailif and pryncipall burgesses agreðe to mete there agayn on tuesday mornyng following to fynishe their purpose for the eleccyon & swearing of the rest of xxiiij And then deptid for that tyme

On the said Tuesday morning the Balief and all the principall burgesses (saving M^r hudson) come to the said hall and sent for such as they thought meet some of them that went away the day before & some others w^t whom having conferens It was confessid by divers of them that the day before deytid to the nomb^r of ix or x that they were not privye of the Intencyon or meanyng of Powell & his company but went with him for company and were sorry for their misusage and offred themselves to become newe men at the comanndement of Mʳ Balief & his bretherne wheruppon the Balief & his brethern the pryncipall burgesses seing & accepting them conformybly recewid them & tendered the othe onto them which well liked and willing did sweare The names of them which deptid and were ther agayn recevid & did sweare were thes Jo. Rigeley Jo. Biker Roger hurlebutt John Grene John Rey Thomas Cawdrey To which were added by a newe Eleccion John Griffyn Willm Townesend Tho. Bewfoo henry Byrde Willm Martlyn Roger Weale & Willm Stevyns who also did take the othe and were sworne

Sʳ Willm Wigston Recorder 7th Eliz.

Whiles thies thyngs were doing the other chieftaynes namely Powell Jenkes ffrekulton Oliver Brookes Staunton & Burges posted abrode to learne counsell And Purfloo postid to mete Sʳ Willm Wigston being then Recorder comyng from Coughton, and by the way makith grevouse compleint unto him against the Balief & burgesses affirmyng that they doo & wold use the comoners very evill & unhonestly wheruppon the said Sʳ Willm Wigston comyng to the towne alighted at the Baliefs house and there brake unto him and principall burgesses the compleint made by Purfloo desiring to here the matter at large whervnto the Balief & (folio 17) principall burgesses graunted unto Whervppon Nycholas Purfloo was callid and willid to say what hee coulde And so fyndyng himself greatly grevid that hee & the xxiiij might not have anctorytie as well as the pryncipall burgesses in graunting or devysing of things he said he thought they had wrong and desired reformacyon Wheruppon the Chr (Charter) being showed to Mʳ Recorder and the mysdemeanoʳ of Purfloo & his complyces openid before his face The said Sʳ Willm Wigston much blamed Purfloo & his fellowes And tolde him that he had not to doo in those matters And therfore exhortid him & them to to be quyet & use themselves more honestly towards their officer & supiors Nevertheless did entreat the Balief ernestly to remyᵗ this offence procedid of ignorance & trustid theruppon to fynd emendmᵗ in the psones which he hartely desired And so by the Intercession of the said Sʳ Willm theis misdoers were spared of ponishmt"

Anno Dno 1568.

xij Rege Eliz.

Thomas Powell elected Bailiff

Thomas Powell was chosen Bailiff on 29 Sept. & took the oath on All hallows Day following.

Ro. Philips chosen one of the principall Burgesses.

On Palm Sunday 19 March 1569 Robert Phillippes was chosen a principal burgess in the place of Roger Egeworthe "lately departid out of that towne to dwell in Coventry" but being out of town was not then sworn   On Easter Monday 27 March he appeared and "alledged his unmeteness for that company" but his reasons were not considered strong enough & he was sworn in

(folio 18) Copy of a surrender by John Gower Gent. to the corporation of two advowsons of the Vicarage of Stone in Worcestershire of which they were patrons

(folio 19) Copy of Lease of the Vicarage of Stone from the Vicar to John Gower.

(folio 21) 1st Nov. 1570 Thomas Burges was chosen Bailiff.

(folio 22) X° die Deceb^r 1570 in the xiij^t day (sic) of o^r Souarayne Lady Quene Eliz.

"It is this day orderid by the bailief & pryncipall burgesses and dyvers of the comoners that for dyvers great and abhomynable offencis comittid by Agnes the wief of Mr Gaunt w dyvers lewde psons That the said Agnes shall depte out of this towne betwixt this and St Thomas Day thappostell next comyng And that she be not suffred any leng^r here in any part of this towne to dwell uppon payne of carting from place to place & from tyme to tyme till she be banisshed & cleane gone"

On the same day there was a grant of a lease of tithes of corn hay hemp & flax of the field of Coton & herdwik in St Nicholas parish to John Fisher

Also a grant to Burges of a close at Woodcote

Also a grant to Frekulton of 3 houses beyond the bridge & 18 acres of arable land at Myton

"It is also agreid that Willm huddisdon shall have the charnell house and Saint Maryes church yard & a litle house in the churchyard for xxj yeres for the rent of v^s by yere

Also a grant to Thos. Powell of a house and land at Radford

Also agreed that J. Fisher should have a patent of the offices of Stewerd Auditor & Surveyor for life

(folio 23) "It was the same day orderid that Richerd Wilkyns having veary leawdly behavid himself in langwage & speche aswell against the said Bailief & corporacion to Richerd Townsend calling the said Richerd Townesend knave as also before the said Bailief & burgesses examyning him in their comon hall That the said Richerd Wilkins shoule be comitted to the stocks their to contynewe during M^r bailiefs pleso^r"

"And this day it was agreid that thies whose names do followe should be the nomb^r of xxiiij assistants to the Bailief & principall burgesses wch xxiiij^{or} should be as it were the mowth of all the comoners   And what they agree unto shalbe taken as the consent of the comoners in any election &c   And they to be callid used continued or dismissed as the bailief & principall burgesses shall finde cause by their behavio^r viz Robert Sheldon Thomas Jenkes humfrey Crane John Rigeley Oliver Brooke Thomas Staunton John Grene John Byker Richerd Tuskott Richerd heynes Roger hurlebutt Thomas cawdrye William Saunders Phelippe Coo John Griffin Roger Weale Thomas Allen Nycolas purflowe henry Chapleyn Thomas Chapman Thoms Shoteswell John Bailies John hicks and Baldewym Benford wherof part being sworne & part unsworne It is agreid that the rest that be not yet sworne shalbe sworne when M^r bailief will

Money being due to Rich. Fisher on his account of baliwick in the 4th & 5th years of Philip & Mary & 9th of Elizabeth a bill for payment under the common seal was ordered to be made

Facsimile of folio 11b.

On the 24th of January 1570 there was a meeting of the Corporation to seal the leases granted at a former meeting, & for that purpose the baliff & principal burgesses "cam togither unto the church & chest." After the sealing & delivery the account is as follows:

"M^d that at the same tyme x^{li} pcell of the xxx^{li} aforesaid into the chest was taken out & delivered to John ffisher therwth to pay the quenes ma^{ty} for the ffee ferme of the said Borough due the tymes of William ffekleton & Thomas Powell who have not yet made their accompts of their said Baliwik"

"And at that tyme it was consentid That Richerd Brook should have the barne & the house wherin Nicholas hunt dwelleth by leace if he woold desire it The said Richerd paing yerely viij^s & that he should repayre the said house & barne And that when he shall have the said leace there be mencyon made wth the leace of the way to the barne wch he confessitt to be thorough the gate leading into his backside

And also that same day Robert Phelips one of the said pryncipall Burgesses being chargid w^t c^r ten misdemeano^r that he should peure M^r henry Goodeve esquyre to treat of a cause betwene him & Richerd Roo for a mayden servant named ( ) Shakesper & so to infringe the libtye of this borough by complayning to the said Mr Goodeve The said Robert Phelipps excuseth himself That he labored not to Mr Goodeve but that his wief did it. It was this tyme pdoned w^{t}hout any fyne assessid."

(folio 24)   LEASE TO JOHN FISHER OF TITHES.

By Indentures dated 12th Dec. in the 13th year of the reign of Elizabeth the Bailiff & Burgesses granted to John Fisher "all & every these offerings oblacions privie tuythes comon tuithes obvencions and othes the tuithes of corne hey hempe flax fruytes herbes pigges geese eggs cockes henes & other tuithes whatsoever & of what kind soever arising within the towne of Warwick and also all and singler the crysomes weddings churchings and buryengs whin the said pish & church of Saint Maryes" &c from the feast of the Natyvitie of our Lord God nowe next comyng for 21 years at the yearly rent of £20

B

LEASE TO JOHN FISHER OF THE TITHES OF THE FIELDS OF COTON AND HERDWIK.

By Indenture of 12th Dec. in the 13th year of Elizabeth after reciting that the "late Dean & Chapter of the late collegiat church of the blessid virgyn Saint Marye in Warwick" had leased to Richard Fisher otherwise called Hawkins their tithes of corn hay &c of the fields of Coton & Herdwick in the suburbs of Warwick & also a tithe barn in the parish of St. Nicholas in a Street called South St unto Richard Fisher for 40 years from the feast of the Annunciation following the decease of one John Carvanell clerk then Dean or as soon as a former lease to the said John Carvanell should be void the said Fisher paying £6 a year with other conditions contained in an Indenture of the 20th March in the 32nd year (folio 25) of the reign of the "late King of ffamouse memory" the Bailiff & Burgesses for a consideration then paid granted to John Fisher the above tithes & barn at the expiration of Richard Fisher's lease for the term of 21 years at £6 per annum

Appointment of John Fisher as Steward general of all the Courts & leets and surveyor & supervisor of all lands houses possessions &c belonging to the corporation And also Auditor & hearer of the accounts of all Accountants accountable to the Bailiff for his natural life at a yearly fee of £5

(folio 26) A bond to Richard Fisher for the payment of £28 13s 10d

A LEASE TO RICHARD HUDISDON GENTLEMAN OF THE CHURCHYARD CHARNEL HOUSE AND BIER HOUSE.

By Indenture dated the 30th of Dec. in the 13th year of Elizabeth the Corporation granted to Richard Hudisdon Gent. a lease of the herbage of the churchyard of St. Mary's and also "the house callid the charnell house & an other house in the same churchyard sett & being on the north side of the said church of Saint Maryes sometyne used for the beere to stond in" for 21 years from the feast of the Annunciation then next coming at the yearly rent of 5s. payable half yearly   Hudisdon covenanted to keep the churchyard walks gates stiles & ways & the houses in good order & not to " suffer any undecent or unmete thing to be laid sett used or frequented in the said churchyard charnell house or bere house"

(folio 27) By Indenture of 30th Dec. in the 13th year of Elizabeth the Corporation granted a lease to Richard Fisher of a tithe barn called the barn of St Lawrence together with a close of land situate near to a Street called West St for 51 years from the feast of the annunciation then next coming at the annual rent of 6/8 payable half yearly Fisher to keep the barn in repair

By Indenture date 30 Dec in 13th year of reign of Elizabeth the Corporation granted houses & 18 acres of land beyond the bridge to William Frekulton for 21 years from the feast of the annunciation for 20s 8d per ann

(folio 28) Lease to Thomas Powell of a house & land at Radford

Lease to William Crofts of a close in Woodcote

The Butchers Book.

The Boochers Book

(folio 29)   "Ordinaunces Constitutions devised consented and concluded uppon by ye Companye & felowshippe of Boochers Dwelling in the Borough of Warwick agreid unto by the Bailief and principall Burgesses of the said Borough for the better victualling relieving & well serving of the Inhtants of the same Borough & countrey adjoyning wth good & holesome victuall wth orders and to be observed & kept at all tymes from henceforth aswell by the Boochers nowe presently occupieing as also by all such as hereafter shall occupie & use markett whin the same Borough ffirst it is ordeyned constituted & establyshed by consent aforesaid that all Boochers dwelling in the same Borough being householders & vsing to kill flesshe to sell & alredie being allowed of the Companye of Boochers shall every year yearly uppon the sonday comonly called midlent Sonday mete togethere at some convenient place & house w'hin the said Borough wch they shall call their hall and there shall choose amonge them one of the same companye & occupation dwelling w'hin the same Borough or suburbs to be warden of that occupation for the yere to come and also shall chose one other of the same companye to be the maister of that occupation for the said yere to come wch twoo psones so chosen by consent off the said Boochers or the greater nomber of them & named to be maister & warden of the companye of Boochers shall & may have autoritie to call togither at tymes convenient when they shall think good all householders being Boochers & dwelling whin the same Borough & suburbes & evry of them into their comon hall or other place convenient there & then to consult reason & devise orders for the well serving of the said Borough & country adjoyning & furnisshing of the same wth good & holesome victualls and for other causes towching the wealth comodity & comon utilitye & proffit of the same occupation and company of boochers

Item it is ordeyned & established that every Boocher dwelling w'hin the same Towne being householder upon warning to him given shall come & appeare before the maister & wardeyn for the time being at such convenient tyme & place as by the said M^r & warden shall be appointed to talk & consult of the causes aforesaid And if any of them being warned doo make default wilfully & doo not come having no reasonable cause to the contrary Or if any denye or refuse to obey any such good order as shalle be made by the Mr Warden & the more part of the same Company That he or they so denieing to come or refusing to obey & pforme such ordinance shall forfit & pay for every such default

Item it is further ordered that no boocher dwelling whin the same borough or suburbes shall take any man or chield to dwell w^t him to thintent to teach such man or chield his occupation except he take him to be his apprentice or covenat Sruint for seaven yeres at the least uppon payne that every boocher doing the contrary shall forfit & loose for every such offence xl^s

Item that every Boocher taking any to be his Apprentice or covent servaunt shall take his said Apprentice or covennt srunt by Indenture And shall bring as well the same Indenture as also the said covennt s'unt before the Bailief & Recorder or Towne clerk of the same Borough for the tyme being w'hin one month next after such Apprentice or covennt srunt is taken into S'uice and then & there shall knoleig the same Indenture & Bargayn before the said Bailief and Recorder or Towne clerk wch Indenture shall be enroled in the Court Roles of the same Borough the same Boocher taking such Apprentice or covennt srunt paing only xii^d to the Towne clerk for enrolling the afs^d uppon payn that every Boocher not so doing do forfit and loose for every offence xx^s

Item it is ordeyned that no person dwelling presently or herafter w'thin this Borough or suburbes of the same whether to be borne in the towne or out of the towne nor any other forrener dwelling out of the said Borough shall in any wise be lycensed by any agreament or composicion to occupie or use the same occupation of Boocher w'thin the said Borough or suburbes except he have bene apprentice or covennt s'unt to that occupation and have srued them by the space of seven yeres at the least as apprentice or covennt srunt and the same to be proved before the Bailiff of the same Borough and the Maister & Warden of the occupation of Boocher by sufficient testymony & witnes before he do use & sett up the said occupation w'hin the same borough or suburbes upon payn that the M^r & Wardeyn of boochers admitting or suffring any pson to sett uppe contrary to the ordynance to forfeit & pay unto the Bailiff & Burgesses of the same Borough unto their Hands for every such default Five pounds

(folio 30) Item it is ordenyd & established that no fforener wch alredy is not allowed as one of the companye of Boochers w'in this Towne although he have bene Apprentice or Covennt srunt & srue in the same occupation seven yeres shal be sufferd or admitted to sett upp & use and occupye that occupation whin this borough or suburbes of the same untill he have agreed and compounded wth the Maister & Warden of the same occupation uppon payne that every such boocher occupieng & using to kill & sell flesshe as he shall offer to sell before such composicion or agreem^t had the one half of wch flesshe to be to the bailief of the borough for the tyme being the other half to the Maister Warden & company of Boochers

Item it is ordeyned & constituted that any pson dwelling or wch hereafter shall dwell w^thin this towne or suburbes of the same being not alreadie admitted & allowed as one of the company of Boochers w^thin this borough shall not be admitted or allowed to be one of the company of Boochers of the same borough & to kill and sell flesshe as a boocher of the same borough untill he have first paid or be bound to paye Ten poundes or above by the discrecion of the said Bailief Maister & Warden of the Company of Boochers unto the said Bailief and Burgesses Of wch some of x^li or upwardes the Maister & Warden & Company of Boochers shall have one part and the other nyne partes to goo & be to the chamb^r & use of the same borough Uppon payne that every Maister or Warden compounding or admitting any one for any lesse some to forfit & pay for their so doing ten pounds to the use of the said chamb^r

Item it is agred & orderyd that all & every such pson as hath bene is or shalbe Apprentice or Covennt srunt w^thin the said borough in maner & form aforesaid and served there all the said tyme shall or may uppon request made unto the said Maister and Warden & company of Boochers sett upp use & occupie his said occupacion w^thin the same Burrough & suburbes paing only at his setting upp iij^s iiii^d the third part whreof to be to the chamb^r & use of the said Borough And the other two parts to be to the Company of Boochers

Item it is ordenyd & agreid that no boocher dwelling out of this borough or suburbes shall bring in any fleshe to be sold w^thin the same borough or suburbes except it be uppon the Saturday only And that he shall not sett any such flesshe to sale before the officers of the same borough callid the flesh tasters have first sene tastid & allowed the same flesh to be good & holesome victuall for sustence of mans body And also that euery such bocher bringing in flesh shall bring in the hide skyn fell & tallowe comyng of the said flesh uppon payne that euery one bringing in flesh to sell & not bringing w'hall his said hide skin fell & tallowe to forfeit & pay for eury default that is to say for euery hide not brought xx^d ffor euery calue skin iiij^d for eury shepes skyn or fell viij^d & for evry beastes tallowe ij^d which seuerall forfeitures shalbe presently leauied & taken by the said flesh tasters of such flesshe as the said Boochers offending bring to the markett The one half of wch forfeiture to be to the chamb^r & use of the borough the other half to the maister warden & company of Boochers

Item it is ordereid that no fforrener dwelling out of the towne bringing flesh to be sold w'hin this borough shall neither in the markett tyme nor after the markett is done in any wise goo about in the said borough or suburbes of the same to sell the same flessh to the Inhabitants or people there but shall mak sale therof openly in the markett place Uppon payne to forfeit & loose the flesh so offrid to be sold out of the markett the one half wherof to be to the balief of the said borough the other half to such pson as shall find or take him so selling flesh contrary to this order

Item it is ordenyd that no boocher dwelling out of this borough being not alredy admittid shall from hensforth be admittid to bring in any flesh upon the Saturday as is aforesaid untill he have first compoundid w^t the maister & warden of the company of boochers and doo paie or be bound to pay the some of twentie shillings for his fyne The third part wherof to be to the chamb^r & use of the towne the other twoo ptes to be to the maister warden & companye of Boochers

Item it is ordenyd that euery forren Boocher dwelling out of this borough w^h herafter shalbe admittid to come in & sell flesh upon the Saturdaie as afore is said shall before he doth utter & sell any such flesh be bound to the Bailef & Burgesses of this borough of Warwik in a resonable some such as the bailief for the tyme being shall think convenient w^t condicion that he shall wekely euery Saturday out of lent bring to the said markett flesshe of all sortes acording to the season of the yere and the same shall sell w^t the skyn & tallowe openly in the same mkett And also he shalbe bound that if he mak default & doo not bring in flesh as aforesaid but do absent himself from the said markett three markett dayes togither having no lawfull lett Then that he wilbe contentid from that tyme for ever to be disfranchisid

Item it is ordenyd that no pson dwelling w'in the said borough or suburbes being not allowed to be a Boocher shall kill any kynd of flesh comonly sold in the shambles to thentent to sell the same Rawe by retaile w'in the same borough or suburbes upon payne to forfeit for euery tyme so doing v^s one part wherof to be to the use & chamb^r of this borough the other two ptes to the maister warden & company of Boochers

Item it is ordenyd that in case of any of the boochers using to sell flesh as aforesaid whither he dwell w'hn the borough or without doo wilfully refuse or deny to kepe observe & pforme the Articles orders & constitucions aforesaid or any part of them or do any thing contrary to the said Articles & ordinance or any of them That then the maister or warden of the Boochers for the tyme being shall or may enter into the shoppes howses stalles or stondings of the said boochers offending And shall & may tak the flesh of such as shall offend by waie of distresse and the same flesh shall cause to be priced by the fleshtasters of the (folio 31) same borough and theruppon put the same flesshe to sale and of the money rising or comyng of the same fleshe satisfie all such penalties & forfeitures as the offender hath lost And after that done shall restore the rest of the monye if any shall remayne to the said boocher from whom the said flesshe was so taken

Item it is ordenyd that the penalties forfeitures & Losses wch shall happen and the monye rising therof shalbe leavied by the maister and warden of the company of Boochers for the tyme being And that they ymediately uppon the Levieng of the same shall paie that part wch shalbe due to the use & chamb^r of the towne to the Bailief of the borough for the tyme being And the other part wch shalbe to the company of the boochers they shall kepe in their owne custodie untill the tyme of their Accompt And also that on the said midlent Sonday they shall make their Accompt to the Rest of the company of Boochers And shall deliver all such monye as shall then remayn in their hunds to the next Maister & Warden of their said occupacion and so from one to An other successively for ever

Item it is ordenyd concludid & consentid that the said boochers shall not at their metings or consultacions devise or doo any thing contrary to good order & quiet governemet of the comon weale of this borough or countrey adiacent neyther shall determyn any thing against the good usage & lawes of this land but shall doo all things to the benefiting of this borough the countrey and themselves so farre as the same is agreable to the lawes aforesaid   And in case any matter of doubt or controversie happen to arise emongs them That then the same shalbe orderid & determyned by the Bailief & Burgesses of the borough aforesaid

ffynally It is agreid concludid & consentid unto that incase any thing be done by the said boochers contrary to the good custome & lawes of this land or the quiet governemet of this comon weale Or in case that the bailief and principall burgesses shall see cause to redresse or reforme any thing or Article abovesaid Or to adde or encrease other orders to their above writen That the said company of Boochers uppon Request made to the maister or warden of Boochers or either of them shall surrender and deliver upp into the handes of the Bailief & principall burgesses for the tyme being this book & all the orders constitutions and agreamets abovesaid And also that the said Bailief and principall burgesses for the tyme being may determyne all or any the articles above writen and the same make void Or in their places to make newe as occasion & tyme shall require by their discrecions wch being devised & agreid upon by the said bailief & Burgesses or the greter nomb^r of them and knowleig therof given in writing to the maister or warden of the boochers for the tyme being shalbe from hensforth taken & reputid as ordynances & orders to bynd the said company of boochers & any of them This book or any thing therin contenyd to the contrary notwithstonding In witnes of all wch Articles and agreamets made by consent aforesaid

The said Bailief & Burgesses have to thes presents put their comon seale the xxx^th day of Deceb^r in the thirtenth yere of the reigne of o^r soueryne Lady Elizabeth by the grace of god &c.

The Election of two Burgesses to represent Warwick in Parliament in 1571.

"M^d That ffrancis Willoughbie Esquire for this yere a^o xiij^o Eliz. R^e being hiegh Sheriff of the countie of Warw^k by Edward Catesbie gent his undersheriff directid his precept to the Bailief & Burgesses of the towne & borow of Warwik for the election of two sufficient burgesses of the same towne to be elected & sent to the parliament to begin at Westm. the second day of Apriel in the said xiij^th yere of the reigne of o^r said souereign Lady Ladye Quene Elizabeth The teno^r of which precept Insuith"

Here follows a copy of the precept in Latin, which precept given under the official seal of the said Francis Willoughby, & dated the 8th of March in the 13th year of Q. Elizabeth, was directed to the Bailif & Burgesses of the Borough of Warwick commanding them to send two burgesses to parliament on the 2nd of April.

"M^d that Besides this precept there was brought to Mr Bailief of this borough a lre of Request to the same Bailief and Burgesses directid from the ryght honorable therle of warwik towching the election of one of the same two burgesses The teno^r of wch lre ensuith

(folio 32) "To my loving freends the Bailief and the rest of the company of the towne of warwik

After my hartie comendacions I have recevid lres from my l.l. of the counsaill importing the great desire her ma^tie hathe of good choice to be made of wise discreit & well disposid psones to serve for knights & burgesses in this pliament nowe somonyd by her hieghnes order to begyn in Apryll next And being therby requyred on her ma^tys behalf that I for my part (to avoyd some enormyties) will take care that the Burgesses w'n that towne to be chosen be to all respects mete & worthie those Romes I have thought good like as to signifie thus much unto yo" so to pray you to consider thereof acordingly And albeit it may be there is no want of hable men emong y^r selves for the supply of the matter yet the speciall opynion I have upon good cause concevid of my friend Mr Edward Aglionbys sufficiency dothe move me to recomend him unto yo" for one of yor burgesses being a man not onely well knowen among yo" but one I dare undertake yo" shall finde veary forward in thadvauncement of any thing that may tend to the comon profit & comoditie of yor towne Wherof not doubting but you will have due regard I bid yo" haitely farewell At Westm the xixth of ffebruary 1570 yor loving friend

A. Warwik" [a]

By virtue of which precept "Thomas Burges then bailief of the said Borough callid a hall or meting of the principall burgesses & others the comoners of the said Borough in the Burges hall in Warwik aforesaid and there the xxvith day of March 1571 being Monday the said Bailief aforesaid w^t William huddisdon Richerd ffisher John Butler Richerd Roo Thomas Oken John ffisher Thomas Powell Symon yong & Robert Phelips principall b^{r}gesses togither w^t Robert Sheldon Richerd Tuskit humfrey crane Roger Weale Thomas Jenks Thomas Allen Willm chandes & John Ridgeley Assistants after the reading of the said precept & lres have electid named & chosen Edward Aglionbie Esquire & John ffisher gen to be their twoo burgesses of the parliament of the said Borough wch place and Rome the said John ffisher being present refusid disabling himself both for want of creadite wisedome & health wch not w'stonding the said Bailief and Burgesses earnestly requesting the same John to take upon him the same place & Rome the rather for that they having nowe great cause to chose & appoynt a faithfull & trustie man   have thought him to be of all most metest & therfore eftsones both entreatid and pswadid him to take the same uppon him and to

[a] This nobleman was known as the "good" Earl of Warwick. His monument is in the Beauchamp Chapel.

prepare himself therunto w^t all convenient spede wch by much entreaty & pswasion being lothe therunto the said John acceptid w^t thanks giveng for their good willes desiring them to contynewe their good opinions towards him & promising to do the best in him lieth for the benefit of the said Towne wch he said should be put forth acording to his simple hability praing them to accept of his good will eftsones beseching thr company to apoint some other & meter man & to discharg him in respect of his late & yet present sicknes being then very weak And towards their charges he wold give them x^{li} wherof they woold in nowise allowe but willid him to prepare himself And for that purpose causid to be made a paire of Indentures the one pt wherof sealid w^t the town seal was c'tified the teno^r wherof ensueth

Then follows an Indenture, which testifies to the Election of Messrs. Aglionby and Fisher.

" After wch Election & Indenture so sealed & delivered to the said Sheriff, The said John Fisher being veary weak in bodie prepared himself, and on the Thursday following toke his journey to the said Parliament Where he attendid from the last day of Marche 1571 being xiij^o Elizabeth untill the xxixth day of may following being tuesday on which tuesday the said Parliament was dissolvid. In all wch meane tyme neither the said Bailief nor principall Burgesses did neith^r send or wryte to the said Burgesses or either of them although the same John Fisher had from tyme to tyme addressid lres to the said Bailief & principall Burgesses w^t such advertisements and namely of one especiall matter wch was of the noble disposicion of the right honorable therle of Leicester towards the said towne & countrye In that it had pleasid him to be suto^r not only to the quenes ma^{tye} but also to the whole parliamet to have licence & warraunt to erect & found an hospitall either in the towne of Warwik or Kenelworth and to give towards the mayntence therof lands tenements hereditaments & possessions to the yerely value of twoo hundreth pounds by the yere wch should have ppetuytie for ever and that the lands tenements possessions & hereditaments so to be by him given should be assured by auctorytie of the said parliamet A thing both notable & to be thankfully acceptid of by all the whole countrey which his sute it pleasid her heighnes most favorably to heare & likid also the whole state of parliamett besides that they most gladly consented And so in thend the said parliament was by the quenes ma^{ty} most benigley w^t roiall assent graciously confirmed this thyng being thought to the said John a cause of g^t joye encouragd him oftener to write thereof & of some other occurrants but all in vayne for he could never receve any answer by writing or woord of any his lres from the said Bailief wch grounded in the said John no litle discouragement of this service quid significat querendum est de discrecioribus in nullis enim consolatus fuit"

A VISIT OF THE EARL OF LEYCESTER TO WARWICK.

Conference towching the receving of therle of leycr at his comyng to kepe St Michaells feast

(folio 33) MEMORAND That uppon c'ten knowledge had of my Lord therle of Leicesters coming downe into this Countrye to lie for sixe or seaven daies at Mr Thomas ffishers [a] house called the pryory nere Warwik It was considered by the Bailief Thomas Burgeis and such other of his Assistants principall Burgesses of this towne as then were in the towne that it was requisite to offer some present unto his L & therle of Warwik who as the saing was should have come downe with him togither wth many other noble Lords & Ladyes

Wheruppon the said Bailief appointed a meting & sent for all the principall Burgesses to be at their house in the churche on tuesday the xxv^{th} day of September 1571 there to consult & confere of such causes as then they had to do

---

(a) Thomas Hawkins alias Fisher was a man high in favour with the Duke of Northumberland, and had a grant of the Priory made to him. Being also enriched with other possessions, he pulled the old monastry down to the ground, and built the present house, which he called Hawkins's Nest or Hawk's Nest. He was a man of ability and courage, and at the battle of Musselburgh Field in Scotland, where he had command of a regiment, he distinguished himself by the capture of some colours.

When the Duke of Northumberland was plotting to place Lady Jane Grey on the throne, Fisher had a large sum of money entrusted to him for the payment of forces. After the Duke's seizure he hid the money in Bishop's Itchington pool, and was, by authority of Queen Mary, questioned about it, but, according to Dugdale, "denying it stoutly and put upon the rack, was so extreamly tormented, that his fingers were pull'd out of the joynts, yet would never reveal it." He died Jan. 12th, 1576, and was buried in St. Mary's, where a handsome tomb was erected to him and his wife in the North Transept; which tomb was destroyed by the great fire.

uppon which sending for thither cam Willm huddisdon Richerd ffisher Richerd Townesend John ffisher Richerd Roo Willm ffrekulton Thomas powell and Robart phelippes to attend on the said Bailief for the purpose aforesaid At wch assembly It was openyd that the comon speche was that the Earles of Warwik & Ley^r wth many other Lords & Ladyes woold be the next thursday night at Mr Tho ffishers nere Warwik And therfore it was thought mete that some thing might be prepared to be presentid to thes L^ds for two speciall causes the one for that therle of Warwik is Lord of the borough & beareth the name thereof And the other for that therle of Leicester his brother being in gr^test favo^r wth the prince was honorably mynded to doo great good not only to this borough (as he before had done to Coventry) but also to the whole Countrye wch his good will so had aperrid in suing to her Ma^ty & obtayning of her & the whole parliament Licens & graunt to erect & build in Warwik or Kenelworth one hospitall and to endowe the same w^t lands & tenem^ts to the yerely value of twoo hundred pounds wth his honor able doings manifesttid his godly heart and disposicion towards this poore borowe & Countrye And therfor not to be altogither forgotten of us especially having so inst an occasion by their coming so nere the towne And so in conclusion it was demanded whither it were thought good to this house to present any thing or not Whereonto it was answerid by Every man that it was very necessary to yeld some present to their L^d in token of o^r good willes & dutys wherupon it was askid what might best serve that turne to be presented And uppon informacion given to the house that the said erle of Leicester was well

A yoke of oxen psented to E Leisister & E Warwik

provided of muttons It was agreid that a yok of good oxen should be prepared & bestowed on the said Lords at their comyng And that the mony remayning in M^r ffrekultons hands viz ix^li xix^s & od mony should serve for that purpose if it might be by him conveniently spared wch was not then so ready And therfre it was by the whole companye agried that x^li should be taken out of the chest to serve this turne And that the same should be delivered to Richerd ffisher and Richerd Townsend to provide therw^t the said oxen The wch being agreid It was movid among them whither they thought it convenient to mete the same Lords on the waye or not

The Lords being but subjects must not have such dutys as princes Therefore not fitt to goe out of ye Towne but to be ready in ye Towne to offer welcomb

to w{ch} it was answered and agreid that the said Lords being but subiects must not have such Duety as the prince whom they do wayt for but at the boundry of the libties of this borough therfre it was not thought mete to go out of the towne but being ready in the towne to offer welcomyng to the said Lords w{t} their said present That being agreid upon It was demandid whither it were necessary to yeld thanks to the said Earle of Leicester for his honorable good mynd toward this country and borowe and to move his hono{r} to found his said hospitall in the said borowe as a place convenient And whither the towne woold offer unto his L any part of their burges hall & buildings there towards the pformance of so good a woork Or not To which it was answered & resolved not to give any thanks or to tak knowleig of his disposition that waye unless it might lik him either by himself or some about him to give occasion thereof And if it happenid that any such matter should by the said Lord or any for him be movid or any request made for the said hall or any thing thereabouts Respit should be disired by us before we should mak any direct answer in those matters And so it was concluded that such as had keys should be at the church by seaven of the clok the next morning to tak out the said ten pounds for the purpose aforesaid w{ch} was done And the said x{li} was delivered to the said Richerd Townsend who with the said Richerd ffisher (folio 34) travalid in the said Busynies and hearing of c{r}ten fatt oxen that were to sell at henley park they went thither where they found such as served their turne w{ch} oxen were to be sold by John Butler of Warwik being one of the principall burgesses and in great creadit and trust w{t} the said Earle of Leicester So after the oxen were viewid they returned to Warwik to speak with M{r} Butler to knowe the price w{ch} was holden at xj{li} And so in conclusion the said John Butler sold the said oxen And being given t understand for what purpose they were bought and of the whole discourse and entencion of the Bailief & Burgesses towching the meting of the said L. of Leicester & presenting the said oxen to him the said John Butler otherwise advised bothe the said Bailief & such as he talked withall and tok uppon him to appoint a more meter & fitter tyme bothe for the psenting of the said oxen and the Bailief attending on the said Lord wch should be on Friday morning promissing that he wold in the meane tyme solicite o^r good willes to the said Lord to the better contentacion of the said noble men & for the better aceptans of the present & to the great comodity of the towne wheruppon the Bailief resolved to do in all thyngs as the said Butler had devised And therefore disappointed the first agreament to the no litle detryment of the said Borough and defacing of the said not only Bailief but all the principall Burgesses ffor so it hapind that the said Earle of Leicester having in mynd his form^r intencions & good woork and knowing that the Bailief & his brethern could not be ignorant of his said devise for that one of the same company being of the Parliament house was privie & consenting to the same devise and had some speche w^t his Lordshippe thereof expected the not only attendance of the Bailief and his said company but also that they woold have mett him on the waye and recevid him w^thout the towne in some semely manner the rather for that he cam downe so nobly acompanyed and to shewe himself so honorably amongs them Insomuch as the Wensday night lieng at Sr John Spencers he spake somewhat thereof to such as were about him Whereof the next day a litle Inkling was given thereof to J^hn ffisher being bothe his man & one of the principall burgesses of the said borough wch knowleig was brought to him by message as he was riding beyond Radford on the hiegh way to do his duety to the said Earle his M^r but w^t all was signified that he should kepe it to himself Whereon the said ffisher musing as he rode, & revolving the conferrence before thought it mete to advise the said Bailief to followe his first devise in attending for the said noble men at the Townes End or ells at the crosse ^(a) acompanied with the rest of his principall Burgesses and as many other honest comoners in gownes as might be gotten upon that warning And there to offer their present as a token of their good willes And therupon sent his serv^t in all hast wth that message to the said Bailief who had knowleig of all this by two of the clock in the afternoone But the said Bailief resting uppon thadvise given by the said John

---

(a) There were three crosses, a market cross in the Market Square, another in Bridge End, near to the old bridge, and another nearly opposite the present Court House. The latter would be the one referred to.

driven to give it over   And surely feawe or none of that towne is hable to make any sufficient stok for that purpose besides that skilfull men are wanting w'hout wch also if they had a good stock woold litle prevaile and also the trade of clothing is not greatly enioyed bicause of the dampe & stoppe of entercourse and many other causes   To wch the said Earle said as for skilfull men may be provided either from coventry or some other place if men have desire & care so to doo   And as for the stok his L woold be meane to helpe them to a stock if he might understand it might be well used   but if by his travail a stock might be provided and refused (as in Beaverley it was) he could not like of it ffor at Beverley the said Earle having brought to passe that of him and the gentlemen of the countrye a stock of MM^li was offred to the towne men to be put in use of some trade in this maner that the said townes men should have it delivered to them in mony or wooll at reasonable price to be by them occupied and paid again that tyme twelve monethes and to have it always a yere before hand during six yeres This offer being made to the said townes men they refusid it wch was thought to the wiser sort that it woold have bene bothe a meane to put their Idel poore into woorke and so gotten them a speciall good trade and also woold have resid encrease wherw^th to have had in those six yeres a good round stock of their owne besides the first but this was refusid of them wch sithens they have repentid and woold be glad to have if they might   And so his Lordship said that he doubtid howe if any offer of like were made to o^r towne howe it woold be liked of (folio 44)   To wch the said ffisher aunswerid that albeit he had no comission of them that sent him towching those matters   Yet he doubtid not but that offer whensoever should be made unto the towne wold be not only not refusid but most thankfully acceptid wth such duetifull regard to his L for so honorable consideracion of their prosperous & well doings to the furtheraunce wherof nothing could be better devised insomuch as the comodotes requisite to such trades are bred amongs them at home in the same country   And therfore most humbly besought his Lordship to contynewe his good mynd therin   Wherw^th the Earle said willed the said ffisher to ympart this devise to his companye to thend they may think theruppon   w^ch

D

if it be likid his L said he woold further it to his uttermost   So entring into other concacion his L asked whither I had comission to mak him a dede of the house bestowed uppon him or whether he must have it from the towne and the said ffisher aunswerid that he had no comission so to doo but the dede must come from the towne and passe their comon seale and theruppon he askid what seale we had and of what forme it was wch the said ffisher discribid aswell as he could then remember^(a)   Then his L desired that the dede might be made & sealid wth as good spede as might be wch the said ffisher promissed to be done in all things towching the towne that was for the sealing therof but for the devising and making was requisit to be done by the L counsull to wch his L aunswrid that he had willed Peniston his solicto^r to conferre wth the said ffisher therabouts wch the said ffisher confessid was done and that some question grewe betwene them for the maner of the drawing therof wherin he was humbly to move his hono^r for his pleasure to be signified whither it might lik his lordshippe to have the use putt into the dede or not wch to doo the towne woold graunt acording to his L pleasure wheruppon making a litle pause It pleasid his L thus to aunswer   That he trustid the towne woold bestowe thenheritance of the same house uppon him And so doing hit likid him well that the world should knowe their good willes therin and therfore was veary well content that woords might be put into the dede to signifie the use   which nevertheles he woold never have put to any other use or p^rpose neither woold have desired but for the convenyency of the place And dothe veary much desire his entencion might goo forwarde w^t as good spede as maye be and that he may have his assurance the soner bicause he myndeth to set men on woork there assone as the season will suffer and askid the said ffishers opinion whither he thought v^e m^ks woold make the place readye wch the said ffisher thought woold be sufficient and aunswerid that he trustid his L should save v^e m^ks in having his house &c   And so the said ffisher brought downe the dede devised and writen upp   And making reaport to the bailief & the rest of the burgesses on friday the ix^th of deceb^r of all the aforesaid matters there the

---

(a) The Borough seal represents a walled town with warders on the towers blowing horns. On one side is the sun, on the other the moon.

the said dede was red emongs them and it was agreid that the same should be sealid on the Wensday following and sent upp to the said L w^t as good spede as might be and that one of that company should cary upp the dede and should followe the sute before begonne

THE DEATH AND BURIAL OF THE MARQUIS OF NORTHAMPTON.

The death and buryall of the Marques North^ts

"Nowe whiles thes things were thus in doing happenid a thing thought worthie to be remebrid the rather because it hapned in this place by occasion of the coming of the said Earle to this towne of Warwik And this it was as is afore remebred Amongs many noble personages coming to this towne to accompanye the said Earle of Leicester One William Lord Marquesse of Northampton being of the quenes pryvie counsaill being long before sick and sore trowbled with the gowte cam w^t his ladye and wief to Warwik aforesaid being so payned & feble that he was not hable to goo or stand but was carryed betwene two of his srvnts from place to place upon a stoole for that ppose devised This Marquesse there contynewing was sometyme better and sometymes worse but at no tyme hable to goo out of the chamb^r In so much that the said Earle of Leicester depting w^t the rest of the noble men & others left the said Marques at Thomas Fishers house untill he might be better recoverid and assigned officers to diffray the chardges of his dyet & other things whiles he should be there wch was longer than was expected ffor so it hapned that god had apointed his tyme that on saint Simons and Judes day about iiij^or of the clock in the after none the said late Marquesse gave up the ghost veary cristianly by all reaport leaving behind him a Ladye Marchionesse a straunger borne in Swecia the doughter of a knight whiles he lived whose name was woolf this lady being bothe yong and faire cam into Englond attending on the Lady of cicilia & here left behind at the request of this late noble man and was placed to attend the quenes ma^tie her privie

This was Sr Willm Parr whom Henry 8 created Earle of Essex & Ed 6 created him Marquesse of North^ton

13. Eliz. 1571

chamb^r untill such tyme as god wold suffer the said Marques (having then a wief a live though divorced from him) (folio 45) to be cowpled wth her in marriage as he was in dede uppon the death of the late Ladye Bowser This Marquisse so decessid not the richest man in Englond nor of sufficient living to make his said Ladye any jointure It was doubtid howe and by whom he should be buryed ffor the said Lady had not wherew^h to beare the chardge and therfore Order was give that his corps should be enchestid and kept until the quenes pleasure therein might be knowen And after that some demaund towching that matter was made to the Erle of Pembrooke (his sisters sonne) his L. offred towards the funerall c^li (as it was said) wch being thought not sufficient to bear those chardges It pleasid her Ma^ty to tak the whole charge uppon her and appointid howe all things should be done giveng great chardge to the heraulds to see his obsequies pformed wth all solempnitie acording to his honorabls callng and therfore apointid Garter the king at Armes Norrey and Lancaster being herralds to be at thes funeralls and appointid such clothe & other things as was necessary to be taken out of her great wardrobe to the doing therof And assyned John ffortescue esquire m^r of her said wardrobe to see the diffraing of all maner of charge towching that buriall All which things being put into order the said m^r ffortescue and Garter & the other heralds cam to Warwik on Sonday the second of Decembr 1571 and there delivered to divers gentlemen and others their liveryes viz of black clothe v yards for evry gentleman & for evry srvnt man ij yards and prepared all things against the funerall apointid to be on the Wensday following being the vth of Decebr At which funerall was said should have bene the Earle of Pembrook chief mo^rner The lord Barklay & lord Vaux and the Bisshopp of Wo^rceto^r to have done the obsequies but howe soever it hapned neither the Earle of Pembrook Lord Vaux nor bisshop cam not So as the L Barkley was chief Manye other knights and gentlemen were away wch were said should have bene there But such as were there were placid by the heraulds And whan all things were made redy the corpes was set furth in maner folowing viz. before the corpes went priests & ministers to the nomb^r of xx or thereabouts then follow^d William Beaumont in a black gowne & whood bearing the standerd of the late Marquesse then yong Mr Lane bering his banner Then followid Lancaster in his coat of armes and berith his coat Armo^r Then Norrey who berith his sworde & targe Then followeth Garter who beareth his hed piece & crest Then cometh the corpes being borne of eight gentlemen in black gownes on the coffin was laid a lardge paule of the quenes being of cloth of silver and bandekin hangi l about with eskuchiens wch was supportid by ffoure other gentlemen about the corpes were carried by iiij^{or} other gentlemen in black gownes iiij^{or} bannerroles of dissent And then followe the mourners viz The Lord Barkley which mo^rn^r assisted by Mr Willm Gordge the pencioner Then followe Sr Richerd Knyghtley and Sr Robert Lane in black gownes Then S^r ffulke Grevile & M^r clement Throkmton Then Mr George woolf my Ladyes brother & one Mr Wake all in black gownes & whoods   Then followid other gentlemen & yomen of the said Maquesse to the nomb^r of x or therabouts gentlemen in gownes & yomen in coates of black Then M^r clement Throkmton's srvnts to the nomb^r of xx all in black though not of that livery   Then followed M^r ffrekulton ye bailifs deputy and the rest of the principall burgesses w^t divers comoners of the towne and then lastly srving men in their Maisters liveryes   In this order they procedid till they cam to the church where was prepared in the bodie of the churche a hearse stonding upon iiij^{or} pillers railid the pillers being by estimacion xij foot hiegh covered w^t black clothe having a tester of black clothe on wch were fastenyd v seuchions of his Armes in metall The valance of black vellet & russet taffata w^t a fringe of black silk uppon the pillers were fixed skutchions of his armes to the nomb^r of xij about the valence w^h like scuchions to the nomb^r of xj on the topp over the valence were sett fourth pennons of his armes in mettall upon sarcenet to the nomb^r of xl w^thn the hears was a table sett wheron the corpes was laid for the tyme of the srmon on the pawle laid on the corpes was laid downe his coat Armo^r his sworde & targe and his helmet and crest being a maydens head stonding on his helmet w^t a wreathe or Role of black & yealowe sarcenet having mantells of black vellet hanging downe on either side w^t knoppes guilt & w^t tarseltes of black silk fringe (folio 46) Then was song a psalme and that endid the srmon began wch was made by Mr Raffe Griffin preacher whoo took for his Theame thes woords viz   certamen bonum decertaui cursum consummaui fidem seruaui quod surperest reposita est michi Justicie corona quam reddet michi dominus in illo die qui est iustus Judex: non solum autem michi sed omnibus qui diligunt aduentu ipsius &c[a] wherein bothe learnedly and eloquently he sett fourth the lief of man to be a warfare and ffyht impugned by many enemyes namely the devill the world and the flesh And howe evry cristian man ought to fight against them & with what armo^r he should be furnisshed and then the victorye folowing that is the crowne of glorye wherin also did much recomend the vertue of this late Marques how strongly he had shewed himself even till the last end & gaspe most cristianly by his testimonye as an eye witnes and the assured hope he had in his rest besides declared the great losse had happenyd by his taking a way not only to that good lady his wief but also to all his srvnts as well gentlemen as others whom he recomfortid on that he was deptid to God &c which srmon so endid they pcedid to the funerall in maner following ffirst come the thre heraulds in order Lancaster norrey and Garter and after them John watts as gentleman ussher to my L Barkley Then the lord Barkley who was assisted by Mr Willm Gordge bering his trayne and all the other morners attending on the said lorde who was so conveid from the hearse into the Quire where at the comunyon table stod the vikar of saint Maryes after he had begonne the comemoracion of the comunyon so farre till he cam to the sentences for Relief of the poore whereof whan he had redd two or three verses he staid being so apointed by the heraulds and taking of a bason there prepared in his hand he recevid the offring brought by the said lord barkley and others and the offrings were in this manner ffirst the said lord being brought upp as before is said offred for the Estate a purse of gold being v^{li} Then after curtesye made aswell by the said lord as the herralds & others the said lord & others are conveid again to their place about the hears And then Garter making lowe curtesye to the said Lord barkley the said L arriseth again & followeth Garter who bringeth him to the comunyon table again where the vikar holding still the bason the said Lord offreth xii^d for himself wch done the said Garter conveid the said Lord again to his place at the head of the corpes stonding

(a) II. Tim. c. iv., v. 7, 8.

still in the body of the church and after obeyzance done Garter stondeth still Then come Norrey and Lancaster and making curtesy the to Sr Richerd Knyhtley and Sr Robart Lane they two arrise to whom the two herralds deliver the coate Armo^r wch is holden betwen the said Sr Richard & Sr Robart and is brought in sollempe maner & offred at the comunyon table to the Vikar w^h done they are conveid to their place by Norrey but Lancaster stondeth still at the table Then Norrey takith the sword & delivereth it to S^r ffulke Grevile who w^t Mr Throkmton be brought in former maner to the comunion table there they offer the sword to the Vikar as before and so are brought again to their place Than Norrey delivereth to Mr George Woulf and Mr Wake the targe who taking it betwene are conveid by Norrey to the said comunyon table & there offre it and so are reduced to their places Then Norrey delivereth to Sr Richerd Knyghtley and Sr Robart Lane the headpiece and crest which betwene them they bring upp and offer as aforesaid Then bothe Norrey and Lancaster goo downe conveng the said Knyghts to their placs And this done Norrey bringeth upp again Sr Richerd Knyghtley & Sr Robart Lane to the table where they offer pieces of silver Than Lancaster bringeth up S^r ffulke Grevile & Mr Clement Throkmton who also offer Then Norrey bringeth up Mr George Woulf & Mr Wake who likewise offer Then Lancaster bringeth up M^r ffortescue Mr Olney Mr Butler and Mr Mousewold who were the supporters of the paule and thes all offer and depte again to their placs Then doth Norrey bring up Mr Willm Lane who offreth up the great square banner Then Lancaster bringeth up Willm Beaumont who offreth up his standerd Then Lancaster bringeth up all the Marques men who offer in order first Mr Oddel Rowse Mr Snobal having white staves as officers then all the rest of the gentlemen & so the yomen Evry man in his order and office who after they have offred depte downe again After all thes offrings done & a fewe prayers said & a psalme sung during the tyme of the offring The corpes (folio 47) is by eight gentlemen assisted w^t the iiij^{or} supporters taken up from the table w^{t}hn the hearse and brought upp attendid on by the foure gentlemen that bare the banner Roles till they come to the place made for the grave being right agaynst the tombe in the quier on the north side of the same tombe betwene the doores of the vestry and the chapter house where the same corpes is enterrid togither w{t} the white staves of the officers & many teares there to rest till God otherwise provide   And so thes obsequies done the Lords and gentlemen repayre to M{r} ffisher's to dynner   And ther had a veary great feast all at the chardge of the quenes ma{ty} till dynner was done   Then on the morrowe the coat Armo{r} helme crest targe and sword were hangid up & so were the Standerd banner and banner Roles over the place where the bodie lieth   And so all thes thyngs finnisshed the herraulds claiming the hearse & all about it to be their ffees woold have taken the same downe the next day but uppon entreaty to let it stond they were content to sell it to Jo. ffisher who gave them eight pounds therfore   In w{ch} bargain he had none of the cloth w{ch} was hangid on the utter Rales neither about the sides of the church but only that about the hearse w{ch} he bought not so much for the value therof as for that the country people resorting to the towne might see the honorable order of part of the said funerall w{ch} stonding is also a bewtifieng of the church"

The Assistant Burgesses Rebel.

Memord   That on Sonday the xvj{th} of Deceb{r} 1571 Robart Phelippes bailief made his Acompt of his burgers office for the yere past by w{ch} Acompt appeared his Receipts to be iiij{xx} vj{li} vj{s} wherof his payments to be Lxix{li} viij{s} iij{d} besides some supers as in the same Acompt appeareth   At this Acompt were present Willm huddison Richerd ffisher John Butler John ffisher Richerd Brook Symon Yong Willm ffrekulton Thomas Powell and Thomas Burgeisse chief and principall Burgesses and of the comoners were psent John Grene John Ridgeley Thomas cawdrye Thomas Allen Philipp Coo Richerd Tuskott humfrey crane John Griffin Bar hurlbut John Bikar Nicolas Purflowe John hicks Thomas chapman henry Chapleyn Roger Weale   Baldwin Benford & John Balies who hearing the said accompt declarid were required to goo togither and to elect and chose of the principall Burgesses one such as to them should be thought metest to execute the office of Burgeis and to receve the rents due to the said borough acording to the accustomed order wch choice the principall Burgesses were contentid to give to the said comoners the rather to signifie their good opinions of them and therby their favo^r they bare them wch was of the said comoners lightly regardid as may appeare ffor ymediately uppon the request made unto them to goo togither to make choice as aforesaid Their prolocuto^r John Grene being as it may be thought prepared to that p^rpose As the mouthe of all the said comoners said That wheras they were requested to chose a newe burges of the principall burgesses he & his company thought themselves therin greatly restrayned to mak their choice in that maner and shewed that they all desired to knowe whither the principall burgesses might not make choice w^thout them wch was told them they might but bicause of their more frendly neighbo^rhood It pleasid Mr Bailief and the principall burgesses to associat them in thes cases more of curtesy than for any necessitye Wherunto the said Grene aunswerid Than is o^r being heare in vayne & to no p^rpose and therfore desired they might have licens to depart Wherunto M^r bailief told them that their being there was not in vaine but veary necessary being required so to be by him who may call them or any of them at any tyme for his assistance as nowe they were to mak choice of a burgeis as before tyme they had used to doo Wherunto the said Grene aunswerid in the name & for the rest That they had bene often callid to this acompt of the Burgeis from yere to yere and being there they have seen that yerely there hathe bene brought in mony as the Remayne of evry mans acompt But after the same hathe bene so brought in they could never be pryvie What cam of that monye neither in whose keaping it was nor howe it was bestowed neither were they made privie of the graunting of any thing by the said borough but were used as ciphers not to be reconid of Besides that there be other things wherein he & his company were desirous to be resolued And thinkith that there might be better order in their Accompts then is used To wch they were willed that if they found themselves in any thing grevid they should utter their mind reasonably towching the points of their grief Wherin the bailief and principall burgesses promised to resolve them as they were hable Then said Grene one matter is (folio 48) That where they heare allowance of c^s given for a fee to M^r ffisher There desire is to knowe whither the same hath bene used to be allowed there or not & so the said Grene pawsed Whenunto it was willid him to procede if he had any mo questions or other matters as if he had they should be aunswerid togither Then said he an other thing is that where there is a chardg of & confession of the Recept of c^{r}ten lands callid the corporation lands They think it good that the said lands should be declaried what lands they bee and where they lie to thend they may be known And other matters they have wch be but mocions or warnings as things whrof they have not much to doo And that is y^t as he & others of his felowship use to travail abrode they heare of some fault found in the maisters of the towne for not using the mony of Mr Willingtons & Mr Whately so well as should be ffor saith he it is knowen that the same monye is to be lent out but as farre as they can heare there is but litle delivered out And therfore they heare say the same mony shalbe callid back again out of their handes And so there pawsid again Saing thies be the grieves wch they mislike Wherupon Mr Balief required them to wthdrawe themselves for a tyme till he & his company might confere towching their aunswer & satisfieng wch they did And not long after they were callid again before the said balief & principall burgesses who had apointid Jo. ffisher to aunswer them in this manner That M^r bailief and his companye had considered of their mocions And had very well accepted their resonable behavio^r in declaring their griefs in such quiet maner & therbye contentid the rather to doo what may be to satisfie their demaunds And first as towching the monye brought in as the remayne of euery burgers acompt his pleasure is they should understand the same hath bene diffraid and laid out for divers purposes in such wise and for such causes as uppon this their soden requests can not pticulerly be declared but bicause they might have some gesse therof he desired them to call to mynde the coming of the Quenes ma^{ty} to this borough wch was no small thing besides that howe from tyme to tyme yerely the towne hath bene chardgid wth presents bestowid upon noble men & others and w^{t}hall praid them to consider howe the ffee fermes being yerely v^{li} for the bailiwik might be aunswered if that monye should not helpe that waye especially for thies vij or viij yeres in which feawe estreates or none at all were leavied Wherof if they had consideracion they should not nede to ask that question   And as towching the allowance given to John ffisher it is in respect of sruice to the towne aswell for matters towching the bailiewik as the Burgarshippe wherin they are many ways to use him and therfore have given him that fee to be paid either by the bailief or burges as he shall require and monye srve wherin saith the said ffisher of himself besides his commission That if the having of that fee be grevous to the towne he will not so chardg them but wilbe content bothe to leave his said fee & patent And the busynes he takith in hand   And towching the pticuler declaracion of the lands callid the corporacion Lands   Mr Bailief desirieth them all to have that opinion of him & his company that though the same be not for length of writing pticulerly sett furth   Yet willith them to think that they be not ignorant what the same lands be nor where they lie or that they kepe not a good record therof registred in the burgers book wch was pticulerly red unto them And lastly towching the mony of Mr Willington & Mr Whateley he takith their warning in that point in good part but for aunswer   Lettith them knowe wth those monyes they shall not nede to trowble themselves neither wth the care to see the same disbursed wch is reported to the trust of divers who be bound for the same monye and disposing therof unto whom whan it shall please them to call for it a Reconing shall be made to satisfie them that have to doo therwth which they have not And therfore Mr Bailief and his company frendly require them not to trowble their heads any further about those matters   but to goo to that matter which they come for   That is to make a newe election of some one of the principall burgeisses to be the burgeis for the yere to come who may be such a one as may padventure satisfie their (folio 49) desires aforesaid   And therin M^r bailief & his company are pleased to graunt them free choice of any of them otherwise then before they have had for before this tyme they had twoo of the principall burgeisses prescribed to them of wch they should choose one but nowe they may elect any one of the twelve   To wch the said Grene replied saing that if they might not choose where they woold either of the principall burgesses or comoners it was no free choice and then they were resolued to choose none at all but to leave the choice to the said M^r bailief and his companie especially for that they were no better reconed of and that there being there was not nedefull and therfore desireth there might be no such nomb^r of xxiiij which they took to have bene a nomb^r apointed by the corporacion & assistants to the bailief w^thout whom the bailief and his company could not pfitt any thing   And insomuch as they pceve it is otherwise they mynd not nor will trowble them any long^r either at this tyme or any other tyme neither for the choice of the burgeis or any other matter as they had hitherto don thinking themselfs apointid by the said corporacion   And so offred to depte   But M^r bailief & his company eftsones required them to goo to that election & let thies matters passe at this tyme   And an other tyme whan leasure might serve they should be better and more fully satisfied although therin the said bailief & principall burgesses should therby make them privie of all their private accompts not only of the bailiwik but otherwise wch for their satisfieng & quieting they woold be pleasid to do whan they might   Wherw^th it was demaunded of them their veary entencions & meaning what it was   Whether they did not think & look for to be privie and consulting to the graunting of all Leaces & things doon by the towne   To wch they made aunswere it was their meaning & they lookid for no lesse   Then said Thomas cawdry more stowtly then wisely & more like a chorle than a choser we will be pryvie to all things orells we will chose no burges nor will not tarry heare come sirs letts us goo and so wth some lewde maner & behavo^r he went away w^t wch ill demeano^r   Mr Bailief bare to much in respect of some friendship belike   And so the said comoners were depting again till Mr Bailief comaundid them to tarry and to withdraw themselves into the windowe aside for a tyme whilest the said bailief and principall burgesses conferring togither agreid That it should be ones again offred to them to mak choice of a burges of one of the principall burgesses which if they refusid to doo they should be suffred to depart And the election should be made by the bailief and principall burgeisses w^thout the comoners   So therupon they were eftsones callid to the said bailief and principall burgeisses and were by them required to goo togither and mak choice of a new burgeis in forme aforesaid wch the said comoners refused to doo unlesse they might have free choice aswell of some of themselves as of the other Wheruppon it was said unto them that both M^r bailief and the rest of the principall burgeisses were veary sorry to see their obstynate behavio^r and wilfull proceadings wherin they had shewid themselves so pversly & frowardly as they had doon uppon some speciall purpose belike but for so much as they were so maliciously myndid they should know that the bailief and principall burgeisses had sufficient power of themselves to doo any thing there to be doon w'hout them And therfore willid them to depart away if they psistid in that mynd as they said they all did and so deptid And whan they weare goone it was agreid that there should bee no such numb^r of xxiiij but some feawer nomb^r should be callid of such as woold be conformable to reason And that Robart Phelips being bailief should have the receving of those rents this yere And that from hensforth the bailief for the tyme being should supplie this office of burgeis w'hout any other choice to be made by such comoners ffor it was thought that the bailief being of sufficient hability and bound to aunswer them was most metest to have the chardg therof And so the remayne was left in the said Mr Phelips hands for that tyme At wch tyme also John ffisher make accompt of the x^li deliverd unto him out of the chest in January last past by wch acompt it apeared that he had paid that x^li for the fee ferme of the bailiwik for ye tyme of M^r ffrekulton & Mr Powell And that he had paid more for ffees about that matter ffourten shillings wch was (folio 50) promised to be paid to him And then the said John offred to the said bailief v marks wch he before had in the absence of the bailief recevid of M^r ffoscue for the bureing of the Lord Marques of Northampton in the church of saint Maryes wch five marks is delivred again to the said John ffisher to be chardgid in the next yeres acompt.

The Deed of the burgers halle given to th'erle of Leycester sealid & agreid to be sent upp

M^d   That on Saint Stevins daye being the xxvj^th day of Decemb^r 1571 The bailief and principall burgeisses being viz. Robart Philips bailief Richerd ffisher Willm huddisdon Richerd Townesend Jhn ffisher Willm ffrekulton Thomas powell & Thomas Burges being assemblid in the church thought it mete & agreid that the Dede made to the Earle of Leycester of the gift of the burgers hall &c should be sealid and sent upp to his L for his neweyers gift   And therfore agreid to send one of the said Company of burgeisses wth all viz. John ffisher who not refusing the travaile desired the rest to send to Mr John Butler being then at Kenelworth & to offer him that busynes the rather bicause he having dealt somewhat in that matter before that tyme being best likid of to my Lord should best be heard of his L offring further that if M^r butler refusid to goo the said John ffisher woold take uppon him the delivery therof upon wch mocyon the said bailief sent to Mr Butler desiring his company both for his consent to the sealing as his advise for the dispach therof to the said Earle   Wherupon a messag was p^sently made to the said Mr J. Butler who reading the lre wrote an aunswer to the said bailief to this effect   That the said bailief & his company had veary well don to pcede in sealing of the dead and to send it spedily to my Lord   neu^rtheless thought that the said bailief & his company had not forgott his former offer & promise towching that matter but inasmuch as they had appointed an other messenger belike more trustie he was content although he had never deceavid the towne or never woold wch lre being so recevid the said M^r balief callid his Assistants again and made them privie to the said aunswer wch was veary straunge to them all who did well remeb^r that the said J. Butler at his being togither w^t the said bailief and principall burgesses said That he could in no wise goo upp before neweyeres daye but w^thin six or seven days after wold be content to goo himself or to be ioyned wth any other of that company and to do his best in that sute   And therfore the said bailief and burgeisses agreid to seale the said dede and to dispache John ffisher therw^th so as the same might be deliverid to the said Earle on newyers daie at the farthest   And theruppon they sealid the dede   The teno^r wherof ensuith viz.

The copy of the deed of the Burges halle giben to therle of Leycester wheron to founde his hospitall

Omnibus cristi fidelibz ad quos hoc presens scriptum puenerit Balliuus et Burgenses Burgi Warwici in com̄ Warr saltm. Cum prenobilis Dn̄s Robertus comes Leicestr Baro de Denbigh utriusq ordinis sci Georgii et sci Michis miles Magister equor dn̄e n̄re Elizabethe dei gr̄a Ang̅l &c Regine ac unus a privato sui consilio Ex sua charitate bona disposicōe ac mero motu suo quoddam hospiciū siue hospitale infra burgu Warwic pred fundare et erigere in auxiliū et sustentacōen pauperum (deo favente) cum omni celeritate decreverit Sciatis igitur nos predcos balliuū et burgenses &c unanimi assensu et consensu n̄ris dedisse concessisse feofasse et confirmasse ac p presentes pro nobis et successoribus n̄ris dare concedere et confirmare predco Dn̄o Roberto comit Leyc heredibus & assignatis suis ad opus et usum & intencioem predict totam illam domū siue aulam n̄ram voc siue cognit p nomen seu n̄oia de le Burgers hall siue le Guild hall in Warwic pred unacum pomario siue gardino n̄ro eidem domui adiacen ac omibz aliis domibus structuris edificiis et easiament quibuscumq situat & existen infra portum siue Januam exteriorem ip̄ius domus siue Aule Ac eciam totam illam capellam n̄ram nup nuncupat Capellam sci Jacobi situat fundat et existen desuper quendam portum siue Januam vocat le westgate burgi pred cum omibz suis p̄tinen uniusis Que quidem premissa quondam fuer parcello possessionu nup Guild sce Trinitatis & sci Georgu in Warwic pred ac modo sunt in tenuris siue occupacoetz pred balliui et Burgenss & quodam John ffisher et Thomas Jenks siue assignat suor habend tenend et gaudend pred domu siue Aulam pomariu gardinu & Capellam pred cum ombz pred structuris edificiis et easiament uniusis predco dno Roberto comiti Leycestr et heredibus suis ad opus et usum pred inppetuum tenend de capetalibz dnis feodi illius p suicia prius debit & de Jure consuet Et nos predt Balliuus et Burgenss predcam domū Aulam capellam et cetera p̄missa p̄fat Dno Roberto Comiti Leycestr & heredbz suis ad opus & usum pred contra nos et Successores n̄ros warrantizabm̄ et inppetuum defendemus p. presentes Sciatis insup nos (folio 51) prefatos balliuū et Burgenses nominasse ordinasse constituisse in loco n̄ro posuisse ac p. presentes nominamus ordinamus et constitum et in loco n̄ro posum̄ dilc̄m et fidelem n̄rm John ffisher generosum n̄rm verum et indubitatum

Attornatū dantes et concedentes prefato Attorn̄ n̄ro plenam et sufficien potestatem facultatem et auctoritatem ad intrand pro nobis et noīe n̄ro in pred domū siue aulam pomariū gardinū capellam et cetera p̄missa seu eor aliquam pcellam ac seisinam inde capiend Et post   seisinam sic capt et ht plenam et pacificam possessionem et seisinam om et singlor p̄missor pfat dno Roberto Comiti Leycestr aut suo in hac parte   Attornāt siue attorn̄ suis de nobis et p nobis ac noīe n̄ro tradere et deliberare p pentes secundum tenorem uim formam et effcm huius presentis doni siue consessionis   Ratum et ḡtum hentes et hituri totum et quicquid d̄cus attorn n̄r faciet in hac parte   In cuius rei testimoniū huic presenti scripto n̄ro sigillum n̄rm̄ coe apponi fecim   Dat xxvj° die Decembr anno regni pred due Elizabeth dei ḡra Anglie ffranc & hibnie Regine fidei defensoris &c quarto decimo *

This dede being so sealid and offred to the said John ffisher to carry the same   And the l̄re from M^r butler being considerid of the said John ffisher desired of the said bailief & burgesses that it might please them ones again to send to M^r butler and to comytt this chardg to him if he woold tak it uppon him (as it semid he woold) wch the said John ffisher did chiefly tavoid the displeasure wch haply might folowe if the said offer of M^r butler should be refusid who being nowe a tenderer of the sute for the benefit of the towne & in great favo^r w^t the said Earle might haply become a hinderer therof   In avoiding whrof It likid the said bailief by the advice of his brethern the said principall burgesses eftsones to write to the said M^r butler to this effect   That where he had by his l̄re pcevid his good contentacion to travaile for the towne w^t their dede to therle of Leycest^r and that he had offred the like before   That neither he the said bailief nor any of the principall burgesses could remeb^r any such offer made but doo remebr that he said he could not goo till after the twelve dayes were past   Wherupon they had orderid as before they had writen to send upp Jo. ffisher w^thall   Nertheles if it pleased him to tak that travaile uppon him they thought him for divers respects the metest   And therfore required him to come by nyne of the clok the next morning to Warwik to conferre wth the said Bailief and principall burgesses

* See Appendix a.

herof w{ch} lre being sent to the said M{r} butler he wrote his aunswer that he was glad that the said bailief and burgeisses had forgotten his promise & offer and astowching his comyng by nyne of the clock that morning he could not bicause it was nyne of the clok or the lre cam to his hands and his busynes was such as by no meanes he could come till the after none And then woold be w{t} them and do anything they should comaund him Therupon the said bailief apointed a meating of the burgesses in the church again the after none Where after evensong the said bailief & m{r} butler w{t} the rest of the principall burgesses viz Robart Phelips bailief John butler Richerd ffisher Richerd Townesend John ffisher Willm ffrekulton Tho. Powell and Thomas Burgeis being assemblid the said bailief eftsones ymparted to the said M{r} butler of ther form{r} procedings and determynacion and the consent of the house towching his going upp to my said Lord w{th} the said dede and howe they thought it good that the same were presentid to his L before or on newyers day at the ferthest And bicause they had sutes to make to the said Earle towching the peuring of the other chappell & other things to the said towne It was thought metist to require him and John ffisher to followe the same and therfore desired them bothe to ioyn togither and to ride upp presently so as they might be there before neweyeres daye wherunto the said m{r} butler aunswerid that it was very well that the dede was sealid and desired that he might heare it wherupon it was red by Jo. ffisher And after the reading therof M{r} butler said he woold be content to travell either nowe or any other tyme whan they should appoint but said at this tyme he hath no other busynes thither And saith further that he thinkith my Lord shalbe so busyed at this tyme as he shall be at no leasure for thes matters (folio 52) and thought that a better tyme woold be after the twelve daies and so such as should be sent about this busynesse should have conveniet tyme to folowe the sutes ymediately uppon the delivery of the deede w{ch} advise was well likid of and so acceptid That although some woold have had the dede sent upp presently yet the greater nomb{r} concludid the same should be staid till after the twelve daies were passid And then the same should be sent upp by the said John Butler and

E

John ffisher who promised their travailes to thuttermost And so that matter was for the tyme so staid Nevertheless to returne to the conferrens on saint Stevins daye It was agreid that the book for the company of the poyntmakers Glovers and Skynners being newely made and enlargid in divers points should then be sealid wch was doon The teno^r of wch book ensueth

Ordynaunces &c

The poyntmakers
Glovers & book
Skynners

A declaracion of all the constitucions ordyndts & agreamets of the Glovers poyntmakers and Skynners w'in the borough of Warwik and suburbes of the same constituted ordenyd & agried uppon by the company and fellowshipp of the Glovers pointmakers & Skynners of the said borough Agreid uppon & consentid unto by the Balief & principall burgesses of the same borough wch orders are to be obsruid fulfillid & kept at all tymes from hensfurth aswell by the Glovers pointmakers & Skynners nowe presently occupieng as by all such of those occupacions as herafter shall occupie & use markett whin the same borough ffirst it is constituted ordenyd and agreid by the whole assent and consent aforesaid that all the Inhabitants being housholders of the said misteries or crafts of Glovers poyntmakers and skyners shall yerely uppon Saint Stevins day assemble themselves and mete togither in some convenient house in the same borough which they shall call the Skynners hall And at that place & tyme they shall evry yere elect and name one of the same artes or crafts to be maister of that crafts for one whole yere then to come And in likewise shall then and there elect & name one other of thes crafts to be warden for the yere After whiche election & nonacion the said maister & warden shalbe fully auctorised by this booke for that yere to warne call & comand at conveniet tymes all the residue of the same severall crafts being men and householders to come to the same hall where they advisedly may talk consult conclude and agree of and uppon all such matters as shall concerne these seuerall crafts and the welth of the said borough

Item it is ordenyd and agreid that euery householder of the said misteryes or crafts of Glovers Poyntemakers & Skyners shall upon sufficient warnyng to him or them first given by the said M^r or warden come to the same hall and there to attend to thentents beforesaid And if any of them upon such warning refuse to come thither having no sufficient excuse for his or there absence at that tyme or being there present obstinately refuse to agree to any such good order shall forfeit for euery such offence xij^d

Item it is ordenyd and agreid That no Inhabitant w^thin the said borough or Suburbes being of the same craft or mistery of Glovers Poyntmakers or Skynners shall in any wise hire receve or take to his sruice any man or chield to dwell w^t him to thentent to learne him in any of the said misteryes or crafts except to take him to be his Aprentice or covenut srunt for the terme of Seaven yeres at the least And that he shall take him by Indenture And shall cause the same Aprentice or covenut srunt to be brought w^t his Indenture before the bailief & Stuard of the same borough within one moneth next after such Aprentice is taken And there the said Apntice or covenut srunt shall acknowleig himself to be bound by the same Indenture to his said Maister for the terme comprisid in the same Indenture wch said Indenture shalbe enrollid by the towne clerke there paing to him therfore xij^d And if any man of the said misteryes do contrary to thies ordendts to forfeit for euery tyme so offending twenty Shillings.

Item it is further establisshid ordenyd & agreid that no man of the said Arts or crafts of Glovers Poyntmakers or Skyners shalbe admittid by the said M^r & Warden to sett upp the said crafts or any of them in the said borough or Suburbes Except he have bene Apprentice or covendt srunt to one of the same occupacion by the space of seven yeres at the least and have servid in the same accordingly wch he shall prove before the said Bailief M^r and warden by the testimony of some honest psones before his admission to sett upp And that provid he shall first compound agree & pay to the said (folio 53) Master warden & feloshippe for his said admission & setting upp three poundes sixe shillings & eight pens at the least to be paid at such resonable daies & tyme as he & they can agree for the same And if any person doo contrary to this Ordinance he shall forfeit and paie to the same M^r warden & felowshippe ffive pounds Provided alwaies and it is agreid that it shalbe lawfull for euery man that hath bene prentice or covennt srunt to any of the said occupacions or crafts in the said borough and sruid there his whole terme as is aforesaid making request to the said Maister and Warden to sett upp & occupie the said Artes or craftes or any of them where he hath bene brought upp Payng to the said M^r and Warden at his setting upp three shillings & foure pens

Item it is ordenyd & agreid that no man of the said crafts or other facultie shall in any wise uppon the market daies holden in the said Borough buie any Shepe skins that is brought to the same market to be sold before the skynnes be brought or laid in the market place uppon payne to forfeit for the first offence & so doing euery skyn so brought contrary to this ordinnce And for the second tyme or more oftene so offending to forfeit & paye Ten shillings The moytie or half value therof shalbe to the chambr of the said borough and the other moytie to him or them that so shall find and tak the thing so bought contrary to this ordnnce

Item it is further ordenyd & agreid that no pson or psons shall buye any maner of Shepes skyns in the said market Except he or they be of the crafts aforesaid or one of them uppon payne to forfeit the same skynnes so bought The one moytie wherof to be to the use of the chamber of the borough The other moytie to them or him that shall tak the same skynnes so bought Provided alwayes and it is agreid that it shalbe lawfull for any persone inhabiting w^{t}in the same borough or suburbes to buy such and so many Skynnes so brought to the market or laid in the market place so as he or they convert the woolle therof into clothe or yarne to be for their owne wering and not to sell the same agayn

Item it is further concludid & agreid that no fforrener of any of the said occupacions or arts shall buye any skynnes brought into the said market before he or they become a brother wth the company of the said crafts in the said borough and paie quarterly to the said M^r warden & ffeloshippe iiij^d uppon payn that euery man buying any skynnes & being no brother as is aforesaid shall forfeit to the same Mr Warden & ffelowshippe Ten shillings to be levied furthw^th by them so offending after one warning first given therof.

Item it is ordenyd & agreid that if it fortune any man of the said occupacions w^tin the said Borough or suburbes having Apprentice or covennt s^runt being bound by Indenture shall happen to die before thexpiracion of the terme & yeres of such Aprentice or covennt s^runt That then the said Aprentice or covennt s^runt serving out the rest of the yeres not determyned wth the widowe of the his late maister or wth any other by his M^r or Mystres apointm^t shall and may at his libtie making first request as is aforesaid And paing iij^s iiij^d Sett uppe in any of the said occupacions or craftes as well as though his Maister had lived out the terme of his yeres comprised in the said Indentures.

Item it is agreid That if any woman w^tin the said borough or suburbes fortune to bury her husbond wch at the tyme of his death of any of the said crafts or occupacions And after happen to marry an other man being not of eny the same crafts but dwelling w^thin the said borough or suburbs And after such marriage wold sett upp or occupie the same crafts or occupacions or any of them That then he shall first compound & agree w^t the same M^r & Warden before he sett up & occupie them or any of them Orells he shall forfeit for euery moneth to the said Mr Warden & felowshippe twenty shillings.

And it is further agreid That if any person or psons w^thin the same borough or suburbes shall in any wise offend in any of these ordnncs And will not uppon demaund made by the M^r or warden pay such somes of monye as by him or them is lost or forfeited for not obsuing the said ordynauncs That then it shalbe lawfull to the said M^r and warden to enter the house or houses of any such offender or offenders and there to take some part of his or their goods &

catalles in the name of a distresse And the same to deteyne untill such tyme as he or they have paid (folio 54) the same mony so forfeited or lost by breking any the said ordnes or agreements And if the offender or offenders in them or any of them will not pay the mony so lost as is beforesaid w'in one moneth next after such distres taken That then at the next court day to be holden in the said borough after the said moneth The same distres to be brought by the said M^r & Warden into the said court before the Bailief and Recorder there and the same distres there shalbe prasid by iiij^{or} indifferent men after which presement so made it shalbe lawfull to the said M^r & warden to sell the same distres and satisfy themselves of the monye so forfeited or lost And the rest to redeliver to the owner or owners of the same.

And it is also agreid that uppon the said feast of Saint Stephen in cristmas evry yere after election and nomacion of a newe maister & warden made as is aforesaid the said olde maister and warden shall mak a full and a pfect acompt of all such somes of money as they have recevid by any defalte forfeiture agrement or otherwise as is beforesaid And after the said Acompte so fully made and finished they shall deliver the moytie or one half therof w^t the surplusage of the precedent acompt to the said newe M^r & Warden And the other moytie and half of the said monye lost & acrewing by defalte forfeiture or agrement to the bailief of this borough for the tyme being to the use of the chambr of the said borough.

ffinally it is likewise agreid cencludid & consentid unto That incase any thing be done by the said Glovers pointmakers & Skynners contrary to the good customes and Lawes of this Land or the quiet government of this comon weale Or in case the Bailief and principall Burgesses shall see cause to redres or reforme any thing or article abovesaid or to adde or encrease other orders to thies above writen That the Bailief and principall Burgesses for the tyme being may determyn mak voide & frustrate all or any the Articles abovewriten and in there steed to make newe As occasion & tyme shall requyre by there discrecions wch being devised & agreid upon by the bailief and principall burgesses or the greter nombr of them and knowleig therof given in writing to the Maister &

warden abovesaid shalbe from thensfourth taken & reputed And shalbe in dede ordynces & orders to bynd the said company of pointmakers glovers & Skyners & evry of them this book or any thing herin contenyd to the contrary notw'stonding In witness &c

The Walkers & Dyers book

A declaracion of the constitucions and orders agreid upon aswell by the company & felowshippe of Walkers and Dyers w'hin this Borough of Warwik as consentyd unto by the Bailief and principall Burgesses of the same Borough by the said walkers and dyers to be observid fulfillid and kept &c

ffirst it is ordenyd & consented unto that the Inhabitants & householders of the same misteryes & craftes of walkers and dyers dwelling w'hin this borough or the suburbes of the same shall yerely uppon the feast of purificacion of saint Marye the virgin assemble and meat togither at some convenient house w'in the said borough w'ch for the tyme shalbe callid the walkers & dyers halle and then & there shall yerely choose & name one of their sevrall artes to be M^r for one whole yere next to come and twoo other psons of the same Artes to be wardens for the yere to come w'ch said M^r & wardens so chosen & named shalbe auctorised by this book to warne call & gather togither at tymes convenient all the rest of those craftsmen being householders within the said borough & suburbes to come to that halle where they may consulte & agree upon such resonable articles and good orders as shalbe for the benefit & comodytie of their sevrall artes & misteryes and the comon weale of the same borough & countrey adiacent

Item it is ordenyd & agreid that euery householder of the said misteryes & craftes of Walkers & dyers w'in this borough or suburbes upon resonable warning to them given by the said M^r & Wardens shall come to the said hall and give his & there attendance there for the causes beforesaid And incase they or any of them upon that warning refuse to come having no reasonable let or cause of excuse for his or ther absence Or being there doo refuse to consent & agree to such good orders as by the company & felowship of walkers & dyers or the greter nombr of them w't the M'r & wardens shall then & there be devised & agreid upon That then evry pson so absenting himself or refusing to come or being present refuse to agree to such good orders as shalbe devised shall forfeit and pay for euery such offence xij'd

Item it is further agreid & ordenyd that no Inhabitant w'tin the said borough or suburbes being of the said crafts of walkers and dyers shall in any wise receve or take into his sruice any maner of person or psons to dwell w't him to thentent to learne him his said misterye or craft except he tak him to be his Aprentice for the terme of seven yeres at the least And that he shall tak such person by Indenture and shall bring in the said Aprentice w't his Indenture before the balief & Recorder or town clerk of the same borough for the tyme being w'tin one moneth next after he have so taken such aprentice there to acknowledge himself to be bound by the same Indenture to his said master for the terme & under the condicions conteynid in the said Indenture w'ch Indenture shalbe enrollid before the said balief & Recorder & Towneclerk the towne clerk taking for such enrolment only xij'd upon payn that evry pson not pforming this Article to forfeit & paye Twenty shillings

(folio 55) Item it is establishid and agreid that no man of the said crafts of walkers and dyers being a forrener shall sett up or shall use the said Artes or crafts or either of them w'tin the said borough or Suburbes except he have been Aprentice to the said craft and sruyd therin seven yeres at the least w'ch shalbe duely provid before the bailief of this borough for the time being and the M'r & warden of the said craft before any such forrener be admittid or suffred to set up as aforesaid And after such proofe made he shall compound w't the said M'r & Warden of the said craft And shall pay to the said M'r & Warden three pounds at the least for his said admission to be paid at such resonable tymes & dayes as shalbe agreid upon by the said M'r & Warden so it be w'tin one yere next after such admission Provided alwayes and it is fully agreid that it shalbe lawfull to any pson that hath bene Apntice w'in the said borough or suburbes to ether of the said crafts & srng out his yeres of Aprentiship making first request the said M^r & Wardens to sett up & use his said occupacion w'in the same borough & suburbes paing only three shillings and foure pens.

Item it is agreid & ordenyd that no pson or psons being a forrener of the misteryes of walkers & dyers shall come into this borough or suburbes and fetche any kind of cloth either brode or narrowe of any thinhabitants of the said borough or suberbes to mylle or dye the same unles he or they do compound w^t the M^r & Wardens of the said crafts for his freedome w'hin the said borough uppon payne that evry pson offending this Article shall forfeit & pay for euery such offence twenty shillings.

Item it is agreid & consentid that none of the said walkers or dyers shall at any tyme sett up or ocupy any other occupacion or arte than such as he hath bene brought up in & bene Aprentice unto Uppon payne that who so doth shall forfeit for euery moneth so doing ffoity shillings

Item it is further ordenyd concludid & agreid by assent aforesaid That if any person or psons dwelling w'hin the said borough or suberbes Or any forrener being of either of the said occupacions shall in any wise offend in breking any of thies ordynaunces & agreements And will not uppon demaund therof made by the said M^r or wardens pay such some of monye as is by them lost as aforesaid That then it shalbe lawfull to the said M^r & wardens by Auctoryty of this book to enter the house or houses of any such offender or offenders And there to take some part of his or there goods for a distres And the same to take away & deteyne untill such tyme as he or they have paid such mony as is lost & forfeited by him or them And if such offenders or offender will not paye the mony lost as is aforesaid w'in one moneth next after such distres taken That then the said Maister & wardens shall bring the same distres so by them taken into the next court to be holden w'hin the said borough next after the said moneth And there in the presens of the bailief & Recorder the said distres shalbe praysid by iiij^{or} indifferent men After wch praisement the said maister & wardens shall sell the same distres And of the mony rising therof shall satisfie themselves of such some or somes as have bene lost & forfaited And the rest if any remayne they shall deliver to the owner or owners.

Item it is further agreid consentid & ordenyd that of all such mony as shall rise of the fynes agreements forfeitures & penaltyes above delivered the one moyty and half shalbe to the use of the chamb^r of this borough And the other moytie to the use of the said Mr Wardens & company of Walkers & dyers.

Item it is ordenyd concluded and agreed that uppon the said feast of purificacion of saint mary yerely after such election of newe maister and wardens The olde M^r & wardens shall make a full pfect & iust acompt of all such somes of monye as they have recevid for any default forfeyture agreement or otherwise as is aforesaid And after theire said Acompt so fully playnely & clerely made the said late maister & wardens shall deliver the moytie & one half of all such mony as hath or shold haue come to their handes by reson of such default forfeiture agreament or otherwise to the bailief of the said borough for the tyme being to the use of the chamb^r of the said borough And the other moytie and half wth the rest of the same monye as remaneth upon the precedent Acompt they shall deliver to the newe M^r & wardens so by them electid & chosen putting in sufficient band for the redelivery & true aunswering therof at the end of the said yere.

Item it is finally agreid concludid & consentid that incase any thing be doon by the said Walkers or dyers contrary to the good customes and lawes of this land Or the quyet government of this comon weale Or that the M^r & wardens of the said Walkers & dyers do not yerly pay all such mony as should yerely come to their hands for & to the use of the chambr of this borough as aforesaid Then this book and all Articles therin conteynyd to be void Or incase the bailief and principall burgesses shall see cause to redres or reforme any thing or article abovesaid or to adde or encrease other orders to thies abovewriten that the Balief and principall Burgesses for the tyme being may determyne make voyd

& frustrate all or any the Articles above wryten And in their places to mak newe as occasion and tyme shall requyre by their discrecions which being devised and agreid uppon by the bailief and principall burgesses or the greater nombr of them And knowleig therof given in writing (folio 56) to the M{r} & wardens abovesaid shalbe from thensfourth taken and reputid and shalbe in dede ordynnes & orders to bynd the said company of walkers & dyers & euery of them This book or any thing herin contenyd to the contrary notwithstonding. In witnes of all w{ch} Articles & agree{ts} made by consent aforesaid The said bailief & principall burgesses have to thies presents put their comon seale the sixt day of August in the xiiij{th} yere of o{r} sovegn Lady Elizabeth by the grace of god &c.

Mem. of the election of Rob{t} Philippes as one of the principal burgesses on Sunday, 19th of March, 1569.

Mem. of election of Rob{t} Philippes to be bailiff on 29th Sept., 1571.

Mem. of election of Thomas Jenks to be a principal burgess on 1st August, 1572, and on the same day the election of Edward Aglionby, Esquire, to be Recorder in the place of Sir William Wigston, Knight, "whose age & wekeness was such as he could not supply that office"

Mem. of election of Thomas Jenks to be Bailif on 29, Sept., 1572.

Mem. of election of John Dyche & Humphrey Crane to be principal burgesses on the 2nd of November, 1573

On the 18th of January, 1574, it was agreed "That Richard ffisher shall have fforty Ronell Okes & all the wood callid (   ) being in the tenure of Robart Tibot of hatton & two yeres tyme for the felling therof paing therfore ffive pounds

Wood sold to Richerd ffisher

Item that Robert Philips shall have an advowson made to him of the psnage of Russhok for the presenting of one hable pson to the said benefice at the next avoydance The said Robert Philips giveng for the same a vj{li}

advowson of Russhok grnted to Robart Phillipps

Item that the plate remaning in the chest shalbe taken out valued & sold

Reuercion of the moyty of the tuithes of Muyton graunted to John ffisher

Item that John ffisher shall have the Reuercion of the moytye of the tuithes of the felds of Myton after thexpiracion of a leace nowe in esse paing therfor as an other will give

Advowson of Stone graunted to Thomas Powell

Item that the Advowson of the Vicarage of Stone be grauntid to Thoms Powell thadvowson of Russhok & the bargayn of wood sold to Ric ffisher shalbe sealed the next morning

(folio 57) Be it remembrid that on sonday the second day of August 1573 in the xv^{th} yere of quene Elizabeth The bailief & pncpl Burgesses of Warr being assemblid in their counsaill house in the church of saint Maryes have after long delibacion

election of John Rigeley to be one of the principall burgesses

electid and chosen John Rigeley one to be a principall Burgess of the said borough in the place of Thomas Oken decessid late one of the said principall burgesses And have theruppon agreid that the said John Rigeley shalbe callid to that company on tuesday next after the buryall of the said Thomas oken Wheruppon the said Tuesday being the iiij^{th} of August aforesaid The said John Rigeley being callid before the said Mr Bailief & pryncipall burgesses he declarid his inhability & insuffissiency to that office And therfore praid the said Mr Bailief & principall Burgesses to pcede to a new election and to dismisse him Nertheles his said excuse was not thought sufficient And therfore resolued to have the said John Rigeley And so tenderid to him the book where he was before the said bailief & Burgesses sworne this iiij^{th} of July (sic) 1573.

Copy of a conveyance of land at Snitterfield to Bartholomew Hales.

(folio 58) Copy of a lease dated 4th of March, 1573, to Thomas Powell, Draper, of a house in the High Pavement for 51 years, at an annual rent of sixteen shillings, and subject to his doing all repairs.

𝔗𝔥𝔢 𝔅𝔞𝔨𝔢𝔯𝔰 𝔟𝔬𝔬𝔨   (folio 59)   A declaracion of the orders & ordynaunces deuised consented & agreid uppon by the Companye & ffelowshippe of Bakers dwelling w^thin the Boroughe of warwicke & Suburbes of the same & concludid uppon aswell by the Bailieff & principall Burgesses of the same borough as also by the Bakers there nowe Inhabiting by them & their Successours Bakers of the said borough & suburbes for ever herafter to be inviolabely obseruid & kept as hereafter ffolowith

ffirst it is ordeyned establisshed & agreed by thassent & consent aforesaid that all householders of the crafte company & ffelowshippe of Bakers within this borough shall yerely uppon Saint clements daye convent & assemble themselfs in some convenyent house wh^tin the same borough wch for that tyme shalbe called the Bakers halle And then at the same place shall nomynate & choose one of the same crafte companye & ffelowshippe dwelling w^thin the same borough or Suburbes to be Maister of that crafte for one whole yere than to come And lykewyse than & there shall nomynate & appoynt two others of the same crafte company & ffelowshippe also dwelling w^thin the said Borough or Suburbes to be wardens of that crafte for that yere to come To wch master & wardens power & auctoryty is given by this booke to warne & call the rest of the same craft being householders w^thin the said Burrough or Suburbes at tymes convenyent to the said hall where they maye consult reason & detmyne such matters as shall concerne that Arte or crafte for the comen weale comodytie & profytt aswell of themselfes as of the said burrough & countrey adiacent.

Item it is ordeyned & agreed by thassent aforesaid that yf any of the said crafte companye or ffelowshippe being choosen nomynated & appoynted to be master or warden of the said crafte as is beforesaid shall refuse & will not take uppon him or them to serve in that place for the tyme of the same yere folowing That then he or they that so shall wilfully refuse having no reasonable cause to the contrary shall forfeyt & paye for his said wilfull refusall Sixe shillings & eight pence

Item it is ordenyd & agreed that evry householder of that mistery or crafte w'hin the said Borough & Suburbes shall attend & come to the said halle at such tyme as they shalbe comaundyd upon warning to them gyven by the said master & wardens to thentents beforesaid And if any of them having no lawfull lett doo obstinately refuse upon such warning given to come thither or being there after such good orders or ordynaunce made agreed on & sett downe in writing doo refuse denye or w'hstand any good order that there shalbe concludyd or agreed on by the master wardens & the greater parte of the rest of that crafte that then he or they & evry of them so obstinately refusing to come or being present w'hstanding or not obeing such good ordynaunce shall paye for evry such defalte two shillings & sixe pence.

Item it is also establisshed & agreed that no Baker w'hin this Burrough or Suburbes shall receve or take into his sruice any man or chielde to dwell wth him to thintent to learne his mistery or crafte Except he take hym to be his Apprentyce or covenant servaunt for the terme of seven yeres at the least uppon payne that evry suche offence shall forfeit & paye ffourtie shillings

Item it is further agreed that no Baker dwelling w'hin the same Borough or Suburbes shall take above one Apprentice or covenant sruant to dwell wth hym at once Except it be in the last yere of such yeres as his former Apprentice or covenant servante hathe or ought to serve And than yf he wille he may take one other to be his Apprentice or covenant sruaunt for seaven yeres to come or more wherin it is ment that none of the said householders being Bakers may have one Apprentice at one tyme sauyng in the last yere of the former Apprentice And that evry of the said Bakers taking any Apprentice or covenant servant for yeres shall take the same Apprentice or covenant servant by Indenture And shall bryng the same Apprentice or covenant servaunt togyther wth his Indenture before the Bailief & Recorder Steward or Townclerk of the same Borough for the tyme being w'hin one moneth next after such bargain or taking into sruice of such aprentice or covenaunt sruaunt So as the said taking may be acknolegyd before the said officers or any two of them And the Indenture enrolyd by the

Towneclerk emong the Court Roles or Recordes of the said Borough The townclerk taking for such Inrolment only twelve pence uppon payn that evry Baker retayning any Apprentice or covenant servant and not pfourmyng this Article shall forfeit & paye Twenty Shillings.

Item it is ordenyd that no man whither he were borne in the said Borough or out of the said borough shalbe admytted by the said master & wardens to sett upp the Arte of bakyng or suffred to use the same crafte w^thin the said Borough or Suburbes Except he have been Apprentice or Covenant sruant & served in the same craft by the space of seven yeres at the least And that to be duely puyd (proved) by good witnesses before the Bailief of this borough for the tyme being & the maister & wardens of the Bakers before his admission uppon payne (folio 60) that the maister & wardens of Bakers suffring any such pson to use & occupie the said Arte w^thin the said Borough or Suburbes the space of one moneth shall forfeit & paye to the chamber of the said Borough for evry such defalte foure pounds whereof the master shall pay fourtie shillings & the two wardens other fourtie shillings.

Item it is further agreed & establisshed that no fforener wch is not alredy admytted as one of the company of bakers of this borough Although he haue beene Apprentice or covenant servant out of this borough shalbe suffred or admytted to sett upp and to use & exercise the said Arte w^thin this Borough or Suburbes before he compound wth the maister & wardens of Bakers & paye unto them ffoure pounds of good englissh money at the least wch Some of foure pounds shalbe paid at such dayes & tymes as they & the partye compounding can agree So it be w^thin one yere next after such composicyon uppon payn that evry such fforener baking to sell w^thin the said borough or suburbes before such composicion had shall forfeit & loose all such bread as he baketh to sell w^thout composicion & lycens.

Item it is agreed that the said master & wardens of bakers w^thin this borough shall quietly suffer evry such pson as hathe beene Apprentice or covenant sruant to the said Arte in the said borough or suburbes & there srued the space of seven yeres or more as is above lymytted after thexpiracion of his terme to sett upp & occupye the said Arte or mistery w'hin the said borough or Suburbes So as the same pson first make request therof to the said maister & wardens & paye to them at his ffirst setting upp three shillings & foure pence.

Item it is further agreed that if it fortune any man being a householder of that company of Bakers w'hin this borough or Suburbes having Apprentice or covenant sruant as aforesaid to dye before the end or thexpiracion of the terme & yeres of such apprentice or covennt sruant That then the said apprentice or covennt srunt being bound & inrolled as abovesaid sruyng out the rest of the yeres to come in his Indenture w'th the widowe of his late maister or w'th any other of that companye by his maister or mistres Apoyntment shall & maye at his libertye after thexpiracion of his said yeres (making ffirst request to the maister & wardens of that occupacyon & paying to them three shillings & foure pence as abovesaid) sett upp occupye & use his said occupacion or crafte w'hin the said Borough or Suburbes aswell as thoughe his maister had lyved out the terme of yeres comprised in the same Indentures

And further it is agreed that if any woman w'hin the said Borough or Suburbes fortune to burye her husbond who at the tyme of his deathe was one of the feloshippe & companye of Bakers hauinge Apprentice or Servaunt that can skyll of baking That the said woman during her widowhedd shall or may use the said Arte or crafte of baking w'hin the said Burrough or Suburbes paing such scott lott & other duetyes as her husbond should or ought to have doon iff he had lyved And if any such widowe be afterward maryed to another man being of the same Arte And not admytted of the said company of Bakers of this borough Although he be dwelling w'hin the said Borough or Suburbes And after such mariage woolde sett upp the same crafte or occupacion It is agreid that neither the man nor woman so married shall use or exercise the said Arte w'hin the said borough or suburbes untill he have first compoundyd w't the said maister & warden of bakers as aforesaid uppon payn that evry pson offending & breaking this Article shall forfaite & loose all such bredd as he or she baketh to sell before such agrement & composicion

Item it is agreed that evry baker w'in this borough & suburbes shall bake horsebred in such sorte that he shall not sell above three horseloves for a peny if he sell but one penyworth at once uppon payn that evry pson doing the contrary shall forfeit for evry tyme offending thre shillings & fourepence.

Item it is agreid that no Baker of the said Borough shall from henceforth in any wise bake any kind of bred uppon the Sondayes (except it be for great necessitye or urgent cause wch cause he shall first declare to the bailief of this borough for the tyme being & the said maister & wardens And that cause knowen to be true & lycence obtenyd he or they may bake on the Sonday And otherwise whatsoever baker offending this Article shall forfeit & paye for evry tyme so doing Sixe shillings & eight pence.

(folio 61) Item it is agreid that none of the said Arte or crafte of Bakers of this Borough shall carry out of the same Borough or Suburbes any kinde of Bread to be solde to any market towne or other place Saving to Coventrye on Wensdayes & ffridayes to Southam on mondayes & to Rugby on Saturdayes uppon payn to forfeit for evry tyme doing the contrary Sixe shillings & eight pence Except it be to gentlemens houses buryalls & weddings And that not to be done w'hout request first made to the maister & wardens of that company & licence of them obtayned uppon payn to forfeit for evry tyme doing the contrary Sixe shillings & eight pence.

Item it is ordeyned & agreid that all the Bakers of the same Borough shall wey all such corne & grayn as they shall send or delyver to be ground at any mille uppon payn to forfeit for evry tyme sending corne & not weyng it ffyve shillings.

Item it is further agreid that if any man of the same crafte of bakers of this borough having Apprentice or covenant sruant wth hym for yeres as it is aforesaid shall happen to misuse the said Apprentice or covenant Serunt That then it shalbe lawfull to the said Apprentice or covenant sruant to complayn to the maister & wardens of that company of & for the misdemeanor of his said master uppon wch complaynt it shalbe lawfull to the said maister & wardens of that company to call the maister of such Apprentice or covennt sruant before them to examyn the said misdemeanor And if by examynacion it appeare that the said maister hath misused his Apprentice or covenant sruant Than the maister & wardens of the said companye shall for the first misdemeanor give him warning of the same faulte wth exhortacyon that he use not the same agayn And if it appeare that the said maister doo eftsones misuse his said Apprentice or covennt sruant Then it shalbe lawfull to the said maister & wardeyns to take such Apprentice or covennt sruant misused from his said maister & to put him to serve some other honest man of that crafte to serve out the rest of his yeres notw'hstonding any Indenture or bond made by any such Apprentice or covennt sruant or by any of his frynds to his said maister And uppon the determynacion of the same yeres so served out The same Apprentice or covenaunt sruaunt shall or may be admitted to sett upp his said occupacion or crafte as is beforesaid in like maner as yf he had sruyd out his yeres wth his first maister

And it is also agreid & concludid by consent aforesaid that yf any pson or psons w'hin the said Borough or Suburbes shall offend in breking any of the ordynnes in this booke conteynyd & will not furthwith pay such some or somes of money as he or they haue lost by the same offence or offencs Then it shalbe lawfull for the said maister & wardens for the tyme being by auctorytie aforesaid to enter the house or houses of such offenders or offender & to take some part of his or their goods & cattalles in the name of a distress or otherwise to distreyn the cattalles or goods of evry or any such offenders though it be out of their houses so it be w'hin this Borough or Suburbes And the same to deteyn untill such tyme as he or they have payd such some or somes of money as he or they have lost or forfayted by breaking any of the said ordynnes or Articles And in case he or they so offending will not quietly paye the same some or somes of money w'hin the space of one moneth next after such distres taken Than the said maister & wardens shall bring the same distres before the Bailief & the Recorder Steward or Townclerk or any two of them sitting in the court the next court daye holden w'hin the said Borough next after the said moneth And then &

there the said distres shalbe praised by two indifferent psons uppon w{th} praisement the said maister & wardens shall or may make sale of the thing or things praised & shall take such some or somes of money therof as have been lost or forfeited by the said offender or offenders & shall deliver the rest & overplus of the money (if any be) to the owner & owners so offending and distreynyd as aforesaid.

And it is further agreid that uppon saint clements daye evry yere the said maister & wardens shall call all others of that craft of the said Borough & Suburbes to the said halle And there in psence of them all shall make a full & pfytt Accompt of all such somes of money as they have recevyd that yere for any default agrement or otherwise as aforesaid And after that Acompt fully made & detmyned The said maister & wardens w{th} the rest of that craft shall than & there choose one of that crafte to be maister & two others to be wardens of the said craft company & ffeloshippe for the yere to come And then after the election & choice of the newe maister & wardens the olde maister & wardens shall delyver over to the said newe maister & wardens the one half of all such money & other things as have come to their hands that yere hapnyng or rising of or for any composicion agrement forfeyture payne (folio 62) or penaltye whatsoer togither also w{th} such stock as the said maister & wardens recevyd the yere before (the said newe maister & wardens putting in band for the true Acompting & aunswering of the said stock & receipts at the yeres end The other moytie & half of all somes of money & other things levyed or rising of any composicion agrement penaltye or forfeiture the said olde maister & wardens shall delyver & pay to the hands of the bailief of this borough for the tyme being to the use & behafe of the chamber of this borough ymediatly or w{th}in seaven dayes next after the levyeng of the mony rising or hapenyng uppon or for such composicion agrement penaltye or forfeiture And shall at some covenyent tyme betwene Martilmas & saint clements daye yerely acompt before the Audytor of this borough for all such somes of money & other things as haue risen & happenyd w{th}in the tyme of their offices for by reson of any composicion or penaltye or otherwise as aforesaid uppon payn that evry maister & warden not pforming this

Article shall forfeyt & pay to the bailief of this borough for the tyme being to the use of the chambr of the said borough for evry defalte negligence or offence ffive pounds

And also it is ordenyd & consentid unto that the said Bakers shall not at their meetings or consultacions devise or doo any thing contry to good order & quiet government of the comon weale & subiects of this borough or countrey adiacent neither shall detmyne any thing against the good usages & lawes of this land but shall doo all things to the benyfiting of this borough the countrey & their selves so farre as the same may stand & be agreable wth the good usages & lawes aforesaid And in case any matter of doubt or controuersye happen to arise emongs the said bakers That then the same shalbe referrid to be orderyd & detmynid by the Bailief & principall Burgesses of the borough aforesaid for the tyme being.

ffinally it is agreid consentid unto & concludid that incase anything be done by the said company of bakers or any of them contry to the good customes & lawes of this land or the benifite & quiet government of this comon weale Or incase the Bailief & principall Burgesses of this borough for the tyme being shall see cause to redresse reforme or emend any article or thing in this booke specified or to adde or encrease other orders to thies abovewriten That then the said maister & wardens & company of Bakers upon request made to them or any of them by the bailief of this borough for the tyme being shall & will surrender & delyver upp into the hands of the said bailief & principall burgesses for the tyme being this booke & all the orders constitucions & agrements abovesaid to be by them reformid redressed emended or newe made as the tyme & case shall requyre.

And otherwise if it happen that any maister or wardens of the said company of Bakers wilbe obstinate or so wilfull as to refuse or not to delyver upp this book uppon request made as is aforesaid That then it may & shalbe laufull for the said Bailief & principall Burgesses for the tyme being at their pleasures to detmyn all & evry or any of the Articles abovewriten & the same make voide or in their places to make newe as occasion & tyme shall require by their discrecions wch being deuysed determyned & agreid upon by the Bailief & principall Burgesses aforesaid or greter nomber of them & knoleige therof given in writing to the maister & wardens of the said company of Bakers for the tyme being shalbe from thensforth taken and reputyd ordynnes & orders to binde the said company of Bakers & evry of them to the pformance therof from tyme to tyme This booke or anything herin conteynid to the contry notw^thstonding In witnes of all wch articles agrements & conclusions made by consent abovesaid The nowe Bailief & principall Burgesses aforesaid have to thies presents put their comon seale the Laste daye of August in the ffiveteuth yere of the reigne of our souereign ladye Elizabeth by the grace of god Quene of Englond ffraunce and Ireland defender of the faithe &c 1573

M^d that the Bakers book in fourme aforesaid mad was sealid in the counsell house where the chest stondith the xiiij^th daie of June 1574 being in the sixtenth yere of quene Elizabeth Than being therat present the balief & all the principall Burgesses namely humfrey crane bailief Richerd ffisher Richerd Townesend Richerd Roo John ffisher Richerd brook Symon Yong Thoms Powell Willm ffrekulton Robart phillippes Thomas Jenks John Diche & John Rigeley at wch tyme the sute brought by John ffisher & other overseers to Mr Oken's will against Robert philips & Thomas cawdrey was treyted of.

(folio 63) GRANTS OF ADVOWSONS OF CHADDESLEY AND STONE.

A sale of wood underwood upon a close at Hatton called "pyrry croft" "togither also wth ffortye Ronell Okes growing in and about the hedgerows" to Richard Fisher for £5.

(folio 64) Precept of the Sheriff Henry Compton to the Bailiff & Burgesses for the election of two representatives for parliament, 14 Elizabeth, and Indenture of the election of Thomas Dudley and John Fisher.

(folio 65) Grant of advowson of Russhok

The visit of Queen Elzabeth.

The second coming of the Quenes Maiesty to Warwick 12 Aug. 14 Eliz. 1572

Be it rememberd that in the yere of O^r Lord God one thousand five hundred seventy and twoo and in the fourtenth yere of the reigne of o^r souireigne Lady Quene Elizabeth the xijth day of August in the said yere It pleased the said souireigne Lady to visit this Borough of Warwik in her hieghnis pson whreof the Bailief of this Borough and the principall Burgesses being advised by the ryht honorable Therle of leycest^r the said Bailief andprincipall Burgesses aforestated w^t some other of the comoners after the election of Edward Aglionby to be there Recorder in plaice of Mr Willm Wigston Knyht prepare themselfe according to there bounden duty to attend her heighnis at the uttermost confynes of their Libtye towards the place from whence her Ma^{ty} should come from dynner wch was at Ichington the house of Edward Fisher being six miles from Warwick where it pleased her highnies to dyne the said xijth of August being Monday The direct way from whence leading by Tachebrok and so thorough Myton feld And therfre it was thought convenient by the said bailief Recorder & Burgesses to expect her Ma^{te} at the gate between Tachebrok feld & Myton feld Nertheles the weather having bene very fowle long tyme before And the way much staynid with carriage her Ma^{ty} was led an other way thorough Chesterton pastures & so by Okeley & by that meannes cam toward the towne by ffourd myll wheroff the said Bailief Recorder & Burgesses having woord they left there place afretaken And resorted to the said ffour myl hill where being plaiced in order ffirst the Bailief then the Recorder then evry of the principall Burgesses in order kneling And behind Mr Bailief knelid Mr Griffyn preacher her maiesty about three of the clok in her coache acompanyed w^t her Lady of Warwick in the same coche & many other Ladys & Lords attending namely the Lord Burghley lately made lord Tresorer of Englond The Earle of Sussex lately made Lord Chamberleyne to her Ma^{ty} The lord howard of Effingham lately made lord pryvy seale The Earle of Oxford Lord gret chamblyn of Englond Therle of Rutland Therle of Huntingly lately made president of the North Therle of Warwik Therle of Leyester M^r of the horse and many other bishops lords ladyes & great estates aproched and came as nere as the coche could be brought nyegh to the place where the said Bailief & company knelid and there staid causing evry part & side of the coache to be openyd that all her subiects present might behold her wch most gladly they desired (folio 66) Whereupon after a pause made the said Recorder began his oracion to her Ma^{ty} and spack as hereafter folowth

The oracion made to the q. maty

The maner and custome to salute princes w^t publik oracions hath bene of long tyme used most excellent & gracious souereyne Ladie begonne by the greek confirmed by the Romayne & by discourse of tyme contynued even to thes our daies And because the same were made in publik plaices & open Assemblies of Senators & counsaillors they were called both in greek & Latyne pæaegyricæ In thes were sett fourth the comendacions of Kynge & Empors in the sweet sound whereof as the eares of evill prynces were delighted by hearing there undeservid prase So were good prynces by the playsaunt remberance of their knowen & true virtues made better being put in mynde of their office and goverment To the pformance of thes oracions of all the three stiles of Rhetoryk or figure speech the hieghest was requyred wch thing considered most gracious Ladie abasshith me very much to undertake this Interprice being not exercised in thes studis occupied & travelling in the comon & private affaires of the Countrey & y^r heyghnies service here The Maaestie of a prynces countennce such as it is reported to have been in Alexander in the noble Romayne Marius in Octavius the Empero^r & of late tyme in the wise & politique prince King Henry the seaventh yor graundfather & in y^r noble and victorious father King Henry the eight whose lookes appallid the stout corages of their beholders The same also remaining naturally in yor hieghnes may soone put me bothe out of countenance & remembraunce also which if it happen I most humbly beseech yor hieghnies to laie the fault there rather than to any other my folly neclegence or want of good regard of my duties who coulde not have bene brought to this place if the good will wch I have to declare bothe myne owne duetifull hart towards yor highnes and theirs also who inioyned me this office had not farre surmounted the feare & dissability wch I felt in my self But the best remidie for this purpose is to be short of spech which I entend to use in this place who having spoken a feaw things towching the auncient and present estate of this borough & of the ioyfull expectacion which thinhabitants of the same have of y^{or} graces repayre hither ffor if I shoulde enter into the comendacion of the divyne gifts of yor Roiale person of the Rare vertues of yor mynde ingrafted in youe from yor tender yeres of the prosperous Achievem^t of all yor noble affaires to the contentacion of yor hieghnies & the wealth of yor Domynyons I should rather want tyme than matter & be tedious to yor hieghnies when I should bothe to myself & others have seemed so skant in praises And yet if wee should forget to call to remembrance the great benefits receved from God by the happy and long desired entraunce of yor maiesty into thimperiall throne of this Realme after the pitifull slaughter & exile of many of yor hieghnies godly subiects the Restauracion of Gods true Religion the speadie chaunge of warres into peace of dearth & famyne into plentie of an huge masse of dross & counterfeit monye into fyne golde & silver to yor hieghnies gret hono^r whose prosperous reigne hitherto hath not bene towched with any trowbelous season (The Rude blast of one insurrection except) which being soone blowen over & appeasd by Gods favo^r & yor ma^{ts} wisdome hath made yor happy goverment to shyne more gloriosly even as the Sonne after dark clowdes appereth msre clear & beautifull If this I saie weare not remembred wee myht seme unthankfull unto God unnaturall to yor maiestie of w^h thyng I woold saie more if yor ma^{te} were not present but I will leave considering rather what yor modest eares may abide than what is due to yor vertues Thanking God that he hath sent us such a prynce in deede as the noble Senator Caius Plinius truly reported of the good Empero^r Fraianus calling him in his presence w^{t}out feare of flattery castum sanctum & deo similimū principem But to return to the auncient estate of this towne of Warwik wee reade in olde writyngs & autenticall cronycles the same to have been a citie or walled towne in the tyme of the Brytayns called then carwar & afterwards in the tyme of the Saxons that name was chaunged into Warwik We reade also of noble Earles of the same namely of one Guido or Guye who being Baron of Wallingford becam Earle of Warwik by marriage of the Ladie ffelixe the sole doughter & heyre of that house in the tyme of King Athelston who rayned over this lande about the yere ef o^r lorde God 933 We reade also that it was indowed with a Bysshoppes See & so continued a florisshing citie untill the tyme of K. Etheldred in whose dayes it was sackid & burnt by the Daynes & brought to utter desolacion the comon evill of all barbarous nacions overflowing civill countreys as may appeare by the famouse cities & monuments of Germanye ffraunce & Italye defaced & (folio 67) destroyed by the Goathes Vandales Normanes & Hunnes Synce this overthrowe it was never hable to recover the name of a citie supported only of long tyme by the countenance and liberality of the Earles of that place especially of the name of Beauchampe of whom yor maistie may see divers noble monuments remanyng here untill this daie whose noble services to their prynces & countrey are recorded in histories in the tyme of King Henry the third King Edward the first second & Thirde and so untill the tyme of King Henry the sixt about whose tyme that house being advanced to dukedom even in the toppe of his hono^r failid in heires male and so was translated to the house of Salisbury which afterwards dekayd also and so this Erledome being extinct in the tyme of yor hieghnis grandfather King Henry the seaventh remaned so all the tyme of yor noble father o^r late dred souereyne King Henry the eight who having compassion of the pitifull desolacion of this towne did incorporate the same by the names of Burgesses of the towne of Warwik endowing them also w^t possessions & landes to the value of Liiij^{li} xiiij^s iiij^d by yere inioyning them w^{t}all to kepe a vykar to serve in the church and divers other Ministers w^t a skolemaister for the bringing up of youth in learnyng & vertue The noble prynces Quene Mary yor hieghnis Sister folowing thexample of her father in respect of the Auncientnes of the said towne by her lres patent augmented the corporation by creating a Bailief & xij principall Burgesses w^t divers other libtes and franchises to thadvauncem^t of the poore towne and the ppetuall fame & praise of her goodnes so long as the same shall stand your maiestie hath graciously confirmed thes lres patent adding thereunto the greatest hono^r that ever come to this towne sins the dekay of the Earles Beauchamps aforenamyd by giving unto them an Earle a noble & valiaunt gentleman lyneally extracted out of the same house And further of your great goodnes bountfullnes yor ma^tie hathe advaunced his noble & worthie brother to like dignytie & hono^r establisshing him in the confynes of the same libtie to the great good & Benefit of the Inhabitants of this towne Of whose liberalitie (being inhabilid by your hieghnis only) they have bountifuly tastid by enioyng from him the erection of an hospitall to the relief of the poore of the same towne for ever besides an annuall pencion of ffivetie poundes by yere bestowed by him upon a preacher w^tout the wch they should lack the hevenly foode of ther soules by want of preaching the towne being not hable to fynde the same by reason that the necessary charges & stipend of the minister & other offices there farre surmount their yerely Revenues notw^tstanding the bountifull gift of yor noble father bestowing the same to their great good & benefyt Such is yor gracious & bountifull goodness Such are the persones & fruytes rising up & springing out of the same To which twoo noble psonags I know yor mai^te presence here to be most comfortable most desired & most welcome And to thinhabitants of this towne the same doth bode & pronosticate the conversion of their old fatall dekaye & poverty into some better estate & fortune even as the comyng of Carolus magnus to the olde Ruynes of Agnisgrann nowe called Achi in Brabant being an Auncient citie buylded by one Granus brother to Nero was the occasion by the pitifull compassion of so noble a prynce to reedifye the same and to advaunce it to such hono^r as untill this day it recevith every Empero^r at his first coronacion But what cause soever hath brought yor Maiestie hither either the bewtifulnes of the place or yor hieghnes gracious favo^r to theis parties surely the incomparable ioy that all this countrey hathe recevid for that it hath plesed yo^u to blesse them w^h your comfortable presence can not by me be expressed But as their duetifull hartes can shewe themselves by externall synes and testymonyes so may it to yor mat^ie appeare the populus concourse of this multitude the wayes & streites filled w^t companyes of all ages desirous to have the fruicion of your divine countennce the houses & habitacions themselves chaunged from their old nakid bareness into a more fresshe shewe & as it were a smyling livelynes declare sufficiently though I spak not at all the ioyfull hartes the singler affections the readie & humble good willes of us yor true harted subiects And for further declaracion of the same As the Bailief and Burgesses of this poore towne doo present to yor miestie a simple & small gift comyng from large & ample willing hartes though the same be indede but as a droppe of water in the ocean Sea in comparison of that yor ma^{te} desurth & yet in their substance as much as the twoo mytes of the poore Widowe mencioned in the Scripture So there hope & most humble desire is that yor highnes will accept & allowe the same even as (folio 68) the said twoo mytes were allowid or as the handfull of water was acceptid by Alexander the great offred unto him by a poore folow^r of his mesuring the gift not by the value of it but by the redie will of the offerers whom yor maiestie shall finde are readie & willing to any sūice that you shall ymploy them in as those that be greatyst And thus craving pardon for my rude & lardge speach I make an end desiring God long to contynewe yor ma^{tie} happy & prosperous reigne over us even to Nestors yeres if it be his good pleas^r Amen Amen

The Oracion ended Robart Philippes Bailief rising out of the place where he knelid approched now to the coche or chariott wherein her Matie satt & coming to the side thereof kneling downe offred unto her Ma^y a purse very faire wrought and in the purse twenty pounds all in souereynes wch her maiestie putting forth her hand recevid showing w^thall a very beming & gracious countenance and smyling said to Therle of Leycester " My lord this is contrary

the q. annswer   to yor promise " and turnyng toward the Bailief " I thank you & yo^u all w^t all my hart for yor good willes And I am very lothe to take any thing at yor hands now because youe at the last tyme of my being here presented us to o^r great liking & contentacion And it is not the maner to be always presented w^t gifts and I am the more unwilling to tak anything of you because I knowe that a myte of their hands is as much as a thousand pounds of some others Nevertheles because you shall not think that I mislike of yor good willes I will accept it w^t most harty thanks to yo^u all praying God that I may pform as Mr Recorder saith such benefit as is hoped " And therew^thall offered her hand to the Bailief to kisse who kissed it and then she delivered to him agayn the Mayse wch before the oracion he had deliverd to her Ma^{ty} wch she kept in her lappe all the tyme of the oracion And after the mace delivered she called Mr Aglionby to her

And offred her hand to him to kysse w^thall smyling said " Come hither litle Recorder It was told me that you wold be afraid to look upon me or to speake so boldly but you were not so fraid of me as I was of you And I nowe thank you for putting me in mynde of my duty & that should be in me" And so thereuppon showing a most gracious & favorable countenance to all the Burgesses & company said again " I most hertely thank yo^u all my good people

This being done Mr Griffyn the preacher aproching niegh her Ma^ty offred a paper to her and knelid downe to whom she said " if it be any matter to be answerd we will look upon it & give yor answer at my Lord of Warwiks house" And so was desirous to be going The contents of Mr Griffyns writing was as hereafter followth in verse

verses deliu^d to the q by Maister Griffin p^cher	t	triste absit letum dignare amplectier ome	n
	v	t firmo vitæ producas stamina nex	u
	e	xplorans gressu cepisti incedere cale	b
	l	urida sulphurei qua torquent tela ministr	i
	i	n capita autho̅ru lex est ea iusta resultan	t
	s	it tibi demonstras animi quid in hoste fugand	o
	a	gmina c̅u fundas regno nocitura maloru	m
	b	ella geris parce illicite non suscipis arm	a
	c	xempla illo̅ru nunq̅m tibi mente recedun	t
	t	urpe quibus visum magna cum clade preess	e
	a	lma vernis vultu sed Christus pectore fertu	r
	v	ere vt feruescat cor religionis amor	e
	i	n verbis pallas factis Actrea tenetu	r
	r	ara vt Penelope regia nescia Debora vinc	i
	o	men triste absit defuncta propagine viue	s

       Gloriæ Anglo̅ru modo non cadente
       te cadit flos sed perit ipsa radix
       regio in ex te solio quiescat
           Septifer hæris

(folio 69)

    Apparent tenebræ occidente sole
       alternantq̄ vices quies laborq̄
    postq̄m federa desiere pacis
       squalet terribilis lues Mauortis
    Queq̄ olim Nemesis reciprocatur
       que sunt ante pedes videre tantū
    non prudentis erit futura longe
       quam sint prospicere : est opus laborq̄
    est solum patriæ salutis ardor
       quo post funera Regīu relucet
    Nomen sidereo nitens vigore
       nec c̄u corporis interit ruina
    Hec quorsum ? an patriæ studere cessas
       quo cessas minus hoc magis supersis
    omnes vnisono ore vota fundunt
    at vitæ statuere terminos dii
    atq̄ equo pede pauperū tabernas
    pulsat mors tetra principuq̄ turres
    viūnt prole tamen sua parentes
    Sed quid plura ? deo regente reges [a]

[a] Far from thee be sadness and disaster! mayst thou deign to take hold on this for thy lot— the living-out of a happy life in a firm established union, departing from the path, which, till now, thou hast trodden—unwedded. May the lightning-bolts, which ministers of darkness may hurl (against thee) recoil upon the heads of them that cast them—for that is law and justice.

May it be thine to show thy courage in putting thy foes to flight, when thou pourest forth thy hosts to shatter the power of hostile nations: yet avoid thou the waging of war; take not up arms save for just cause; and let not the example ever leave thy thoughts of those who thought it shame to win their way to power only through deeds of blood.

Fair art thou to look upon : but let Christ be Lord of thy soul, that thy heart may be ever ardent and sincere in its love for things of holiness. Let it be truly said that in thy words thou art wise as Pallas—in thy deeds as kindly as Astrœa, (in virtue) as renowned as royal Penelope : (in courage) as Deborah, knowing nought of defeat. May never harm befall thee—and when thou art dead mayst thou live again in thy children

If thou shouldst fail us, not only fades the flower of the glory of England's sons, but its very root is cut off : but in thy person may it rest secure on thy royal throne, (while) thou remainest to wield the sceptre.

As the sun sinks the shades of darkness fall, and rest and labour take their equal share : after the bonds of peace have fallen away, War, grim destroyer, stalks throughout the land, and future

Thes verses her maiestie delivered to the Counties of Warwik riding w^t her in the coache and my Lady of Warwik showd them to Mr Aglionby And Mr Aglionby to this writer who tok a copie of them

Then the Bailief Recorder and principall burgesses w^t ther Assistants were comanded to their houses wch they took w^t as good spede as they might and in order rode two & two togyther before her Ma^ty from the ffourd mil hill till they cam to the castell gate And thus were they marshallid by the heraldis and gentlemen ushers first the Attendantes or Assistants to the Bailief to the nomb^r of xxx two & two togyther in coates of puke ^(b) laid on w^t lace Then the xij principall Burgesses in gownes of puke lyned w^t satten & damask upon footclothes Then two byshoppes Then the lords of the counsaill Then next before the Quenes Ma^ty was placid the Bailief in a gowne of skarlet on the ryht hand of the Lord compton who then was heigh Sheref of this Shire And therfore wold have carried up his rod into the towne wch was forbiden him by the herals & gentlemen ushers who therfore had placid the bailief on the ryht hand w^t his mace And in this maner her hieghnes was conveid to the castell gate where the said principall burgesses & assistants staid evry man in his order devidyng themselfes on either side make a lane or Rome where her Ma^ty should passe who passing thorough them gave them thanks saying w^thall " it is a welfavored & comly company " what that meant let him divyne that can The Bailief nertheles rode into the castell still carrieng up his mace being so directed by the gentlemen usshers & heralds and so attending her

The order of marshalling & Ridyng to the Castell

Fate will drink its deep revenge, though now we see it not, nor ever look beyond the path we tread. 'Tis no wise man's part only to look upon the future : let him, too, regards the things that *are*. There's need of work to-day, need for the kindling of a deep desire for the welfare of our land ; desire, through which, tho', he who sits upon the throne may die, his name, shining in starry splendour is still borne brilliant, nor ever dies, tho' his mortal body perish.

But whither tends my song? Shouldst thou then cease to love thy country ? Nay! the more thou lovest it the more thou shalt reign supreme (in its heart) : all with unanimous voice shall raise their prayers for thee. But the gods have allotted the span of mortal life, and dark death treads alike in the cottage of the poor, and the palace of the Prince —yet parents live again in their children. Need I say more ? While God shall reign (in heaven) ; thou (on earth).

I have to thank my friend F. Burrow, Esq., of the Inner Temple, for the above translation or paraphrase.

(b) a dark colour between black and russet.

Ma^ty up into the hall wch done he repaired home on whom the principall burgesses & comoners attended to his house from whence evry man repayred to his own home and Mr Recorder went w^t Jho. ffisher where he was simply lodged because the best lodgings were taken up by Mr Comptroller That Monday nyht her Ma^ty tarryed at Warwik and so all tuesday On Wensday she desired to go to Kenelworth leaving her household & trayne at Warwik And so was on Wensday morning conveid thorough the streates to the North gate & from thence thorough Mr Thomas ffishers grounds ^(a) & so by Woodloes the farest way to Kenelworth where she rested at the chardge of the L of Leycester from Wensday morning till Saturday night having in the meane tyme such princely sport made to her Ma^ty as could be devised On Saturday nyht very late her Ma^ty returned to Warwik And because she woold see what chere my Lady of Warwik made she sodenly went unto Mr Thomas ffishers house where my L of Warwik kept his house and there fynding them at supper satt downe awhile and after a litle repast rose agayne leaving the rest at supper and went to visit the goodman of the house Thomas ffisher who at that tyme was grevously vexid with the gowt who being brought out into the galory end woold have knelid or rather fallen downe but her Ma^ty wold not suffer it but w^t most gracious woords comforted him so that forgetting or rather counterfeyting his payne he wold in more hast than good spede be on horseback the next tyme of her going abrod wch was on Monday folowing when he rode w^t the lord Tresorer attending her Ma^ty to Kenelworth agayn reaporting such thyngs as some for their untrueths & some for other causes had bene better untold but as he did it by counsell rashely & in heat so by appearance at leysure coldly he repented what these things meane is not for evry one to know But to retourne her Ma^ty that Saturday nyht was lodgid agayn in the castell at Warwik where also she restid all Sonday whence it pleasid her to have the countrey (folio 70) people resorting to see the daunce in the Court of the castell her Ma^ty beholding them out of her chambr wyndowe wch thing as it pleased well the country people so it semed her Ma^ty was much delightyd and made very myrry That after noon passed and supper done a showe of firewoorks

(a) The Priory.

prepayrd for that ppose in the templ felds was sett abroche the maner whereof this writer can not so truly sett fourth as if he had bene at the being than sik in his bed but the reaport was that there was devised on the templ diche a forte made of slender tymber coverid w^t canvais in this fort were apointid divers psons to serve as soldiers and therefore so many harnesses as myht be gotten w^thn the towne were had wherew^h men were armed & apointid to shewe themselfs Some others apointed to cast out fire woorks as squibbes & balles of fyre Agaynst that fort was another caselwise prepared of like strength wherof was governo^r the Earle of Oxford a lusty Jentleman w^h a lusty band of gentleman Between these forts or against them were placed c^rten battering pieces to the nomb^r of xij or xiij brought from london and xij skore chambers (a) or mortys pieces brought also from the towne at the chardge of therle of Warwik Thes pieces & Chambers were by traynes fyred & so made a great noise as though it had bene a sore assault having some intermission in wch tyme therle of Oxford & his soldiers to the nomber of cc w^t qualivers & harqbuzues likewise gave divers assaults Then the fort shoting agayn & casting out divers fyers terrible to those that have not bene in like experience valiant to such as delighted therein and inded straung to them that understood it not ffor the wild fyre falling into the Ryver of Aven wold for a tyme lye still and than agayn rise & flye abrode casting fourth many flasshes and flambes wherat the quenes ma^t tok great pleasure till after by mischaunce a poore man or two were much trowblid ffor at the last whan it was apointed that the overthrowing of the fort should bee A Dragon flieng casting out huge flames & squibes lighted upon the fort and so set fyre thereon to the subv^rsion thereof But whether by necligence or otherwise it happed that a ball of fyre fell on a house at the end of the bridge wherein one henry cowy otherwise called myller dwellid and sett fyre on the same house the man & wief being both in bed & on slep wch burned so as before any reskue could be the house & all things in it utterly pished (perished) w^t much ado to save the man & woman & besides that house an other house or two nere adioynyng were also fyred but reskued by the diligent & carrefull helpe as well of therle of Oxford M^r ffulk Grevile & other

(a) a kind of short cannon.

gentlemen & Townesmen wch repared thither in greater nomb^r than could be orderid And no m^rvaile it was that so litle harme was done for the fire balles & squibbes cast upp did flye quiet over the castell and into the myds of the towne falling dwne some on houses some in courts & baksides and some in the streats as farre as almost of Saint Mary church to the great perill orells great feare of the Inhabitants of this borough And so as by what meanes is not yet knowen foure houses in the towne & suburbes were on fyer at once whrof one had a ball cam thorough both sides & made a hole as big as a mans head & did no more harm This fyere appeased it was tyme to goo to rest And in the next morning it pleasid her Ma^{ty} to have the poore old man & woman that had ther house burnt brought unto her whom so brought her Ma^{ty} recomfortid very much And by her great bounty & other courtiers There was given towards their losses that had taken hurt xxv^{li} xij^s viij^d or therabouts wch was dispnsed to them accordingly (folio 71) On Monday her maiesty taking g^t plesure in the sport she had at Kenelworth wold thither agayn where she restid till the saturday after and than from thence by charlecot she went to the Lord comptons & so forwards   In this meane tyme the Earle of Warwik keping house at the pryory to his great chardge the Towne offred unto his L a small present That was a fatt ox & x muttons or wethers fedd wch it semyd his L tok very courteously So as in the end at his going away it plesed him to apoint iiij^{or} bucks to be given & deliverd to the Bailief & townesmen to make myrry w^thall and in mony (   ) wch both were pmised by his officers but nothing delivred And thus briefly I thought good to towch some part of her ma^{tys} repaire hither though for want of understanding of many things omyttid and by reson of long sicknes being not hable to put the same in writing all things be not remebred But the writer thinkith it better to reaport somewhat than leave all undone the towne having bene at so great chardge as may apeare by the Bailiefs acount where the comon charge is set forth pticularly

G

RESIGNATION OF THE STEWARD

On the 29 September 1573 Thomas Hankinson alias Jenks the Bailiff & the principal Burgesses met to elect a Bailiff for the coming year and according to the charter sent two names to the commoners who chose Humphrey Crane "Wheruppon John ffisher who for divers causes him moving" (then follow these words, which have been erased but are just legible "mislikid the choice of the said humfrey crane to that office namely his ignorance his wilfulness his blind boldness his inconstantnes before showed in divers matters") (a) "desired of the then balief and such principall burgesses as were present that they wold dischardg him the said ffisher of that company as a man not mete nor hable to shew himself as his place required wherwhall he remembred an offence before taken by the comoners misliking as it might seme that the said John ffisher should have any fee allowid him for the Stewardshippe to wch office as he was desired & ernestly requestid So from the same he most hartly prayd he myght be nowe again dischargid being neither hable to discharg the same as he woold nor well allowed of as he thinkith he ought ffor wch cause he protestid openly before all the company that he had not recevid any fee for the yere past respecting the great charge the towne was put unto otherwise and the unwillingness of the people whom to satisfye the better he was content to forgoo both the fee & office And thrupon he deliverid his patent to the Bailief Thomas Jenks who though he semid unwilling in showe to receve the same yet w^t a tikling hart as his wavering countenance (folio 72) declared glad of such an offer willingly recevid the same & kept it wth him Nevertheles afterwards uppon some fowle causes falling out every day against him he afterwards desired the frendship of the said John ffisher aswell to himself as towards the towne using such honyed woordes as he thought might pleas the delicat tast of a sweet eared & simple soule In so much that he by divers of that company the frends of the said ffisher was somewhat allured to contynewe his place ffor his better enioyng wherof they offryd to him his patent agayn w^t many desires to take the same But

(a) Humphrey Crane in Sep. 1565, refused to be a principal burgess, and obstinately departed v. p 7.

Election of humfrey crane to be bailieff

he refused so to doo having deliverid the same opnly Yet grauntid for his frends sakes especially his brother Richerd & Thomas Powell who earnestly travellid w{th} him to have regard to the present weakened state of this towne to contynewe still and do as before he had doon otherwise offred to lay to his charg whatsoever evill or overthrow should happen (as things consentid to) by the said John ffisher making w{th}all frendly request & great promises to the said John ffisher for his tarryeng & contynuance Wheruppon he was in dede pswadid So as he may have a new patent of those offices which he had delivred Wherof the balief being aduised semed to be very glad and p'msed that he woold in all things herafter be ruled & well advised and very desirously semed to crave the ayd of the said J. ffisher as one w{th} out whom he could not do any thing nor wold deale whout his counsaill but all mere woords & as I take it no meaning but sure I am no dede folowid Albeit the said J ffisher endevored himself to answer for & defend the said bailief in such cases as were laid to his charge by divers many causes and enformed aswell to S{r} Jo. Hubond knight as to therles of Warwik & Leicester which obiections being for a tyme blowen over tyme requyred to have a leet w{th}in this borough to be holden whn a moneth after michilmas acording to the statutes w{ch} leet the said bailief Required the said Jo. ffisher to kepe as Steward w{ch} to doo the said ffisher refused having no patent nor warrant therof ffor w{ch} the said Bailief said their should be no lett for he should have a patent the next morow This was agried unto by most of the principall burgesses And a patent should be made & sealid But after that the day of leet was agried upon & knowleige therof given in the church The patent was no more thought upon by the said balief as it semed till the day of the leght cam And than the bailief comyng to the said ffisher to goo to the hall to begyn the leet The said ffisher required his warraunt according to his former promise Wherupon the bailief answerid the default to be in the rest of the principall burgesses who having keys were dispersid & could not so sodenly come togither But desired the said John ffisher to kepe that leet And the next day he shold have his patent sealid Wherat the said ffisher stickid as one that was very unwilling to enter into any matters aptening to a coralty w{th}out sufficient warrant Yet at the last upon a promise made by the most of the principall burgesses that they wold seale his warrant he pceded by warrant of their woords Thes things being thus handlid and the leet holden the xiiij^th day of October no more woords were made of this patent but hangid in suspence or rather oblivion from that day forward although every day almost betwixt that day & Symons & Judes day the said bailief was wth the said John ffisher sometymes for matters of the towne & sometymes for his owne Afterwards the bailief having a charge to speak to Mr Thoms ffisher aswell for tharrearages of the rent going out of c^rten land sometyme mathew ffaircliffe as also for the arrerage of a rent or tenth going out of combwell Both which the said Thomas ffisher should of right pay as this writer thinkith And also three yeres tenth of the first corporacion graunted by King Henry theyght of wch tenth being vj^li xiij^s iiij^d by yeres paymet had bene made to the said Thoms ffisher for three yeres by Burgesses of this borough for wch the quene was unaunswerid And therfor divers proces awardid against the Bailief & burgesses who were compellid to pay & be bound to pay £xxiij vj^s viij^d for tharrearage of the said tenth Wherof part remaned in their hands but xx^s for three yeres had bene paid to the hands of the said Thoms ffisher & others by him apoint^d (folio 73) to receve the same And other vj^li xiij^s iiij^d was allowed to Richerd Brook burgesse of this borough for the eight yere of the quenes ma^ty that now is Who said he had paid the same though he cold not show the acquitance but did allege that he thought the same was put into the comon chest and therfore desire that a serch might be made there So likewise M^r ffisher denyed that he had recevid any more but two yeres tenths unaunswerid And for the rest going out of Mathewe ffaircliffes lands he said that he should pay but x^s by yere wheras the towne required xiij^s iiij^d as might appere by his dede of purchase requyring the balief to serch his records better And as for combwell he refused to pay any Therfore the bailief reporting this aunswer to the burgesses it was thought mete that the dede of Mathe ffaircliff should be sought up And that the said M^r ffisher might be satisfyed therein before the going out of this bailief out of his office Wheruppon it was

Ductyes by Thomas ffisher esquire

Richard Brooke demaunds vj^li xiij^s iiij^d uniustly

agreamt that the burgesses having keys sholde goo to the chest

agreid that on thursday the xxix^th of october so many of the company as had keys should mete at the church by eight of the clok in the morning to goo to the chest for the p'poses abovesaid Wheruppon there met Thoms Jenks Bailief Richerd ffisher

their names that mett

Richerd Townsend John ffisher Richerd Brook Robart Philips and John Rigeley And Willm ffrekulton and Symon Yong sent their keys Thies being togither openid the chest Where the found the dede of the said ffairclif made to the burgesses for the said xiij^s iiij^d as also the dede of ffaircliff made to divers ffeffes of trust Emongs whom one Thoms Shotteswell was one & alone the Lyveng ffeoffee to the uses of the said Martyne & (   ) his wief during their liefs & after their decesse to the use of the Burgesses of Warr. to the mayntenance

Mathewe ffairclough his ordes taken out

of the dues wch being seen it was thought convenient that both the dedes should be taken out the one to shewe and satisfye M^r ffisher The other that a newe might be made acording to the will of the donor to other ffeofes after the lief of the said Thoms Shotteswell wch doon Mr Townesend

the baliff put in remembrance

remembred the bailief of his pmis towching the sealing of a new patent to John ffisher of & for such offices as he before had Wherupon the bailief callid to the said John ffisher asking him whither he had writen & brought w^t him his patent Wherunto the said J. ffisher aunswred that he desired not any further patent or office but that they woold be his sufficient warrant for his doing sins the surrender of his late patent And being so he should have cause to thank them all But as towching any new patent he gretly desired not being very lothe & unwilling to serve w^t such a one as they had apointid bailief whom for his inconstancy & wilfulnes he thought so given to himself that it should be but a trowble to the said John ffisher to serve whall And therfore desired that he might have no patent Nevtheless the Bailief semyd so forward that he wold send for the same home to the house of the said Jo. ffisher if it were not there assuring that he wold not dept till it was sealid Upon wch woords the said John ffisher drue out of his bosome the said patent writen Yelding in respect of some of his frends to take the same at their hands though rather he were to serve at pleasure whout any fee But the patent was recevid and deliverid to

	Richard Brook who red the same wch being likid of The said John ffisher agayn
The sealing of a newe patent of Stewardshipp to John fisher	desired the said bailief & others present that they wold spare the sealing therof and that he might serve at libty and pleas^r whatsoer movid them they wold nedes seal the patent wch the
The patent red by Richard Brooks	bailief deliverid ther to the said John ffisher as the dede of him & the principall burgesses Requiring the said ffisher to tak paynes

& travaile in those offices as before he had done Wherby they should be all beholding unto him upon which woords & earnest request of the rest he aceptid the said patent & gave them thanks for their good wills After this cam in mynde

Arrerage of tenths   the payment of the xxiiij^{li} vj^s viij^d pmisd to be paid this terme as peell of the arrerags and debt of the towne for the tenths of the first corporation for wch John ffisher & Richerd brook were bound in the   And because the bailief said he had litle mony remaining in his hands (folio 74) skarcely so much as wold answer this yeres chardges & fee fermes It was thought

plate taken out of the chest to be sold   good that the patents of two chalices & a crucifix of silver & gilt remaining in the said chest should be taken out and sold

And the mony therof comyng should be ymploid towards the payment of the said debt wh was done acordingly And the weight of the said patens & the crucifix cam to xxxi ounz somwhat lacking wch the said ffisher sold after the rate of V^s the ounz wch cam in the whole unto vii^{li} xv^s "

(There are several erasures and interpolations in the account of the above proceedings, as though Mr. Fisher in preparing the same had wished to be very precise in writing the narrative of his grievances, and the slights to which he had been subjected.)

Copy of Patent of office given to John Fisher

The placing of Jhumfrey Crane in the office of Bailiwik   (folio 75) On Sunday, 1st November, 1573, Mr. Jenks, Bailiff and others met at the Church and went from thence to the Shire Hall to swear in the new bailiff. Robert Phillips and Thomas Cawdrey Executors of Thomas Oken were called up and required to deliver to the Corporation the plate left by Oken ª " of wch plate the said Robt Philips was content to make delivery upon a resonable and but Thomas Cawdrey thought they nedid not so to do wherupon a bond was tendrid to them acording to the will of the said Thomas Oken wherunto the said Cawdry at the first tok exception but afterward upon

the plate delyvered to Humfrey Crane   pswacion he fetchid the plate " Humphrey Crane then took the necessary oaths on assuming office " And so thes things thus doon the whole company returned to the church where Mr Martinus delenus being vikar of Saint Maryes in Warwik prechid showg very learnedly the office of

The diligent cares of the said Bailief in his duty   a good magistrate Thies things being thus set in order And the said humfrey crane placed in his office of Bailief upon what good counsaill this writer can not tell The said humfrey crane ymediatly upon his placing even the next morowe after began diligently to search out this reformacion of such things as were amisse And first determyned

Alehouses   to begyn with the Alehouse kepers and their haunters calling them before him & giveng them gentle pswacions to reform the comon misorders usid in the same And to the end that good myght followe he caused such as he

Sessions of the clerk of the Market   thought mete to be victualers or kepe victualling houses to be bound with suretyes in recoynizaunce to observe the articles of the statute in that case pvided and such other as he thought not to be mete for that ppse he disallowed After that he thought it convenient to trye the measures & weights whin this borough And therefore agreid to kepe his Sessions as clerk of the mket which he did acordyngly and therein reformed many things bothe strikes yards & other waights to the great benefit of the Inhabitants of the said Borough & countrey about Then he diligently weid the bakers bred and then such other things as were convenient In all wch things the said Bailief showing a willing mynde The said John ffisher was much allowed to assist him more diligently wch he did the more gladly that he p'ceivid he had bene before deceivid verely hoping that where he expected the Ruyn of all goodnes by the wilfulnes of

(a) For Oken's Bequest see Oken's Will, post.

the officer nowe he should fynd a comfortable alteracion from evill to better to the comfort of that poore state Nowe when some order was sett in the things abovesaid and after that the monyes given by M{r} Willington & M{r} Whaitley had bene disposed & lent furth acording to their devises the said bailief having a forward mynde to further the good estate of this borough brak w{t} the said ffisher to have a second company of the assistants apointed to be the xxiiij as he callid them which he would fayne have to assist him & the principall Burgesses as before had bene usid and therfore desired the said ffishers not only consent but also opinion in the choice of them Wherunto the said ffisher had no great liking having experience of former tyme in that matter remembring the perilles that might & were like to have growen by the mutyny of such disorderid p'sones of cankerd natures that some tyme had been part of that company ffor avoiding of which like daungers & unquiet brawles he advised the said Bailief either to (folio 76) forbeare any such choise orells if he thought it mete to have a second nomb{r} to appoint such as myght be both for their honestnes & discrecions mete to aunswer that he expectid w{h} could not be if either the nomb{r} of xxiiij or the same psones as before tyme had bene of that company should be admitted And first as towching the nomb{r} of xxiiij the said ffisher thought it not mete to have so many for divers causes partly because it would be very hard to chose out so many fit in all respects whn this borough secondly he doubtid least being such a nombr they would seek to restrayne the said Balief & principall Burgesses of that w{h} by the charter they might or ought to doo & so take the ordering of things into their owne hands but chiefly he was on mynde that by the chr there could be no such company admitted ffor the woords of the Kings graunt be That they the said Balief & principall Burgesses shalbe the comon counsaill of the same borough to order & do all things for the good govern{t} of th'inha'bitants of the same w{ch} being so their nedith no other counsaill Nevertheless because by the charter it is apointed that the comoners shall have the naming of one of the twoo chosen by the bailief & principall burgesses to be bailief for the yere to come hee thought it not greatly

Monyes given by M{r} Willington & M{r} Whatley set out in lone

a second company desired

ffishers opynyon upon that poynt

amisse that an other company might be specially chosen to serve for that purpose & to assist the said bailief & principall burgesses for the eleccion of the Burgesses for the parliament & to attend on the bailief at ffaires & such other tymes as the bailief should call them and so by a convenient nomb^r of resonable men to be aydid & assisted wch might better be done & w^t greter quietnes than if every rude fellowe should have his speche And such a company he thought the charter wold well beare having thies woords That the bailief & xij principall burgesses may by their discrecions elect and name such & so many others to be their Assistants as they should think good So as the opinion of the said ffisher was that this woord so many had relacion but only to the nomb^r of balief & twelve principall burgesses And so yeldid that if twelve of the most honestest comoners such as were tried men resonable & comformable & w^{h}out notable vices or spotts might be allowed it might be suffred yet for the more orderly proceding in thies matter and for the

Consultation towching a second company of Assistants — more sure doing herein advised the said bailief to call a hall or meting of all the principall burgesses & to requyre their opinions in this behalf which the said balief did Wherupon cam togyther the most of the principall burgesses all saving Richerd Brooks & Robart Philips upon wch meting The cause was opened to the said principall burgesses who at the first blussh semid to agree that it was very convenient bothe for sight & otherwise to have a company of xxiiij insomuch as some thought there could be noth^g done or pfited by the principall burgesses w^{t}hout them such was their ignorance But after that the said ffisher had declared to them the woords of the charter & his opinion towching that point that the charter wold not suffer such a nomb^r and withall had remembrid to them the misdemeanors wch in tymes past had bene used by such as acompting themselfs of that nomb^r had hastely & w^{h}out reson attemptid things unhonest and his poore opinion What he mistrusted might herafter happen by those or such like if such or such like nomb^r or opportunyty should be agayn All such of the principall Burgesses that were of experience and had seen the things remembrid confessed that it was not mete to have such a company N^{r}theles bothe to satisfy the apetites of the honester sort that woold be content to be resonably Rulyd and for the better sight of people they wished their might be a second nomb^r chosen of the honest inhabitants of this borough Wherof they doubtid not but they might choose such as wold be bothe conformable & redy to doo their dutyes gladly So at the last it was agried that there should be a nomb^r of xij chosen to be Assistants to the said balief & principal burgesses to do those things that the comon multytude should ells doo That is to say to choose the bailief electid out of twoo psons to be namyd by the bailief & principall burgesses and to assist the bailief & principall burgesses in the eleccion of Burgesses for the pliament But in all other matters or causes whatsoever they should have no voices neither affirmative nor negative no though they were callid to be privy to any cause whatsoever herupon it followid that the names of the most metest to the nomb^r of fourscore or more were red before the bailief & principall burgesses to thend

Election of those twelve that out of those the nomb^r of xij might be chosen & so upon conferrence were namyd thies that folowe Robert Sheldon John Greene Oliver Brook (folio 77) Roger hurlebutt Philippe coo John Griffin John Bykar Roger Weale henry chaplin cristofer Knight Thomas chapman John Balies and then it was agried that those should be callid before the bailief and principall Burgesses to be made privye to thies causes & to their eleccion and further it was agreid that when articles or orders should be devised by John ffisher against the tyme of their calling w^h was apointid to be on Monday the (   ) daie of Deceb^r being Saint Thomas daye then to be showid to the said Assistants wherby they should be bound to the same orders (if they wold consent to be of the company which orders were devised accordingly and on the said Monday all they last namyd saving only John Griffin & John bailie being bothe at Southam) cam before the said bailief & principall burgesses Where was let them to knowe the cause of

Conference w^t the said psons so chosen to be Assistants their sending for wch was that Mr Bailief and principall Burgesses being given t'understand on Michilmas Day that they that were now present being than at the eleccion of the bailief found them selves grevid for that they were not of late tyme callid to counsaill of many things as before they had bene used wh'rof they desired reformacion And

Marginalia: resolution of xij assistants & what auctoryty they shold have

for that ppose the said Bailief & principall B^rgesses willing to satisfy them as they might requyred them the cause of their griefs which than bicause some of the company were away the said comoners wold not utter but praid thay they might put them up to the said M^r bailief & his company in writing wch was well likid of by the said bailief & principall burgesses w^h promise to satisfy them as they might Sithens wch tyme M^r bailief nor the principall burgesses have not seen their petitions but have ptely heard somewhat of their intencions privylie wherof they more mislik than if they had doone as they promised wch was to shewe their griefs in writing Nev^rtheles bicause it should appeare unto them that Mr Balief & his company woold their satisfieng & the reformacion of such things as were not well if any were he had nowe determyned to send for them to understand their griefs And w^thall to let them knowe what good liking he & his company had of their felowshyppe & assistance And therefore had resoluid to pyck out them as the only choice of the whole borough w^t whom they were content to ioyne in so nere friendshippe as to mak them the example of vertue in pserving them to be a company selectid from the rest as most worthy to be associated unto the said bailief & principall Burgesses trusting that they for their partes woold shewe themselfs again to the said bailief & principall Burgesses as aptenid bothe loving neighbo^rs & obedient assistants And so doing the proverb should be fulfilled that pmiseth concordia parve res crescunt like as on the other side by dissencion discordia maxima dilabunter nowe therefore it is their parts if any things be amisse to open the same in this place to thend reformacion may be had as is promised accordingly To this Robert Sheldon after a space spak

grieffs of the Company of xviij utterid That in dede their company had found themselfs grevid in that they had not bene callid to counsaill as they ought & had bene used especially at the burges acompt wherat they think they ought to be & be as privy as the bailief or any of the principall Burgesses bicause the same acompt of burges conc^rnth only things grauntted by the first corporacion wherin they be all made Burgesses as well the worst as best and so they have bene usid untill a yere or two that whan they cannot tell howe they were not made reconing of but put apart he know^h not howe and besides that they think they should be privy to all grauntes & leaces made of any thing that cam by the first corporacion aswell as the bailief & principall burgesses were & should have their voices & consents aswell as any other had And for that cause they spak somewhat on Michelmas day mynding to have deliverid up their mynd in writing alhouliday but bicause much busynes then was for Mr Oken's plate they did then forbeare supposing they should have bene callid to the burges acompt at St Androes tide against w^h tyme they had made a note of their myndes in c^rten articles but bicause they were not then callid they have brought them nowe w^h them And so exhibited c^rten articles in writing As herafter follow^h v^rbatim

Requests of the Company of xxiiij Exhibited in writing

The Requestes made to Mr Bailief & the twelve principall Burgesses of the towne of Warwick by c^rten of the comoners of the same towne late being sworne of the company of the xxiiij to be of the comon counsaill of the said towne to & w^h the said bailief & Burgesses as folow^th viz.

1. Inprms the said company of comoners doo request that there may be a full & whole company of xxiiij chosen & sworne out of the best & chiefest comoners whin the said towne of Warr. to be of the comon counsaill of the said towne to & w^h the said Balief & Burgesses in all matters & causes that may towch & concerne the comon state & welth of the same acording to laudable custome frequented & usid in all other cities & Townes corporate yf the corporation will allowe the same

(folio 78) 2. Secondarely the said company do request That when & so often as any of them shall die or be chosen unto the company of any of the twelve principall Burgesses or otherwise depte out of this borough to dwell in any other place That then & ymediately after whn convenient tyme there may be chosen by the said Bailief Burgesses & xxiiij or the greter part of them others in their Romes to be sworne to be likwise of the comon counsaill of the same towne & so to contynewe from tyme to tyme

3. Thirdly the said company do request that when there is a full & whole company of xxiiij so chosen and sworne to be of the comon consell of the said towne That then after they nor none of them to be amovid from the said counsell by the balief & xii principall Burgesses so long as he or they shall behave themselfes decently & honestly in the said counsell and company

4. ffourthly the said company do request that they may have free speche at all tyme & tymes in the counsell house or hawles to & w^t the said Balief & burgesses w^{t}out any comptrolling of them or any of them so as the same speche be comely decent & orderly & not repugnant to the comon wealth & state of this borough

5. ffivethly the said compeny doo request that if any of them shall not bee of good name & fame or live orderly & decently w^{t}n the said borough according to their calling or shall give counsaill or stirre in any matter thing or cause which may or shall be preiudiciall or hurtefull to the corporacion of this towne or either of them or against the comon state and wealth of this said towne and the same duely provid against him or them That then the same person or psons so dealing to be presently amovid of & from the said company of the xxiiij by the said balief burgesses & xxiiij or the most part of them & never after to be recevid into the said company agayn

6. Sixtely the said compeny doo request that they may yerely bee callid & made pryvy to the burgesses acomptes as heretofore they have bene acustomyd aswell towching the Receipts of the yerely Revenewes & rents of all such lands tents and hereditaments as were given unto this borough by the first corporacion as also of all maner of payments yerely paid and going out of the same to any person or psons whatsoever

7. Seventhly the said compeny doo request that hereafter there may be none of the lands tenements or hereditaments aptening or belonging to this borough alienated or sold away by the said Balief or burgesses w^{t}out the consent & assent of the said xxiiij or the most part of them for the tyme being

8. Eightly they doo request that likewise hereafter there may be no lease or leases graunted & made to any person or psones either in possession or Revercion of any of the said landes tenements & hereditaments by the said balief & burgesses without the like assent & consent of the said xxiiij or the most part of them

Answer to their requests Thies articles were openly red before the Bailief & principall Burgesses & the others then present to w^h It was ymediately aunswerid That the same articles contenid matters unresonable & therefore not to be graunted As particulerly to the first where is requyred to have the nomb^r of xxiiij to be chosen & sworne & to be the comon counsell of this borough to & w^t the bailief and principal burgesses The same is in no wise to be graunted ffor by the charter the Bailief & principall Burgesses are apointid to be the comon counsell of this borough & being so there is no reson to alter the Kings graunt besides that if there should be xxiiij apointid were more than the charter wold bere though not of the comon counsell for the charter saith the balief & principall burgesses may at their libtye chose other so many as they are whern is to be notid that if any nomb^r be chosen it may not excede the nomb^r prescribed likewise the woord—may—is to be notid wherin is ment that it is not of any necessitye that there shalbe a second nomb^r but at the pless^r of the bailief & principall burgesses And it is well seen & found that the Balief & principall Burgesses be wel inough hable & doo sufficiently pforme that office aswell yea & better it is thought than if there were a greater nomb^r as by example of the xxiiij hath bene well tought & therefore they are resoluid to have no such nomb^r of xxiiij wherin also the experience of Mr Okens ffeofement may suffice wherin it is puided that the bailief & principall Burgesses & three of evry ward shalbe at the doing of all his busynes And when or how that may bee to have xxxvj or xxxvij psons to come or especially to agree togither Is doubtid of Besides whan there is xij or xiij of one side & xx or xxiiij on the other side you woold look that the greter nomb^r should take place and so if yor requests were grauntid youe that clayme to be but comoners woold rule the balief & his company wch should be yor hed & Ruler.

And as towching yor second request that such of the xxiiij as shold be namyd & sworne should not be displacid but continewe in ther Romes still is very hard to be graunted ffor so should the bailief & principall Burgesses graunt youe more than to them is promissed ffor there is none of the principall Burgesses Recorder nor Bailief that hath or may clayme to have that ppetuytye after his election But is in case & must be content (folio 79) to be amovid & displacid if the rest see cause or so doo agree & so be the woords of the charter

And as towching the free speche in counsailles & metings there is no doubt that whan youe or any of yor are alowid to come & speke in counsells using yo^rselfs as shall apteyn free speche being not fryvolous or inconvenient may be herd so farre as may be graunted that is so long as it excedith not the bonds of reson and is not out of the matter in hand but restith w^thin the lymytts of the matter proposid wherin also youe must more playnely understand my meaning that is you may speak in such things as your speche shalbe requyred & not otherwise but to showe your opynion w^thout that ye shall have any effectuall voice either affirmative or negative to consent or dissent but only a speche to shewe yor opynion as aforesaid

And to that ye requyre that any psons of that company misbehaving himself towards the corporacion should be duly reformed youe may be well assured that y^r request herein may & shalbe graunted though not in that maner for we are persuadid & so mynde to see that doone w^thout the consent or making pryvy of so great a nomb^r as xxiiij

And as towching the Burgers acompt nowe all & every of youe might have bene pryvy therunto if yor selfes liked & so were till some such as hath litle reson & lesse understanding refusid so to be which bicause he or they could not have their own willes wilfully refusid bothe to heare or tarry at the same acompt as some of youe can tell and his behavio^r was taken to be all your consents ffor so many as were then present deptid w^h him showing your selfs like to him wch was the cause why youe were not sins callid especially seing we were of o^r selves

sufficient to determyne those causes And ye may be well assured we had rather &
will in dede provide in those matters w'hout yo' pryvite & company rather then by
calling yo" to fall into such quarrells & questions as neither Reason nor concord
will suffer

And lastly to yo' last requests as towching the restraining of us from making
of any leaces or the depting w' any of the landes or hereditaments of this borough
without yo' counsent is a thing in no wise to be graunted ffor as wee take o'selfes
namely M' Bailief & the principall Burgesses to be the governers & comon counsell
of the borough & all things therto aptening So to ioyne you w' us or rather to
admyt that yo' request were in myne owne opynion madnes or at least might be
taken a iust cause to deprive or depose us from having any thing to doo in any
such graunts ffor examyne youe the cause truly & see as is before said whither
youe that desire to be callid the xxiiij should have yo' willes before us or no first
yo' nomb' is greter yo' auctoryty all one the meanest of you as great as balief yo'
mindes padventure as wilfull as o's Then it folow'h that yo' auctoryty in evry
singler pson being asmuch as any of us yo' nomb' being greater than ours must
allure us to consent will we nil we & so should it come to passe that the foot
should govern the hed & the meanest him of best calling & most experience
wherunto be ye well assured we neither can nor will yeld But to conclude yf
youe that nowe be present whom M' Bailief and his company have chosen out to
be men of best order & discrecion can agree to attend on M' Bailief at tymes
convenient and yeld you resonable assistants in such causes as the said M'
Bailief shall ympart unto you as tyme & occasion may requyre Then ys he plesid
& it is his speciall desire to have you as his especiall friends to supplie those
things w'ch are to be done quietly & by order wherin as is before said he woold
have you to knowe that having ones experience of yo' resonable conformytie he
myndith to ympart w' you such necessory causes as conveniently he may but to
be bound to you not to pced in graunts & other things specified in yo' articles he
thinkith not convenient nor resonable for causes afore showid wherfor if you can
agree first to be the nomb' of xij as nowe ye are apointid ye shalbe well aceptid

of us all & welcome to us as bretherne friends & ptakers of o^r cares & travells wherof we trust by youe to be somewhat easid as further ye shall knowe whan we may understand howe ye like of or can agree of the nomb^r & choice alredy made wherunto we pray you first to answer And yf youe can or doo like of that nomb^r & choice Than shall youe see what orders or articles we have devised for your better quyet & comely behavyo^r wherin we mynd to deale w^t you as with ourselfes to prescribe youe some (folio 80) c^rten lymytts for triall in the beginning wch if you excede not but observe as we trust you will being resonable we shalbe more encouragid herafter to pticipate more w^h youe as is aforsaid but first we expect yor answer of liking or misliking the choice alredy made

Replicacion — Then after a while Rbart Sheldon and said ffirst as towching the nomb^r of xxiiij it woold be a comly sight to have them as it is in Stretford in Northampton & coventry and I wold wish their were so many if it might be but if the charter will not beare it then as you will Then spak John Grene & said wheras you are not willing that we should be privy to the burges acompt and say that it is long of o^rselfes that we were not sithens callid yt is not so but long of you that doo misuse us in woords whan we coome there caling us

britt brekith out into flambes — by the names of undutifull subjects rebelles & such like names wheras the wors of us is as honest as any of you Stay there said Jo. ffisher comparrisons be odyous Nay said Jo. Grene as honest as the best of you Nay said J. ffr. it becomith not youe to compare w^h the wors of us Yes saith J. Grene as the best of you It becometh saith J. ff. youe of all worst to spek that for my self I wold be loth there were any nerenes of your honesty to myne for you have excedid the bounds of honesty as might wel appere when it was by yor pilde hed he is said J G a lieng knave that saith so Than said J. ff I say that the poks made youe to have a pillid head & beard Thowart a lieng knave saith J. G. Therwth Jo. ffisher held his pece & then said J. G. agayn he is a lieng knave that so reportith of me herwth the whole house was trowblid till at the last they weere both comandid to silens after wch being doon & the said J. Grene somwhat said unto by the Bailief & some of the principall burgesses it was agayn

H

demaundid of the rest of the comoners whither they likid of the determynacion towching the nomb^r & choice wherupon they desired to have licens to goo togither & to conferre of this matter & then to give their aunswer which was graunted And therupon the said comoners went into the church where comonyng about half an houre they returnid to Mr Bailief & principall burgesses of whom being demaundid how they likid of the nomb^r & election the said comoners aunswerid that forsomuch as it was doubtid lest the corpacion woold not beare to have xxiiij they were well liking of the nomb^r of xij but they wold have bene glad to have bene the full nomb^r of xxiiij if it might have bene And as towching the choice they all agreid that those that were chosen were honest men but yet there were men unnamyd that both for their age & substance might be well placid And then said Thomas Chapman that he was unmete to be of that company & therfore desired to be sparid so said Phillippe coo that there were auncient & welthy men that might better supply the plaice & therfore desired to be sparid Towching wch allegacions it was told them that it was true that there were others wch for the substance or age might supplie the place but wanting other such virtues & conformyties as is iudgid to be in them they were rather preferrid And then was offred unto the said comoners a draught or minute of c^{r}ten orders & articles towching their behavo^r wch was openly red to them wherin also was contenyd the forme of an othe wch they should also swere at their admission wch articles being somwhat long I leave here to write bicause they are writen in the book of constitucions & orders of the burrough of Warwick And because the same articles contenid many things to be obsrvid of the comoners then callid assistants the said comoners desired to have the pusing & consideracions therof untill Wensday following wch was graunted Then spak J. Grene and said that wheras it had plesid Mr Bailief & his Maisters to name him emongs others as one of the assistants he thought himself gretly beholding to them but forsomuch as there were others more mete that be left out and also for other causes so desirith them all to p'don him and chose some other in his Rome wherunto Mr Bailief aunswrid

[margin notes:] Conferens of them elected. Consent to have xij. mocion. Aunswere declaring causes of their election. Orders devised for the xij Assystants.

that forsomuch as they had ably determynid their choice they could not nor woold not alter the same Wherunto the said J. Grene replied & said that he woold not be sworne nor was mete for the said company and therfore desired them to hold him excusid for he knew causes in himself that he could not serve that turne And therfore pray'd eftsones to be dismissid wth their favors Or to lay such fyne upon him as they thought mete wch he woold rather pay than be of that company wch woold not be graunted

(folio 82) (sic) And so for that tyme the company departid On Wensday acording to promise cam before Mr Bailief & his company All the company of xii assistants saving John Grene who as the rest said had given his consent to doo as the rest woold doo And being so togither it was askid of them howe they likid of the Articles deliured to them who aunswerid that they were very good & mete to be put in use w^t such addicions as they had put to them wch was not past a woord or twoo & the alteracion of one penaltye Than said Jo. ff. are you contentid to have them engrossid so as you may put yor hands to them they said yea Then said J. ff. you did see what disord^r happenid the last tyme of yor being here by some of yor company Therfore it was very meet to have an order to restrayne such lewd speech wherunto the said company agried desiring that like as an order was made for the conformyty of their company So a like order might be to promiss the principall burgesses it they should give any such causes at any meating W^{ch} also was consentid unto And therupon the said orders were drawen And so that night agreing to mete the next day for the assig of the said orders wch in the meane tyme should be engrossid into parchement they for that tyme departid The next day after evening prayer being cristmas even Mr Bailief & the gretest part of the xij principall burgesses assembled themselfs before whom cam also the said xij assistants then newly namyd To whom was deliverid the articles engrossid togither w^t the mynit drawen which articles they redd and therupon Robart Sheldon began to use a fewe woords towching the first of the said articles Wherin it is said that the Bailief & principall Burgesses may use & wherin saith

Acceptance & liking of the orders by them elected

some cavell made after consent

the said Robart Sheldon it semyth that Mʳ Bailief & the rest may choose whither they will call them to all things or no To wᶜʰ it was aunswerid the woord <u>May</u> was in the first draught & therfor not altered sins the first agrement wᶜʰ they confessid but they wold wisshe it should be turnid to shall or should In no wise said Jo. ff for so the Bailief & his company should be bound to call you to all things wᶜʰ you knowe was not ment neither that whan you are callid that you shall have any affirmatyve voyce or negative saving in the election of the bailief as afore is said & the election of the burges for the parliament Nevtheles upon yoʳ diligence & honest behavoʳ it may be & it is very like some of you shalbe

Subscribing the articles of ordrs   callid to more things than I think you all desire Well said they wee are content and herwᵗʰ agreyd to put their handes to the

said articles wᶜʰ they did and after that evry one of them in the presence of Mʳ
wthole iij assistants chosen   Bailief & the rest laing their handes upon a sruice book swoare the othe contenid in the said articles wᶜʰ doone J. ff usid a fewe

Exhortacion to concord   woordes to put them in mynde of their duty aswell towards the bailef and his company as also ech one to an other pswading them to unyty & brotherly concorde and to put from them rancoʳ & malice if any had bene in any

Remitting of offence   of them And wᵗʰall direktg his speeche to Jo. Grene said I am for mye own part sorry if I have offendid you & so doo pray you forgive me if I have so done like as on the other side I utterly remit any thing you have spoken or done against me and so I wisshe it might be amongs you & us all for so we shall by gods grace come togither after a better sort & wᵗʰ one mynd & so shall one be partaker of an others goodnes to all oʳ comforts and wᵗʰall I wish you to stick togither as brethen & frends for so shall you be made more strong & hable to resist any thing practzid against you and in case not to care for the malice of the worser sort who padventure whan they shall see you preferrid before them will utter their cankrid fruit of there malicious hete for wᶜʰ you shall not nede to care so long as you doo well wᶜʰ I wish to you all as to myself Then spak John Grene & said And I for my part doo forgive youe any thing done against me Wherwᵗʰ all the company semyd to be glad to see unytie & concord Then Mʳ Townesend & Mʳ Ric. ffisher movid that a lik reconciliacion might be betweene

Robert Phillippes & Robart Sheldon & John Bailies who had before that tyme concevid some unkindnes chiefly growing upon woords wch after some color on bothe partes loosed promised ech to other their good willes whereof I pray god make a sure knot and kepe us in good liking one of another

A graunt to make the Company of Tayler's a reformyd Book After this the company of Drapers made request to Mr Bailief & principall Burgesses that they woold please to reforme their book of the said occupacions especially in making the somes of composicion of straungers greater wch was grauntid togither w^t other reformacions & addicions

The Booke for Drapers & Taylers (folio 83) A declaracyon of all the constitucyons ordynnes & decrees of the misteryes or crafts of Drapers and Tailors of the borough of Warwik in the county of Warr. made constitutid & ordeynid aswell by thassent consent & agream^t of the balief & principall burgesses of the same borough as by thassent Consent & agream^t of all the companyes of Drapers & Taylors nowe inhabiting & occupyeng the said misteries w^thin the said borough & suburbes ordeynid to be from hensfforth truly observid & kept of them & euery of them & their Successors Drapers & Tailors w^thin the said borough & Suburbes as ffolowith

ffirst it is ordeynid constitutid & establishe^d by consent aforesaid that all Drapers & Tailors of this borough being housholders shall yerely in the feast of saint John the Evangelist assemble themselves and mete at some convenyent house w^thin the same borough wch shalbe callid the Drapers & Tailors hall And then and there shall chose one of the said companyes dwelling w^thin the said borough or suburbes to be Maister of those occupacyons for the yere to come And also shall at the same tyme elect & chose twoo others that is to say of either occupacyon one to be wardens of the said companyes for the yere to come wch psons so namyd and chosen maister & wardens of Drapers & Tailors shall have auctoryty to call togither at tymes convenient when & as often as they shall thinke mete by their discrecyons all Drapers & Tailors being housholders inhabiting w'hin the said borough & suburbes into their said hall There & then to consent reson & devyse for the benefyte comodytie & true dealing in the said crafts or misteryes and good orders emongs themselves

Item it is ordeynid establisshid & consentid unto That euery Draper & Tailor dwelling w'hin the said borough & suburbes being housholder upon somons or warning to him gyven shall come & apeare before the maister & wardens of the said companyes for the tyme being at such convenyent place & tyme as by the said maister & wardens shalbe apointid And if any of them so warnyd doo make defalt wilfully and doo not come having no resonable cause to the contrary Or if any deny or refuse to obey any such good order as shalbe made by the maister & wardens & the more part of the said companyes That he or they absenting themselfes shall forfeyt & pay for eury tyme absenting himself Twelve pence And eury one refusing to obey such good orders or ordynnces as shalbe made by the said master wardens & company shall forfeit & pay for euery such defalte Sixe shillings and eight pence

Item it is ordeynid & agreed that no pson being of either of the said artes or misteryes of Drapers or Tailors dwelling w'hin this borough or suburbes shall take or enterteyn any man or chield to dwell w'th him to thentent to teach such man or chield his occupacion except he take him to be his Aprentice or covennt sruant for seven yeres at the least uppon payn that eury pson doing the contrary shall forfeyt & pay for evry such default ffourtie shillings

Item it is agreid that evry of the said Drapers or Taylors taking any Aprentice or Covennt srunt shall take his said Aprentice or covennt srunt by Indenture And shall bring aswell the same Indenture as also the Aprentice or covennt srunt before the Bailief and Steward or Towne clerk of the same borough for the tyme being w'hin one moneth next after the taking of such Aprentice or

Covennt srunt into sruice And then & there shall knowleig the same Indenture & bargayn before the said balief and Steward or Towneclerk wch Indenture shalbe enrollid in the Court Roles of the same borough the same Draper or tayler taking such Aprentice or covennt srunt payng only xij^d to the Towneclerk for enroling therof upon payne that evry Draper or Tayler not so dooing shall forfeit loose & pay for evry defalt xx^s

Item it is agreid consentid & orderid that no psone or psones of either the said crafts or mysteryes dwelling w^thin the said borough or suburbes shall take or receive into his sruice any Journeyman to work any maner of work by the garment or week or otherwise but by the yere half yere or quarter of the yere at least according to the statute in that case provided And also that evry psone of of either of the said artes reteyning or taking any such Journey man shall give knoleige therof to the Maister & Wardens ot the said Artes or misteryes w^thin eight dayes after such reteyning or hiring of any such Journey man to thentent that such Journey man shall not depart his said sruice untill the ende of his terme upon payne that whosoever shall hire receve or enterteyne any Journey man contrary to this order shall pay for evry default Twenty shillings

Item it is agreid consentid & orderid that no psone dwelling presently or or which herafter shall dwell w^thin this borough or suburbes or libtyes of the same whither he were borne in the towne or out of the towne nor any forrener dwelling out of the said borough shall in any wise be licensid by any agreament or composicion to occupy & use either of the said crafts or misteryes of Draper or Tayler w^thin the said (folio 84) borough or suburbes except he have bene Aprentice or covennt srunt to one of the said artes and have servid therin faithfully & truly the space of seven yeres at the least as apprentice or covennt srunt And the same to be provid before the bailief of the same borough and maister & wardens of the said arts or mysteryes by sufficient testimony & witnes before he doo use & set up his said occupacion w^thin the same borough and suburbes upon payne that the maister & wardens of the said company of Drapers & taylers admitting or suffring any psone to set up contrary to this ordynance shall forfeyt & pay unto the bailief & principall burgesses of the said borough to the use of the chamber of the said borough for eury such default neglicence or suffrance c̃

Item it is consentid agreid & orderyd That no forrener Whither he dwell in the towne or out of the towne wch before this tyme or at this psent is not admyttid as one of the company of drapers or taylers of this borough although he have bene Aprentice or covennt srunt & srued in the same occupacions or one of them seven yeres shalbe suffred or admyttid to sett upp & use & occupy his said craft w^thin this borough or suburbes untill he have agreid & compoundid wth the maister & wardens of the said arts or misteryes upon payne that eury such psone setting up or using either of the said crafts w^thin this borough or libertyes before he have so compoundid shall forfeit or pay for eury day so dooing ten shillings

Item it is consentid agreid & orderyd That from hensforth eury psone that shalbe admyttid & allowid of the companyes of Drapers & taylers of this borough wch hath bene or shalbe a forrener & borne out of this towne That is to say such a one as hath bene Aprentice to one of the said Arts w^thin this borough & suburbes & sruid therin truly & faithfully seven yeres shall before he be admyttid or allowed to be one of the said company & to use & exercise his said crafte in the said borough or suburbes shall pay or be bound to pay as herafter is expressid That is to say yf he have bene Aprentice or covennt srunt to the said art or mistery of Drapers & sruid the same occupacion in some citye Borough or corporate towne the space of seven yeres and so provid Then he shall pay before he be admyttid to exercise his said craft w^thin this borough or suburbes the some of vj^li xiij^s iiij^d to be paid presently at his admissions or w^thin one yere next after his admission as to the balief of this borough for the time being & M^r & wardens of that arte shalbe thought good And if he have bene Aprentice or or covnnt srunt to the arte of Taylers and sruid in the same occupacion in some cyty Borough or corporate towne the space of seven yeres & so provid Then he shall pay before he be admyttid to exercise his said craft w^thin this borough or suburbes the some of three poundes sixe shillings & eight pence to be paid presently at his admission or w'hin one yere next after such admission As to the bailief of this borough & M^r & warden of the said occupacion shalbe thought good uppon payne that the maister and wardens of the companyes of drapers & taylers compounding or admytting any one for any lesse some to forfeit & pay for their so dooing to the use of the said chambr of this borough Ten pounds

Provided alwayes that if any forrener wch was or shalbe borne w'hin this borough or suburbes wch hath sruyd or herafter shall serve as Aprentice or covennt srunt in either of the said Artes in any cyty Borough or corporate towne the space of seven yeres & that provyd be desirous to be admyttid to be one of the said company of Drapers & Taylers w'hin this borough & to set up & use his art in the said borough or suburbes such psone may by the discrecyon of the bailief of this borough for the tyme being & the M^r & wardens of the company of Drapers & Taylers be admyttid to set up paing as herafter is declared That is to say yf he have bene Aprentice or covennt srunt to the art of Drapers then paing Lxvj^s viij^d in maner & forme above declaryd And if he have bene Aprentice or covennt srunt to a tayler Then payng xxxiij^s iiij^d in maner & forme as is abovesaid he shall & may be admyttid & allowed as aforesaid

Item it is consentid agreid & orderid that all & eury such psone as have or hath bene is or shalbe Aprentice or covennt srunt w'hin this borough & sruid or shall serve the said occupacions or either of them therin within the said burrow or suburbes as above is declaryd by the space of seven yeres shall or may after thexpiracion of his terme upon request made to the M^r & wardens of the company of drapers & taylers set upp use & occupye w'hin the said borough or suburbes the said arte wherin he hath bene brought up Payng only at his setting up three shillings & foure pens

(folio 85) Item it is further consentid agreid & orderyd that yf any forrener being a tayler & not of the company of Drapers & Taylers of this borough doo fetche any garment or other woork to be made out of the towne of any psones dwelling w'hin this borough Or if any such forrener doo woork any garm^t or other thing aptening to the art of a tayler closely w^thin any mans house w^thin the towne borough or libtyes eury such forrener shall forfeit & pay for eury tyme so dooing Sixe Shillings & eight pens And that eury Inhabitant of this borough setting any such forrener in woork in his house shall forfeit for eury daye three shillings & ffoure pens

Item it is consentid agreid & orderyd that if any psone of either of the said Artes or craftes having any Aprentice or covennt srunt in maner & forme before declaryd shall happen to mysuse his said Aprentice or covennt srunt So as the same Aprentice or covennt srunt doo complayne to the said maister & wardens of the said company of drapers & taylers Then the said maister & wardens shall call before them aswell the maister of such Aprentice or covennt srunt as the said Aprentice or covennt srunt so complayning And shall examyne the cause & mysdemeano^r And yf it fall out by examynacion that such Aprentice or covennt srunt hath bene misused the said M^r & wardens shall for the fyrst tyme gyve warnyng to such maister misusing his said srunt to emend that fault But if it happen the same M^r of any Aprentice or covennt srunt eftsones to misuse his said srunt agayne Then it shalbe laufull to the said M^r & wardens of Drapers & Taylers to take the same Aprentice or covennt srunt away from his said maister And to place the same Aprentice or covennt srunt wth some other honest man of that craft or art to serve out the rest of his yeres And to set such fyne upon him so misusing his said Aprentice or covennt srunt as to their discrecyons shalbe thought mete And that such Aprentice or covennt srunt so agayn placyd & sruyng out his yeres shalbe dischargid of his sruice to his said form^r maister & shalbe made free & be suffred to sett up in like maner as if he had sruid out his yere wth his said first master notw^thstonding the covennt or Indenture to his said maister

Item it is consentid agreid & orderid that if it fortune any man of either the said artes or crafts w^thin the said borough or suburbes having Aprentice or covennt srunt by Indenture shall happen to dye before thexpiracion of the terme & yeres of such Aprentice or covennt srunt That then the said Aprentice or covennt srunt srung out the rest of the yeres not determyned wth the widowe of his late maister if shee kepe herself widowe or wth any other of the same art or craft by his maister & M^ris apoyntment during the rest of the yeres comprised in the Indentures shall & may after thexpiracion of his yeres at his libtye making request and payng three shillings foure pens as is aforesaid Set up & use his said art or craft as well & in like maner as if his maister had lived out the terme of yeres comprised in the said Indentures

Item it is agreid consentid & orderyd that yf any woman w'hin the said borough or suburbes happen to bury her husbond wch at the tyme of his death was one of the company of Drapers & taylers Such woman during her widowhed shall & may use & exercise the arte wch her late husbond at the tyme of his death did use But if it happen any such woman afterward to marry an other man being not of the same company of Drapers & Taylers although he be dwelling w'hin the said borough & suburbes And after such marriage would use & occupye the said art or craft It is consentid & agreid that neither such man nor woman shall set up exercise or occupy the said art or craft except he or she have first compoundid in maner & forme abovesaid wth the said maister & wardens of the said company of drapers & Taylers uppon payne that who so dothe contrary to this ordynnce shall forfeit & pay for eury weeke so doing Twenty shillings

Item it is further agreid consentid & orderyd That if any psone or psons w'hin the same borough or suburbes shall in any wise offend in any of thies ordynncs or any other good orders that shalbe made emongs the said maister wardens & companyes of Drapers & Taylers And will not upon demaunde by the m^r & wardens pay such soms of monye as by him or them is hath bene or shalbe lost or forfeited for not obsruing the said ordynncs & orders That then it shall be laufull for the said m^r & wardens of Drapers & taylers to enter the houses shoppes closes or ffeilds w'hin this borough or libtyes of any such offender and offenders And there to take some part of his goods & cattalles in the name of a dystres And the same to deteyne untill such tyme as he or they have paid the monye or somes so forfeytid or lost by breaking any of the said orders or agreaments And if the offender or offenders in them or any of them will not pay the mony so lost or forfeited as before is said w'hin one moneth next after such distres taken That then at the next court to be holden in the said borough after the moneth (folio 89) (sic) The same distres shalbe brought by the said m^r & wardens into the court before the bailief Recorder or Steward or Towneclerk or any of them there present And the same distres shalbe presyd by foure indifferent men After wch thing so done it shalbe laufull to the said m^r & wardens to sell the same distres And of the mony therof rising to satisfie them selves deteyning so much monye as hathe bene forfeited & lost And the overplus yf any be they shall delyver to the late owner or owners of such distres

Item it is also agreid consentid & orderyd that the one half of the monye rising happening or growing of for or by reson of any composicion agreament fyne forfeyture payne or penaltye wch shall or should come to thands of the m^r & wardens of the said company by reson of the orders abovesaid shall goo & be to the Bailief & principall Burgesses of this borough to the use of the same borough And the other half or moyty to the use of the company of Drapers & Taylers of the said borough

And it is also consentid agreid & orderid that uppon the said feast of saint John the Evangelist eury yere after the election & nomynacion of a newe maister & wardens in maner & forme above declaryd made The olde maister & wardens shall make & declare before the newe maister & wardens & the company then present a full pfitt & iust acompt of & for all such somes of monye & other things as they have or ought to have recevid for any default forfeyture composicion agrem^t or otherwise And after their said accompt so fully playnly & clerly made the said late maister & wardens shall ymedyately delyver the moytye & one half of all such monye as hath or should have come to their hands by reason of such defalts forfeitures or agreaments or otherwise to the bailief of the said borough for the tyme being to the use of the chambr of the same borough And the other half or moyty togither wth the rest & remayne of the precedent acompt they shall delyver to the newe maister & wardens so by them electid & namyd putting in sufficient band for the redelivery & true aunswering therof at the end of the said yere And for the more pfit aunswering of such somes of mony as shalbe due to the chambr of this borough It is also agreid consentid & orderyd That the Auditor of this borough for the tyme being shall & may ones in the yere at the least call to accompt the said Mr & wardens of Drapers & Taylers wch said mr & wardens upon resonable warning to them given by the said Auditor shall bring before the said Auditor all their books of orders acompts & reconings and shall accompt before him for the mony due to the said chambr upon payne of forfeyture of this book & graunt to be sealid at the will & plesure of the bailief & principall Burgesses of this borough for the tyme being

ffynally it is concludid consentid & agreid that in case any thing be doone by the said Mr wardens & company of drapers and Taylers contrary to the good orders customes & lawes of the land or the quiet governmt of the comon weale of this borough Or that the Mr & wardens of the said Artes of Drapers & Taylers doo not yerely pay to thands of the bailief of this borough for the tyme being all such mony as should yerely come to the use of the chambr of the said borough as aforesaid That then this book & all the Articles herin conteynid shalbe voyd Or incase the Balief & Principall Burgesses shall see cause to redresse or reforme any thing or article above writen or to adde or encrease other orders to thies above writen It is also agreid consentid & orderid that the bailief of this borough & principall burgesses for the tyme being may detmyn make voyd & frustrate all or any the articles above writen and in their places to make newe or to the same to adde others as occasion & tyme shall requyre by their discrecions wch being devised & agreid upon by the bailief and principall burgesses or the greter nombr of them And knoleige therof given in writing to the maister & wardens abovesaid or to one of them shall from thensforth be taken & reputid and shalbe in dede ordynnces & orders to bynd the said company of Drapers and Taylers & eury of them This book or any thing therin conteynid to the contrary notwthstonding In witnes of all wch articles orders constitucions agreaments & consents the said bailief and principall burgesses have to thies presents put their comon seale the last daye of decembr in the sixteenth yere of the reigne of our souereign Lady Elizabeth by the grace of god of Englond ffraunce and Irelond Quene defender of the faith &c

(folios 90-91) Copies of Covenant between W. Willington and the town as to a sum of £80, and a lease from the Dean and Chapter to John Rey of a house in Northgate Street, not far from the Churchyard, Date 34 Hen. viii. (in Latin)

(folio 92) Whereas John Speede Citizen of London and Servant to o^r gratious Sovaigne the Kings ma^{tie} hath heretofore made and p^{r}sented to his highnes a card or mapp of the whole empire of great Britaine and now intendeth by gods pmission and assistance to add to all and euery pticuler Sheire and Countie of this Realme the true platforme and scituation of all such cityes and Sheire townes as are yet undescribed wth all the auncient and honorable Armes of those most noble families that have had the Dignities and titles of Dukes Marquesses and Earles of euery seuerall County citty and place therin conteyned and created since the Normaines conquest And also such memorable and worthy monuments as concerneth euery of them with such Antiquities as therin are yet seen and remaininge or els hath bine there found The true descriptions of wch he can no way effect or perfectlie pforme (as he informeth us) wthout the p^{r}sent veu and sight thereof These are therfore to pray and desire all and euery of yo^u to whom it shall apptaine to suffer the said John Speede and all such others as he shall imploy herein quietlie to effect and finish this comendable worke wch he hath in hand in all and euery place of this kingdom wherunto he shall be occasioned to repaire wthout anie of your letts or hinderances so as alwayes the said Speede and his assistants in this busines doo giue no occasion of offence and doo well and honestlie beare and behaue themselues according to the lawes and Statutes of this Realme whereof not dowbtinge of yor good regard to be had hereunto we bid you hartelie farewell ffrom the court of Whitehall the 17 of June 1607

   R Cant J. Ellesmere Canr & J. Dorset
               Northampton
   E Lomes   E Wotton & J Stanhope
               J. Herbert

A REQUEST FOR A LOAN

Decimo octauo die Sep- (folio 93) My requests for my streinght and asistance in my trade tembris 1607 of cloathinge in your towne are together wth the continuance of the loue and favour of the right wor^{ll} S^r ffulke Griuill the right wor^{ll} m^r Baylyff and the rest of his bretheren only two

first the free Lendinge of 200^{li} uppon good security

Secondlie the time viz fiue yeares My reasons prouinge the laufullnes of my requests are these and first for the first request : I shall loose the benefitt of all my worckfolke wch I haue trayned upp and brought them fitt for my purpose : Also chardge and hinderance in remouinge And lastlie the trouble and hinderance wch cannot be avoyded but I must undergoe till I haue brought the people fitt for my trade

And to countervayle & to ballance these things I am by reason thereof moued to make my first request

And concerninge the second thing viz the tearme of v yeares I shalbe long before I can fetch the compasse of my tradinge to bringe my cloath marke in request beyond the Seas And if I should repay it in very short time as at ij or iij yeares end it would be either as quicklie or before my cloath were knowne in other lands for it is euident that our merchants will not delight to buy our cloath till the very wearinge of it in other lands doe giue testimonie unto it

Moreouer I thinke this time to be reasonable because the money that is giuen to our Cittie of Hereford is lett from x yeares to x yeares unto cloathiers

And to conclude I doubt not but at the end of these yeares : when my good carryage & honest dealinge wth all people of all sorts shall appeare : your worshipps I trust will continue my good freinds when I shall giue noe cause to the contrary : the mightie god continue and encrease all the tokens of his loue towards you

      Your wo^{rs} in all that I may
         Richard Taylor

(folio 94) Michaelmas Day 1574 16 Elz. Richard Townsend was elected Bailiff.

The sealing of twoo dedes

The one to demand the C£ given by Master Oken

The other acquitance for the same

M^d that the said Michilmas daie in the after none the said bailief & principall Burgesses that is to say humfrey crane Bailief Richard ffisher Richerd Townesend Richerd Roo John ffisher Richard Brooks Simon Yong Thomas Powell Robert Philippes Thomas Jenks John Dich & John Rigeley having conferrens of other causes concerning the said Burrough emongs others agreid to seale w^t their comon seale twoo dedes the one being an acquitance for one hundreth pounds bequethid to the towne by Thomas Oken the other a lre of Attorney auctorising humfrey crane to receve the said hundred pounds of thexecutors of the said Thomas Oken bothe wch were left of trust in the hands of the said humfrey crane At wch tyme divers matters happenid & be talked of so whotly that it is better to leave the report than to write

The teno^r of the twoo dedes ensue

(folio 95) The two deeds

Conference howe the said mony should be ymploid

Be it also remembrid that on Monday the xviij of October the bailief & some of the principall Burgesses namely humfrey crane bailief Richerd ffisher Richerd Townesend Richerd Roo John ffisher Richard Brookes Simon Yong Thomas Powell & John Rigeley principall burgesses assemblid themselfs in their counsell house in the church to consult howe the above said hundred poundes might best be ymploid acording to the mynd of the giver and for the most comon proffit of the poore Inhabitants w^{thin} this towne & suburbes Wheruppon it was agreid that if the same mony might be ymploid & used by some skilfull in making of cloth or yarne It would be very beneficiall bicause the poore & Idle people of this borough might therby be set on woork & so deserve & get their living Wherfor it was agreid that the said some of C^{li} should be offred to V that had some experience in yarne & spinning & they to have xx^{li} a piece if they could find good sureties to be bound both to use the same money in that trade & also to repay the same at twoo or three yeres end The men herunto namyd were John Rigeley Thomas Reynoldes Barthilmew Twycrosse Edward Brown Thomas Porter and it was further agreid that they should be sent for by Mr Bailief to know whither they woold have it & whither they could find suretyes for so great a some Wheruppon Mr Rigeley being present was content to be the name for twenty pounds wch his wief & her sonne Broun should occupy

Request made to discharge Richard Townsend of the Baliwick

After that matter determynid upon Ric. Townesend by Ric Brooks movid the company present to have consideracion of him & not to rest upon him to be bailief the yere to come alleging his inhability & saing that there were secret causes wch movid him so as in no wise he could nor wold take that office upon him at the tyme apointid And besought the resonable consideracions therof wch being not grauntid nor utterly denyed It was requyred of Mr John Rigeley whither he would take the office upon him who semyd utterly unwilling therunto affirming w^thall that he would not tak an other mans leaving & so w^t much a doo at that tyme the matter restid

A meting for conferrence towching the election of an other to be balieff

On Wensday the xxvijth of October Mr Bailief sent to the principall Burgesses to mete at the church that day at Evening prayer to confer of such causes as they should then have to doo wheruppon that night the said Bailief & all the principall Burgesses (saving Richerd Roo & Symon Yong) mett together where the bailief showid that the cause of their assembly was to desire them to have consideracion of some election of some to be bailief for the yere to come bicause Mr Townesend who was electid woold in no wise tak the office uppon him But wold yeld himself to such fyne as should be cessid upon him wheruppon It was demaunded of the said Mr Townesend being present what cause movid him to refuse to take upon him the said office who answerid that he was in debt or so otherwise chargid that he was not hable to shewe himself therein as otherwise he woold and therfore (folio 96) besought the said bailief & company to spare him for this tyme

I

yelding himself to any ffyne they should or wold put upon him ffor he was determyned not to take it Wheruppon after long entreaty made to the said Mr Townesend aswell by the said Mr Bailief as all the other principall burgesses present w^t many promises of their good willes & helpes to him the said Townesend

The absolute answere of refusal to be Bailief

absolutely answerid That he wold rather leave the towne & goo dwell in some other place than take the office uppon him the yere to come & therfore besought them of sparing & to apoint some other for he in no wise wold medle w^t it Than earnest request was made to John Rigeley being present who before stood in election wth the said Ric. Townesend That he would prepare himself to tak the office uppon him at Allholoday next who answerid that Mr Townesend had bene therunto apointed and he should have it for him ffor he wold in no wise medle w^t it & said that he thought himself not well delt w^t that he should be required therunto Wherupon John ffisher seing the said Rigeley so earnest said that in his opynyon it was not mete he should be therunto apointid Inasmuch as the said Rigeley had utterid c^rten woordes very suspicious and as the said ffisher toke them very Iniuryous to the comon weale of this borough And for his better satisffieng as well of himself as other desired the meaning of the said Rigeley to be signified to this house towching the same

Woords Suspicious spoken out of the house rehersid

woords wch were thes that if it lay in the diche meaning the corporacion there it should lye for hym And if it were in the diche he doubtid not but he woold lyue so cyvilly that he should be as fit be towchid as any in this towne whatsoever And should be as sone herd and aswell taken & acceptid with the best and wold be in as good credit & adding further that if he were bailief he wold have in his owne keping such bookes as be hidden from them wch speches had before passid the mouth of the said Rigeley to John ffisher & Thomas Powell uppon communycacions & earnest request privately made by them to the said Rigeley to tak the office upon him which they did the rather bicause there should be no stay or obstacle at the tyme of open meating And the said ffisher desired to be satisfied of thes meanings & what opinion the said Rigeley had in good or evill conceit of the contynuance of the charters & corpacions Adding that he thought it his duety to c^rtify the house therof wch speaches so utterid were much mislikid and it was desired by the whole company present That the said Rigeley might answer the

Rigeley answere in excuse

same Who present said I inded spak half a woord to M^r ffisher And he makyth the whole of it And further said that in dede he thought that if there were no corpacion he should live as well as he doth nowe Nevtheles he ment nothyng in his so saing nor spak so much as was reportid Wherupon Mr Powell being also psent affirmed that the said Rigeley utterid those woords & more Than said the said Rigeley yf I have spoken any thing that offendith you I am sorry for I ment no harme in it But if youe put me to be bailief youe doo me wrong And I will trye my freends before I tak it uppon me for I think youe doo more than youe may doo And I will bring it in question So

Question of pparatiue before eleccion

in conclusion he semyd very unwilling at that tyme Wheruppon it was thought good that a question might be made in the house (not as an eleccion bicause it was thought the eleccion could not proply bee before alholoday when Ric. Townesend either should take the office & be swoorne or refuse) But as it were a preparation for the furtheraunce of thelleccion when that should bee And therfore it was demaundid of all the principall Burgesses present whom they thought to be mete to be in election And so John Diche began who namid Ric. Brooks & John Rigeley than Mr Rigeley namyd Richerd ffisher & John Dyche then Tho. Jenks namyd Richerd Roo & John Rigeley So the choice semyd very different wch being pceivid that it was likely to grow to some long spech and that night was come It was movid & thought good that on Fryday morning after there should be a newe meting against wch tyme

A confference aswell of the bailief and principall burgesses as the xii assistants

warning should be given to all the principall burgesses & to the other xij assistants to be togither in the church on that fryday morning by seven of the clock for further advice in this matter which warning was given accordingly And (folio 97) that fryday morning aswell the said bailief and principall burgesses as the other xij assistants cam togither into their house where it was openyd unto the xij assistants That where Richerd Townesend had bene on Michilmas day last namyd by them to be bailief for the yere to come The said M{r} Townesend had made great request to M{r} Bailief & principall Burgesses to be dischargid of that eleccion and that it might pleas them to consider of his estate present w{ch} was not such as men belivid and that therfore it might please them togither w{th} the assistants to spare him for that tyme Showing to some prvately such causes as partly pswadid some of that company to think his allegacions to be true and therfore to be considerid Nevtheles bicause the said Assistants were part of the bodye & had voices in such elections It was thought meet by the said M{r} bailief & principall burgesses that they the said Assistants should be callid & made pryvie of his said sute before any resolution or aunswer were made to him to thend that the said Assistants hering thallegacions of the said Townesend might assist & advise the said balief & principall burgesses their good advice in the case & what they thought should be convenient in their further procedings and this was thespeciall cause of their sending for w{h}all giving them tunderstand that their being togither that day onely a meane to be quiet on Alholoday when might arise some trowble padventure towching thelleccion if M{r} Townesend should then refuse to be sworne & none other in the meane tyme presentid w{ch} thing if shoulde happen the whole company might be notid very necligent by the multytude for no better looking to a matter of such moment for avoiding whrof they are now callid Heruppon it was demaundid of the said M{r} Townesend whither he contynewid in that mynde of refusall who notw{th}stonding earnest request made unto him by humfrey crane Bailief & the rest of the principall burgesses & assistants to take the office uppon him affirmid that he woold in no wise so doo for divers causes

R. Townesends refusall & submission to the fyne before thassistants

knowen to some of that company w{ch} he woold be lothe to shewe openly But earnestly besought them all to apoint some other for this yere submitting himself to the order of the house for his fyne wherin he also requested them so favorably to use him as he might think himself beholden to them And so they should have him redy to doo any thing that lay in his power otherwise he must be freed to get some other habitacion for he was determynid not to take thoffice upon him Then was it thought good that the Assistants should consider emongs themselfs wch of the principall Burgesses were meet to be in election ffor wch purpose they were desired to goo togither & to

circumstance in their Conference

comon of that matter for the better ayde of the bailief & principall Burgesses who being somewhat divided in opinions referrid their willes to their good advices Than the said Assistants desired that inasmuch as this case is rare and the first that hath happenyd sins their incorpating & specally stonding upon such weight as wherby the comon quiet may be disturbid far want of due regards That it woold please M^r bailief and his company to signifye their opynyons singularly one by one before the said Assistants before they went togither to thend that they hearing the opynyons of that company to whom the matter proply aptenyd might the rather be inducid to doo that to them belongid the rather bicause that choice should be made by the Bailief & principall Burgesses onely To that it was aunswerid That albeit Mr Bailief & his company had callid the said Assistants for their better ayde in this case yet the meaning is not That any absolute election should be presently made ffor that may not be untill the manifest refusall of Mr Townesend to take his oth on Alhallonday But this conferrens was onely a premeditacion of their affections for avoiding of inordynate and inconsiderate actions that might otherwise happen the said Alhalonday and so desirid them to tak it Neuertheles forasmuch as they had desired to heare their dividid opynyons It was agreid that the principall Burgesses & M^r balf should & woold yeld the same And so John Rigeley began & namyd Ric. ffisher & John ffisher John Dych namyd Richerd ffisher & John Rigeley Thomas Jenks namyd twoo others & so in conclusion all or the most were namyd some by one some by another So as in the end the said Bailief & principall Burgesses eftsones referrid the censideracions therof to the said assistants who went togither into the Lady chapell and there conferrid of that busynes wch helde them so long as they spent full twoo howres before their returne Whan it was lookid for that they woold have namyd John Rigeley for one

to stand in election But what cause movid them to the contrary this writer doth
not knowe But in conclusion uppon their returne they agreid & said that in their
opynyons (as they thought euery one of the principall burgesses very meat &
woorthy to stand in election) yet for some causes them moving
their opynyons were that it was convenient that Richerd ffisher
& John ffisher should be (folio 98) in election & one of them to tak upon him that
office for the yere to come wch signified & some pause made Jo.
ffisher said ffor my part I am greatly to thank you that youe have so good
opynyon of me as to think me worthy to be put in trust wth that office Neuertheles
I mervaile not a litle that you have no further consideracion than to name me
who bothe for my Inhability almaner of wayes & for my other suices am unfitt
for that purpose especially knowing that being Steward of the borough & so also
serving the office of towne clerk or Recorders deputy am occupied diversley in
thaffaires of this borough wch if I doo some other must besides that as you all
know I have bene returned & contynew yor burges for the pliament wch is apointid
to begyn agayn in March next so as that wayes also I am to serve for the towne
in an other place besides that I have to doo for the shire diversly all wch I wold
surely have remembrid to you before your going furth if I had any thing doubtid
of this matter as in dede I did not Assuring you that I doo not speak this in
excuse to be holden from the said office of Bailief ffor therin or in any thing I am
hable I am very willing to serve the towne to thuttermost of my powr But
considering myne Insufficiency as well for lack of health as for that I can not
serve many places at ones And that bothe the place in the pliament house &
office of Steward & Towneclerk is to be supplied orells some perill may ensue I
trust you will have consideracion in your further election Than
said R. ffisher And I had thought that you woold have thought otherwise of me
and not to seek to charge me still this wayes ffor as you all knowe I have borne
the office of Bailief twise and so hath no man ells doone And for those twoo tymes
I have bene at some charge Besides that in the tymes whan I was Bailief I laid
out above fforty pounds for the towne wherof the towne oweth me yet almost
Thirty And not long ago I laid out mony about the Repayring of the bridge above

Side notes:
The opynyons of the iij Assistants shewid
J. ffisher
R. ffisher

twenty nobles wch I was content to give towards the repr̄ng of the Boothehall And I trustid you woold have had some consideracion of me And besides this is an evill president that Mr Townesend being chosen & namyd Bailief should thus give it over And they are not his freends that doo p̄swade him to yt But it is no matter Let me have the rest of my monye that the towne owith me besides the xx nobles And I will not see it lye in the dych yf it cost me x^{li} wherupon it was p̄mised that he should have that mony assone as it comyth in And theruppon yt was told to Mr Townesend openly that his fyne should be no lesse than is in the book of orders wch was Ten pounds After wch doone The book of orders were redd before the bailief & principall Burgesses & xij assistants who all allowid the same saving that in one Article towching the bailief sending for one to sitt w^t him at the courtes That one was emendid by consent of all & made twoo at the least &c wch things so doone The Assistants desired a copy of their orders bicause they woold kepe them more c^rtenly wch was p̄mised And therupon deptid

The mony owing by the towne to Ri ffisher p̄mised to be paid

The fyne agreid uppon to be paid by Richerd Townesend

Aligacion of one Article in the book of orders

The refusall of Ri. Townesend to be bailieff on Alhalow-day 1574

Be yt remembrid that on Alhallouday the first day of November 1574 humfrey crane bailief & the xij principall Burgesses & xij Assistants of this borough assemblid themselfs in the Shire Hall w^thin the same borough being for the tyme their hall & counsaill house Where was offred to Richard Townesend the book to be sworne for the office of Bailiwik for the yere to come who openly before them all & a great nomb^r of other the Inhabitants & other Straungers did utterly refuse to tak uppon him the office & to be sworne Wheruppon it was told him by John ffisher that if he wold so refuse he must suffer such ponishm^t as by the charter & their orders were to be laid upon him wch was to be fynid and to be comyttid to warde To wch the said Townsend said he wold yeld himself to their order trusting that they woold use him so as they might have him a neighbo^r emongs them & one of their house Wherupon it was askid of all the principall burgesses what fyne they would lay

Ri. Townesend yeldith him to the orders of the house

upon the said Ric. Townesend for his such refusall And it was agreid by them all that no whit of that was agreid upon by the book of orders should be diminished and so also said the Bailief wch was eftsones by the said John ffisher declarid to the said Ric. Townesend and that he must not think any uncurtesy to be sent to warde till such tyme as he had paid the fyne To wch the said Richerd Townsend aunswerid that he trustid they wold not use him so for if they so did he wold refuse their company & come no more in the house And therupon said I trust you will tak my bond for my fyne wch I trust will not be so much Wherupon Mr Willm hudson offred to be surety for the said Ri. Townsend that he should pay his fyne at crstmas next And gave his woorde before the whole company that if the said Townesend did not pay the said x^{li} for his fyne at cristmas he the said W^m hudson wold pay yt for him (folio 99) W^{ch} promises of the said Richerd Townesend & W^m hudson the bailief & principall burgesses aceptid as a good assumption for x^{li} Therupon it was agreid that a new election should be And bicause the tyme passid and the preacher tarryed for the returne of the bailief & his company to the church It was requyred of all the principall burgesses that they would procede to their election w^t their voices as spedely & w^t as fewe woords as might be So it began wth John Rigeley who namyd Richerd ffisher & John ffisher So did John dyche and so from one to another thorough the whole company wch the bailief humfrey crane confirmid Wherupon the xij Assistants being a litle wthdrawen were callid before the Bailief & principall burgesses To whom it was declarid openly That where before that tyme on Michilmas day an election had been made of twoo psones to stond in election for to tak upon one of them the office of bailief this day acording to the ch^r and that they the said Assistants had namyd & chosen one of them namely Richerd Townesend to be bailief for the yere to come The said Richerd Townesend had partly shewid causes but determynately had refusid to take upon him the said office & to be sworne referring himself to be for his said Refusall orderid as to the said bailief

& principall burgesses should be thought mete So as now they are to procede to a new choice And thern M{r} bailief & principall burgesses had considerid of twoo of that company namely Richerd ffisher & John ffisher referring the namyng of one of them to the said Assistants to take the office of bailwick upon him for the yere to come praing them therfore to goo togither & to make their choice of one of those twoo & to present his name w{t} as good spede as may be Wheruppon the said assistants w{th}drew themselfs agayn And tarrieng not long they were agreid And returnid to the said bailief & principall burgesses before whom they namyd & apointid Richerd ffisher to be bailief for the yere to come w{ch} Richerd ffisher being required to seale the bonds aswell for redelury of M{r} Oken's plate (a) as for the true aunswering of his Acompt so did And was theruppon sworne & placid Bailief w{ch} office he protestid he did tak uppon him w{th} no desire of glory or any such like cause but onely to shew his good will to the towne & his neighbo{rs} whom he woold not suffer to p'ish as long as his poore powr might stand in stede And so deptid to the church.

Richerd ffisher the third tyme sworne bailliff

Not long after Thomas ffisher Esquyre (b) brother of ths said Richerd sent for the same Richard and requyred of him the payment of c{li} due by the said Richerd to him upon the bgayn of the leefield w{ch} hundred pound the said Richerd paid to the said Thomas at w{ch} tyme the said Richard desired John ffisher their brother M{r} Crane & Phillipp coo to goo w{t} him to see the mony paid and the writings betwene them sealid w{ch} was done acordingly And uppon the payment of the said mony the said Richerd & John ffisher put their other brother Thomas in remembrance of his promise before that tyme made to the said John ffisher & humfrey crane whiles the said humfrey crane was bailief & afterward to the said Richerd & John of his consent & contentacion to aunswer the mony due by the said Thomas ffisher to the towne of Warwik w{ch} were thes somes viz. ffirst for the Rent resuid of the first charter at vj{li} xiij{s} iiij{d} by yere by the said Thomas Receiud & not answerid to the quenes ma{ty} for three yeres viz. v{t} vj & vij{n} of her ma{ty} reigne a xx{li} Then for vi yeres rent of combwell at vj{s} viij{d} by

(a) Oken's plate is still given into the custody of the Mayor.
(b) This would be the Thomas Fisher referred to in note a on p. 29.

yere due at michelmas last a xl^s Then for vj yeres rent going out of the lands sometyme math farecloughs xiij^s iiij^d by yere due at Michilmas last iiij^{li} So in all xxvj^{li} All wch the said Thomas had yeldid to pay uppon conferrence betwene him the said Thomas and the said humfrey crane late Bailief & the said Jo. ffisher who by shewing c'ten bookes dedes & writings satisfied the said Thomas therin & in all other doubts before tyme risen & in questions towching the tuithes of Lynnen fields &c. Uppon wch mocyon made by the said Richerd ffisher bailief &

Thomas ffisher Esquire paide xxvj^{li} aswell for arrerage of Rents due to the towne as for other duptyes

the said John ffisher The said Thomas ffisher was contentid And did paye the said xxvj^{li} as aforesaid to the said Richerd to the use of the said towne of Warwik taking for the said paym^t an acquitans signed wth the hands of the said Richerd ffisher John ffisher & humfrey crane And further did then promise that he woold apoint his rents of the cambwell & mathew ffarecloughes land should be yerely aunswerid by such as should be tenn^{ts} to the same & that they should not eftsones be in arrerages wch mony so recevid by the said Richerd ffisher was afterward on Sonday the vijth of Novembr brought into the church where in the counsaill house before all or the most part of the principall Burgesses then present The said Richerd ffisher confessid the Receipt thereof And putting them

Richerd ffisher his good will towards the townes quietnes

in remembrance of their promises made unto him towching the satisfieng of himself of the first mony should come to his hands Offrid nevertheles the lenger forbearing of his owne (folio 100) some lenger tyme to sett the towne out of debt towards the quenes ma^{ty} And theruppon deliverid the monye before them all to John ffisher therwth to satisfye such arrerages as the towne was cast into the said rent resruid of the first corpacion wch xxvj^{li} the said Jo. ffisher then recevid of the said Richerd ffisher in   towardes these causes ffor wch all the whole company gave the said Richerd great thanks recomending him as a father in all his doings towards the towne Not long after the said Ric. was sruid w^t a subpena to aunswer before the L of the counsaill in the starre chambr upon a bill of piury preferrid by Tho. Staunton the yog^r So as he was forcid to go to london & tarried there contrary to his mynd After that it was remembrid that by agrement betwene Robert

the Acquitans for iiij^xx^li giben by Maister Oken sealid

Phillippes & Thomas cawdrey executors to Thoms Oken & the overseers of the said Oken's will The said Executors should pay to the hands of the balief of Warwik for the tyme being iiij^xx^li given by the said oken to the uses of the townes of Stretford & Banbury It was therfore thought good that an acquitans should be made redy before hand (if the said Executors should tender the said monye at the day wch was the xxiiij^th^ of dec^r^ And also that a lre of Attorney should also be made redy giveng the said bailif auctority to demannd & receive the said mony wch both were made & agreid uppon And were sealid on St Thomas day before cristmas And at that tyme also

The book for mercers sealid

was sealid an other book of articles granted before that tyme & enlargid in some cases towching the orders emongs mercers haberdashers Grocers and ffishmongers The tenor^s^ of wch writings followe

the mony giben by Maister Oken deliverid out

The same day that Richerd ffisher bailief was sruid w^t^ the suppena aforesaid being the xx^th^ day of Novembr he caused the mony given by Mr Oken to this towne that is to say the hundred pounds remaining in humfrey crane late bailiefs hands to be delivered out in lone to such as promised & took uppon them therwth to sett poore people on woork acording to such orders and devises as before had bene devised ffor wch bondes were taken

The book of orders for mercers haburdasshers Grocers & ffishmongers

A declaracyon of the constitucyons Ordynaunces & decrees of the misteryes & crafts of mercers haburdasshers Grocers & ffishmongers wthin the borough of warwik and Suburbes of the same made ordenyd constitutid & agreid on aswell by the balief & principall burgesses of the same borough as by all the mercers haburdasshers Grocers & ffishmongers nowe Inhabiting there from henceforth iustly & truly to be observid fulfilled & kept of them & eury of them & their Successors mercers haburdasshers Grocers & ffishmongers as herafter Ensuith ffirst it is orderyd agreid & constitutid by assent & consent aforesaid That all Inhabitants being housholders w'thin this borough & suburbes and being alredy of the same misteryes or crafts of mercers haburdashers Grocers & ffishmongers ffree shall yerely uppon saint Johns day in cristmas assemble them selfes & mete togither at some convenient house within the same borough which they shall call the mercers halle and at that place & tyme they shall yerely elect choose & name one person being of that Artes or craftes to be maister of those Artes & craftes for one whole yere then next to come And in like sorte shall elect choose & name twoo other persons of the said crafts to be wardens of the same Artes or craftes for the same yere to come by which eleccyon & nomynacion the said maister & wardens shalbe auctorized by this booke for the tyme of their offices to warne call & comande all others & residue of the same craftes being housholders of the same borough to mete at the same halle there & then quietly & orderly & peaceably to devise & make good orders for the true dealing in the said craftes & misteryes to the benefiting of them selfes & the comon weale of this borough & countrey adiacent

Item it is orderyd established & consentid unto That evry housholder of the said misteries or crafts of mercers haburdashers Grocers & ffishmongers shall uppon sufficient warning to him or them first given by the said maister & wardens or their knowne officer come to the same halle & there attend to thintents aforesaid And if any of them uppon such warning given refuse to come having no reasonable lett to excuse him or them for his or their absence Or being there present doo obstinately refuse to agree to such good & wholesome orders as shalbe ordenyd made & consentid unto by the maister wardens & more parte of the company & ffelowshippe of the said Artes craftes or misteryes shall forfeit & pay for eury tyme so offending Three shillings & foure pence

(folio 101) Item is ordenyd establishid & consentid unto That none of the Inhabitants of the said borough or suburbes being of the said craftes of mercers haburdashers Grocers & ffishmongers shall in any wise hire receve or take into his service any man or chield to dwell wth him to thintent to learne or teache him any of the said misteryes Artes or craftes Except he take him to be his Apprentice for the terme of seven yeres at the least and that he shall take him by Indenture And shall cause the same Apprentice to be brought with his Indenture before the balief & Recorder or Stuard or Towneclerk of the said borough for the tyme being within one moneth next after he hathe so taken him by Indenture And then & there the same Apprentice shall knoleige himself to be bounde by that Indenture to his said maister for the terme comprised in the same which said Indenture shalbe enrollid togither with the said recognicion by the Towneclerk there who shall haue for evry such Inrolment xij^d And if any person of the said misteryes Artes or craftes doo contrary to this ordynance he shall forfeit & paye for eury tyme so doing ffourty shillings

Item it ordenyd establishid & consentid unto that no man of the said Artes of mercers haburdashers Grocers & ffishmongers shalbe admittyd by the same maister & wardens to sett upp or occupye in any the said misteryes or crafts in the said borough or suburbes Except he haue bene Aprentice or covenante servaunte to all or one of the same craftes by the space of seven yeres at the least which shalbe provid before the maister & wardens and the balief & Steward of the same borough for the tyme being by sufficient testimony of honest persons before his admission to sett upp as aforesaid And that doone that he shall first compound & agree & pay or be bounde to pay w^thin sixe moneths after his said admission to the maister & wardens for his admission & setting upp Ten pounds

Provided always and it is fully agreid that it may & shalbe lawfull for evry man that hath bene Aprentice or covenaunt sruant w^thin the said borough or suburbes and sruid in the said misteryes or craftes seven yeres as aforesaid making suite & request to the said maister & wardens & ffelowshipp for the tyme being to be good unto him to sett upp & occupye in of the said Artes or craftes w^thin the said borough or suburbes payng unto the said maister & wardens before his setting upp iij^s iiij^d

Item it is condiscendid concludid & agreid that if any man being of the same Artes or craftes or any of them dwelling w^thin the said borough or suburbes fortune at any tyme to descede or depart to dwell out of the same borough & suburbes and doo discontinewe his occupyeng in the said borough or suburbes & doo dwell in other place or places by the space of seven yeres being not in the sruice of his prince or countrey nor being not in prisyn or beyond the Seas but in health & at libertye And after would come again & dwell & exercise the said Artes or craftes or any of them within the said borough & suburbes That then he shall first compound & agree wth the said maister & wardens for his readmission Orells he shall forfeyt & paye unto them for evry weeke that he occupieth any of the said Artes or craftes before he haue compoundid Thretten shillings & foure pence

Item it is agreid consentid & orderid That if it happen any man being of the said Artes or craftes dwelling within the said borough or suburbes to dye having Apprentice by Indenture before thexpiracion of the terme & yeres of such Apprentice That then the said Apprentice or covennt sruante serving out the rest of the yeres not detmynid with the widowe of his late master if she kepe her self widowe or wth any housholder of the same Artes or craftes by his master or mistres apointment during the rest of the yeres comprised in the Indentures shall & may after thexpiracion of his yeres at his libtye making request & payng Three shillings & foure pence as aforesaid sett upp & use the said artes or craftes or any of them aswell & in like maner as if his maister had lived out the terme of yeres comprised in the said Indentures

Item it is agreid consentid & orderid That if any woman w^thin the said borough or suburbes happen to bury her husbond which at the tyme of his deathe was one of the company of mercers haburdashers Grocers & ffishmongers Such woman during her widowhed shall & maye use & exercise the Arte which her late husbond at the tyme of his death did use But if it happen any such woman afterward to marry an other man being not of the same company of mercers haburdashers Grocers & ffishmongers although he be dwelling w^thin the said borough & suburbes And after such mariage would use the said arte or craft It is consentid & agreid that neither such man nor woman shall sett upp exercise or occupye the said Arte or crafte Except he or she have first compoundid in maner & forme abovesaid wth the said maister & wardens of the said company of mercers haburdashers Grocers & ffishmongers uppon payne that who so doth contrary to this ordynaunce shall forfeit & paye for eury weeke so dooing Twenty Shillings.

Item it is further concludid & agreid that no fforrener of the said Artes or craftes or any of them shall in any wise uppon the market dayes holden in the said borough tyll over his or their heades or make any back shewe in any parte of the markett place (Except it be in the boothe halle) And if they or any of them doo contrary to this ordynnce to forfeyt for evry tyme to the master & wardens the some Ten Shillings

Item it is further agreid consentid & ordenyd That if any persone or persones w^thin the same borough or suburbes shall in any wise offend in any of thies ordynnces or any other good orders that shalbe made emongs the said master wardens & companyes of mercers haburdashers Grocers & ffishmongers and will not uppon demaunde by the maister & wardens pay such somes of money as by him or them is hathe bene or shalbe lost or forfeytid for not observing the said ordynaunces & orders That then it shalbe laufull for the said maister & wardens of mercers haburdashers Grocers & ffishmongers to enter the houses shoppes closes or ffields w^thin this borough or libties of any such offender or offenders and there to take some parte of his goods & catalles in the name of a distres And the same to deteyne untill such tyme as he or they haue paid the money or somes so forfeytid or lost by breaking any the said orders or agreaments And if the offender or offenders in them or any of them will not paye the money so lost or (folio 102) forfeytid as before is said with in one moneth next after such distres taken That then at the next Court to be holden in the said borough after the moneth The same distres shalbe brought by the said maister & wardens into the court before the balief Recorder or Steward or Towneclerk or any of them there present And the same distres shalbe presid by ffoure indifferent men After which thing so done it shalbe lawfull to the said maister & wardens to sell the same distres and of the money therof rising to satisfye themselfes deteyning so much money as hath bene forfeited & lost And the overplus if any be they shall delyver to the late owner or owners of such distres

Item it is also agreid consentid & orderid That the one half of the money rising happening or growing of for or by reason of any composicyon agreament ffyne forfeiture payne or penaltye wch shall or should come to the handes of the master & wardens of the said company by reason of the master & wardens of the said company by reason of the orders abovesaid shall goo & be to the balief & principall burgesses of this borough to the use of the same borough And the other halfe or moytye to the use of the company of mercers haburdashers Grocers & ffishmongers of the said borough

And it is also consentid agreid & orderid That uppon the said feast of saint John the Evangelist evry yere after the eleccion & naming of a newe maister & wardens in maner & forme above declaryd made The olde master & wardens shall make & declare before the newe maister & wardens & the company then present a full perfytt & iust Accompt of & for all such somes of money & other thinges as they haue or ought to haue recevid for any default forfeyture composicion agreament or otherwise And after their said accompt so fully plainly & clearely made The said late maister & wardens shall ymediately deliver the moytye & one half of all such money as hath or should haue come to their handes by reason of such defaltes forfeytures or agreaments or otherwise to the balief of the said borough for the tyme being to the use of the chamber of the same borough And the other half or moyty togither with the rest & remayne of the precedent Accompt They shall deliver to the newe maister & wardens so by them electid & namyd putting in sufficient bonde for the redelyvery & true annswering therof at the ende of the said yere

And for the more pfytt annswering of such somes of money as shalbe due to the chamber of this borough It is also agreid consentid & orderyd That the Audytor of this borough for the tyme being shall & may once in the yere at the least call to Accompt the said maister & wardens of mercers haburdashers Grocers & ffishmongers which said maister & wardens uppon reasonable warning to them given by the said Audyto^r shall bring before the said Audyto^r all their bookes of orders Accompts & reconyngs and shall accompte before him for the money due to the said chamber uppon payne of forfeyture of this booke & graunt to be seasid at the will & pleasure of the balief & principall burgesses for the tyme being

ffinally it is concludid consentid & agreid that incase any thing be done by the said maister wardens & company of mercers haburdashers Grocers & ffishmongers contrary to the good orders customes & lawes of the lande or the quiet governement of the comon weale of this borough or that the maister & wardens of the said Artes of mercers haburdashers Grocers & ffishmongers doo not yerely pay to the handes of the balief of this borough for the tyme being all such money as should yerely come to the use of the chamber of the said borough as aforesaid That then this booke & all the articles herein conteynid shalbe voyd Or incase the balief & principall burgesses shall see cause to redresse or reforme any thing or article abovewriten or to adde or encrease other orders to thies abovewriten It is also agreid consentid & orderyd that the balief of this borough & princypall burgesses for the tyme being may determyne make void & frustrate all or any the articles abovewriten And in their places to make newe or to the same to adde others as occasion & tyme shall requyre by their discrecyons which being devised & agreid uppon by the balief & principall burgesses or the greater nomber of them & knowleige therof given in writing to the maister & wardens abovesaid or to one of them shall from thensfurth be taken & reputyd and shalbe in deede ordynaunces & order to bynde the said company of mercers haburdashers Grocers & ffishmongers & evry of them This booke or anything therin conteynyd to the contrary notwithstonding In witnes of all which articles orders constitucyons agreaments & consents The said balief & principall burgesses haue to thies presents putt their comon seale the xxjst daye of December in the seventene yere of the reigne of our souereigne Lady Elizabeth by the grace of god of Englond ffraunce & Irelond Quene defender of the faithe &c

K

(folio 103) (On folio 103 there is an account of a meeting between the bailiffs of Warwick and Stratford-on-Avon, to confer respecting the legacy of £40 left by Thomas Oken of Warwick to Stratford. These matters are not entered in the Black Book in chronological order relating as they do to the carrying out of certain directions contained in the Will of Thomas Oken, an account of whose death, and a copy of whose deed of feoffment and will are given on subsequent folios. On the 23rd of December, 1574, as before related in folio 100, the Executors of Oken paid the two sums of £40 over to the Bailiff of Warwick.)

Wheruppon on the morrow after the said Richerd ffisher then bailief did write his lres sevrally to the bailiefs & officers of the said townes of Stretford & Banbury signifieng that the monye bequethed to their townes by Thomas Oken was in his hands redy to be delivered to them acording to the will of the giver uppon such bands & condicions as the said giver apointid And therfore earnestly desired them to come or send such of their company as they could trust & thought mete to conferr wth the said bailief of Warwik & his bretherne towching the said condicions & bonds Wheruppon w'thin twoo or three dayes after the bailief of Stretford namyd (a blank) Plymley Adryan Quynye of the same towne & Henry Byers of Sherborne their understeward or towneclerk came to Warwik where conferring wth Richard ffisher bailief & John ffisher Steward of Warwik certen

Articles delivred to the bailiff of Stretford towching the ymploying of the mony given by master oken

articles were by the said John ffisher drawen in maner of an Indenture & showid to the said Bailief & other officers of Stretford Who desiring to ympart the same to the rest of their bretherne desired to have a copye therof wch was grauntid acordingly and was deliverid to the said Bailief & others who shortly after conferring togither aceptid the condicions And were content to be

Acceptance of the Articles

bound for the pformance therof under their comon seale and agreid to send or fetch the monye on tuesday the fourth of January And then to bring wth them their seale to confirm & seale aswell their part of the Indenture of covennts as also an obligacion for pformance of the same At wch day cam from Stretford the said (   ) Plymley then bailief

Andryan Quyny than Alderman Lewes ap Williams ( ) hille & ( ) Tyler all of the company of bailiefe & wth them cam Barbo^r of the beare & Nicolas Banister of the second company and henry Rogers their tounclerk & the S^rjaunt who all were well recevid by the bailief of warwik & feastid & had to beare them company the most part of the principall burgesses & some other of their assistants of warwik And after dynner the books being lookid uppon & examyned Adryan Quynye semid somewhat in the name of the rest of his company to stick at the sealing of the bond thinking it hard that they should bothe be bound to such condicions & also a bond w^thout wch they ment as he said to pforme as much as in them lay to doo for the pformance of all things To wch it was aunswerid That if they mislikid any thing nowe it was very late having before that tyme had the mynit in their hands & consideracion three or foure dayes & returnid the same wth desire to have it writen upp wch now being so don can not be alterid And more it was told them playnly that unles they did yeld both to the covennts & bond they should receve no mony ffor so was the will of the giver who putting his trust in his neighbours desirid to pforme the trust as nere as they might & yet w^t as great favo^r showid to them of Stretford as might be ffor though it be true that they be men knowen of good credit honest behavio^r upright dealing & such as upon their credits might be trustid in as great a matter as this yet forasmuch as they be but men & therfore varyable & mortall & therfore must dye And the thing yet contynnueng It is not to be taken amisse that some matter be devised in writing to tye their posterytie & successors for the pformance of the covennts being bothe resonable & easy to be pformid by carefull & good men whose travailes in that case being also but easy shall greatly benefyt their poore neighbo^rs wherunto we are all bound So in thend they agreid and the books were sealid & deliverid and the mony paid And they of Stretford sent mery homewards.

circumstance in the fetching of the mony for Stretford

The book betwene Warwik & Stretford for xl^li giben by Maister Oken sealid The xl^li delurired

(folio 104) Copy of the Indenture of Covenant

> To my loving frendes Mr Bailief & his brethern Burgesses & cobretherne of the borough or towne of Banburye

The tenor of the first lre to Banbury

After my hartie comendacions Thes are to let you understand that the monye given by o^r sometyme good neighbo^r Thomas Oken decessid for the reliving of yor towne of Banbury is nowe redy & in my hands to be deliverid acording to his will wherof I wold be glad to be dispatchid acordingly And therfore thes are to to desire youe to send over such one of yor company as you think meet to conferre wth me & my bretherne about the condicions & covents to be agreid on for the same And so I bid you hartely farewell ffrom Warwik the xxiiijth day of Decebr 1574

> Yo^r loving freend
> Ric ffisher balief

Thes lres deliverid to the caryer that went to london thorough Banbury to be delivred to the bailief of banbury were not deliverid but brought again Wheruppon the said bailief of Warwik wrote ymediately upon the returne of the carryer an other lre of like effect & somewhat more The tenor of wch ensueth

> To my loving freends the bailief & Rulers of the borowe of banburye

The tenor of the second lre to Banbury

After my harty comendacions Thes are to let you understand that the monye given by o^r sometyme good neighbo^r Thomas Oken decessid for the reliving of yor towne of Banbury is nowe redye and in my hands to be delivred acording to his wille wherof I wolde be glad to be dischargid acordingly And for that purpose did write my lres desiring some of you to come hither to conferre wth me & my bretherne about the condicions & bondes for the same wch lres be not come to yor handes (as I understand) but returnid to me So as I take that to be the cause that I have not heard from you towching that matter albeit I have heard saye some of yor company had woord by mouthe to be here about those matters in the begynnyng of the last weeke Nevertheles having a care to be dischargid of the trust reposid in me & the rest of my brethern And being desirous that the good wille of the giver might take effect wth spede I nowe send you a mynute or draught in paper of such condicions as by the will of the said Oken youe are to be bound unto which it may please you to consider of & accepting therof & ratifieng the same by yor comon seale & bringing the same hither wth you youe shall receve the monye ymediately Otherwise if you make any sticking at any part or matter conteynyd in the said mynute Youe shall doo very well to send such one or twoo of yor companye as you shall think mete to conferre wth me & my bretherne of doubtfull poyntes (if any be) wherin we will resolve you the best we can And so bid you farewell this last of Decembr 1574

Yo^r loving freend
R. ff

W^th this lre was a messinger promptly sent to whom was delivred the mynute of the covenants & bonds agreing verbatim w^th (folio 106) that aforewriten agreid uppon betwene Warwik & Stretford (Saving in the title of the corpacion) and the some wherin they should be bound should be an hundreth marks & one article or clause wherin the bailief & his company of banburye should at evry foure yeres end bring & tender the said xl^li before the bailief & principall burgesses of Warr. and putting in suretyes have the same xl^li back agayn All wch points were thought to be very requisite at the least to be offrid unto them all though if any reason had bene shewid to the contrarye by them of banbury The books should have bene reformed as were they of Stretford.

This lre & mynute being so delivered to the bailief of banbury they returnid the messinger w^t answer by woord of mouth that shortly the bailief of

Warwik should here from them Wheruppon about a sevenight after the balief of banbury wrote a lre to the bailief & his bretherne of Warwik the tenor whrof ensuith

      To my very freend M^r ffisher bailief of the borough of Warr and to his bretherne hedde burgesses of the same borough geven spede from banbery

the tenor of the first lre recevid from Banbury After my most hartie comendacions & having recevid yor lres & perusid the contents therof I wth the rest of my brethern have considered therof and of the drawfts of assuraunce in paper which ye will to be executid to yor use acording to the deades will In wch draught forasmuch as there are many streight clauses tending to ympossibilities & Inconveniencs (as wee suppose) our desire is therfore to see the last will of Thomas Oken (wch ye saye is in effecte & meaning acording to yor said draught to thentent conferring the said draught & last wille togither wee may use thadvise of o^r learned counsaill therin and theruppon I wth some of my brethern meane wth speede to repaire to youe & eyther fulfill the effect of yor said lre & draught orells ympart unto you & yor said bretherne our myndes & meanings in the same and of the causes (if any be) of misliking veryly trusting wee shall finde ye readye & willing acording to yor lre to reform all Inconveniencs extremyties & Impossibilities and content yourselves wth such reasonable assurance as may be for yor discharge & the laufull execucion & fulfilling of the reasonable meaning of the last will of the said Testato^r wherin ye shall give me & my bretherne (who are chargeable & must stand chargid wth the mony occasion to think well of yor indifferencye towards us and also o^r poore neighbo^{rs} to whose use the same shalbe to be much beholding to youe wherfore for that o^r meaning is speedily to deliver you of the said legacyes acording to o^r expectacion y^t may please you to be a meane wee may have a true copie of the deades will made redye and we will send for the same and paye for the charges of writing Trusting ye will take thes lres acording to o^r meaning to be no delay but onely a necessary request for our safety in o^r dealings uppon whom the burthen is like to lye So for this tyme wee leave to trowble you comytting you all to the mercifull governaunce of the almighty who graunt us all his grace ffrom banbury the vj^th of January 1574

Yo^r loving freend Thomas Dyxe
balief of banbury

Conference uppon receipt of the lres from Banbury

Thes lres thus sent to the bailief of Warwik from the bailief of Banbury wth excuse of that they had no soner aunswerid our former lres to them bicause that the same (as they said) were delivered to the bailief of banbury at such tyme as the greater nombr of his cobretherne were from home namely at Oxford at the quarter sessions The bailief of Warwik calling togither all his brethern the principall Burgesses (emongs whom was Robart Phillippes one of thexecutors of Tho. Oken) and making them all privye to the lres that had passid on both sides desiring their opynions & advises what further to doo in this case It was thought meete and was agreid uppon by all aswell the bailief as all the principall burgesses present namely by Richerd ffisher bailief Richerd Townesend Richerd Roo John ffisher Richerd Brook Willm ffrekulton Thomas Powell Robart Phillippes Thomas Jenks humfrey crane John Dyche John Rigeley and John Grene That they the Bailief & his bretherne of Banbury should be aunswerid playnely that they should not have the said xl^li except they woold yeld to those condicions wch agreing well both wth the will & meaning of the said Oken was by them to be yeldid unto ffor otherwise said Robart Phillips they were not worthy of it And he said that he hard Mr Oken saye & precisely will That if either they of banbury or of Stretford would not make such assurance as might be most strongly made against them they should not have it but that the mony should come agayne to Warwik and that Mr Oken gave him great charge to see therunto Wheruppon the said Bailief & pryncipall Burgesses wrote their other lre and putting ther euery man his hand to it sent the next day to banbury this aunswer The tenor therof Insuith

To the wo^r^shipfull Mr Bailief & his bretherne of the borough of Banbury

the tenor of the third lre sent to Banbury

W^th^ like hartye comendacions having considerid of yor lres of the sixt of this moneth for aunswere towching the ffourtie pounds bequethed by Mr Oken wee understand that you have conferrid about the mynute of the covenuts sent unto you for disposing the same acording to his wille Wherin you conceve harde (folio 107) dealing of us towardes you in devising many streight clauses tending to ympossibilities Inconveniencs & extremyties And therfore you doo requyre a copie of Mr Oken's wille to shewe to yor Counsell wth the said Mynute Wherein as youe give us cause to think youe mistrust us and that wee doo more than reason or auctorytie servith us So to deliver you a copie of Mr Oken's will wee think it unnecessary bicause there is many things that towchith you not nor mete to be knowen to all men Nevertheles seing o^r^ creadite is so slender wth you as not to be believid by that wee have alredy sent you Youe may (if you list) send to the Arches to see the Recorde wch may better satisfy you than any copye that wee can make Assuring you that whan you have so doon wee will look for the veary same Covenuts in effect to be assured under y^r^ common seale (if you have any) or the seales of some sufficient of you such as wee shall thinke meete before you receve the monye And bicause the givers mynde was the mony should be ymploid for the benefit of poore Artificers wth as good spede as may be wch also is our care & desire wee do earnestly prey you to sett aside all delays answere us directly by yor lres under yor handes whither you will receve the mony uppon the condicions alredy sent you in the said mynute or not And that wee may receve yor resolute aunswere in writing by this bringer whom wee purposely send for the same Otherwise wee will ymploye the same monye according to the mynde of the said Oken & his trust reposid in us where the same wilbe more thankfully taken And so we bid you farewell from Warwik the ix^th^ of January 1574.

Thes lres were sent to Banbury by (   ) Skott who had charge & comaundm^t to deliver to M^r bailief of Banbury and to tarrye there for aunswere three or foure dayes And the said Skott made such spede that he delivered the

dillitory aunswere made by the baliff of Banbury to the berer of the lres from Warr.

said lres to the bailief there on Monday in the presences of divers of his company & bretherne comyng wth him from the Court House wch they presently lookid on and after that gave him aunswer that the most part of his bretherne were out of the towne so as he could make none aunswere presently to wch he said that he had comaundm^t to tarry for aunswere and so he woold if it were twoo or three days To wch the bailief made aunswere that should not nede but if he wold dept home aunswere should be sent after him by some of their towne very shortly wth wch aunswer he returned

The comyng of the Bailiff of Banbury to Warwik

Wheruppon The baileff of Warwik expecting the comyng of some from Banbury either wth lres or wth some message herde nothing from them untill the monday after loosonday at wch tyme the bailief and some others of Banbury having occasion to come to Warwik to speak wth one in the gaole that either had robbid their church or recevid the goods stollen out of the church that Monday night late sent to the bailief of Warwik desiring that the next morning he & his companye woold heare them of banbury towching the aunswering of their last lres & the order to be taken

Conferrence

between them for the xl^li given by Mr Oken Wherupon the bailief of Warwik sending for his company and bretherne mett in the church the next morning being tuesday and the quarter sessions day by seven of the clock whither they sent for the said bailief of Banbury & his companye who comying thither namely Thomas Dyxe bailief (   ) Bentley (   ) Jackson & one other whose name this writer know^th not after some gratulacions on Both sides It was openid by some of banbury that the cause of their comyng nowe was to requyre the monye given to their towne by Thomas Oken Wheruppon It was demaundid by them of Warwik whither they of Banbury had brought wth them the Covennts & bonde under their comon seale writen up in such maner as the same were sent to them or not and it was tolde them that if they had brought the same so pfectid wth them they should have the monye home wth them albeit their negligence had well deservid to have the same holden from them besides their writings & messages were such as desruid litle favo^r or frendshippe at any of their handes whom they had chargid wth great misbehavio^r in that they should offer them to be bounde to matters ympossible inconvenient & extreme wch termes in writing they had not before that tyme been acquainted wth neither had at that tyme given them any cause either to say or think so of them besides that the bailief of Warwik & his bretherne had iust cause to ymagine that they of banbury had no great desire to have the monye for if they had they woold not have usid so many dilatory aunsweres as they had done neither forgotten their promises to come or send aunswer in short tyme after the recept of the last lres wch they of banbury might presently have aunswerid if it had pleasid them w^thout excusing the same bicause it was the quarter sessions at Oxford ffor so the bailief & his company of Warwik might nowe more iustly have aunswerid them that this tyme was very inconveniently apointid for their comyng to Warwik being the sessions day at Warwik whan both the bailief of Warwik himself & most of his company had to give their attendance by reson of their offices Nevertheles they woold not give them any occasion of misliking but being they are nowe come yf they have brought such assurance wth them as may be likid of the mony shalbe redyly deliuerid to them w^thout more delaye otherwise they are not to have the same monye Except they can showe some matter that might otherwise move them of Warwik who doo desire to know (folio 108) what movid them of Banbury so to charge them To this Bentley answerid that to some of their company in banbury it was thought very harde to enter into such covennts insomuch as they who should be bounde should take litle or no benefit by it nevertheles he thinkith not that any such termes were usid but if any such were usid It was the fault of the wryter & no entent of the bailief and his companye wheruppon for their better satisfieng they desired to see their lre wch was shewid them there presently

Than (   ) Bentley againe said it is otherwise than I understood it notw^tstanding some of o^r companye doo think that by Mr Oken's wille it is not required to have any such straight covendts as to be bounde that the monye shalbe gatherid in euery three or foure yeres Or that they should be bound to bring the same mony to Warwik euery foure yeres or that they should procure a precher to make a srmon eury yere for iij˹ iiij᷎ or that in any case their should be either covents or bonds made more than acquytance testifieng the receipt of the mony ffor seing it is to be deliverid out unto poore young occupiers and that none of any wealth should take any benefit of it it is thought hard that they of the better sort should be bound to aunswer for the misbehavo' of the other And it might happen that some of those that have the mony in use may be so evill husbondes that the mony may be spent wch then woold be requyred at their hands that were bound besides if they should bring it to Warwick they might haply be robbid and so the losse lye in their necks And so padventure they should not get a precher that woold comend the said Oken for iij˹ iiij᷎ And so their bonde should be forfeitid And so in the rest of the covendts divers advauntags may be taken contrary to the meaning of the said Oken In consideration wherof they are now come to desire M^r bailief of Warwik & this company to deliver them the monye and to take their acquytance for the discharg therof w^thout any more or other covennts And not to urge them further than Mr Oken's meaning was by his will wch they also desired to see for their better satisfieng To that it was aunswerid that as towching the wille forsomuch as towched them therin they might see it in the Arches where there was no doubt but they had sought orr this tyme And as for the acepting of their acquitance w^thout any further condicions or bonds they were resoluid not to doo nor deliver any mony except the same condicions & bonds were made in the very same maner as was sett downe in the mynute sent unto them ffrom wch they woold not varrye w^thout better resons showid to them uppon wch point a question was made and euery mans of Warwik his opinion was askid who presently before the bailief and them of Banbury sevrally signified their opynions that the draughts of the covennts & bond were agreable to Mr Oken's devise & will & were so resonable & indifferent as not to be alterid or changid And therfore absolutely determynid that w^thout the pfeting of those assurances the mony should not be delivered And so aunswering euery of their of banburye's allegacions by sufficient & pbable reasons after many woords spent on both sides It was desired by them of banbury that they might have tyme to ympart their aunswer of them of Warwik to the rest of their bretherne of Banbury Wheruppon they should have resolute aunswere from them wth as good spede as might be To wch it was grauntid And that bicause the terme grewe on and therfore some of both the companyes might for that tyme be at london or elsewhere from home at the comyng of them of Banbury wch they woold not willingly should be The tyme of aunswere was untill after that easter terme wth this promise made by them of Banbury that before their comyng they woold send woord a seveninght before to the bailief of Warwik & his company to thend that all the whole company might be togither And so for that tyme they deptid and they of banbury lieng at Robert Phillips house at their going away said (as this writer was informid) that they woold never speke to have that mony at the bailiefs of Warwiks hands or at that towne But at thexecutors hands of whom proply they ought to requyre it And so deptid

After wch tyme the bailief of Warwik & his bretherne hearde no more from Banbury untill the Wensday or thursday before Whitsondaye At wch tyme a lre was brought to the bailief of Warwik by the Serjaunt of Banbury the tenor wherof ensuith

    To the Wo^rshypfull the bailief Aldermen & Burgesses of Warwik thies be deliuerid

After o^r hartie comendacions Thies are not only to shewe unto youe That (god willing) certeyn of o^r companye uppon frydaye next wch shalbe the xx^th of this present Maye shall repayre unto you at Warwik by eleven of the clock in the forenone of the same daye Then & there to take some reasonable order wth youe towching the fourty pounds given unto o^r Towne by Mr Oken but also hartely to desire yowe That ye (to that purpose) will observe that tyme at such place in Warwick as ye shall apoint Thus trusting ye wyll so doo We bid you hartely farewell ffrom Banbury the xvij^th of May 1575

    Yo^r loving freends The bailief Aldermen & Burgesses of Banburye

Aunswere by mouth to the Serjeant of Banbury

Thes lres so brought the bailief of Warwik answerid by woorde of mouthe That divers of his bretherne & company were then from home and that it woold be whitsonweek or ever some of them came home and therfore he could not give so resolute an aunswere as he woold And promised that so sone as he might gett his company togither he woold conferre wth them and theruppon wth as good spede as may be send to M^r bailief of Banbury And wth that aunswere the s^riannt deptid

After wch tyme viz. saturday in Whitsonweek John ffisher being newly come from the bathes and made pryvy of this last lre aduisid M^r bailief of Warwik to write to the bailief of Banbury acording to his promise wch was done acordingly in thes words following

To the wo^rshipfull Mr Bailief Aldermen & Burgesses of the borough of banbury

The tenor of the fourth lre sent to Banbury

After like harty recomendacions having receuid yor lres dated the xvijth of Maye instant declaring yor entencion to have bene here the fridaye following to take some reasonable order w^t us towching the ffourtie poundes bequethid by Mr Oken at wch time some of o^r companye namely John ffisher o^r Steward was from home whose absence was the onely cause that we aunswerid not yor expectacion at that tyme Thes are therfore to lett youe understand That wee are content according to former promise to deliver you the said xl^{li} uppon Saturday next (if youe then will please to come over to us and put in such assurance & bonde as at yor last being here wee resolued uppon Otherwise yor Journey shoulde be in vayne wherof we premonish youe and therfore desire you as our good neighbors to send us your resolute aunswer by this bringer Whither ye will yeld to those condicions or not and whither ye mynde to bring us the writings engrossed or not trusting ye will send us aunswere in writing of all things by this bring^r ffor otherwise it is like we shall not attend youe And so we youe fare hartely well At Warwik this xxviij^th of Maye 1575

       Yo^r loving freends the bailief & principall burgesses of Warwik

W^ch lres so sent awaye and delivered to the bailief of Banbury Annswere was made to them the next day as followith

       To the wo^rshipfull the Bailief & principall burgesses of the borough of Warwik give this

The tenor of the third lre receuid from Banbury

After like harty recomendacions having receuid yor letters bering date the xxviij^th of Maye wherin wee finde that you wilbe redy to paye to us on Saturday next the xl^li wch Mr Oken bequethid unto us if it might please us to come over to Warwik on saturday next and to deliver youe such assurance wth such condicions as at our last being w^t you at Warwik youe did requyre orells as we pceve by yor lres o^r labor is like to be in vaine to this we annswer yf it may pleese you to make paymet unto the xl^li wch Mr Oken hath given unto us by his last will & testament and to take of us such good assurance & bondes as by the wille we may be required or by the same will is by any way ment that then hearing from you we will as duety bindeth us be wth you uppon yor day apointid or any other daye the next week following and then and their to doo euery acte & dede as we are chargeable for the same this we are to desire yor laufull frendshippe in the same and this we pray you that we may heare from you or it be long orells we must take yor lres for denyall of the same & if not we shalbe constraynued to come by yt as we maye This we bid youe most hartely farewell from Banbury this xxix^th of this instant May

       Your loving freends The Bailief Aldermen & Burgesses of the borough of Banbury

Uppon the Recept of thes former lres recevid from Banbury Mr Bailief & his company of Warwik thought good to cesse any further writing back agayne referring them rather to any order that by law might be set down in this matter than to bestowe their tyme to write so frivolesly And so the matter restid for the tyme But about half a yere after one ( ) Bentley of Banbury having occupied to come to Warwick for other matters spak wth John ffisher about that mony and emongs other many woordes to litle purpose askid of the said ffisher When they shoulde have their mony given to their towne by Thomas Oken To wch ffisher aunswerid saing Mr Bentley you knowe Mr Oken willid that xlli should be deliverid to yor towne for the use of poore men and to thend the same should be ymploid as he ment he devised & ordenyd that Bonds should be taken of yor towne for the pformannce of such condicions as were devised wherby the poore & nedy might tak the benefit of that his good devotion which condicions & bonds being agreid uppon the mony wilbe redy at any time

Speches passid betwene Bentley of Banbury & John ffisher in Robart Phillips Alley

And ye knowe that to that effect & end meny lres have passid betwene you & us but you mynd not as it semith to come to any Such order and therfore in or opinions ye think the mony will not plesor yor towne and we therfore are contentid for it helpith or poore very well & we can be content to kepe it untill you pforme & doo that is ment by the will of Oken which being done ye shall not be long wthout the mony Nay said Bentley you wooll not let us have it But we will have it in spite of yor nose in spite of yor tethe & so adding many ymprop termes shewid his great courage but ffisher considerid that Bentley was an old man and it was in weather somewhat warme & towards evening and therfore said lesse But in the end told him they should knowe howe they cam by yt before they had it This passid on untill lent after And Mr Knight the Baker & John Knight of the red lyon in banbury & an other cam to Warwik and brought with them Mr Westen the Attorney about what causes this writer knoweth not But after the Assises (folio 110) were endid on the Saturday Mr Knight & the others of Banbury

The comyng of John Knight Baker of Banbury & others to Warwik

cam to M{r} John Grene then Bailief of Warwick from M{r} Bailief & his bretherne of banbury signifieng further that he had a message to them of Warwik from them of Banbury & therfore desired that M{r} Bailief wold apoint him a tyme to deliver his message to him & his brethern the maisters of Warwik w{ch} did conc{r}ne a legacy bequethed by Thoms Oken decessid Theruppon M{r} bailief apointid to heare him & the rest for the next day being sonday in the after none & bicause that John ffisher was then trowblid with his desese & not hable to come out of his bed he desired them of Banbury to come to the said ffishers house where the rest of his company should mete to here them which doone M{r} bailief the next morrow told the said John ffisher of his determynacion And so that after none
message doon by John Knight from the Balif of Banbury
their met M{r} Bailief M{r} hudson M{r} crane & one or twoo of the principall burgesses besides And thither came the said M{r} Knight & the others of Banbury who there eftsones did comendacions from M{r} bailief & his bretherne of Banbury and said that the said M{r} Bailief & his bretherne of Banbury had willid them to desire the xl{li} given to their towne by Thomas Oken decessid might be delivered to M{r} Bailief & his bretherne of Banbury according to the will of the dead and that it wold please
answerid M{r} Bailief of Warr. & his bretherne to give them such direct aunswere as might satisfy them of Banbury To that M{r} Bailief of Warwik aunswerid that towching their demaund of the xl{li} he & the rest of his bretherne had bene well pleasid to deliver long ago acording to the deads wille And that M{r} bailief and his bretherne of Banbury might have recevid the same at their pleasures if they woold have doone that on their parts was to be doone which was to give bond & condicions under their seale for the using the said mony acording to the devise of the giver But that to do M{r} Bailief & his bretherne of Banbury refused and therfore ment not to have the same (as might be gathered) And therfore that mony is now otherwais distributid out to them that are more thankfull & that do good w{t} it To that M{r} Knight aunswerid that M{r} Bailief of Banbury & his bretherne had not refused to take the mony but desired it often nor refused to make bond for the weil using of the same But uppon such drafts of covents as M{r} Bailief of Warwik had sent to Banbury It was thought that M{r}

Bailief of Banbury & his company should be bound to things almost ympossible to be kept & at least very hard to be obsruid wch points they desired to be reformid & then they woold have done that had become them To that it was aunswerid by Jo. ffisher that at such tyme as the first mynute or draft was sent to banbury M^r bailief of Warwik then wrote to Mr Bailief & his bretherne of Banbury that if they mislikid any thing in the devise It might please him to apoint such as they might trust to come to Warwik to open their doubts & they should be resonably satisfied which they did not but wrote aunswer that the devise had in it many points very hard unreasonable & ympossible &c termes to move resonable men having given no such cause ffor the devise is yet extant & the draf remaning w^t them of Banbury which if they will they may shew otherwise an other true copy of the same is kept wherin no such matter will appere and is determyned uppon to be graunted unto by

(This is the end of the first half of folio 110, and at the bottom of the page is the following note :—

nota { Looke more for this matter in the Leaf notid where ye may see them 173

And so this is carried forward to the second half of folio 173, the intervening leaves being filled up with various other matters, which will appear on subsequent pages of this volume. For the sake of the narrative I bring this folio in here, instead of keeping it in its proper order. At the head of the leaf is written, " this followith the leaf 109)

(folio 173) Mr Bailief & his bretherne of Banbury before they shall receve the mony Except by Law they shall otherwise recover it as it is like the will seke the meanes they can by any extremytye having of late given out that they will have it in spite and therfore the opinion of ffisher is that they shall come by yt as they may To that said Mr Knight I think no man so folish as to give out any such woordes of spite for there be other meanes by order of Lawe to come by yt But

Banbury   Mr Bailief of Banbury dothe gently & frendly desire you Mr Bailief here & the rest to deale as resonably w^t them as w^t others and that youe will not

L

urge them to be bound further than they may well performe and so doyng they will make any resonable bond that may be for yor dischardg and so to have yor loving & neghorly good willes as youe shall have o^{rs} To that point Mr Bailyf & the rest of Warwik present made aunswer That the woords of spite were given out largely by Mr Bentley whose age was cause of his more bearing w^t But as towching the mony & the bonds & covennts They are resolued to have the condicions devised to be put in writing & under seale before the mony be paid Except they shalbe otherwise therto compellid by lawe which if they will attempt they are ready to answer them And uppon such condicions & bonds sealid they wool be as redy to deliver them the mony though to the hinderance of the poore of their owne towne who presently have the same mony in use Therwith Mr Knight drew out the first draft sent to banbury and callid to Mr Weston saing Mr Weston you know the poyntes wch Mr Bailief of Banbury & his bretherne think very hard I pray you open them here Wherupon opening the books he said It was thought very hard that the mony should be brought evry foure yere to Warwik and hard also that Mr Bailief & the company now present should be bound for the doings of them that were to come & to or three such light poynts wch being aunswerid by them of Warwik to the satisfaccion of them of banbury as it semid Mr Knight desired that he might ympart the answer of Mr Balief of Warwik to Mr Bailief of Banbury and that he might have the draf back agayne w^t them to shewe at Banbury Wherin if some small poyntes should be reformed by them of Banbury it woold please Mr Bailief of Warwik somewhat to yeld to them so as the same might not be hurtfull to the devise of the giver And also they desired to understand whan they might come for the mony if they agreid uppon the articles So it was agreid they should have the mynute or first draught w^t them to consider further uppon but so as they chaungid none of the effectual matter but for the dayes of bringing the mony or c^ttificat of the names of such as should have the use therof there should be no sticking though they were altered to tymes more convenient to them of Banbury And for the mony if Mr Bailief & his bretherne of Banbury could agree to those condicions & to be bound acordingly as before was offred They should uppon such bonds & condicions recevid under their seale receve the mony at holyrood day next But to thend that their travaile should not be in vayne it was requyred and agreid unto that the devise or draft of the Indentures should be sent back from Banbury to Mr Balif of Warwik before Easter to be examyned & considered uppon And uppon thes conclusions resting The said Mr Knight & others of Banbury went home resonably satisfied (folio 174) So Easter being come & the mynute not sent back It was thought that they of Banbury woold not yeld to the condicions But w^thin a fortnight after The S^rjant of Banbury bringeth lres to Mr Bailief of Warwik the tenor wherof ensuith

To the wo^rshipfull their very freendes the Bailief & principall Burgesses of the borough of Warwik in the County of Warwik this be deliverid

the tenor of the fourth lre recebid from Banbury.

After our hartie comendacions Trusting that ye are all in good health which we pray god may contynewe to his good plesr Thies are to shewe you that wee (although not in so short tyme as we apointid) have sent agayne the book unto you altered in some resonable poyntes as ye may see and have sent withall the leaf correctid hartely desiring you as o^r freends That you will peruse the same and send it back agayne unto us in such sorte as ye will not alter yt And appoint unto us a daye that wee to the finishing herof may mete togither at Warwik And wee god willing will observe yt praing you eftesones to use frendly & reasonably that we shall coveunt as wee hope ye will And thus comytting you to god we bid you hartely farewell for this tyme from banbury this xxixth of Apriell 1577

Yo^r frends to then powers the bailief Aldermen & Burgesses of Banbury

This lre was brought by the S^rjaunt of Banbury & delivered to Mr Bailief who having openid the same about xj of the clok brought it to John flisher and w^thall the mynute or draft alterid much in theffect & especially for the payment of the monye at Warwik and divers points very materyall which pcevid John ffisher drewe the condicions correctid of newe And so making M{r} Bailief privie The messenger was dispatchid w{t} a lre from M{r} Bailief signifieng that from that draft they woold not dissent and therfore if they could like therof they might engrosse the bookes & bringing the same under seale uppon trynyty Sonday they should have the mony Trynytie Sonday came and none came from Banbury But on the morrowe being Monday about v of the clok at night cometh John Knight thelder baker Roland Merik Alderman Willm halhed & John Knight the young{r} J. holder & w{t} them one wiese their towneclerk who all affirming the disseas of M{r} halhed of Banbury bailief did his comendacions w{t} the rest of their bretherne who had sent them to conclude uppon such condicions & bonds as were promised for the receving of M{r} Okens mony Wheruppon it was demaunded whither they had brought those assurancs w{t} them who said that they had brought that should satisfy M{r} Bailief as they trustid but for the booke were not yet ingrossid bicause they trustid that some poyntes or wordes uppon resonable conferens might be alterid Wheruppon the next morning being tuesday the quarter Sessions M{r} Balif having sent for the principall burgesses into the chapter house had conferrence w{t} them of Banbury who made many questions of matters not worthy to be doubtid of And so in thend the bookes being agreid uppon were apointid to be engrossid by the said wise who did the same that day And the next day being wensday a newe meting was apointid for the finishing & sealing of the bookes & payment of the mony all which was done acordingly The said Aldermen & Burgesses of Banbury having brought their seale w{t} them sealid their part in the chapter house whiles M{r} Bailief & his bretherne of Warwik went upp to the chest where they sealid the counterpayne of the covennts.

(folio 175) Copy of Indenture of Covenant

(folio 176) Copy of obligation upon the covenant

      Copy of warrant of Attorney.

The conclusion & mony paid to them of Banbury

And uppon the delivery of thes writings sealid as aforesaid the said John Grene having paid to the said John Knight Roland Meryk Willm halhed & John Knight the said ffourtye pounds in the chapter house in the church of saint Maryes in Warwik on the Wensday morning the fourth of June aforesaid as well they of Warwik as of Banbury were agreid & after Brekfast lovingly & frendly deptid evry man to his whome

The names of them that were present are indorsed on the book of the Indenture of covennts

(On several occasions the Bailiff of Banbury came to Warwick and tendered the £40; the last record of this in the Black Book is on folio 315, where it is stated than on the 6th July, 1714, the Mayor of Banbury came to Warwick and tendered the £40 according to Oken's Will. One of these visits, made during the Commonwealth, is related circumstantially, and although out of order as regards the folio, I have placed it here, as by so doing the matters in connection with the bequests to Stratford and Banbury are kept together. The account is as follows :)—

22 June 1657

The tender of 40ᵗʰ by Banbury And of 40ᵗʰ by Stratford upon Avon

(folio 286) Mᵈᵈ that on Saturday 6ᵗʰ day of June 1657 Mʳ John Webb of Banbury & Mʳ Richard Lunt of Stratford upon Avon came to Mʳ Robert Warner then bailiffe of Warr. at his house in the Church Street & in behalfe of their sevrall Corporacions desired a day might be agreed on for the tender of the two sevrall 40ˡⁱ given by Mʳ Oken to their sevrall boroughs & which evry 4ᵗʰ yeare they are to tender to the bailife & burgesses of Warr. Mʳ Bailife sending for some of his brethren monday the 22 of June was appoynted at the house of Moses Holloway called the great Swan (a) in Warr: At which day & place by 10 a clocke Mʳ Nathanaell Wheateley Maior of banbury & Mʳ ffrancis Smith bailife of Stratford upon Avon with their sevrall companyes came Mʳ bailife of Warr & his

---

(a) This may have been a house on the site of the present "Warwick Arms Hotel." The supporters of the Earl of Warwick's Coat of Arms are two Swans. Or it may have been a house on the south side of Jury Street, near to the East Gate, as old inhabitants well knew the "Black Swan Hotel," now converted into private houses in this Street.

brethren went to them & after some freindly salutacons & a glasse of wyne or two they went to S{t} Maries Church in Order viz{t} the bailife of Warr with the Mace before him the Maior of Banbury & the bailiffe of Stratford in one ranke then M{r} Ainge of Warr M{r} Allen of Banbury Hickox of Stratford in the second ranke & soe a Warwicke man a Banbury man & a Stratford man 3 in a ranke all alonge M{r} Maior of Banbury brought with him M{r} Maunder minister of Cropredy[a] who preached the Sermon After that ended they returned all to the Swan to dynner where M{r} Venour[b] minister of S{t} Maries said grace & concluded with the Lords prayer according to M{r} Oken's will: dynner ended the Maior of Banbury tendered theire 40{li} to the bailife & burgesses of Warr upon the table which was not Counted but accepted & retorned to him the like was done for Stratford And sevrall noates were subscribed by the bailife & Burgesses of Warr then p{r}sent testifying the sevrall tenders the Copyes whereof hereafter follow This being done the reckoning was brought up which came to 6{li} 16{s} 6{d} at 2{s} ordinary & for wyne tobacco &c which was paid equally: by the bailife of Warr; the Maior of Banbury & the bailiffe of Stratford by 45{s} 6{d} a peece.

Warwicke Borough
A noate under the hands of the Bailiffe & Burgesses of Warr. testifying the tender of 40{li} by Banbury vide ante 175 176{b}

M{dd} that the day & yeare above written the some of 40{li} given by M{r} Oken deceased unto the Towne of Banbury to be lent unto poore Tradesmen there was this day brought in and tendred here according to M{r} Oken's Will & Covenants Indented thereupon made & this tender was made by M{r} Nathanaell Wheateley Maior M{r} Will{m} Allen M{r} Nathaniall Hill M{r} John Webb M{r} Richard Halhead M{r} Aholiab West M{r} Thomas Robbyns & M{r} James

---

(a) Cropredy is about three miles from Banbury. The Rev. W. Wood, D.D., present Vicar of Cropredy, has kindly furnished me with the following particulars with regard to Mr Maunder. It appears that he was Vicar of Cropredy in the year 1654, although the date of his appointment is not known. His predecessor was Edward Bathurst, Scholar of Trinity College, Oxford, who appears to have been ejected by the Puritans, probably when "Triers" were sent round the Parishes for the purpose in 1654. If so, Mr. Maunder was appointed in his place. He held the living for some years after the Restoration, as is evidenced by entries in the register of the dates both of the births and baptisms of several children of Mr. Bernard Maunder and Mrs. Mary as late as 1688.

(b) There is a note at the beginning of the earliest existing register of St. Mary's, to the effect that Richard Venour was presented to the living by Robert Rich, Earl of Warwick, and was inducted on the 20th of July, 1639.

West Aldermen & M{r} William Stokes M{r} John Hams M{r} Edward Welchman M{r} Henry Smith & M{r} John Russell theise Burgesses of Banbury aforesaid unto the psons whose names are subscribed beinge the bailife & burgesses of Warwicke

Banbury is bound not only to tender y{e} 40{li} but to give a noate also of y{e} names of the pties & their sureties that haue it

       Robert Warner bailife
       Christofer Ainge
       George Weale
       Abraham Greene
       Willm Harmer
       Willm Ley
       Roger Edes
       Thomas Greene
       Edmund Makepeace

There is a similar memorandum in the case of Stratford, the marginal note being as follows:—

The like noate for ye tender of 40{li} by Stratford See y{e} Indenture before 104 They are not bound to tender y{e} money but to give a noate of their names y{t} have it with y{e} names of their sureties

The tender was made by Francis Smith Bailiff William Hickox Thomas Greene Thomas Tayler Richard Lunt William Greene Aldermen Michael Jonsone William Caudwell Chamberlaynes Richard Ainge and John Wilmore Junior Burgesses

(folio 110)

A note of Tho. Okens good dedes before his death

    In the name of God amen
So let your light shyne before men that they may see your good woorkes and gloryfie your father wich is in heven
ffor so much as euery good woork is said to come of god and that the same doo give glorye to the heavenly ffather being ministred by men of good faith and that a light is to be shewid

openly and not to be put under a busshel This writer is encoragid the rather to take some paynes truely to sett furth as nere as he can the good and charitable woorkes of Thomas Oken sometyme of the towne of Warwik mercer who being borne in the same towne of a poore linage and growen to some resonable wealth by his good diligence & Industry being a man of resonable great age having neither weif child nor many kinsfolks knowen disposid such goods lands & tenements as he had before p^{r}chasid to divers good uses & purposes as hereafter shall appere And to thend that the same should be ymploid in dede acording to that devise he had he was advised by learned counsaill to put the same in feofments to such uses as he had devised And therfore made a deed first to convay the land to c^{r}ten p'sons to the use of others &c & so after other feoffm^t The teno^r of wch dedes insuith

(folio 112 to 117) Copy of Oken's deed of foefment

(folio 117 to 120) Copy of Oken's Will

Thomas Oken.

(Of all the old Warwick worthies no name is so well known or so much cherished in the town as that of Thomas Oken. As a great many pages of the Black Book are taken up with copies of his deed of feoffment and will, and with accounts of his last moments, and the various proceedings in connection with his charitable bequests, a few words about him will not be out of place. In the Castle Street, Warwick, which branches off from the main thoroughfare, there stands a small gabled half-timbered house, facing up the street in the direction of St. Mary's Church; it is at the head of a block of buildings, having the road on one side of them, and a narrow passage on the other: on the side of the passage opposite to this house, there is another quaint building, and the two together, with their surroundings, form a very pleasant quiet picture. In the first-named house dwelt Thomas Oken. As you approach Oken's house, you have a charming view of Guy's Tower of the Castle, rising among the trees of the

Castle Grounds, and here the street makes a gentle curve, and after crossing Castle Lane, is brought to a termination by the wall enclosing the Castle Grounds. In Oken's day this wall did not exist, and the road was continued under the Castle walls, until it joined the lower end of Mill Street, opposite the old stone bridge mentioned in the description of Elizabethan Warwick in the preface.

Of Oken's life but little is known. He was born of humble parents, in Warwick, and carrying on the trade of a mercer, amassed a considerable fortune, and became a man of some importance in the town. We do not know the date of his birth. He was married to a wife whose christian name was Joan, and who died in his lifetime, without leaving issue. Another old minute book states that he died on the 30th July, 1573, and was buried on August 4th. From the tablet in St. Mary's Church, we learn that he was Master of the Guild of Holy Trinity and St. George, whose Hall was the building now known as the Leycester Hospital, in the 37th year of Henry VIIIth, *i.e.*, in 1546. He was elected Bailiff in the year 1557. Thus we see that he lived in the reigns of Henry VIIIth, Edward VIth, Mary and Elizabeth, and possibly during a part of Henry VIIth's reign. He was without doubt a man of importance in his native town, and one whose opinion and words were listened to with respect, as on folio 40 of the Black Book there is a report of a speech by him. If hand-writing is any indication of strength of character, we may conclude that he possessed it, as his signature is in a good firm hand. In sketching his life, I will briefly mention some of the great and startling events and changes which must have come under his notice in Warwick. He witnessed the dissolution of the Collegiate foundation of St. Mary, by Henry VIIIth, and the incorporation of the borough by the same Monarch, and these must have furnished food for much conversation with his friends and neighbours. He was a witness of the Reformation, of the introduction of the Prayer Book, of the Restoration of the Mass under Mary, and of the re-establishment of the Reformation under Elizabeth. In order to show how these events manifested themselves to Thomas Oken, I give some extracts from the accounts of the Churchwardens of St. Nicholas Church, Warwick, which date from 1547. The registers of St. Mary's, Oken's Parish Church, of that date are lost, but we may assume that the same alterations were being carried out there, as in the Sister Church. The following entries were made in Edward VIth's reign:—

    Item payd to Henri brien & bosewarthe for
      Takyng down the Rodesolar............ ....xij^d
    It. r.c. of master brokys for ye tymber of ye
      rode lorfte & ye tymber of ye hye auter &
      for bokes hyllynges & for a olde cowfer.......... ....xij^s
    It'm payd to mr. skerrow ffor the nwe
      commu'n böke other called the booke
      of mornyng praer & evyny'g praer.....................vj^s iiij^d

The following entries made after Mary had ascended the Throne, show that Oken saw the re-introduction into worship of many things which had been removed:—

    It'm payd for a hope off lyme to occupy
      to the settyng off the holi water stoke............ .....j^d ob.
    It'm for mendyng the loke off the stypulls
      dore & the holy water pot hangulles......................iij^d

There are also entries of payments for a sepirclor, for a sensor of brass, for frankenscence, and for work about the Sepulcur.

    It'm payd to Harry warde for Mary and John
      & ffor other worke yt ys to say bordyng up
      off the holle there as the rode loffte stode............vj^s x^d
    It'm payd to mictyng ffor payntyng off the
      same Images................... ....iiij^s iiij^d
    It'm payd to ales broke wydow ffor the
      tymber off the rode lofte the whyce hur
      husband bought off the parishe whan
      ytt was takyn doyne........... ....vj^s

And many other entries as to torches, tapers, wax, mending the rood loft stairs, and as to a scaffold for the rood loft.

Oken heard the merry peals of the bells of St. Nicholas when Elizabeth was proclaimed as appears by this entry—

It'm in brede and aylle to the ryngeres
at the generalle prosessyon ffor quyne
Elisabethe..viij^d

As one of the principal burgesses he would be present at St. Mary's at the celebration of the Feast of St. Michael, by the Earl of Leycester, and at the burial of the Marquis of Northampton, and, also if his health permitted, he would go forth with the Bailiff to meet Queen Elizabeth when she visited Warwick, in August, 1572. Judging from the sums of money which Oken bequeathed, he was evidently well to do, and from the gifts of plate, goblets, and spoons, left by his Will to the Corporation, and the "depe silver goblett of parcell gilt" left to Anne sometimes called Agnes Catur his servant "for taking paynes for him when he had the Ague and the gowte," we may conclude that he kept a good table. In his declining years he appears to have lived quietly, and to have done but little business, as it is stated in the Black Book that at the time of his death he had but few wares in his shop, and that his household goods were not of much value. By his Will he left directions for "his body to be buryed in the Parishe churche of Saynt Maryes Warwick against Saint Annes Altar hard to the walle and there I wille to have a little Tombe of stone and on the said Tombe in the stone wall I will to have an epitaph of brasse w^h twoo pictures one of myself and the other of my wieff w^h thes woordes graven under, 'Jesu have mercy uppon me, Jesu have mercy uppon me'" The Oken brass fortunately escaped the fire of 1694, and may be seen placed against the east wall of the north transept of St. Mary's Church. He is represented in a civic gown, and she in a plain gown, with a scarf tied round the waist. He died possessed of real property in Warwick, Baddesley, Beausale, and Harbury, which by deed of feoffment he had conveyed to Trustees in trust for various objects. To the poor, by this deed, he devoted an annual sum which to this day is paid weekly to several recipients. He saw how valuable and necessary were good roads and bridges as means of intercommunication, and a good water supply for health and cleanliness, and so he devoted annual sums for the repairs of roads, and the Edmondscote bridge and cleaning of wells. He devoted an annual amount to Education. Church music he sought to encourage for he directed "12s to be distributed to and amongst three children or young men for the singing or saying of such laudable airs as should be used in the parish church of St. Mary, by sufferance of the laws." To this day 12s. is paid to St. Mary's Choir, which sum is of course now out of all proportion to the present income of the charity. He devoted 3s.4d. a year to the herdsman, to look after poor men's cattle on the Common. The tramp question appears to have occupied his thoughts, for he left 3s.4d. a year to the beadle among other things "to keep and avoid from time to time such vagabonds and sturdy beggars out of the said town as there should resort." Among other things he left "20d to the young men of St Mary's parish to make merry w'thall at the cutting down of the Whitsuntide tree yf any then shalbe standing at the Hiegh crosse of the said towne of Warwik and that they the said young men at the end of their mirth shall saye the Lord's prayer and give thanks for the presuacion of the quenes Mate her heirs and successors and the good estate and contynuance of the said towne of Warwik." He wished to promote conviviality and good fellowship, and so he appointed a feast day. On that day he directed that "one learned man should make a sermon" for which he was to receive 6s.8d., and after Service he provided for a dinner for the bailiff and twelve principal burgesses, and twenty-four wardsmen. "And in the end of the dynner to saye the lordes prayer and to praise God for the soule of the said Thomas Oken Joane his wief and all cristian sowles departid out of this transitory world." I have only now to remark that Oken's estate produces, at the present time, about £600 a year; that his name is honoured and kept green in Warwick; that the annual Sermon is preached on Oken's feast day, in St. Mary's Church, before the Mayor and Corporation, and such others as choose to attend; that the preacher receives 6s.8d. for preaching; and that on the evening of the same day the feast is held, the Mayor presiding, at which feast Oken's plate is placed on the table, and after dinner the Vicar of St. Mary's says the grace in the form prescribed by Oken; and that the first toast of the evening is drunk in solemn silence, and is "The pious memory of Thomas Oken and Joan his wife." Oken's chest, which is massive and ponderous, and provided with many locks, is now in the Court House. From the narrative on folios 120, 121 and 122, it appears that the last moments of Thomas Oken were not quite so peaceful as might have desired, and that his soul took flight in the midst of an unseemly jangle, which perhaps he knew nothing about, as he was almost, if not quite, insensible for some hours before his death.)

Extracts from Thomas Oken's Will.

(folio 117) In the name of God amen the xxiiijth day of Novembr in the yere of o^r lorde God 1570 I Thomas Oken of the towne & borough of Warwik marcer being at this present tyme in good mynde & memory thankes be to almighty God, ffor dyvers & good consideracions doo ordeyne & make this my last wille & testament in maner & forme following ffirst and pryncipally I give & bequethe my Sowle to almighty God my onely maker & Redemer trusting thorough the meritts of his passion to be savid and my body to be buryed in the parish church of Saint Maryes in Warwik against Saint Annes Alter harde to the walle and there I wille to have a litle Tombe of Stone and on the said Tombe in the stone wall I will to have an Epitaph of brasse w^t twoo pictures one of my self and the other of my wieff w^t thes woordes graven under Jesu have mercy uppon me Jesu have mercy uppon me

Item I give & bequeath to the comunyon table for my tuithes necligently forgotten ffive shillings

Item I will my bodye to be brought to the churche & there to have such service as is apointid by the churche as may be to the glory of God & to the comfort of my Soule And the vikar if he will fetche me to the Churche to have ij^s for his paynes And euery minister that is there that day to have xij^d And euery chield that servith in the Quyer that daye iiij^d

Item I will to have sixe poore men & sixe poore women to bring my bodye to the church and they to have euery one of them sixe yardes of black Rugg or black coton and that to be made redy to their backes Also I will whan the comunyon is doone that they twelve shall have iiij^d a pece to pay for their dynners And they to dyne all togither in some honest house And at thend of their dynner they shall give thanks to God and saye the lordes prayer

Item I will that the Vikar or some learned man doo declare Goddes woorde to the people that daye and he to have for his paynes vj^s viij^d and other vj^s viij^d to Mr Griffyn if he will take paynes to declare Gods woorde to the people some other day and in thend of their sermons to give thanks to God for the soules that be departid in the faith of criste

And after service is doone I will my Executors to make pparacion in some honest place where they think necessarye and there to have the bailief & his bretherne & their wieves and the xxiiij^{ty} & their wieves wth other at the discrecion of myne Executors & overseers to make them such chere as the tyme will serve for and at thende of their dynner to give God thanks & saye the lords prayer

Item I wille that within three or ffoure dayes after my buryall be dealte xv^{li} that is to saye to fivetene score of the poorest householders in Warwik that is to saye xij^d a house and the (folio 118) same tyme twelve monethes I will there be other xv^{li} so to be dealt after the same rate that is xij^d a house Item I will that my Executors or Overseers doo see the bestowing of it wth their owne handes

Also I give to xxx^{ty} poore maydes to their mariages x^{li} that is to saye vj^s viij^d a piece untill the monye be distributid at the discrecion of myne Executors & overseers

Item I forgive Jone Alwoode late wief of Thomas Alwood of Buckingham vj^{li} xiij^s iiij^d And also I give her more to helpe her wthall in mony iiij^{li}

Item I give to John Ruggs of Reding xx⁵ & his bill of debt iiij¹ⁱ

Item I forgive to euery tennt that I have at my decesse a quarters rent whither it be tenement or cotage

Item I give to Anne catur my servaunt in mony for taking paynes for me whan I had the Ague & the gowte x¹ⁱ & a depe silver goblett of parcell gilt that was sometymes her Auntes

Item I give to the foure men that shall beare my bodye to the church xij⁴ a piece that is to saye John bykar Shomaker Robert Oldams Laurence Oldams & hughe Waterson And if it happen that any of thes be from home Then I will that John Jervys be one & he to have for his paynes aforesaid xij⁴

Item I give to Thomas crosse a letherne doblett and a payre of hose and to his wief ij⁵ in monye

Item I will the poore mans chest stand fast by where I shalbe buryed contynually to put in all my bookes & writings wᵗʰall such other Jewells as shall come to their hands Also I will that the bailief & three of his bretherne shall have foure lockes & fowre keys and also ffoure honest men of the ffoure wardes that is to say in euery warde one other foure locks & ffoure keys And I will that my Executors shall apoint some other chest to stand in the place

Item I give & bequethe to the towne of Warwik a hundreth powndes to purchase or buye some piece of grounde to lay to the comons if they can come by it And if they can not than I will that the mony shall remayne to the towne & borough of Warwik for this Intent & pʳpose That is to saye to ten honest comoners and they to have x¹ⁱ a piece orells to five honest comoners and they to have xx¹ⁱ a piece for three or foure yeres at the discrecion of the bailief & his bretherne and such as shalbe put in trust and they to putt in twoo or three sufficient Sureties for it and yerely to paye out of the same viij⁴ the pounde that is to saye iiij⁴ of (folio 119) euery pounde to the poore and the other iiij⁴ in euery pounde to the Bailief & his bretherne for their paynes taking to make merye once in the yere calling to them such as they shall think good Also I will that if it happen any of the said parties wch hath any of this monye to depart out of the towne or doo dye that then the monye be taken & put to some other man that is an honest comoner putting in sufficient sureties And also that if any suretie dye or depart the towne that then the party wch hath the monye shall put in newe Suretyes.[a]

Item I give to Gilbert Blount an oulde Aungell

Also I will that he that makith my grave shall have xij^d for his labr

Item I will that the viij^t ringers shall have for their paynes viij^s

Item I give to Margarett Cooke a hart of silver & gilte weing foure ounz & better Also I give to Mr John ffishers wief a french crowne

Item I give to Mrs Grene a french crowne

Also I will that there be prepared xij lether bucketts to be in some place alwayes in redynes if there be any casualtye of fire

Item I give to the Bailief of Warwik & the burgesses of the corpacion from yere to yere euery one for his yere being bailief for one yere putting in sureties to them that I have put in trust successively one gilt goblett weing xvij onz and also one other goblett of pcell gilt weing xvj oz and also one other goblet weing x ounz & a half quartern also one salte of parcell gilt weing ix oz also xij silver spones w^t gilt typpes weing xiiij oz three qters also vij other silver spones playne weing xij oz & a half Also I will & bequethe that if there be no bailief of the corpacion of the Towne of Warwik That then thes goblets Salte & spones shall remayne to the xij principall burgesses & to their successors for euer Also I will that if there be any Act of parliament that shall touch or pluck awaye any of their order of feloweshippe and brotherhood Then I will that it remayne to the gret bridge in Warwik & to the mayntennce of it

(a) The Corporation with this £100 bought a piece of land from Sir John Puckering, and added it to the common. Dugdale states that the piece of ground was called Michaells piece. From this title it would be ground near to St. Michael's Church, which was in the Saltisford, and of which the remains, consisting of the eastern gable, and a portion of the roof, now form part of a blacksmith's forge. Sir John Puckering purchased the Priory estate, which was adjacent to the Saltisford Common.

Also I give to the bailief of Stretford and the Aldermen & to their successors bailiefs & Aldermen xl^{li} for this Intent & purpose that is to saye to 8 honest occupiers w^t hin the towne And they to have v^{li} a man for three or ffoure yeres togither at the discrecion of the bailief & his bretherne And they to pay yerely out of the same to the poore people iiij^d for every pounde and to the bailief & his bretherne other iiij^d for every pounde And that to be given at twoo tymes in the yere to the poore that is sixe dayes before Cristmas & sixe dayes before Easter and the other iiij^d of evry pounde to the bailief & his bretherne for this Intent and purpose that the Bailief & his bretherne shall once in the yere a learnid man & hee to declare Gods woord and he to have for his paynes taking iij^s iiij^d when the Sermon is done the Bailief & his bretherne to mak mery wth other at his discrecion & they to have x^s and in the end of their mirth to give thanks to God and to saye the lords prayer And that the bailief & his bretherne shall put to their towne seale wth good warrantie for the ymploying the mony to that use that it is given orells to remayne again to the use of the towne of Warwik And also that euery man in Stretford that shall have any of the said monye shall unto the Bailief and his bretherne put in twoo or three sufficient sureties for paymet therof after the order of Mr Willington's booke And also that the bailief and his bretherne shall euery three or ffoure yeres when the monye is deliured upp Then to send a certificat to the Bailief of Warwik and his bretherne who they bee that have and theire names wherby it may be knowen that the monye it is ymploid to that use wch it is given for

Also I give to the towne of Banburye xl^{li} to be deliured to eight honest occupiers that is to say v^{li} a man in such order & wth such condicion as is aforesaid unto Stretford

Also I chiefly will & requyre my Executors Overseers & those wch I shall put in trust as they shall aunswere betwene God & their consciens to see that if there be any thing or any woorde in this my last will & testament that is not well that then I will that they shall make it well and assure as the lawe may make it Wherby that thes goodes & landes may proffit to that intent & purpose as it is given for

Item I will that Mr John ffisher gentleman yf he pay his hundreth pound acordingly at his day apointid that then I will that he shall have his leases & writings agayne that I have of his and my Executors to receve a bonde wherin I am bounde in five hundreth pound And that said hundreth pound I will that it shalbe the hundreth pound to discharge & buy the land for the comons and to be aplied to & for that use that is in the Articles above recitid and if not Then I will the rent to be resued for the space of sixe yeres to that use and after the said sixe yeres the rest of the rent specified in the Indenture of Covennts during the yeres I give & bequeath it to my Executors & to Annys catur suant out of the said Rent xl^s yerely if she live so long

(folio 120) Item I give to Annys Catur my seruant the house during her naturall lief that I now dwell in payng the lordes rent wch is vj^s viij^d a yere keping the repacions and also the kitchin pcell of my free lande Yelding & paing therfore yerely to the towne ij^s iiij^d a yere & keping repacions And also I give to her all such ymplem^{ts} as be nowe in the house to helpe her to begyn house so that she give Jone her Sister parte at her discrecion of euery thing somewhat

And to this my last Will & Testament I doo order & make myne Executors Robart Phillippes & Thomas cawdrey of the towne of Warwik And for their paynes taking I will they have either of them ffourtie poundes a piece

And I make myne Overseers to see that my Executors doo truly performe this my last Will & testament I doo orden John Butler John ffisher William ffrekulton & Thomas powell gentlemen myne overseers and for their paynes taken herin I give them ffourty shillings a piece And likewise I doo make Robart Sheldon and John Grene overseers as the rest and give to either of them ffourty shillings a piece

And I forgive Robart Sheldon & his mother for his father's debt w'h is five nobles

Item Nicolas Marell shall have ij˚ for Gods sake only

And also I give to Thomas Harrys wief for Gods sake only other ij˚

Item I have a peare of currall beades in keping of Ales ffraunce and I will that my Executors doo deliver the same beades having sufficient discharge for the same

The last moments of Thomas Oken

Circumstances towching Th. Okens last Will

After w'ch dedes so made sealid delinerid and season of the land taken by the ffeoffes And his said Will put in writing by the sonne of Robart Phillips and in the lief tyme of the said Oken openly red before him in the presence of manye namely Raffe Griffyne preacher a gentleman for his great learning & rare lief singulerly recomendid Thomas Powell Thomas Cawdrey Mary ffisher Margaret cawdrey John bailies And by the said Thomas Oken pronouncid to be his last will & testament w'ch hapned the rather for that the same Thomas Oken being somewhat weeke & waxing very sick sent for divers his freends of which some came namely Mr Griffyn & others who both pswading him to take his sicknes as the gentle visitacion of almighty god and to dispose & sett some order for his tempall goods w'ch the said Oken said he had doone And theruppon callid for his will to be brought before him wheruppon his srunt Agnes catur fetchid out of a (   ) twoo roles of paper writen w'ch being shewid to the said Oken he said "their is my will" w'ch being openyd theyre appered twoo willes being both writen and bearing one date And being redd examyned and conferrid openly togither before & in the presence & hearing of the said Oken & others present and the one red by (   ) and the other lookid upon by (   ) It fell out that there were some fewe legacyes more in the one then was in the other and that they differed in a very fewe woords ells though not much in substance The difference wherof appearing to those present It was told by Mr Griffyn or M^r powell or both to the said Oken that there were more legacyes in the one than were in the other And therfore askid his mynd which of those should stand

The woords of T. Oken to declare the last will

for & be his last will To the wch The said Oken being in very pfett sence & understanding & well hable to expresse his mynd by woordes aunswered and said That that hath the more in it Wheruppon bothe the said papers being rolid up agayne were deliuered to the mayde to be laid upp wch was done acordingly And so the said Oken languishing & waxing more febler in thend wthin xx^{ty} houres after decesid making no other will in writing Though in the meane space (as this writer is enformed) uppon mocyon made unto him to be good to the s^runt Agnes Catur he gave her the lease of his house and his whole terme that he had in it and all other things in the

howe J. ffisher did first understand of the trust reposid in hym by T. Oken

said house (mony plate & writings exceptid) Before whose depting Thomas powell came (folio 121) to John ffisher & tolde him that Mr Oken was very sick and was desirous to speake w^t him and that the said Oken had made his will wch he had hearde wherin he had putt him wth others in some trust as his overseers to his Executors and by the same will had given very large legacyes but howe the same shalbe pformed he doubtid fearing least the will being made by a boye without any further counsell had not in it sufficient woordes & forme And said further that he

The care of T. Powell to haue the will pformid

peevid that Mr Oken had some care that waye for he had often callid for Robt Sheldon as though his mynde had bene to have either alterid some matter in the wills orells to have had some further advise therin ffor wch cause the rather the said Mr Powell desyred the said John ffisher to tak the paynes to goo to Mr Oken Wheruppon the same ffisher togither wth the said Mr Powell went to Mr Oken whom they found as though he woold slepe but in great passions & many tymes solenly awaking To whom the said ffisher spak and after he had askid him howe he did The said ffisher said to the said Oken "I understand you were desirous to speke w{th} me" "Yea" said he "but nowe it must be an other tyme" and so slombring as it were the said ffisher deptid from him leaving there such as gaped for that they had long longid for (as it may seme) by their doings sithens And afterwards the said Oken falling euery houre weaker & weaker at last lost his speache wheruppon the said M{r} Powell came eftsones to the said ffisher and told him therof making great care that the will might take effect acording to the mynde of the man which he fearid woold hardly be performed except some carefull men woold tak some paynes therin Wheruppon the said ffisher as one put in trust (but specially having a great desire that the towne of Warwik & other who were to tak benefit therby might receve that comodytie w{ch} was ment unto them thought it good to travaill their acording to his hability and sending for Willm ffrekulton an other of the overseers the said ffisher & powell went to M{r} balief then being Thomas

<small>The comyng of the oberseers to the house of Tho. Oken</small> Jenks{(a)} desiring his assistance in this case And so the said M{r} Jenks ffisher Powell & ffrekulton came to the house of the said Oken before he was dead but spechles where at the dore they founde M{r} Griffyn of whom they askid the state of the said Oken who declarid his opynion that he was no use of this worlde and so farre spent that he had nowe no sence uppon w{ch} woordes the said ffisher brake out & said "I am enformed that M{r} Oken hath made a large will & disposed his goodes to many good & charitable purposes And that youe M{r} Griffen have seene his will" All which the said M{r} Griffin confessid wishing that the same might take the same effect ffor w{ch} pupose said ffisher wee are nowe come mynding to further the same asmuch as we may wherin also we pray yo{r} furtherance & helpe And forsomuch as I understand that he hath put me w{th} others in some more trust than I lookid for (though it be litle) and that I never hitherto have bene privye to his state I beseche you be some meane that I may see the will w{ch} being writen twice as I here I woold the one part might be in such keping as herafter might be

(a) In the Margin of folio 138 he is called Thomas Hankinson, als Jenks, and under the former name he is entered in the list of Bailiffs.

a Rule to order & rule such as he hath put in trust if they willd otherwise deale than they should which oppynyon was liked of all the companye who consentid to goo toguther unto the house & to treate wth Thomas cawdrey & the wief of the said ffillippes (because that Phillips himself was then from home) So they the Bailief Mr Griffyn John ffisher Thoms Powell William ffrekulton went into the house where they founde divers others acompanyeng the said cawdrey Phillips' wief & others To whom the said ffisher spack saing "Mrs Phillips & neighbo^r cook I peeve that Mr Oken god comfort him is not like to recover But hath disposid his mynd very godly and charitably as I have heard say And hath made his will wherin he hath put you specially in trust as Executors to pforme the same and wth you others as I am enformid myself Mr Powell M^r ffrekulton & others as overseers your partes & ours are to be so myndfull therof as acording to the trust reposid in us we may so behave o^rselfes as bothe to please god & satisfie thexpectacion of the world ffor myne owne part I doo knowe very litle or nothing of Mr Oken's state of wealth and yet lesse understood till this day that he wolde repose any trust in me that waye (though sometimes he woold saye he myndid so to doo) wch than I took but as his phrase to please some men w^thall And as I knowe not herof So youe bothe do knowe that I am in debt to Mr Oken & do owe him C^li for wch he hath sufficient assurance & such things in pawne of myne as I loke to have agayne upon the paym^t of the monye ffor wch causes I thought good to speak w^t you before this company praying you to let me see the wille to be therby bothe satisfied and also to understand what part & office I have to doo therin wch I will be redy to pforme god willing to the uttermost of my powr (folio 122) Than spak Mrs Phillips sayng "Yea forsoothe Mr Oken hath made his will & sett all things straight I warraunt you youe nede not care he was a fery wise man and hath left all things well" I am the more glad said ffisher And I pray you let me see the wille for my satisffyeng To wch she answerid "the will is layd upp and I woold be lothe to medle w^t yt tyll my husbond come home" And so said cawdrey likewise Yet at the last upon some further perswacions usid the willes were brought fourth by the said Phillips wief and cawdrey who before

Speche usid to Margery Phylips & Tho. Cawdrey

the maner of Comyng by the Will

that tyme had taken them and all the keys of chests cupboards & other plaices from Mr Oken's mayde So the same wills were openyd & redd the one being lookid uppon by Mr Griffyn the other redd by John ffisher who founde the difference in maner as before is reportid And when the willes had bene so redd they present agreid to put their hands unto them to thend they might testify what they had seene And so Mr bailief made his mark Mr Griffyn John ffisher Thoms Powell & Willm ffrekulton put to their hands & mark wch done the same willes were rolid up again as before they were and either bound about wt a string the knot of wch string was coverid wt waxe and sealid in the psence of the said cawdrey Phillips wief & many others And after some dilatorye speche usid The said ffisher holding both the said willes said "Mrs Phillips yor husbond & Thomas cook are put in trust specially by Mr Oken wh matters of no small weight but such as require faithfull & carefull paynes who being now from home it stondith you uppon to have the more care And therfore to thend you that be Executors may both the better knowe what ye should doo & in what maner I think it convenient (the case stonding as it doth) that you should have one part of the will yn keaping untill yor husbond come home till wch tyme I trust youe will all agree togither And for the other part I bicause there be many things that towch the towne I will desire Mr bailief here safely to kepe "Naye by gods blood" said Thomas cawdrey "I will have that" & snatched at it "Neighbor cook" said ffisher "the will shalbe furthcomyng and as safe as if you had it" And therwth the said ffisher deliverid to Phillips wief the one paper and to Mr Jenks the other wth which doing bothe the said cawdrey & his wief and the wief of the said Phillips were much movid insomuch that cawdrey said there should none be carried out of the house and that he woolde have it And wt that the doore was shutt And cawdrey snatching at the part that was in Mr Jenks hand tare a piece of the paper at the end wch notwtstonding Mr bailief being eftsones requyred safely to kepe so did This trowblid so much the unresonable

One paper delurid to Phillips wief

Cawdreys Words & behavyor upon the witholding the will from hym

The behavyour & owtrage of Phillips wief Cookes wieff & cook

woomen that they stickid not to say that if Mr Oken did ever speak agayn the towne should have no one grote of his goods nor land neither if they could helpe it And therwth went into the chambr where the man laye in extreme passions And there cryed out rubbid him using all the meanes they could devise to torment him & so to make him speak if it were possible using such outcryes & scriches that not only all the house was trowblid & disquietid but also a great part of the neighbors in the streat woondrid to here them All wch did nothing move the bailief & his other company to yeld them their desire but rather gave them cause to think no good intencion in such persones as were grevid wth that indifferent dealing The parfitt & last will so come by was brought awaye by the said Mr Jenks then bailief who kept the same in his possession almost three moneths after In wch meane tyme bothe the said ffisher and other the overseers had often bene in hand wth Phillips & the said cawdrey to performe the same acording to the trust

And first of all ymediatly uppon the death of the said Oken the very next morning after (by wch tyme the said cawdreye & Phillips wief had somewhat let downe their collor) they came to the said ffisher signifieng the death of the man & that they were myndid to kepe him unburyed twoo or three dayes untill the comyng home of Phillips (whom she said she had sent for) and the better to kepe the body they had caused him to be openyd & bowellid & otherwise prepared aswell as they might And therfore desired thadvise of the said ffisher bothe what provision should be made & in what maner the corps should be buryed and what in the meane tyme was to be done wth his goods In all wch points the said ffisher gave them his best advise wherof they semed to allowe & followe till the comyng home of the said Phillips who cam home the fryday night about ix or x of the clock and making no long abode at his owne house went from thens to the house of the said Oken to bewaile the corpes wch he could not long behold for sorrow as I suppose In such maner that

Ro. Philips care after he came home

nothing could comfort him but the present sight of the old gold and glittering silver he knewe to be there & wch he in his boots spurres & all wth his companyon so hastid as scarcely woold drink before he might have some fruicyon that way And so (folio 123) going into the Inner chambr where the mony & plate laye they twoo wth the sonne of the said cawdrey (their clerk) shutt fast & lockid the doore to them And than openyd the chestes and did further what likid them dividing the shares wth which the Mayde Anne cater mislikid and tolde them playnly that they did not acording to the trust reposid by her late M^r to whom they had made promise that all the overseers should be present & privye wth them at the openyng of his chestes to thend it might appere what they should receue and that there was sufficient to dischardge all things wherof they made than little regarde newes of this behavio^r was brought to Thomas Powell who told Jhn ffisher therof and they twoo sent for William ffrekulton and so they three about eleven of the clok came into the house where they found bothe the wiefs & divers acompanyeng them resonably merye whiles their husbonds were otherwise occupied And so the said ffisher

The maner of comyng & speches of Jo. ffisher Tho. Powell & W. ffrekulton to th'executors

powell & ffrekulton passing by them went to the chambr doore wch they found made fast not only w^t lock but w^t other things barred w^thin At wch doore they knockid twoo or three tymes before any bodie woold speake notw^tstonding that the said ffisher & others had callid to them by name At last the said ffisher callid for something to breake downe the doore and w^thall gave a great russhe wth that said Phillippes Who is there here is said ffisher I & such other as woold come in here is no busynes for you said Phillippes Well said ffisher open the doore orells I will breake it downe What woold you have said Phillips we

The maner of Phillips & Cawdrey & their Answers to the over-seers

will come in said ffisher and see yor doings Who are you said Pillips yo^u knowe us well enough said ffisher who are you said Phillips o^r names said they are ffisher powell & ffrekulton Oh said Phillips are yo^u there I crye yo^u mercye and wth that openyd the doore In this meane tyme they had shuffled upp all their geare & put

it into the chests agayne so as when the dore was openid nothing was abrode
Than said ffisher M{r} Phillips youe were put in trust by M{r} oken truly to execute his will w{th} this yo{r} ptener and he hath left you no doubt a great substance to do it w{th}all as I gesse knowing him to be to wise to give away & bequethe so much w{th}out he had it so to do and to thend it might appere he left sufficient his mynd was (as we are enformed) that youe should have witnesses w{th} you at the opening of his cofers w{ch} he willid to be those that he put in trust as overseers o{r} selfs that be here & some others as you knowe In which his meaning was to discharge you of the speach that otherwise might growe of youe by such as perhappes woold saye theire came more to yo{r} handes than did orells perhaps least you should forgett what you founde wherein as the man ment bothe honestly & well So in aunswering the trust he reposid in youe It had bene well doone if you had followid his mynde therin w{ch} youe have not doone but w{th}out making any pson more than yo{r} selves pryvie have sought the umbles of all An evill token in the begynnyng that you will procede extraordmarely Therfore we are come nowe to you to requyre you to deale so as bothe may aunswer his expectacions and be yo{r} owne discharg and lett us be privie of his state w{th} you w{ch} if it fall not out so largely as is lookid for wee shalbe hable uppon viewe therof to reaport acordingly Otherwise if it be a M{l} more we are not to ympech you of it nor mynde in dede to be yo{r} hinderance of any one pennye Well said Phillippe I knewe M{r} Okens mynde herein sufficiently before and I think you have litle to do in the matter knowing that we be Executors who must tak the charg therof Yet said Agnes Cater my maisters mynde was that there should be no one chest openyd untill all his overseers were present aswell as youe Well said Phillips you may holde yo{r} peace youe medle more than nede Well M{r} Phillips said ffisher your chardge is not small for by that I gesse by reading the will the legacyes will come to iiij{c} or v{c li} and howe that may be resid in this house is to be consideridof ffor you knowe well he had nother oxe nor shepe horse cowe nor calf nor any maner quick catell he had no corne his wares in the shopp of little value & howshold stuff not much woorth & yet that

Speach usid to there-entors by John ffisher And their Aunswar

given away The substance therfore that must aunswer this must be reisid of monye plate Juells & debts wch if be so much as to satisfye all things & content you to It is right well And it stondith youe uppon to consider of it in tyme In good faithe said Phillips I think there be litle enough and so said cawdrey also Well said ffysher and the rest if you doubt of it It is not amis if youe lett us see & be privy wth you Otherwise we must think that you deale not well and must nedes report that having alredy riflid as you have done you found that you will not be acknowen of By my trouth saith Phillippes I doubtid at the first howe wee should be hable to aunswer so many legacyes as be in his will and was in great feare of it untill we found in Mr Okens owne hand writing in twoo places what his monye was & nowe we fynde that his monye & his writing agreid and therfore wee think there wolbe verye (folio 124) nere enough to aunswer euery man save o^r selfs And as for us seing he hath put us in trust wee will prove his will if it cost us xl^{li} a pece of o^r owne purses (of this John ffisher took some hold who and the rest of the companye well knew that before that tyme xl^{li} was not easily to be sparid by them bothe who were redier to borrow before than to lend Than said ffisher why should youe say that you woold doo it if it cost you xl^{li} a piece It is well knowen that M^r oken wold not put you to it to procure yor owne charge but for you some benefiting and therfore say not so Yet sayd they both we think (as farre as we can peeve yet) that we shalbe scarce savers & yet bestowe all o^r labo^r That were against all reson said ffisher but if you think so we will devise away that you shalbe bothe savers & gayners & yet dischargid of the trowble to howe so said Phillips Mary said ffisher if it be true that you report that Mr Oken did leave notes in writing of such monye as he had And that you fynd the monye acording to his writing deliver us those writings & the monye plate Juells & all other things that he left w^thout keping any thing from us And wee will take uppon us to pay to either of you for yor xl^{li} one hundreth marks a piece And wilbe bound and put in sufficient sureties to pforme all the rest his will in a short tyme and to discharg you of all things You will not said Phillips & his partener We will said the other & you shall have the vj^{xx} marks tomorrowe next Well said they bothe you might haply be so decevid but inasmuch as he hathe put us in trust we will take it uppon us what soever come of it Well than said ffisher we eftsones requyre you to lett us be pryvie to y^r doings orells wee might reaport you meane not well I trust said Phillips you do not mistrust us and tomorrow if you will you shalbe privy for we will make a note & shew it to you To be privy that way said ffisher will not satisfy us who are in trust as well as you though not in the same office and wee doo assure our selves That if you doo otherwise than you should we shalbe trowblid wth complaints against you wch we woold prevent if it might be and so save your creadites & our owne to And therfore to be short if you will not make us privye we will kepe you from seing any further this night & so long as by some further auctorytie we will have more witnesses wth us Why will you do so said Phillips I trust you think that we are Executors and owe to tak order for the pformance of the will and no man can clayme any thing from us but by the will And than why should any man be pryvy wth us ffor if wee tak uppon us to be Executors wee must pay the legacyes whither we fynd so much or not And if we fynd more it is our owne & no man can take it from us There is none of us said ffisher that desireth any thing from youe nor we woold not have desired to be privy if the dead man had not so specially desired but insomuch as he so willid and that for so good a purpose (as we gather) surely we mynd to doo our parts and doo what we may that his good mynd may be pformed Why said Phillips we mynde to pforme his will to the uttermost That well apperith saith ffisher whan youe breke it at the first Whie said Phillips what woold ye have us to doo ffulfill the mynd of the man that put you in trust said ffisher bothe in making us privy & so pforming the rest ffor if you will not doo it we will see it doon Than said Phillips yf you will give us leave we will do all things as you woold have it in tyme What tyme said ffisher Marry said Phillips we will prove the will in the begynnyng of the next terme at the ferthest And we will not have one peny of the legacyes unpaid betwixt this and candlemas next howe may that appere said ffisher mary said Phillips we will be bound to yt And theruppon here I give you my hand wherupon M^r powell & M^r ffrekulton & the said ffisher somewhat relentid and were movid the rather to yeld to their Request So as the said ffisher said to them will you in dede prove the will in the beging of michilmas terme next w'hout further delaye & paye all the legacy before candlemas next Yea by God will we said they And therupon gave to the said ffisher powell & ffrekulton their hands promising by the faith of a cristian man and as they are honest men they will prove the will before michilmas terme end and pay all legacyes before candlemas W^{ch} for that tyme satisfied the said ffisher powell & ffrekulton who theruppon left them & cam away about two of the clock in the morning wheruppon the said Phillips & cawdrey returned to their busynes agayne contynewing there till the break of day And than began to part the plate & mony & put the writings into chests & carried them from theire to theire owne houses leving than the body behind them to be kept wth fewer kepers by all their companye Nowe after the buriall done the said Phillips & cawdrey begon to quarell wth the mayde of the said Thomas Okens saing that she had conveid divers things from them and denyeng her to have any right to the household stuff & other things given by her said maister and saing that she should have nothing there but what they woold give her Wheruppon she complanyd her aswell to Mr Griffyn as to the overseers Who theruppon came to the house (folio 125) to take some order for their quietnes where after some woords of unkyndnes utterid betwene thexecutors wiefs & the said mayde The said Mr Griffyn & overseers qualiefieng them sett them at one (as it semyd) and orderid that the mayde should have all the houshold stuff as beds bedsteds shetes & aptens &c and all brasse latten pewter and all thapparell of the said Thomas Okens given to her & all fourmes tables stools &c and also all lynnen all wch was presed by Indifferent men and on Inventorye was therof taken & deliverid to the said Executors all wch did amount scarcely to viij^{li} and also she should have the woode both in the backside & at the doore all wch was iudgid to be given her by her said late maister But as towching the wares the shoppe being also of very litle value they were apointid to be to thexecutors

faithles p'mise of the Executors to probe & fulfill the Will in short tyme

Thexecutors begyn to quarell

Agrement betwene the Executors & Mr Okens mayd

who therupon took them saving such as of their owne acord they gave to the mayde being in dede   And so after all the house serchid thorough by the said Executors they contentid themselfs wth those things they founde & were apointid to them and so fell to good agream^t wth the said Mayd Agnes Catur And yeldid that she should have all things given by her said maister and all that nowe was allottid unto her as houshold stuff And also of their owne mocyon & freewill they gave her over & besides the things allottid unto her a ring of gold that was her said maisters wch being in their owne possession & keping they deliverid unto her in the psence of (   )
and so acordid for a tyme in good & frendly maner But afterwards whan they had gotten asmuch as they could into their handes and that they thought themselfes so sure of all things as no man coulde procure or acquyre any thing from them w^thout sute of law (wch sute they thought no man woold comence partly for that where any thing was given by the will to any pvate persons) they were so poore or of so smale value as they thought were not hable to sue for the same and those things that were of any value were given to comon uses and therfore no p'vate pson woold be either at charge or care to follow for the same they satt downe by yt and would neither prove the will nor pay any legacy therin bequethed Wherof

Complaynts made to the overseers

Exhortacons & requests made by the overseers to the Executors

complaynt being made by divers to the overseers the said overseers & specially John ffisher exhortid the said Executors by all frendly meanes that they could devise to have care of their conscience & creadites both wch were towched bicause they did not behave themselfs acording to the trust in them reposid neither in proving or Executing of the will wch was much notid and grevously complanyd upon Wherunto they aunswerid that they woold prove the will assone as was possible and woold aunswer euevry bequest & legacye acordingly assone as they could get in the debts that were owing to M^r oken which they said were many To wch such answeres they   untill michilmas terme cam whan the said ffisher supposid that they woold have provid the will acording to their former promise wch terme come & gone they did prove no will In that meane tyme cam the chaunge of the bailief of warwik to whom & his successors Mr oken had bequethd c'ten plate It was therfore thought good by the bailief and the pryncipall

<small>delury of the plate</small> burgesses that a demaund should be made for the said plate to be deliverid openly on Alholowday wch was done acordingly which plate the said Executors very unwillingly as it might seme did then deliver after some fryvolos excuse & after a bond made unto them by humfrey crane than newly sworne bailief to whom the said plate was deliverid to be kept & usid for his yere of

<small>demaund of the C^{li}</small> baliwik After wch tyme whan the bailief & pryncipall burgesses mett in their counsaill house for such causes as they had to doo for the towne emongs other things the said ffisher for & in the name of the rest requyred the said Phillips one of thexecutors to pay the C^{li} due to the towne & the other legacyes bequethed to the use of the said towne by the said M^r oken wch the said Phillips said they could not yet pay bicause they could not gett in the debts wherin he desired the ayde of Mr Bailief & the overseers for such things specially

<small>dilatory annswers towching the pving of the will</small> as were owing in & about the towne wch was promised acordingly At wch tyme it was demaundid of the said Phillips whither they had provid the will wch he confessid that they had not done as yet But woold prove it in candlemas terme wthout any doubt and will pay all things by Easter or sone after Wherunto they were ernestly advised in avoiding that fowle speche that went on them After wch tyme the said overseers many tymes requyred the said Executors to prove the will & pay the legacyes to such poore people as thought long for the same wch they also very earnestly & often promised to do spedily So the tyme passid on untill hillary terme came when the said Phillips and the said ffisher & others having for their private causes sevaley to do at london went upp thither togither where by the waye the said ffisher was earnestly in hand wth the said Phillips to prove the will & dispach the things they had to doo wch the said (folio 126) Phillippes promised to doo wth many protestacions wheruppon the said ffisher verely trusting pswadid therunto the rather by the often & colored promises of the said Phillips was many tymes fayne to aunswere to such as came unto him complaning of the said

Phillippes & cawdrey for not doing of their office & duety of Executors That they
the said Executors wold pforme all things to thuttermost and
the said ffisher aunswerid so long for them that it was thought
that he was ptakr of the spoile And therfore the rather defendid
their cause to the great preiudice of others wch opynion being
concevid of many at the last one emongs others a man very frendly to the said
ffisher namely his own brother Richerd ffisher uttered in the hearing of the most
part of the principall burgesses the most part of which were of the same opynion
though the forbare to utter so much that the same John ffisher was the only cause
that things were not shewn as they should be wch being grevid of by the said
ffisher Who was free from any such either corrupcions or pticipacions aunswerid
for him self for that tyme as trueth was that neither feare nor gift had so blindid
him as to suffer that reaport or conceipt of his frends And
therfore took occasion to move the then M^r bailief to call the
whole companye togither aswell the principall burgesses as the others that were
assistants by order of Mr Oken's will Uppon pretence to call for such dedes of M^r
Okens land as was missing wch being doone and thexecutors there the said John
ffisher openly demaundid of them when the mony due to the towne by Mr Oken's
gift should be paid and whither the said executors had provid the will acording
to their pmise to which they aunswerid as before that they woold aunswr every
man assone as they could And that they had put the will to probacions and they
would take such order as no man should take cause to complayne for they would not
leave one peny unpaid erre it were long Thes said ffisher be yor dilatory aunsweres
by wch they that should take benefite be hinderid and those that trust you be
deludid I meane emongs others my self who giving creadite to yor flattering
pmises see that litle or nothing is doone and therwith those that should take
benefit greatly complayne and think me as bad as any But take some direct way
wherby it may apere that you will in resonable tyme doo that you should doo
orells I will declare myself as I am and the fault shalbe knowen where it is for
I tak both God and you to witnes I am clere from any maner of reward or intent

evill opynion conceivd in Jo ffisher for the defaults of the Executors

Jo. ffisher declarith himself

to hindr so good a devise and am as forward as I may be to further the same to the uttermost of my power & hability To that said Phillips who doth complayne of us we are redy to doo all things assone as we may And this shall not nede ffor before witsonday there shalbe never a grote to pay wch promise evry man wisshid to be true though they had litle hope of it This so passid and Easter terme come the said ffisher remembring what had bene said to him & doubting what might further be ymagyned if thexecutors should play their acoustomed parts having other occasion to be at London went to the office in the Arches where the will should be if any were provid namely Mr Argalles office and sought there for the will of the said oken where none could be found nor any offred to be provid Wheruppon it was thought good by the said ffisher Thomas powell & Robart Sheldon Overseers That a scitacion should be taken out of that court to call them to the probacion wch was doone acordingly wth thexecutors satt And after that an Excommunicacion taken out wheruppon they appred And after some tyme spent by asmany dilatory dayes as might be at last after Easter terme the said Executors put unto the said court A copye writen in paper in wyde lynes

a fyne feate of Executors   being the copye in effect of the true will saving something lacking though not in dede the true will wch true will than remanid in the custdy of the said ffisher And in that coppye there were striken out divers lynes conteyning at least twoo hundreth pounds & above wherof these were parte C^{li} given to Warwik xl^{li} given to Stretford xl^{li} given to Banbury the leace of the house given to Agnes catur & such other which coppy being seen by the said ffisher upon his second comyng to the said office semyd to him very straunge and therfore the said ffisher askid whither it was put in as a will to be provid And who so put it in To that the clerks made aunswr that it was put in to be provid as the will of Thomas Oken and that a litle halting man had brought it in by a proctor then the said ffisher said I am suer the Executors will not prove or be sworne to this will Yes said the clerks that they will for they have causid it to be writen upp & engrossid and it shalbe sealid to morrow I pray you said ffisher let me see the Ingrossid booke wch was showid by the clerks wch did agree wth that copy in paper Well said ffisher if they prove this they are no honest men wth that cam the M^r of the office and askid what the matter was wch the said ffisher told as before (folio 127) wch it semid the officer litle regardid who aunswerid that they must prove such as be brought to them At night the said ffisher meting wth others overseers namely Thoms powell & Robart Sheldon told them what he had seene wherupon the said Robart Sheldon went to the office And requyred to have the sight of the will & thingroced book wch both were shewid to him Wherupon he also desired that he might have a copye of that book so deliuerid into the court wch was promysed against the next day Wheruppon he trustid and went the next day for the same acordingly But in the meane tyme Thoms Powell had spoken wth the said Phillippes and told him of his ill demeano^r spied out by the said ffisher who for the tyme sett a colour of the matter as though there had bene no such thing And theruppon went to the office and took away the said coppye & the Ingroced book and then left the copye of the will which they had in their keping at the death of the said Oken willing that to be engrossid up & provid So as the next day at the comyng of the said Sheldon the first copye & engrosid was not to be had for any mony Thus began their doble dealing to appere manifest wch being so apparaunt movid the overseers to have more earnest care that way And fynding the suttlety of those Executors in procuring the probacion of the will by a procter bicause they woold not be sworne either to the will or to the Inventory The said Overseers thought good to exhibit a bill of complaynte into the chauncery showing the whole distres herof requiring that the said Phillips & cawdrey might be callid into that court to aunswer uppon their othes to those points they should be chargid w^thall towching the said will by that meanes the rather to procure them to do that wch of conscience & trust they should otherwise have done which being done and subpenaes sevrally taken out & srud bothe the said Phillips & cook cam in & aperid but before they had aperid there they had gotten day in the court of Arches to bring in the Inventory in michilmas terme wch they did of purpose to defraud the mening of the will and to deferre the paym^t of any man ffor so they were pswadid that so long as they might have tyme to kepe out the

causes mobing the overseers to comense sute

Sute Comensed by bill in the Chauncery

prety practises

Inventory they nedid not to pay any legacye wch they sought asmuch as they might Upon their appearaunce in the chauncery an aunswere was lookid for by the overseers compl wch could not be gote untill the last day of the terme And than the put in a demurrer supposing the bill of complaynt to be wthout cause Remedy wherof none could be untill the next terme So in the next terme the court was movid for a better aunswr And therupon it was orderid that they should put in an other aunswr by ( ) wch day came and then an other demurrer offred Than the said Executors procuring divers s^riant & counsellors to come to the barre movid the Lord Keaper for an order therin who hearing briefly the substance of the cause sett downe an order that the deffendants should before their going out of the towne put in a sufficient aunswere Orells that attachm^t should be awardid against them To lett this M^r yelverton Attorney for the Executors spake earnestly but was put to silens & the order sett downe as before Wth this order the said Executors were not alitle offendid The knoleige of this order being brought to Jo flisher sick in his bed at london he thought it good in avoyding the corrupcion & wilfull piury that was like the said Executors to fall into that a copye of the true & last will of Thomas Oken than remaning in the keping of the said flisher should be offred unto them And theruppon it was agreid that the said Thomas powell taking some witnesses wth him should goo to the Inne where the said Phillips & cawdrey laye & there to offer them a copy of the said will wch the said Powell taking wth him Ric. hames before divers other psones did saing that he was come to thend the Rather bicause he knew of the order made against them that day in the chauncry to offer them a copy of the true will Whom when they had heard at large they aunswerid that they had the true will & that they wold prove and take no copy at their hands and so wth many colereque woords reiectid the offer of the said overseers And on the next day being the day next after the end of the terme the said phillips & cawdrey put in an other aunswere into the chauncry and were sworne therunto before Sr Ric. Reade

[margin notes: Delatory Demurrers usid for shifts by the Executors / orders grauntid by the Court against them / frenidly & brotherly care of the overseers towards the executors / A copy of the true & last will offred to the executors / the executors doo uttly refuse a copy of the true Will]

Thexecutors put their aunswere into the Chauncry uppon their othes

Ten points wherin the Executors were pinn'd uppon their aunswere

Knight one of the maisters of the said court of chauncry and so cam away the effect of their aunswr consistid chiefly on thes points viz. that the said overseers had comensid their sute of evill will only to trowble the deffs w'thout iust cause that they have disbursid all the monye goods & debts recevid that they have not ymployd (folio 128) the monye to their owne use That they have provid the last wille and that before they were sued in the chauncry That they myndid to have provid the will soner if they had not bene sued That they never denyed to prove the last will That the meane not the hinderaunce of any That they sought no delayes in proving of the will In all wch poyntes they were manifestly piured ffor at the tyme of putting in of their aunswer they had not disbursid all the monye &c They had delivred out upon usury above CC^{li} they had not provid the last will nor any will before they were sued in the chancery They had passid over ix monethes before the offred to prove any will and they had so craftely delt that such as had legacyes of x^{li} they paid onely vj^{li} xiij^s iiij^d taking aquitans for x^{li} they had bene scitid & excoicatid before the provid the will upon wch causes the complaynt was framed Their

A copy of their aunswere taken out

aunswere thus put in uppon their othes & to be seene A copye therof was taken out by the playntiffs after midsomer terme who myndid in michilmas terme following to prosecute the cause But before that tyme they could doo nothing before wch michilmas terme The acompt & Reconing for Mr Oken's lands & howe the proffits therof were ymploid was by the collector yeldid At wch the then bailief & all or the most part of the principall burgesses & xxiiij others apointid by M^r okens devise were present Emongs which John ffisher was who after dynner endid recomending the good acts of the said Oken

ffisher & phillipps fall out

who was cause of that then meting wisshid that thexecutors had doone their parts no worse than the collectors wth that Robart phillips being at the boorde said they meaning himself & cawdrey thexecutors had done as well & as truely as the collectors or any other & more truely to Nay said the said ffisher you have not done so but have done most falsely & farre otherwise than you ought to have done Wherin said Phillips In all things said ffisher and mainely in that you have neither paid the legacyes nor provid his will but have most shamelesly sworne that you have provid the will wheras you have provid a false will like wretches & men of no creadit Nay said phillips we are of as good creadite as you and do as truely as youe And have I this for lending thee my monye Lending me thy mony said ffisher thowe hast lent me none but that I pay truely for to thee like a vile usuring knave knave said Phillips Yea said ffisher thowe art a false forsworne & piured knave and that I will prove wth that Phillips began to arrise from the boorde as though he woold have done something But some of the company kept him in wch made him so much more hoate saing have you brought me hither to murder me Nay said they that we have not And so let him goo who threetined many woords against the said ffisher This passing on about a moneth after the said Phillips complanyd himself in the meane tyme to all his freends against the said ffisher and emongs other making his complaynt wth grevous informacions against the said ffisher to Sr Thomas Lucy(a) the said Mr Lucy sent for the said ffisher M^r hudson M^r powell & Robart Sheldon to come to his house to charlecot whither the said company came at their tyme apointid And the said ffisher hearing that the said Phillips had bene often tymes wth the said Sr Thomas thought it not amysse to take such books papers & copyes as tochid M^r okens will wth him therby the better to satisfye him if the matter should come in question So when they cam thither there they founde Willm Edmonds Robert Phillips & Thomas cawdrey So service done & they dyned Sr Thomas Lucy shewid the cause of their sending for and signified what grevous complaynt the said Phillips had made Wheruppon he was desirous to heare the matter and sett them at one if it might be and therupon callid Phillips to utter his grief nowe that the others are there wch he did wth many protestacions & long circumstanc wherin he was so long that he made not onely the said Sr Thomas but the other hearers

Phillips complayneth to Sr Tho. lucy

S^r Th. lucy sendith for ffisher & others

ffisher goeth to Sr Tho. lucy

Sr Tho. lucy hathe the hearing of the cause

(a) This is the Sir Thomas Lucy who prosecuted Shakespeare, and was lampooned by the latter. He built the present mansion at Charlecote in 1558, and died 7th July, 1600. His monument is in the Lucy Chapel of Charlecote Church, and consists of a high tomb bearing the recumbent effigies of himself in armour, and of his Lady.

theffect of philips complaynt against ffisher	weary At last being willid to goo pticulerly to theffect of his matter he shewed howe that Mr Oken made them his Executors and they had provid the will and myndid to pforme the same wth all speed but they were letted by Jo. ffisher & the others who not only vexed them uniustly by sutes of lawe but also threaten them otherwise & will not suffer them to execute acording to the said will To all wch points the said ffisher annswerid in such maner as by aparaunt mater confutid the said phillips & satisfyed the said (folio 129) Sr Thomas Lucy Wm Edmonds and the other pnt that they all thought that the said ffisher & the other overseers had done honestly & none otherwise than they honestly might & should do And so advised the said phillips & cawdrey that they should reforme themselfs & deale more playnly
The executors desire an end	Well the said phillips & cawdrey finding bylike their owne daungerous state desired most earnestly that Sr Thomas lucy should sett an order betwene them Wherunto he was so ynclyned & movid the said ffisher & others to yeld uppon resonable condicions At whose earnest pswacions the said ffisher & others were content to yeld to such order as should
An order & end sett down by S^r Th. lucy & Willm Edmonds	be thought resonable So in thend after long debating & many folish woords spent It was orderid that the said Executors should paye C^li due to the towne of Warwik to thands of the bailief of Warwik then being at or before the xxiiij^t day of decebr following iiij^xx^li to be by the said bailief & burgesses deliuerid out to the townes of Stretford & Banbury And also that the said Executors shall w^thin eight dayes next following after the said agrem^t pay xv^li to be dealt emongs the poore people of the towne of Warwik And that they the said Executors shall w^thin one yere following pay all other legacyes & somes of mony bequethed by the said Thomas oken wch somes & other things be contenyd in the true & last will of the said oken nowe deliuerid by the said ffisher to the said Sr Thomas Lucy And also that the said Executors should at or before the ix^th day of octobr next after the said agream^t paye to the overseers x^li
The executors confirme the order by their hands & seales with their bonde	towards the charges of the said overseers in the sutes towching the same will To wch articles & agream^ts the said phillips & cawdrey put their hands & seales And for the pforming therof

	entrid bond of iiij^{cli} wch condicions the said John ffisher & the
The oberseers accept thorder	other overseers aceptid veryly trusting that those their agream^t & bondes wold so bridle the said Executors As in nowise after to walk out of the waye Wherupon the said overseers surceassid
The oberseers surcease their Sute	to prosecute their sute either in the Arches or chauncery any further Wheruppon the said Executors deliuerid the said xv^{li}
The Executors do pforme part of the order	for the poore and the said C^{li} and the said iiij^{xxli} and also the said x^{li} at tymes acording to their articles But afterwards having in his maliciouse mynde the woordes spoken by John ffisher towching the piury of the said Phillips The said Phillips
Philips commensith sute in the quenes bench against ffisher for the Wloords spoken	thinking to terrifie the said ffisher being than very extremely ill wth the gout in such maner as not hable to goo about his chambr the space of xiij or xiiij weekes The said Phillips being at london in hillarye terme procured out a cap sat out of the quenes bench against the said ffisher returnable in Easter terme following wch writt the said Phillips kept in his hand untill about midlent
Philips maner for the execucion of the pces	

when the Assises grew on & against wch tyme he well knew the said ffisher woold be stirring abrode if it were possible by reason of his offices and therfore about ij dayes before thassises deliuered the same writt to the undersheriff requyring that he woold make his warraunt to a speciall bailief such as the said Phillips should name for tharresting of the said ffisher wch the undersherif refusid to do seing that M^r ffisher was an officer to be occupied the tyme of thassises & therfore than not to be trowblid Besides he was sufficient to aunswer the said phillips w^thout arresting And therfore the said sheriff promised to speak wth him and so to undertake that he should not nede to arrest him Well said phillips yf you go to him I pray you arrest him in his chambr ffor ells you do me wrong Nay said the Sheriff it is w^thin a corpacion & I may not so doo besides he is a sick man & my freend and I will not so use him but I will speak wth him and I dare undertake he shall appere to you Well said Phillips I trust you will do me right and saith to the Sheriff Take hed what you do for I have accions against him for a vj^{li} or vj^s well said the undersheriff I doubt not but he will aunswer you Therupon the sheriff came to the said ffisher about other matters & found him not hable to sitt upp And so after other communycacions told him that he had pces against him at Phillips sute And therwth deliuerid him a copy of the writt who therwth promosied to apyeare and for his better warraunt gave his bond to appeare at the day prefixed And so in the begynnyng of Easter terme being not hable to ride the said ffisher sent up to reteyne an Atto^rney And to put in baile for him wch was done And the declaracion callid for But all that terme no declaracion woold be put in but the first day of Trynyty terme the said phillips declared against the said ffisher (folio 130) in an accion uppon his case wherin the said Phillipps declarid that the said ffisher had slaunderid him in london laing the woordes supposid to be spoken in london by the said ffisher as followth viz. Thowe (meaning the said Phillips) art falsly forsworne & fowly piured like a false knave and that I will approve & stand to it And I trust to see thyne Eares naylid of the pillorye like a false crypling knave and so laid that he was dampnified by reson of those woords to the value of C^{li} this declaracion so put in in the begynnyng of Trynytie terme his Att^rney gat a rule that the said ffisher should aunswer & come to Issue that terme and so that tryall should be in the guild hall in london orells a

ffisher appeauith to aunswer phillips

Philips declarith against ffisher

The Woords layd

to be entrid herof ffishers atto^rney hearing took out a copy of the declaracion & sent it downe to ffisher requiring pfit Instruns for his aunswere Signifieng wthall what was entendid for the triall that terme It was the mids of the terme or this knowleige came to ffisher who at that tyme was not in good case to travaill as was well knowen to Phillips who had bene at london twice in the begynnyng of that terme to further this matter entending to procure the matter should be taken by defalt if the said ffisher apered not (as by reson of his weakenes & infirmitye was most likely) orells if he woold ride in such weather as than fell out to be very fowle his body might be put in some perill and so the said philips hopid to have his will some of those wayes But ffisher having a mynd no lesse to iustify than he had spoken wherby the lewd libtye of so vile a fellow might be the better knowen determyned to aunswer the said phillips to his face if he had the face to stand to his takling and rather chose to adventure the pill of his health than to yeld to so the manace of so lewde a varlet and so took his Journey towards london in the waye taking by extreme colde & Rayne very g^t disseas Nevertheles keping his Journey & comyng to london there he founde the matter earnestly callid upon and a pemptory day to aunswere orells thadvantage of lawe to be taken so as it stood the said ffisher in hand spedyly to look therto Who taking advise of learned counsaill put in his aunswere iustifieng the speaking of the woords at Warwik where in dede such woords as were spooken were spoken and so shewid the cause of the speaking & the points wherin the said Phillips had piured himself upon his aunswer put into the chauncery upon his othe And so the said ffisher being thus urged to declare the honesty & qualities of the said Phillips was advised to bring the triall of his piurye before the lords in Starre chambr wch he did presently after whan he pcevid that phillips owne folly woold not otherwise be reformed wherin ffisher bestowed long tyme & much mony in that sute wch procedid so farre as to have witnesses Examyned & therfore a comission awardid to S^r ffulk Grevile S. Willm catesby knights Thoms dabrugecoure & Ric. Middlemore esquires who pswading the pties to end left examinacions & fell to arbit'ment & in thend awardid ffisher but only xx^{li} As may apeir by bookes lieng in the tresury to long to be writen.

ffisher aunswerith and iustifieth the speaking of the Woords at Warwik

ffisher comensith sute by bill in the Starre Chambr

the whole discourse of pledings interrogatoryes & Awarde of this matter lieth in the tresury behind the ladie Chapell (a)

loke for this towards thend of this book

But to returne to the goverment of the towne & the travailes of the bailief And first as towching the sute of Staunton against Richerd ffisher Bailief & Thomas Powell for the piury supposid against them The said Ric. ffisher & Thomas Powell at the day prefixed in the writt appearid in the Starre chambr and took out a coppye of the bill put in against them wch conteyned in effect no more than the said Staunton had laid against them in his sute brought against them in the comon lawe wheruppon it was thought good that the court should be movid therin And

The sute betwene Th. Staunton p. & Ri. ffisher & Th. Powell def. endid

---

(a) This is the small room at the East End of the Beauchamp Chapel, originally the Vestry to the Chapel, and now used as a Library for the Clergy. None of these pleadings, &c., are now there.

that it should be declarid before the lords howe that the said Staunton had before that tyme brought sevrall accions against the said ffisher & powell for the self cause at the comon lawe wherin they had ioynid Issue wth him And so procedid to triall w^t powell uppon wch tryall the said Staunton was nonesuit The other accion being also at Issue & redy to be tryed was yet hanging wch being showed to the court order was sett downe that if Staunton could not disprove that allegacion by a c^{r}ten day the cause should be dismissed that Court of the comon lawe where they were at Issue And theruppon gave the said ffisher & powell day to aunswer the next terme being hillary terme nowe in the meane tyme Staunton fynding bylike the weaknes of his cause made meanes to S^r ffulk Grevile Sr John hubond & others to have the matter treatid of in the countrey and procured Mr Griffyn the preacher to further the same whoso disposicion being very godly enclined to quiet solicited the said Ric. ffisher earnestly to yeld that the matter might come to hearing before some gentlemen in the countrey wherwth the said ffisher being greatly movid being also a man not given to sutes or lawe yeldid to the said Mr Griffyn who than travelled more earnestly aswell to Sr Thoms. lucy & others to take some payne in this matter who also being right godly disposed willingly grauntid to bestowe his travaile & labo^r So in thend it was agreid That S^r ffulk Grevile & Sr John hubond for Tho. Staunton And Sr Thomas lucy & Mr Edward Aglionby for ffisher & powell should have the hearing & ordering of the matter Mr Griffyn being as it weare the umpyer or Assistant Wheruppon on wensday after the twelveth day being the morow after Epiphany Sessions the said gentlemen & parties mett (folio 131) at Warwik about that cause where after many witnesses brought in by Staunton to further his cause though wth litle proof as by the sequell may appere And the words spoken & sworne by ffisher & powell openyd the said gentlemen grew to end wch was in effect as followith ffirst that the said Staunton ffisher & powell should be freends and that all the Sutes betwene them should cease and should be w^{t}hdrawen in euery court at the costs & chardges of Thomas Staunton and that from thens fourth the same should never be revived And bicause by the Evidence given by ffisher & powell Thomas Staunton took losse of the lease bought of harry ball And that therby also the towne was benifytid It was orderid that Staunton should have vj^{li} xiij^s iiij^d towards his charges to be yeldid out of the comon stock of the towne and so an end though not greatly likid of to ffisher yet by the earnest pswacion of some freends acceptid And so that matter determynid & set downe in articles subscribid wth the handes aswell of the said gentlemen as the parties wch order now remanith in the custody of Sr Thomas lucy

(The following extract refers to the visit of Queen Elizabeth to Kenilworth in the year 1575, when she had the magnificent reception by the Earl of Leicester which is described in Scott's "Kenilworth.")

The carefull diligence of the bailieff to further the quenes sruice

The quenes being at Kenel

The somer folowing it pleasid the quenes ma^{ty} to make her progresse into Northtshire Warwikshire Staffordshire Worcestershire & so to returne to Woodstok in oxfordshire In wch journey her ma^{ty} lay at Kenelworth (   ) dayes and her houshoulde at Warwik by reson wherof great diligence was to be given by the Bailief of Warwik as well for the good goverm^t of the towne as for the dutifull expediting of such things as by him were to be done for the furtherance of her ma^{ts} sruice divers wayes as by dispaching of lres by post wch cam very thick as also by providing & furnishing her ma^{ts} officers wth all maner of cariags wch were also very many by reson of her ma^{ty} & her houshold lieng asunder & by reson of so many removes apointid & not kept And by reson of horses prouidid for such as had comission to tak horses wch were so many that for a monethes space & more xxxiij horses xxx horses & when they were fewest xx horses wold skarce suffice to serve comissions some to Kenelworth some to Lichfeld some further And as in this so in all things ells his Suice was not onely expectid but also at all houres of day & night required Wherin he so well behavid himself that her Ma^{ty} was well sruid to the good contentacion of her officers & his good recomendacion which procured to him further chardg (as this writer gesseth) ffor the yomen officers of the court attending her person lieng at Kenelworth hearing of the paynfull sruice

& willingnes of the bailief of Warwik took paynes to visit him as her Ma^ts lyvetennt & good officer and bringing wth them a cast of their office by courtly meanes devised the opening of his largesse So as in fees (as they callid them) that way It cost him x^l marks or xxx^li as may apeire by his Acompt therof of which chardg the said Bailief was not willing to ask any allowance but woold have borne it of his owne purse contrary to all reson if some his freends had not earnestly pswadid him to the contry Such was his benevolent mynd towards the towne wch he know^th to be greatly chardgid otherwise as by presents given to therle of leycester to the countyes Warwik & others Who as they acceptid well of the proffers of the towne yet much more reconyd of the carefull sruice of the officers Besides that the chardges of his howsekeping & calling of frends & neighbors togither was such as none before him & is to be fearid fewe after him will compare (the only fault this writer fyndith) in him is the overmuch pittie he shewith to the poore of whom as the better sorte are to be comfortid & relivid so the worser or as I may call them the worst is to be seuerely ponishid wherin the said Bailief was very myelde a fault to be borne whall I confesse.

A PRINCIPAL BURGESS PUT IN WARD FOR A VIOLENT ASSAULT.

Willm ffrekulton being one of the principall Burgesses comyttid to warde

In this Bailiefs tyme it hapnid that one of the company of the xii principall Burgesses was comyttid to warde the very circumstance & maner wherof this wryter can not wryte because he was not then in towne But as the case was after revealid to him wch was thus Willm ffrekulton being than one of the principall burgesses being a freend to one Richerd Graunt who ought a some of monye due uppon an

The cause

obligacion to John hicks baker came to the said hicks the very day at when the mony should be paid & told the said hicks that Mr Graunt had not the mony redy to pay him according to his bond And therfore desired the said hicks to forbeare the mony & to give him day for a c'ten tyme after Wherupon hicks (as himself said) doubting what might come of it if he should assigne any other day answerid that his day was come and he had occasion to use the mony

& woold not give any leng^r day wherwth the said ffrekulton misliking after some other misbehavio^r in harkening at the windowe of the said hicks & otherwise at last callid hicks Knave & offred to strike him in the streat wherwth hicks being movid after he had suffred many indecent proferres at last callid the said ffrekulton Evesdroper & so by multiplieng of woordes proceded to knave wherby (folio 132) some blowes were stirred but at that tyme no harme done by the providence of some others in the company This haping late at night & profferrid to the said hicks in executing of his office (as he said) being at that tyme a constable The next morning the said hicks complanid hereof to the Bailief who willing him for the tyme to be quyet and not to seek any further for justice or remedye (for the said hicks was myndid to have procuried warrants for the peas against ffrekulton from the Justice of the peace of the shire) promiseed that he wold speak wth M^r ffrekulton & take order betwene them And so the same day the said Bailief meting M^r ffrekulton told what complaynt had bene made & told him his opynyon what great fault it was for any of them to be quarellers Whereuppon ffrekulton confessing the matter & partly submytting himself promissed the said Bailief that he woold never medle with hicks nor none other but specially not with hicks And theruppon the said ffrebulton gave to the said Bailief his promise & faith & in token thereof gave him his hand Whereuppon the said Bailief assured hicks that he had taken order that ffrekulton woold not hurt him Uppon which assurance the said hicks forbare any further sute and also went quietly about his busynes nothing mistrusting any ill to come the rather allured by that that ffrekulton meting him in the street the next morning bad him god morrowe (though with a feyned hart as it semed) for the self same morning the said ffrekulton understanding that hicks was gone to Wedgenok park[a] about his busynies he postid after him & made such hast as meting a wayne lodid comyng out at the park gate he wold not stay the comyng of the wayne but rode by in great hast and so fynding the said hicks newely come into the park he rode to him & wth a great crabtry cudgell struck him unwares that he fellid him to the

---

(a) Wedgenock Park belongs to the Earl of Warwick, and is about two miles to the north of Warwick. It is high ground here, and at one part of the road the view includes Warwick, Leamington and Kenilworth.

grounde & so lightid & offred him gret violence insomuch that it was thought he wold have slayne him if some helpe had not presently come and partid them wch doone the said ffrekulton rode his way to Stretford and the said hickes was brought all bloody home by his neighbours who complanyng to the said Bailief the said hickes did chardge him that this was long of him for if he had not bene he woold otherwise have provided for the said ffrekulton So after a day or twoo ffrekulton came home agayne for whom the said Bailief sent & chardging him wth this misdemeno^r & falsefieng his faith The said ffrekulton could not deny his promise made unto him that he woold not medle wth hicks But saith he I ment that promise to extend but to yor liberty of the towne And that I did was out of the libtye & so woold seme to kepe his promise Wheruppon the said bailief callid a hall or metyng of the rest of the principall Burgesses who consentid that the said ffrekulton should receve some ponishm^t And at the last it was determyned that he should be sent to the Bailiefs parlo^r in the market place and there to be lodgid for one night Where it was allowid him to have a bed but he refused And being so committid the kyndnes of his frend & Socyatt flattering Phillyppes appeared who contentid him to take such part as the said ffrekulton did & so voluntary of his owne Acorde kept him company that night wch things being passid over yet the said hicks was not satisfyed but requyred surety for the peace & good abearing agaynst ffrekulton & such other proces for the battrye as counsill gave him But Mr Bailief desiring to have an end of such quarrells callid the company together who taking paynes betwene the said parties made an end of the cause & sett them togither as frends ffrekulton paing something xx^s for his folishe furyes.

(folio 132) On the 4th of January, 1575, John Grene was elected a principal burgess in the place of Symon Yong decased

On Michaelmas Day, 1575, John Rigeley was elected Bailiff.

See the Booke Ante 82 b

The said Michalmas daye The M^r wardens & companye of Drapers & Tailors of Warwik put upp a Supplicacion to the said Mr Bailief desiring by the same That their book of constitucions & orders might be enlargid or reformed So as the Article following might be put to the same book wch ar^{le} being considerid & likid of was writen upp engrossid (folio 133) and affilid to the said Book of constitucions and delivered as an order & parcell of the same book The tenor wherof Ensuith

An order unytid to the book of orders for Drapers & Taylers Memorandum That at the speciall request of the Maister wardens and companye of Drapers & Tailors Inhabitants w'in this Borough of Warwik It is orderid agreid & consentid unto by the Balief & pryncipall Burgesses of the same borough that the order & Article following shalbe added & Annexed to the book of constitucions & orders for Drapers & Tailers within the same Borough And shalbe by the same Drapers and Tailers & theire Successours inviolably obsruid & kept as the other Articles & orders uppon like payne & penaltie as in the said booke is expressid & prescribed That is to say That yf any persone wch hathe bene or herafter shalbe free of the said company of Drapers or Taylers w'thin the said borough eyther in respect that he hathe sruid or shall serve w'thin this borough seven yeres as Aprentice or covennt Servaunt or otherwise compoundid or shall compounde for his ffreedome And after have or shall departe out of this borough to dwell or Inhabite in any other place or otherwise hathe bene or shalbe constrayned to goo out of this borough for his evill lief & behavio^r And hathe not or shall not for all the said tyme he shalbe so absent & dwelling out of the said borough paie his quartereges & other dueties to the Maister wardens & companye of Drapers & Tailers of this borough as other the ffreemen of the same company abiding w'thin the said borough have shall & doo comonly use to paye but hathe slackid or shall slack to pay the said quarterege & dueties the space of one yere That then it shall not be laufull for the same persone or persones so having dwellid or shall dwelle owt of this borowe & liberties and witholden or shall witholde his said dueties to be receuid into the said companye agayne or to occupie his arte or science w'thin the said borough before he doo or shall compounde wth the said maister wardeyns & companye of Drapers & Tailors wth thassent of the bailief & burgesses for the tyme being and paye such ffyne & composicion as before is expressid for fforeners The one wherof to be to the chamber of the said borough And the other half to the said M{r} Wardens & company of Drapers & Tailers uppon the paynes & penalties before in the said book of orders is pscribed In witnies wherof the said Bailief & Burgesses have heruto subscribed their handes and deliverid the same as an order the xxix{th} daie of Septembr in the Seavententh yere of the reigne of our souereigne ladye Elizabeth by the grace &c.

The speciall cause of devising of this order was to restreyne one William Wedgewood Tailer who before this tyme about iiij{or} or v yeres Sithens dwellid in this towne where leaving his wief he went to Stretford & divers other places & there marryed an other wief his first wief yet living besides that he is a man very contencious prowde & slaunderous oft busieng himself w{th} noughty matters & quarelling w{th} his honest neighbours w{ch} condicions forcing him to leave place of good governm{t} first went from hence & afterward was compellid to goo from Stretford. Wheruppon taking a house in this towne to the great misliking of the honester sort they provide as much as may be to banish him from this towne the rather for that M{r} bailief & his company are willid therunto in the name & from my l of warwik who hating the Condicions of the man pluckid his livery from him

the copie of my L of Warwiks lre writen to M{r} hudson towching Wedgewood

To my verry freend Will{m} hudson at Warwik give thies

Good M{r} hudson I am given to understand by a letter of yours directid unto George Turvile That one Wedgewood is come agayne to be a dweller in Warwik Who for his ill behavio{r} & dishonest living was afore banishid by my comandem{t} And therfore I am to desire youe in my name to deale w{th} the bailief & maisters of the towne that he may not remayne there for evell example to others in the like case And so I bid youe farewell w{th} my harty comendacions from the court at woodstok this second of october 1575

Yo{r} very freend

A. Warwik

Budbrook Tithes.

An order for parte of the tmythes belonging to saint mary church in Warwik

Be it remembrid that this yere a° dm 1575 and the xvij^th yere of quene Elizabeth Richerd ffisher being bailief & humfrey crane using the place of Burges to collect & gather the rents due to the towne by the first corpacion bicause many quarrells & contentions had bene before rased for part of the tuithes aptenyng to the church of Saint Maryes in Warwik wch were claymed by John butler & John hodgets fermors of the psonage of Budbrook [a] sometymes by Thomas ffisher Esquire as in the right of his house of Sepulcre [b] nere Warwik & som tymes by John ffisher whiles he had a leace of the tuithes aptening to the said church of saint maryes and sometyme by others some such as have no right therunto It was thought expedient by the bailief & principall Burgesses that some order were meete to be given wherby the best title might be knowen And therfore comaundmt was given to such as had corne & gresse growing on the north & northmost parts of that parish where the said controversy grewe that every person should for this yere gather the whole profits of their groundes w^thout setting out or paing any tenths or tuiths for the same to that end that if any having title to the same felt themselves Iniuryed they might tak such course by lawe for recovering their rights as aptenid By vertue of wch comaundmt the tenuts carried away all the profits w^thout setting forth any tnith Wherw^th Thomas Butler termo^r of part of the tuithes of Budbrook seming to mislike demaundid tuithes of some of the tenuts who aunswerid him wth the order & comaundmt given to them against wch he in woordes greatly inveid as one that would cut out his part by weapon but in effect did nothing whiles the fruyts were on the groundes saving as a man that regardith not what might come of it gave a kinsman of his one (   ) Pardy a loode of pease to be taken out of John bonds closse one of those tenuts

(a) Budbrook is about a mile to the North-West of Warwick. The Trustees of Henry VIIIth's Estate possess land in the Parish, and are lay impropriators of the Chancel of the Church.

(b) The Priory, the residence of Thomas Fisher, was formerly the Priory of St. Sepulchre.

that had comaundmt Emongs others Wherupon the said pardy being a poore man & litle knowing of the daunger that might followe borrowing a teame betweene ix & x of the clok in the night in harvest tyme went to the closse of the said John bond where the most part of the pease there that had growen that yere remanyd and out of wch no tuithes were sett or apointid out And fynding the gate of the closse lockid he break the lock threwe downe the gate & toke awaye viij cocks of pease of the said John bonds as the said Pardye confessid before the bailief afterwarde Wheruppon the said John bond complaining And w^thall M^r crane also complaining that the said Pardye had threatned him wth very unfitting & great woords (folio 134) of theffect that if his kynsman Butler or he had taken him on the ground giveng that comaundm^t they wold have dealt very hardly wth him The Bailief sent for the said pardy and for his evill demeano^r that way ponisshid him in the stocks for a tyme though shortly after uppon the submission of the said pardy his ponisshm^t was released & he sett at libty pmising never to medle againe in such matters This passed on w^thout any other further trowble Untill (   ) Nicolles of Southam a freend of the said butlers & a man of my L of leycesters took the matter in hand as it semith (who after my lords being at Kenelworth at Michelmas attendid my said lord to the court to Woodstok And by the way as it semith tok some occasion to move my lord in that matter And did so much therin that he (as himself confessid) procured my said lords lre to the bailief & others of Warwik The teno^r of wch lre ensuith

To my very loving freends the Bailief & maisters of the towne of Warwik

the tenor of my L of Leicesters lres on the behalf of Thomas Butler for tuythes

After my veary hartie comendacions understanding that there is some controrsy presently fallen out betwene my s^runt Thomas Butler of Budbrook and you concerning the tythes of saint Maryes parish in Warwik wch he holdeth by lease of your towne fforasmuch as he & his predecessours by vertue of the same leace have enioyed the same tythes a long tyme and the like quarrell falling out betwene his father & yor Towne about six yeres since was so taken upp by my meanes as that euer sithens he hath quietly gathered & enioyed those tythes tyll nowe of late I have thought good to signify unto youe that I can not a litle mervaile whie you shoulde nowe agayne seek to molest & troble him therfore and w^thall to request youe except he have given other cause than I think he hath to ceasse further disquieteng of him in that wch youe knowe by vertue of that leace to be his right But that he may wth quiet Enioye it as his father did before him I shall hartely thank youe if at my request youe shall so deale wth him and so doo bid you farewell from the court at Woodstok the iij^d of october 1575

      Your loving freend
       R. leycester.

wch lre was by Thomas Jenks & the said Thomas Butler brought to the abovenamyd Ric. ffisher bailief about the vth or vj^th of October who opening the same & making all the principall burgesses that woold come for his sending for privye to the same Examyned euery one of them whither they did remembr that my said lord of leycester had at any tyme before bene any meane betwene the towne & John Butler for those tiuthes To wch euery man present namely Willm hudson Richerd townsend Richerd Roo John ffisher Richerd Brooke Willm ffrekulton Thomas Powell humfrey crane John Rigeley John Dyche & John Grene who aunswerid evry man singulerly that they never herd of any meane made by the said lord of lecester for those tithes But saith John Dyche I remembr that sometyme Moryce had those tuithes wherupon it was axid him whither he knew what right moryce had to them & howe he held them to that he said he could not tell more than that he had them Than steppith upp William ffrekulton and said that he remembrith that he had heard John Butler in his lief tyme in that place chardge Mr John ffisher that if his leace were not good that he had decevid him To that said John ffisher tell all was that his speach or not w^thout more he said saith ffisher that if the woord Warwik were not in his leace than he had decevid him it is true said ffrekulton Asfor that said ffisher I confesse it is true if the woord Warwik be not in his leace it is my fault bicause I wrote it And then being as I am nowe & as I ought to be indifferent betwene the towne & him uppon his speciall desire the woord Warwik was put in togither wth thies or such like woords aptening to the church & rectory of Budbrook of all wch said the said ffisher I made the house privye at the sealing of the lease At wch tyme also said the said ffisher I tolde him that his leace was not good for other causes namely because the name of Balie was not in it And therupon requyred them that were at the sealing to remeb^r whither any such spech were wch divers that then were put confessid So debating long about that matter it was agreid by all the whole company that Butler having no right unto the things It was no reason he should have them in that maner And because his freends had bene often wth M^r bailief to have a direct aunswer to my lorde and they tarried only for the same It was agreid that an aunswer should be made in writing and sent to my lord by one of the company & not by the parties wch was done The tenor of wch ensuith

To the right honorable o^r singuler good lord therle of Leicester one of the quenes ma^{ts} most honorable privy counsaill & maister of her grace horses his most honorable lordship

the tenor of the auns-wer to the Earle of Leycester his lres

Our bounden dueties most humbly remembrid to yor most honorable lordship wee are earnestly requyred in yor honors name in hast to aunswere yor honorable lres writen on the behalf of Thomas Butler towching the tuiths of saint Maryes in Warwick which he pretendith to have by leace and to wch his ffather about six yeres past was restored by yor l. meanes to the towne Wherin as wee suppose he hath enformed yor l amisse so wee most humbly besech yor hono^r to stande (folio 135) indifferent good lorde betwene us & him wth whome for yor hono^{rs} sake & some other freendes we have borne more than of his part hathe or is like by any meanes to be requyted or desirid Towching that yor Lordship was meane to the towne for that matter at any tyme (under your l favorable correction) none of us can remembr neither hathe it bene any our opynyons that he or his father had right to any tuithes aptening to the parish of saint maryes by any lease Parte wherof (though the ffather wrongfully took & was borne wthall for a tyme (though never without chalange) was promised by him to be in value wth other things recompensid And to saie trueth the towne conceivid a great deale better hope of the fathers frendshippe than to stick w^t him in so smalle a thing especially Recompence being promised wch was not performed either by the father or the sonne And as towching the ffathers opynion of his right therunto is manifest in that about a yere before he died he was Suter to tak the same by leace & to give a rent for the same as a thing out of his leace of the tuithes of Budbrook distinct bothe by parish & rent of olde tyme reserued whiles the collelge stoode as by recordes therof playnely apereth So likewise the Sonne sithens the death of his ffather hathe made meanes & offer to give either a Rent or ffyne for the same whose Request being partly graunted & like to take effect is determyned by through his owne defaulte in not obseruing his tyme & promise And nowe seing he clameth hit as his right and trowblith yor hono^r to conceive ill of us we think him more to blame & lesse worthie (saving for yor honours sake) to have any thing at all that he holdeth of the towne ffor be it so that yor honorable lordshippe may please to stande but indifferent good lord betwene us & him that his whole leace may come in question wee doubt not but to frustrate & avoide the same wch if shall happen must be taken to be his owne follye in claimyng that wch is manifestly knowen to be no parcell of his leace Of all wch we woold have bene glad to have made playne declaracion by mouth whan yor good plesure had bene therin knowen had not the earnest labo^r of his frends procured us to write wherin we most humbly beseche yor favorable Exposicion & pardone if any thing have undutifully escapid And so most hartly besech the almighty lorde to blesse you wth all encrease of hono^r & eternall felicitie At Warwik the xvth of october 1575

Yo^r most honorable L at comaundment This lre so written upp was well likid of and presently assigned or subscribed by all present That is to say by Richerd ffisher bailief William hudson Richard Townesend Richard Roo John ffisher Richerd Brook Willm ffrekulton Thomas powell humfrey crane John Rigeley John Dyche & John Grene who theruppon debating whither it were convenient that the parties should have it or not resolved that Thomas powell being one of the company of principall burgesses having then shortly cause to goo to the court should have the carriage & deliuery therof to my lord the rather for that the same Powell knowing the state of the towne might the better resolve my lord of such questions as might rise wheruppon the lre was deliuerid to him And it was agreid that Mr Bailief should give aunswere to such as should come to him therefore That my l was aunswerid by lre wch should be wth his l wthin lesse than a sevenight

<small>orders agreid vppon for putting furth the xl^{li} given by Mr Oken</small>

This matter being so seth downe the said M^r bailief remebred to the house that at cristmas last c'ten mony was paid to his hands wch was given by M^r oken to be disposid uppon c'ten condicions to Banbury being xl^{li} wch condicions they of Banbury had not pformed nor woold as it semith[a] & so the mony lieth dead his desire is to be dischargid of that mony and that the same might be ymploid so as some comoditie might be reised to the poore Wheruppon after long debating it was agreid that the said mony should be lent out to ffoure occupiers such as might & woold sett some poore on work or relieve them in maner as the c^h given to this towne is orderid And so it was agreid that Jo. Griffyn should have x^{li} henry Roo x^{li} Oliver Brooks x^{li} & (   ) x^{li} putting in good sureties for the Repaym^t at the yeares end Thies matters determyned & John ffisher offrith twoo acompts for mony lent out by him for the towne wch was for that tyme reiectid

<small>speaches of Tho Butler and henry Nicolles</small>

the company deptid the most home to their owne busynes And some tarried at M^r bailiefs request wth him That is to say Willm hudson Richerd Townesend John ffisher Richerd Brook at M^r bailiefs house where being mery togither resortid Thomas Butler & (   ) Nicholls his freand requyring aunswer of my l of leicesters lre wch was tolde him by M^r bailief was aunswerid in writing & sent by one of their company to my lord So I supposed you wold doo (said Nicholls) that you woold not mak us privye So we thought most convenient said M^r hudson to aunswer his l "well" said Nicolls "than we will resort thither to knowe the aunswere" "Ye may so

[a] See page 148 and following.

doo" said M{r} Bailief " whan goith the messinger " said Nycolls That said the company we knowe not but the lre shalbe deliverid w{thin} a sevenight Nay said Nicolls if he have the lre alredy it may be deliured in lesse than a sevenight So he may said the company if he (folio 136) had no other busynesse But padventure he hath some busynesse by the way to lett him Well said Butler I am not well used Wherin said M{r} hudson mary saith butler I am ill used at all yo{r} hands to take away my right Youe are misused said John ffisher in dede in that you are suffred to offer the wrong you doo Nay said butler you offer me wrong but I trust I shall have right Why should not I have my tithes as well as my father had my brother Butler (said Nicolls) is many wayes condempnid & iudgid of whither worthyly or no I know not but am most sure nothing hath more harmed him than in sitting down & not aunswering his cause where tyme & oportunytie sruith & has he should but I think he will be from hensforth better advised of that fault Yea I will in dede said Butler And it shalbe well knowen And if it be not in my leace some here are not true but hath done falsely howe meane you by that said Jo. ffisher & by whom speak youe be playne yf you speak & charg me as belick you do bicause I wrote the leace speak out & chardge me as you may & if you goo any further may happ you shall here of it Yea said Butler so you said that if I had come to gither tithes I should not go away did I sayd ffisher tell yo{r} Autor orells &c By my trouth said nicolls it is strainge that you stand w{th} him in that w{ch} you knowe to be his right & w{ch} his father & he had ever quietly Nay said the company his father nor he never had it quietly Sometyme the half was taken from them & sometyme a quarter & alwayes some was w{th}olden Yee said M{r} hudson one yere before John Butler dyed I paid him no tithe for the medow that I have nor have not done this therfore he hath not enioyd quietly John Butler said Tho. butler It might be semed to have callid him w{t} a better name The name said the company was honest & such as an honest man might be content w{th} & so was he whiles he lived content to be callid John Butler & we wish that there were such an other Tho. butler as he was a John butler Well said he if he had lived you wold not have offred him this wrong nor I will not suffre yt Yea may do as please you said the company doing honestly & well &

that wee woold be glad to see in you You are glad saith butler to seek myne undoing & to offer me wrong but I will not tak it as I have done Well said Nycolls yf youe have aledy writen yo' aunswer to my lord I wish it will be there shortly and there I doubt not but we shall know the same though wee may not here wch is small curtesye and I did think that uppon my lords lre you woold not have gone further in trowbling my brother Butler who if there be no remedy must use sute wch is not his case Yea saith butler I will spend a good deale but I will have my right So may you said one of the company And wthall beware in saying for that is not yo' right you bring yo' whole leace in question of onthrowing Nay as for that said he I fere not though I think you will do asmuch as you can but if I loose that I know howe to get an other as good as that Ye are the better at ease said the company Than said Mr Brookes Mr Nycolls M^r bailief & o^r company have considered of my lords lre and the rather at yor & yor freends request aunswerid the same so as we trust his L wilbe therwth satisfyed and I think it were no great matter if you did understand it but bicause it pleasid my lord to write unto us wee thought it o^r duety likewise to aunswer his lordshipp as if you had brought us the message by mouth we woold have aunswered you by mouth You have done well said Nicolls come brother butler let us begonne Well said butler it is no matter but I trust not to lose it so for I trust it will fall out to belong to S^t pulcres & you have no title to it at all Well said John fisher Mr Butler the towne is greatly beholden to such a neighbour & you are worthy to have any pleasure may be showid for yor good opynion & well wishing them And so the said Butler & Nicolls deptid

Not long after the lre afore remembrid was by Mr Tho. Powell carried to the court where having no convenient leasure to speak w^t the said Earle of leycester the said powell left the lre wth one Ambrose of my l chambr to be delivered to his L assone as convenient tyme might serve wch was afterward done as it semith though for a good space after nothing was further done in that matter But afterward in hillary terme following or there abouts Thoms Butler gave out some reaport that the said Earle of leicester was not well pleasid wth

the bailief of Warwik & his bretherne bicause they woold not annswer his l'res Wherof John ffisher being at London hering demaunded of the said Ambrose whither any such lre was delivred by Mr powell to him to be deliverid to my lord and whither my said lord had it or not wth the said Ambrose confessid that he had long sithens delivered the same to my said lorde And that he knewe where the same lre yet is And in that hillary terme or in the vacacion following Thomas Butler lieng at london & in the same house & Inne where Jo. ffisher lay and where they were often at table & meat togither The said Thomas Butler openid his case to some his learned counsill as it (folio 137) may seeme wheruppon he procured out proces aswell against the said ffisher as divers others that had groundes about the ghospell closse supposing them to have put him out of his fee wherof notwthstonding the said Butler woold say nothing to the said ffisher but dissemblid it at london But after whitsontide being at home he made Thomas Wagstaff & other his freends privye of it Yet did not deliver his proces to the Sheriff wherfore the matter lay on slepe Until midsomer even And than Thomas wagstaff came to John ffisher and saith that his brother Butler had sent him to knowe whither Mr Bailief of Warwik & the rest wold suffer him to enioye the tuithes quietly Orells whither they woold be content that Mr Anderson might deside the matter betwene them at the next Assises Orells whither they woold annswer the said Butler by lawe To this John ffisher made annswer to Tho. Wagstaf That he being but one of the company could not wthont the advise of the Bailief & others make any direct annswere but as towching he marvalid that Mr Butler woold so complayne of them and so prosecute to my lorde of leicester informing him of an untrueth in saing that my l had ones taken upp that matter betwene the towne and his father wch being utterly untrue was not honestly done of him to urge my lord to write so wherby he desrueth litle favo^r at the townes hands so after many speches on both sides the said wagstaff & ffisher for that tyme deptid uppon promise made by Jo. ffisher

Tho. Butler prosecutith proces But servith them not

Thomas Wagstaf travellith for Thomas Butler

Communycacion betwene fisher & Wagstaf

Thomas Wagstaf moveth Mr Bailif for Butler

Mr Bailif & the principall Burgesses confer of that matter determyn the answer

that he wold move Mr Bailief & the company for aunswer against that day sevenight But in the meane tyme the said Th. Wagstaff went to the Bailief than Mr Rigeley and as it may seme used the same or very like speche that he had wt ffisher to Mr Bailief who desired tyme to speak wth the company and theruppon he woold give him a resonable aunswer And theruppon the said Mr Bailief not long after had a meting wt the rest his bretherne in the counsell house at the crosse on wensday the xxvjth of June 1576 where was therfore Mr Ridgeley Bailief Willm huddison John ffisher Willm ffrekulton Thomas Powell Thomas Jenks humfrey crane John Grene & John Dyche where uppon opening of the matter at lardge by Mr Bailief It was agreid That aunswer should be made to Thomas Butlers demand That he may procede by lawe in any accion that he hath or may have against any persones of the towne of Warwik for or towching the tuithes of saint mary parishe Warwik And that he may use any proces against them at his plesure & discrecion and that they desire that title or triall be made by lawe rather than any other way wherunto they are content to aunswer him as apteynith And at that tyme other things comyng to remembrance It was agreid by the company present that they and the rest of the principall Burgesses should be their on the tuesday following aswell for the taking & finishing of Mr humfrey crane his three Acompts for his Burges & Bailiefs offices wc to that day could not be agreid unto by the said Mr crane & and the rest stonding uppon divers dispisions & impfections which nowe in thend were thought to be concludid as also to take order howe the poore of the towne may be relivid wth stocks acording to the puision of the last statute(a) as also howe & what euery constable did wthin evry ward of the same towne towards the paymt of the task or x wherin many complained themselfes to be wronged And also to consider whither it wold be convenient for the towne to have the stock of the Shire and so to kepe the Roges

---

(a) 14 Eliz. c. 5, by which statute power was given to justices to levy a general assessment, and this was continued for the Statute 43 Eliz. c 2. "The Act for the Relief of the Poor" re-enacted former provisions. The term stocks included not only money for those not able to work, but also stocks of flax, hemp, &c., to supply materials for the purpose of setting those to work who were able.

to woork that shall be taken in the Shire of all w^c no determinacion was putly taken partly bicause the tyme was spent And partly bicause a nombr of the principall Burgesses being absent should be warned to be their that tuesday following w^c was agreid unto than But on the morrowe after being saint Peter's Even Willm Bond clerk and lately that is to say before Easter before apointid viker of Budbrook after the death of Sr George ffekenton late viker there made humble sute to Mr Bailief & the more part of the principall Burgesses That it might please them to mak him a new presentacion of that vikaredge which he desired ffor that he having bene wth M^r wilson deane of Warwik for his institucion & induccion could not have the same uppon the former presentacion bicause the same was made to the late Bishop of Wo^rceto^r who was ded and therby the Jurisdiccion for the tyme of vacacion in the Archbishop of canterbury the said former presentacion was void and therfore besought a newe to be made in such forme as he had brought from worceto^r by the advise of the officers there wheruppon and the rather uppon the good comendacion of the ptye & his learning recomendid by the said Mr Wilson It was agreid that a newe presentacion should be made in forme as hereafter shall followe But bicause the matter ymportid hast (as the said Bond affirmed) it was advised to the said Bond that he should earnestly labo^r the company to mete for the sealing of the said psentacion wherin he applied him so as procured divers to come into the church togither the next morning by sixe of the clock and such as for other causes could not come he pcured the sending of all their keys saving of Ric. Brooks who than was at london so as evry mans consent was there saving the said Brooks And there was present the next daye being saint Peters day to seale that & the other devise thies psones namely John Ridgeley Balief Willm huddison Richerd ffisher Richerd Townesend John ffisher Thomas powell and Thomas Jenkes came into the church & gave his consent but could not tary from Southam faire So the said company procedid and sealid the same presentacien and w^thall a lre of Atto^rney made to John ffisher to prosecute such sutes as the towne should have for any cause towching their

Request of a newe presentacion to be made of the vicarege of Budbrook

grauntid

sealid

A lre of atturney made to Jo fisher to Comense sutes for the towne lands Rectoryes or hereditam^ts against any persones The tenour wherof shall herafter followe wch lre of Atto^rney was made to the said flisher of purpose to mete wth the fraudulent practizes & extremyties of others as Ric. brokes & Tho. Butler and thies twoo things being thus sealid the said company came down^a to service in the said St Mary church where John Grene who before had sent his key being come the said lre of Atto^rney was showid unto him who consentid to all that had bene done and thought it a very necessary devise allowing very well of the same after he had red it over

the taking of humfrey (folio 138) Thies things thus dispachid and the said tuesdaye come
Cranes accomptes The said bailief and the principall Burgesses namely John Rydgeley Bailif Willm huddison John flisher Thomas powell Thomas Jenks John Grene John Dyche being assemblid in their house at the crosse Thither cometh humfrey crane wth such acquitance billes & papers w^t him to declare his accompts for his collections of the Burgesse chardge and the Baliefs office wch being showid and the Audito^r of this borough casting the same by his confession & such chardg as he could give him The said humfrey crane felle in debt much more than he expectid as he said But yet not so much as afterward uppon proof it fell out to be for uppon inquisicion made the said humfrey crane was found to have recevid divers somes of mony to the use of the borough more than he had sett downe part wherof was for picage^b & stallage And part for Bloodshed & frayes & such casualties and part of occupacions and companyes for composicion mony And part for tuith corne taken out of Lynnen field by him as tuith due to saint mary church in Warwik the value of all which forgotten amountid to cx^s or therabouts

The Auditor is to charge & surcharge Accomptants w^t all he can
as may apeare by his acompt wherw^th he was surchargid and found himself grevid And chiefly complained that he was hardly delt wth being chardgid wth all thextracts which grewe to xxxviij^li x^s viij^d wherof he said he had levyed but vij^li or therabouts and therfore mislikid wth the Audito^r for chardging him w^t the

---

(a) From this remark that the Corporation "came down" into the Church, it would appear that they held their meetings in the Sextry or long room over the Vestry.

(b) Money paid at fairs for breaking ground for booths.

whole wch the said Auditor must of duety doo and leave the house to order the abatem^t as they please So in the end the house was content to dischardge the said humfrey crane of xxvj^{li} chardgid upon xxvj poore men for keping alehouses without licens & so streightid unto him bicause he offirmed he could not levye it And yet the said humfrey crane being not satisfied but still complaining obtayned of the house to be respitid & allowid all the rest of the streits saving only that he before had confessid albeit he could shewe no cause whie the same could not be levied Wherof yet he is dischardgid And so his debt besides came to xiij^{li} xix^s ix^d wch he paid to Mr Rigeley Bailief

Thomas Hankinson als Jenkes obteyned his bill of debt After this Thomas Jenks was granted a release of his debt on account of his having laid out money in repairing the great bridge[a] & on condition that he should recover certain monies due from Robert Phillips

THE GRANT OF THE EASTGATE, ST. PETER'S CHAPEL AND THE SHIRE HALL TO THE CORPORATION.

the obteynyng of the lordes dedes for the Shire halle crosse taverne & saynt peters chapell (folio 139) In the meane tyme whiles thes things were in doing It hapned That the said lordes the Earles of Warr. & leycester w^t other noble men cam to Kenelworth where being John ffisher contynewith an olde sute for the said towne to the said Earles to confirme by their seales & dedes those things they had before long sithens promised to the towne which was the assurance of the shirehall in Warwik the crosse taverne & St Peters chappell w^t thap^rtens and therin used Sir John hubondes frendshipp in furthering the said Sute to the said lordes who being therin earnestly solicitid It stood w^t their good plesures to parforme their former graunts And theruppon the said ffisher left the dede therof w^t Willm Edmonds who shoulde put Sr John hubond in mynde to get the said lordes handes & seales to the said dede in the absence of the said ffisher whose infirmytie was then such

(a) The bridge over the Avon, now in ruins.

as not hable to give his attendance by nightly watches as he was wont But that notw^tstonding the said dede woold not be gott sealid untill the said ffisher were present the cause certen is unknowen but as he doth ymagyne it was deferrid to thend that both it should be thought the matter was hard to be gotten & therby Sr John hubond worthie more thanks in procuring the same And also that they of the towne should think themselfs more bound And therfore the said ffisher was on Sonday the viijth daie of Aprill 1576 sent for in great hast to Kenelworth to knowe the lordes pleasures therin whither comyng the said ffisher going

Sir Jo hubonde's speche to fisher   towards the hall uppon the steares stoode S^r Jo. hubond who espieng the said ffisher comyng up the hill w^t a staff wekely said alowde John ffisher my lordes of Warwik & leycester are pleased to seal the book for Warwik although they think that the towne is not wo'thie therof for they

fishers answer   have bene enformed somewhat grevously against them I am veary sorrye said ffisher to here that ther Lordships should be so informed and wold be more sorrye their lordships should have such causes as I trust they have not knowing that for the better sort there is not a man but wold most willingly doo their dueties in that they might so doo their lordships any plesure or service as if there be of the worse sort any lewde that have misused themselves in any sort towards them is to be & shalbe reformed & yet of their hono^{rs} not to be regarded Well said Sr John hubond nowe youe are come we will goo to my lord of Warwik who is in his chamb^r And

Circumstances   so the said Sr John hubond and John ffisher went togither into therle of Warwiks lodging Where the said Earle being acompanyed wth Sir ffulk Grevile Sir Thomas Tresham & Sir Willm catesbye the said Sr John hubond entring the chamber of the said Earle said my good lord Warwik I have brought you a lame fellowe to see yor lordshippe wch doone the said ffisher doying his duety to the said Earle The said Sir John hubond said John ffisher my lord of Warwik is contentid to parforme the sute to the towne of Warwik hoping that youe will herafter showe yor selfs more duetifully towards him for his lordship hath bene enformed that youe are forgetfull both of duety & good neighborhood To which said ffisher the whole towne think themselfs duetifully bound to yor

honor as occasioned by yor honorable goodnes towards them many ways to be not only at yor honors comandmt but also to pray for yor honors prosperytie for ever and wth willing myndes to shewe their goode harts towards you or any of yors in any way or wt any thing they have I woold they were so said my lord but by gods will I know there be a sort of cullyons & yet some honest men I knowe But I desire nothing that is there but for my mony and asmuch as eury other man will give but it is no matter I humbly beseche yor honor said ffisher change yt opinion and if any have otherwise used themselfs than they ought it may please yor honor to ympute it to lack of understanding rather than any wilfulnes to offend yor lordshipp Well said Sr John hubond I dare assure yor lordshipp that whatsoer is past They will hereafter shewe themselfes more dutifull to yor honor I besech yor honor said ffisher so to think of us and I dare promise both for myself and all the better sort it shalbe so ffor theself said the Earle John I knowe well enough and I woold wish the rest were as well myndid as theself &c And therwth Sir John hubond offring the dede to the said Earle the said ffisher making as manerly curtesey as he could Said the whole towne of Warwik understanding of yor honorable good favor towards them in bestowing uppon them the Shire hall & such other things as pleasid yor honor & or good l of leicester to graunt them do offer by me their simple messinger their most dutifull & bounden thanks for yor honorable good disposicion towards them wherwth their harts wholly wt daily prayers for yor good prospity wth thincrease of all honor the chief good they can wch wth the rest to the uttermost of their small powers I doo assure unto yor honorable Lordship I woold they did said my lord And then calling for pen & Ink he assignid the said dede in the presence of the gentlemen beforesaid and calling also for (   ) Roberts his servant willid him to put his seale therunto which was presently done

the Earle of Warwik's speche to fisher

fisher

Sr Jo. hubond

fisher

my L of W

fisher

the dede sealid & signed by the Earle of Warwik

224   THE BLACK BOOK OF WARWICK.

the copy of the dede from the lordes of Warwik & Leycester to the towne

see the other booke 211 a

(folio 140) Omnibus xxi fidelibus ad quos presentes lre puenint Ambrosius comes Warwic Baro lisley prenobilis ordinis garterii miles Magister ordinacionū Domine regine ac unus a privato consilio suo Et Robertus comes Leicestr Baro de Denbigh utriusq ordinis garterii & sancti Michis miles Magister Equor eiusd dn̄e Regine aliusq eiusdem Dn̄e Regine consiliarius Salutem in dn̄o Noueritis nos prefatos comites pro bono zelo quem erga rempublicam Burgi warwic in com Warr gerim puberumq eiusdem Burgi in bonis lris salubrisq dogmatibq educacoēm ac meliorem execucioem legum & statutor huius Regni Anglie infra eundem burgum exequend tradidisse concessisse & confirmasse et hoc p̄nti scripto nro pro nobis et heredibus nris tradere concedere et confirmare Ballino et Burgensibus dc̄i Burgi Warwic in com Warr. totū illud Edificiū siue capellam nup nuncupat siue cognit p. nomen capelle sancti Petri infra Burgum p̄dc̄u fun lat situat desup quandam portam voc le Estgate Burgi p̄ed ac murum situat iuxta eandem capellam unacum vasta terr. fundo & solo inter predic̄am capellam & murū et tenementū modo in tenura Margarete Haley vidue Ac totam illam Aulam siue domu nup cognit p. nomen de le Stuards place et modo voc le Shirehall in Warwic p̄edc̄a unacu vasto & gardino eidem domui siue Aule adiacen & p̄tn Aceciam totam illam domu siue tenementū voc seu cognit p.

(a) This refers to another minute book which reaches from 1610 to 1662: on the page referred to is the following:—

LANDS CONVEYED TO THE BAYLIVE AND BURGESSES TO THEIR OWNE USE

Impris one graunt dated 22ᵗ May Anno xlijᵒ Eliz. nup. Rne from Willm Spicer gent to the said Baylive and Burgesses of all that mesuage or Tent called the Crosse house & of all that other mesuage wᶜʰ thapputennis called the Shire hall wᵗʰ the garden & peece of Land to the said mesuage adiecent and all that Chappell called Sᵗ Peters Chappell wᵗʰ a piece of wast grounde conteyning by estimacion one Rode and alsoe that other peell of waste grounde where nowe or late are situate the Comon Butts conteyning by estimacion one Rode and which pmises were first graunted by the sd late Queene to the said Baylive & Burgesses for xl yeares and afterwards were graunted in fee to Richard Dawes & Thomas Wagstaffe gent & by them bargained & solde to the said William Spicer gent & his heires & by him graunted and bargained to the said Baylive & Burgesses and their Successors for ever as by the said graunt to them made bearing date as a feofmt made betweene the said William Spicer of thone pte and the said Baylive & Burgesses of thother pte maye appeare

nomen de le crosse taverne[a] in Warwic pred cū omibz et singlis suis mūribus edificiis structuris cellariis Solariis easiamen & ptinen mīusis Habend tenend & gaudend predict capellam murum vastum & predcū domū siue Aulam voc le Shirehall vel Stuards place ac predict vastum & gardīnū adiacen necnon domū siue tenemen vocāt crosse taverne cellar solar & cetera premissa cū omibz & singlīs suis ptinen prefāt Balliuo et Burgen et Succesoribz suis ad opus & usum predict̄ inppm. Ita tamen qd predc̄i Ball et Burgenses et Successores sui pmittent Iustic predc̄e dn̄e Regine heredum et Successorū suor tam ad pacem in com. warr conservand assigs qm alios Justic itinerantes & Iustic ad Assi. ac alios Justic predc̄e domine Regine heredū & Successor suor de tempore in tempus quando necesse fuerit & es oportunū videbitur ad libitum suū in eandem Aulam siue domū vocat le Shirehall licite & quiete intrare et convenire Ac Sessiones suas tam ad Assiss capiend q̄m gaolem de prisonibz in eo existen deliberaud quameciam alias Sessiones suas tam p. pace conseruand qm pro bono regimne & gubernacōe ppti com. predc̄i ibidem tenere ac alia sua negocia circa execūco legum et statutōr huius regni Anglie secundū tenorem comissionū suarn expediend & exequend talibus eisdem et consimilibus modo & forma prout ante hec tempora usi fuerint & consueuerint Sciatis insup qd nos prefāt comites nominauimus constituimus et in locis n̄ris posūm ac p. pntes nominamus ordinamus et in loco n̄ro ponimus dilectos & fideles n̄ros Johem Hubond militem et Willum Edmondes genōsm n̄ros veros & indubitāt Attorn et eor alterum n̄rm verum et indubitāt Attorn Dantes & conceden prefāt Attorn n̄ris et eor alteri comunitim & diuisim potestatem facultatem et auctoritatem ad intrand comunitim aut diuisim p. nobis & nominibus n̄ris in predc̄am capellam Aulam domos & cetā premissa aut eor aliquam parcellam ac seisinam inde capiend Et post hm̄oi seisinam sic inde capt̄ & habit̄ dando plenm et pacificam possessionem et seisinam omn̄u & singlōr pmissōr prefatis Balliuo et Burgensibus aut suo in hac parte

(a) As the Cross stood opposite to the present Court House we may conclude that the Cross Tavern was close by, and as it is mentioned in conjunction with the Steward's Place or Shire Hall, we may also conclude that the latter occupied the site of the present Court House. Some subsequent meetings are described as being held at the Court House, near the Cross. The building now called the Shire or County Hall is in Northgate Street.

P

Attornt siue Attorn suis de nobis & p. nobis ac noibz nris comunitim aut diuisim tradere & deliberare p. presentes Ratii & gratum hentes et habituri totum & quidquid dci Attorn nri seu eor alter facient aut faciet in premiss adeo plene libere et integre ac in tam amplis modo et forma prout nos ipi faceremus si presentes ibm essemus In cuius rei testimonu huic presente charte nre sigilla nra apponi fecimus Dat octavo die Aprilis anno regni Domine Elizabethe Dei gra Anglie ffranc & hibnie Regine fidei defensoris &c Decimo octavo 1576*

W^{ch} dede so made signed & sealid at Kenelworth as aforesaid was delivered to the handes of William Edmonds srunt to the said Earl of Leicestr & one of the Attorneys for delivery of the possesion who kept the same dede in his hands for a tyme after untill he might spare a convenient leasure to execute the same In wch meane tyme the said Bailief & Burgesses understonding the said dede to be so sealid & left w^t the said Willm Edmonds made lre of Attorney under their comon seale to John ffisher giveng him auctoritie to receve season & possession of the things before remembrd to the use of them the said Bailief and Burgesses

posesion delivered by W. Edmondes   Wheruppon & by vertue of the dedes before remembrid the said Willm Edmonds Comyng to Warwik aforesaid the xviijth day of June then next following did deliver possession of the pmisses of the said dede to the said John ffisher to the use of the said Borough[a] in the presence of many psones as by the Indorcemt of the said dedes may appere

---

* See Appendix b.

(a) The East gate and St Peter's Chapel are now in the possession of the trustees of Henry VIIIth's estate. At the present time the chapel and premises adjoining are the dwelling of the Serjeant-at-Mace

THE MYTON [a] RIOTS

the trowbles betwene Ric. Brook and the towne for Myton tithes

(folio 141) In this meane tyme contencion grewe betwene Richard Brookes one of the principall Burgesses of this borough and one John Raye of the same Borough for & about the leaces of the tuithes of Muyton belonging to the said Borough of w{ch} tuithes one John Ray ffather of this John Ray had gotten severall leaces one from the colledge of Warwik whiles it stoode an other or twoo from the corporacion of this borough sithens it was incorporated[b] w{ch} leaces this John Ray nowe living having by the gift of his said father did mortgage to the said brook as apereth by the pleadings betwene the said Ray & Brook in the court of Request where the said Raye had complaned him of thextreme & fraudulent dealing of the said Brookes by supplicacion to the quenes ma{ty} who comitting the examynacion & ordering of the cause to the Maisters of her requests the said maisters held plea therof as may appeare by a decree set downe wherein is shewed the bill of complaint the aunswer of Brookes the replicas of Ray & rejoinder of Brookes & so their ioyning Issue wherupon commission awardid & many witnesses examyned w{ch} as may seme provid so much for the said Ray that the said maisters gave furth their decree awarding therby that Brookes should redeliver to Ray all such writings leaces & bonds as he had of Ray and pay to the said Raye iiij{xx}{li} for the corne & hey of the said tuithes w{ch} the said brookes had taken the two yeres before the decree and that he should deliver quiet possession therof to the said Raye. and that Ray should pay to the said Brookes so much mony as by covennt or specialty was due to Brookes which decree being pronouncid & set furth in writing under the hands of the Maisters of Request was lightly estemid of

(a) Myton is a hamlet in the Parish of St Nicholas, Warwick, and lies midway between Warwick and Leamington. In the time of Elizabeth the only approach to it from Warwick was by way of the old bridge over the river, close to the Castle; at the present time the road to it is over the Castle Bridge, which was erected in the year 1790, the old one having become somewhat decayed.

(b) The first Charter of Incorporation is dated 5th May, 1546. Among the entries of the possessions of St. Mary's in Domesday Book there is the following:—of Turchill the Church of S{t}. Mary in Warwick holds 1 hide in Moitone. Henry VIII{'s} Trustees the representatives of the Dean and Chapter and the old Corporation still possess about 100 acres of land at Myton.

Brookes who woold not be orderyd by the said decree nor pforme any part therof although he was comandid so to do by Iniuncions of the said court Wheruppon attachm' was awardid against the said Brookes who by shiftes wth Sherif sat the said attachm' and woold neither obey decree or other proces but devised a fyne feate to disappoint the same And by reson of a debt wch the said Brookes did owe to the quene in the Excheqnyre he procured a writ of privilege out of the said Exchequier not only to drawe his body thither but also to bring the cause thither wherw^th the Maisters of Request greatly misliking and finding his practizes to tend chiefly to the derogating of their court & auctorytie prosecutid the cause before them And sent out comission by proclamacion of Rebellion against the said Brookes for his said contempts warraunting the same by vertue & force of the pryvie Seale The teno^r wherof ensuith.

the copye of the comission of Rebellion againste Brookes

Elizabeth by the grace of God Quene of Englond ffraunce & Irelond Defender of the faith &c To o^r trustie & welbelovid the Sheriff of o^r county of Warwik And to o^r Bailief of o^r towne of Warwik greting. We will & comaund youe & either of you That in all places w^thin your Jurisdiccions & libties aswell within ffranchises & libties as without whear by yor discreccons shalbe thought most expedient & behovefull youe doo make open & solempne proclamacion in forme following. fforasmuch as the quenes ma^ti o^r most graciouse sovereigne ladie hath heretofore by her hieghnes counsell of her honorable court of Requestes not only made & taken a certen order & decree in a matter brought before her ma^ties said counsell in her hieghnes said court betwene her Subiect John Ray plaintif against Richard Brooke Defendant but also awardid furth of the same court her ma^ties spiall lres of Iniuncion under her hieghnes privie seale uppon the penaltie of a great some of monye for the due parformance of the said decree, the which decree & Iniuncion the said Brook hath in great contempt of her maiestie & her said counsell contempned & disobeide, wheruppon an Attachment was likewise awardid to the Sheriff of this her hieghnes Countie of Warwik to attach the bodie of the said Brook for his said contempt The which he also most like a Rebel & disobedient

Subiect hath comtempned & disobeid to the great & manifest contempt of her hieghnes said counsell & commandments, and to the evill & perillous example of others her loving & obedient subiectes. Wherfore our said souereigne Ladie takith & reputith him as a Rebelle & disobedient Subiect. And therfore willith & straightly chargith all & every her loving & obedient Subiects so to accept repute & take him. And that no man herafter ayd or assist him wth meat drynk monye or Lodging untill such tyme as he have fully obeid & submittid himself unto our said sovereigne Ladie her hieghnes counsell & comaundents And over this that every man doo endevo^r himself by force & vertue of this proclamacion to attache & put under arrest & sure warde the bodie of the said Richerd Brooke whersoever he may be founde ither w^thin ffranchises & libties or without Any ffranchise libertie or privelege whatsoever to the contry herof in any wise notw^tstonding, So to remayne without baile or mainprise untill such tyme as our said souereigne Ladie being c^rtified therof have signified her hieghnes pleasor what shalbe further doone for his due ponishm^t in this behalf And God save the Quene. And our further pleaser is & also wee straitly chardge & comaund youe that by like warraunt & auctorytie herof Yee o^r said Sheriff & balief and either of you doo not only arrest apprehend & attache the bodie of the said Brooke wheresoer ye may finde him within yor severall liberties, But also in like maner ye apprehend attach & arrest the bodies of every such other person & psones whatsoever as either of you shall finde or have sufficient notice that shall contrary to the good meanyng of the said decree made betwene the said parties in this cause bearing date the xviij^th daie of ffebruary last past in any sorte or maner interrupt molest or trowble the quiet possession or occupacion of the said (folio 142) John Ray his Executors administrators or assignes of & in Burgage or Tenem^t situate in o^r towne of Warwik or of & in all & singler the tuithes of corne & heye in the fieldes of Myton in the parish of Saint Nicolas in our said countie of Warwik And the bodie or bodies of every such offenders or offender so being by you attached or apprehendid after his or their apprehension to ymprisone and them safely to deteyne & kepe in prison and to signifie unto us & o^r said counsell what his or their severall offence or offences shalbe herin, to thintent we by the advice of our counsell may tak such further order for his or their further ponishment as the qualitie of the said offence shall merit And that from tyme to tyme youe & either of youe contynewe thexecution herof towching the preservacion of his possession untill such tyme as youe shall receve comaundem^t to the contrary from us & our said counsell And faile ye not herof as youe & either of you doo tender o^r pleasure the advancement of Justice and will answer for the contrary at yor further perilles. Geven under o^r privie seale at our mano^r of Grenewich the vij^th daie of July in the xvij^th yere of our reigne. This Comission under the privie seale was brought by William Wo^rceto^r of Bilton brother in lawe to the said John Ray and by Robart Sheldon his freends and delivered to John Ridgeley Bailief of Warwik before divers witnesses on tuesdaie the xvij^th of Julie 1576 wth speciall instigacion & request presently to publishe & pclame the same proclamacion. Wherin the said Bailief was urged so farre & so much that the proclamacion as before was that tuesdaye being market day about one of the clock in the after none publisshid & at the hiegh crosse proclamed though in the presence of fewe persones which was doone in respect that the said Brookes was one of the company of principall Burgesses for otherwise he had deservid litle consideracion being a man very trowblous deceiptfull & subtill seking to supplant the honest & welmeaning to the private pfitng of himself & such as he favored The condicions of wch brooks being so well or ill knowen to many woold occupy a very great volume in writing which this writer thinkith convenient to let passe lest fraudulent practizes plainly set furth might be an other tyme provid by such of like disposicion to the hurt of many The proclamacion Red & his case lamentid for that a man of so honest calling should so notoriously be openid to the multitude It fell out so as the wief of the said Brooks having knowleig of all that was done being a woman & mete wief for such a husbond & mynding to shew her audacitie & corage procured divers to goo into the fields not only to disavow the order before taken & the dispossessing of Raye But also to possesse & give title to an other one Thomas Oldnall her owne sonne who by secret devises betwene his father in lawe Brooks

Margin notes: delyvery of the Comision to Jo. Rigeley Bailif of Warwik; thexecucion of the Comision; Broke his wief procurith persons to disobey the comission

& him had an assignement or conveyance made of the said tuithes from Brookes uppon a secret & subtill collusn to disapoint the order of the court And this oldnall being at that tyme wt his mr Sr John hubond at the Court or rather coming from thens had by his mothers apointment one James Richerdson a man of very lewde behavior as his deputy & officer to gather the hey then in hand wt

Ray Complanith being understood by Raye & his ffreends viz William Worcetor & Robart Sheldon who for Ray had appointid one Richerd Pardy to gather the said tuithes The said Willm Worcetor & Robart Sheldon togither wt the said Ray complanid to Mr Bailif & signified that the said Richardson was in the field gathering of the tuith hey and that he had reportid he did it for Brookes

Richerson sent for Wheruppon that tuesday night Mr Bailief sent for the said Richerdson who was found gathering tuith hey as had bene before reportid, and by the constable of that ward named John hopkins by the comaundmt of Mr Bailief brought before him the said Mr Bailief & John flisher Steward of the said Borough by whom it was tolde to the said Richerdson how daungerosly he had done to medle in that matter wherin the quenes maty by her counsell of the court of Requests had set an order wch he had transgressed & therfore deservid

Richerdsons answere submission & promise ponishmt acordingly wch if it should be given him were & woold be to towch him much To that the said Richerdson aunswerid that he was comaundid by his Mr Maister brookes to kepe his possession and that he woold do so farre as he might and as for any such order or pclamacion openyd or spoken of by Mr bailief he said he knew not of. Than said Mr Bailief you shall know & see it and therwith shewid him the comission wch than was red in Mr Bailief his house before they came to the Seward who stonding at the crosse there came to him the said Mr Bailief and told him what had bene done Wherupon Richerdson also being come they went home to the house of the said Steward where the whole matter & circumstancs on both sides openyd The said Richardson seming to be sorry that he had gone so farre desired favor pmissing that he woold not medle any more in that matter And so in hope of his reconciliacion was remittid to libty for that tyme The next day being wensday & the xviijth of July The said Richerdson acompanyed wth one Richerd

Richerson & Ri Brookes doo on the morowe let the possession of Raye	Brooks a tanner & a very meet companyon for him encoraged & set on by the malicious Mary Brookes the wief of the first Ric that trowbleth all men like them selves having nothing to lose but their carcasses apt to no good woork like desperate doers went into the fields of myton to gather (folio 143) the tuithe hey and to kepe
Thomas Oldenall his title first spred	possession as they might for oldnall which being percevid by the other side and complaint therof made & earnest request &
Rayes servants complayn	chardge instigatid to the said Bailief for thexecucion of his comission The said Mr Bailief went himself accompanyed wt other constables & officers into the fields where he found the
Mr Bailifs first going into the fielde	said Richerdson and Brooks Tanner keping possession of such tuith hey as was set furth which Richardson & Brookes were apointid in warlik & riotous maner to defend themselves And
Richerdson Ri Brookes tanner Tho. Brokes Mary Brokes	wth them there was the forsaid Mary wief of the said Brookes and Thoms Brooks her husbonds brother & others quarelling about the matter but using no force more than that Mary Brookes satte & stood uppon part of the hey as one shewing her countenance and great woords for thinconagence of the others wch being provid to the said Mr
Mr Baliffs speche	Bailief he said to Richerdson & the other. What meanith this yor outrageous behavior doo you not knowe how greatly ye offend, and had you not warning yesterday, that ye should not medle wt this matter and howe cometh it to passe that ye will still psever in thes outrages to the contempt of her mats expresse comaundmts & proces Ye shall surely smart for it, and get you awaye and suffer Ray to enioy his owne quietly & such other as he hath apointid
there Answer	for that purpose. To wch it was aunswerid generally by all aswell the said Brooks wief as others that he should have nothing to doo there. And that was then doone was done on the behalf & in the tytle of Thomas Oldnall in whose possession & right they were there and that they woold kepe & mayntene, and therwithall as this writer was informed used many other great woords against aswell the bailief as the court from whence the proces came, but bicause this writer heard them not he reportith them not. In thend Mr Bailief

peeving that his spech did not greatly prevaile but rather that the outrage of the
other & the company grewe greater, he tooke out of a boxe the
comission under seale And there in the field openly in the sight
of the said mary Brookes & all the rest openly red the said comission &
proclamacion which notwithstonding they lightly regardid & contynewed their
force offering to put away the srunt of the said John Raye from woorking &
making of the said haye wch the said Bailief seing comaundid them to depte &
suffer the said Rayes srunt to doo his busines wch they woold not doo And
therfore the said Mr Bailief comaundid such constables & assistants as he then
had there to apprehend the said Richerdson & Brookes Tanner
and to bring them wth him and so they did upp into the towne
where the said Bailief and the Stuard examining the said Brookes & Richerdson
what auctorytie or warrant they had for their doings in that matter They
aunswerid that they had bene there in the defence of Thoms Oldnall his
possession wherin they woold stand & maynteyne the same to the uttermost of
their power And that they were sure that they that had apointid them there
woold see them defendid and fetch them out of prison if they should be
ymprisoned. Wheruppon a mittimus was made and the said Brookes Tanner &
Richerdson comyttid whout Baile or maynprise. This so doone & understood to
Brookes & his freends The first Richerd Brookes the causer of
all this came home that night, and having peured a lre from M^r
Sekford one of the Maisters of Request for sparing of execucion of the said
comission so farr only as towching the taking of his Bodie, he shewed himself at
home in his owne house very valiant as one that had not only conquered but also
brought great warraunt bothe for himself & his in this matter
ou^rthrew of the proces & reproch of the officers & offices And
then sent woord upp to the Bailief that nowe he was come home if he woold any
thing wth him, and yet kept the lre wth himself wth wch message being psumptuosly
done the Bailief was somewhat trowblid and came to the Stuard & some other of
his assistants to knowe what was best to be doone wherupon it
was thought mete to stay that night and to call the rest of the company togither

the Comission red in the field

Richerdson Brokes taken & commited

Ri. Brook his comyng from London

Brokes mesage done to the Balif

advise of the asistants

the next morning and so to be further advised wch was done acordingly. And so the next morning being thursday the said Bailief sending for vj or vij of his company conferring of this matter in the end thought it good to send one or twoo of the same company to the said Brookes bothe to give him knowleidge what outrage had bene comittid and what pces & order was sent out against him and to advise him to behave himself so as both the quenes peace may be kept & himself reconsilid And for this p'pose it was thought good that John Grene one of the principall burgesses should goo to the said brooks and wth all to requyre that if he had any dischardge for that matter that he woold let it be knowen, and after the said John Grene was William ffrekulton sent to assist him (folio 144) who comyng to the house of Brookes found him at home and declarid their message, who aunswerid that he thought himself very straightly & extremely delt wth by the Bailief & his company. But as for that comission he doubtid not but to be hable to aunswere the matter well enough and that he had a discharge therof and therwith shewid to the said ffrekulton & Grene the endorcement of a lre but the contents he woold not shewe them. but afterwards shewed the whole lre to John Grene privately which was in effect to spare thexecucion of the comission & taking of his bodye neu^rtheles aunswred that he did not medle in the matter But that was doone was in the title and right of Thomas Oldnall to whom he had set the same tithes And he thought he wold doo what he could to enioy them wth this aunswer the messingers returned And reportid what they had heard And that Thoms Oldnall was there wth some assistance clayming the tuith and sayng that he woold have it if he could orells &c uppon wch returne of the messingers & their report It was thought good that a lre should be writen to Sr John hubond being than at Kenelwerth to adu^rtise him not only what proces & comaundm^t was come to the Bailief but also howe mainly his s^rnt Thomas Oldnall assisted w^t some of his fellowes offred to stand in that quarrell ppared therunto w^t swoords bucklers long staves & other like weapons affirming that they woold have the tuith orells dye on the ground And also that

John Grene Will'm ffrekulton sent from Mr Balif to Brookes

Brokes answer & demenor

the mesengers reaport

Sir Jo hubond being at Kenel was writen unto

the other side Rayes freends being as wilfull were as redy to trye their manhodes w^t the others and so very great like of ymynent perill if some good order were not taken. And therfore that it might please the said Sr John either to call his men away orells be some meanes of pacifieng of so great an outrage redy to be comyttid. wch lre to that effect writen. the same was presently delivred to the said

<small>William ffrekulton sent with the Lre</small>

William ffrekulton as one indifferent & mete to carry the same and so to be put in trust to shewe the said comission & proces to the said Sr John hubond wch proces also was delivred to the said Willm ffrekulton to be carried wth him. But not long after & that before he could make himself ready it was considered as a thing materiall & very necessary to kepe the comission at home least in the mean tyme any mysdemeano^r happening and the bailief having not his warraunt he should be forced to sit downe and suffer that was not mete. Wherupon the comission was requyred of the said ffrekulton and he notw^tstonding dispachid w^t the lre only. Who came to S^r Jo hubond & delivred the said lre from the bailief unto him before his going to dynner wch the said Sr John Reading askid for the comission or proces. which the said ffrekulton said was at Warwik in the keping of Mr Bailief. Then said the said Sr John howe can I give any advise to Mr Bailief if I have not the comission. Therfore go yor way

<small>Sir Jo. his mesage by mouth</small>

home said Sr John and let the bailief & half a dosen of his company come presently to me so as they be here w^thin thes two howres. And I will let them have myne opinion. wth this message Willm

<small>the messengers return & report</small>

ffrekulton returned and cam to the Bailief about twoo or three of the clock and the said Bailief & ffrekulton came to the Steward M^r hudson & M^r crane being in Phillips garden and reported Sr John his aunswer & mynde which being understood It was thought strange first to send for the

<small>the Balifs & assistants resolucion for that tyme</small>

bailief & his company out of the towne and then in such tyme as was not possibly to be observid for the tyme of the messingers comyng home & preparing eury man to ride woold ask more than twoo houres besides that the messinger told the said Bailief & his company that except they did come w^thin twoo howres Sr John woold be gone back to the court and therfore had lien somuch the lenger in the morning & heat of the day that he might travell in the cole evening. Thes messages well considered the Bailief & his company bing loth to lose their labo^r to ride & then come to short w^c was very likely, and being very carefull to preserve the peace asmuch as might be determyned to tarry at home to be in redynes to depress that might ensue so went not to Kenelworth And so that day passid w^thout any harme done more than that the said Oldnall & divers of his fellowes were in the fields wth great Bravery & edge toles to gather & make the hey And on the morrow being friday Thomas Oldnall assisted w^t twoo others of his fellowes came up to the said Mr Bailief and told him that he had ymprisoned twoo of his men and desired to know the cause whie he so did to wch the said Mr Bailief aunswered that he had done that he was comaunded but he knew no men of his ymprisoned for those that were ymprisoned were such as disturbed the possession of John Rey in the tuithes of myton and that he (folio 145) was comaundid in nowise to suffer, nor woold Well said Oldnall Ray gettith no tithes there ner no man ells but myself for it is myne & I will have them orells I will lie in the dust And you shall aunswer yor doings, whereunto the bailief aunswerid I do nothing doubt to aunswer my doings and bicause you pretend a litle that I never herd of before I wish you to beware that you doo no more than you may lest you here therof And therwith shewed them the comission of which the said Oldnall & his company made no reconing and said this towchith not me, but my father, & my father had nothing to do w^t it this twelve moneths & more But sithens Mr Bailief ye stand uppon yor comission here is a dischardge for that and it had bene mete that you had made Mr Sheriff privy before ye had delt in that comission bicause the Sheriff is first in comission before you, and therwithall delivered to Mr Bailief the lre afore remembred. The Tenor whereof ensuith

Oldenall & his felowes walk in the fieldes

Oldnalles speche to the Balif

Mr Balif sheweth the comission to Oldnall

Oldenall delivereth a lre to Mr Balif

the copy of Mr Seklordes first lre

After my hartie comendacions where the quenes ma^{ts} proces under her hieghnes privy seale is awardid unto youe to attach one Richerd Brook at the sute of John Wraye And for that I have appointid to heare the cause of controversy betwene the said parties the first of

August next at Grafton if her ma^{ty} shall then be there Thes are therfore to require you untill that tyme to stay from executing of the said proces and this shalbe yor dischardge in that behalf. from my house nere St Johns this xvj^{th} of July 1576

        Yo^r loving frend
         Thoms Sekford

Indorced & directid

      To my loving frends the hiegh Sheriff of the County of warwik & to the bailief of the towne of Warwik

Oldnall desireth to have the lre agayn & a copy of the comission

wch lre so delivered to the said Bailief after he had red the same The said Thoms Oldnall required to have agayn & that Mr Bailief woold take a copie therof and that doone that he might have the said lre & a copie of the comission to the hiegh sheriff Wheruppon the said Mr Bailief imptid the same & the whole request

the Stewardes aduice

to the Stuard who advised him to kepe the lre for his warraunt whatsoever should happen And as towching copies either of the comission or this lre it was in his choice whither he woold make any or not. but the more to satisfy them it were not greatly materiall if he let them have copies. Wheruppon copies were made both of the comission & lre & delivred to the said Oldnall. which whan were offred to him he litle estemid but would have had the Bailief to have kept & delivered the lre to him. And after this the said Oldnall accompanid

Oldenall & other make hey w^t swordes and Buklers

wth iiij^{or} or v others of Sr John hubonds sruuts having swoords & Bucklers and w^t twoo others wth long pikid staves & pikeforks. The names of w^c psones be not knowen went into Myton field & the closes neer the said field and there gathered & made heye. Wherof Mr Bailief

Mr Balif goeth into the fieldes the second tyme

being advertised taking wth him a fewe such as he thought both sober & discrete namely Richerd Stevins constable Thoms Chapman constable henry Bird constable Richard Smith

Mr Balifs chardge

pewterer Anthony clemens baker & some other went into the

fielde Where meting wth the other persones tolde them they did not well in this unquiet maner to trowble the peace & good quiet of the quenes subiects and therfore willid them to depart and to kepe gods peace & the quenes. Who aunswerid that they were there in get possession of Oldnall and that they ment not to breke the peace onles it were offred to them. but being there they woold not leve the possession and that they woold have the hey orells it should cost some of their lieves and advised the said bailief that he should beware what he did, for he should aunswer his doings and that he had done enough alredy, and that Oldnall wold break the neck of the corpacn And as some of the company reportid They bad Mr Bailief go home orells haply his cote might be torne And that if any man stirred or any thing were done his cote should be first pluckid over his head. And being pswadid by some to leave those woords & outrages S^r Jo. hubonds man namely the cook should say. That if Mr Bailief brought an hundred they woold the next day have ij^c & if M^r bailief brought three hundred they woold have iiij^c. Wheruppon & chiefly in avoiding what otherwise might happen the said Bailief willid John Reyes man being but only one to walk about the field and look to his maisters busines and so returned into the towne. By which tyme it was told that Sr John hubond was not gone to the court but was still at Kenelworth. Wheruppon it was thought good that a lre should be writen unto him aswell to advertise him of all thes things as to as to desire him to call home his men. And theruppon an other lre was writen in this maner

a second lre writen to Sir John hubond

Sir acording to that we were bold to write to you yesterday here w^tin the libties of this borough is like to be doone by Servants of yo^rs great outrage, who arming themselves w^t swoords bucklers & other like unmeat weapons for peasable men doo offer wth force not onely to take away the possession of certen tuithes from one Raye whom we are comaunded to maynteyne in possession But also say they will kepe the possession (folio 146) therof w^t unreasonable force many hundredes which as they excede greatly the bondes of reason So we assure o^r selves they do it without yor consent & privitie (as they say) to the use of Oldnall Our humble desire is that youe will call that riotouse company hens before they excede in accion so farre as they say they entend, to wrong the poore man. ffor otherwise, worse may & is very like to ensue than wee can by any meanes gently depresse. And forasmuch as yo' worshipp is one whom we greatly regard & think o' selves beholden unto and also in comission for the peace keaping wee doo trust veryly yo' wisdome will tak order as no such Riot may be continewed by any towards you But that rather ye will please to be meane to appease the same, which if be not presently doone wee doubt what may followe And the soner it is doone the more we shall recon to be beholden unto yo' worshipp w' whom we wolde have bene glad to have conferrid of this matter but dare not absent o' selves least mischief might happen in the meane tyme contrary to o' good willes Therfore earnestly & hartely desire yo' wo'shipfull & wise order in this behalf. At Warwik this xx^th of July 1576 in hast yo' w'ships to comand. J.R.b WG. R.ff Th p. J.F.

<small>this lre sent by Olivere Brook was not delivered</small>
This lre was sent by oliver Brook to have bene delivered to S' Jo. hubond but the said Brook meting twoo of S' J. hubonds men in Kenelworth lane was told by them that their Maister was riden from Kenelworth but whither they knew not. Wheruppon that messinger returned w' the lre & that aunswer to M' Bailief not long after it was said that S' John was gone but to colshill and that he wold returne that night wheruppon an other messinger Willm Sharples was about ix of the clok

<small>Sent agayn by Willm Sharples not delyuerid</small>
that fryday night sent agayn to Kenelworth w'th further comaundm' that if S' John were not there but at colshill, that he woold ride thither to him The said Sharples went also to Kenelworth where he found not S' Jo. but heard that he wold be there the next morning very early but where he was he could not learne by any meanes and therfore returned w'th the lre. Wheruppon John ffisher considering the tenor of

<small>an other lre sent from Jo. fisher only by his owne man</small>
the former lre & w'thall the corage of the gentleman to whom they had writen and w'thall the malice of Brook who as a subtill and conyng companion woold practize the displeasure he could devise to hurt the towne. Wrote therfore a more humble or gentle lre in his owne name to the said S' John hubond wherin he tempred his stile w'th more

softer mettell though in effect the same matter and tending to the same end, and sent the said private lre of his owne to the said Sr John who was hopid to be at Kenelworth but was not And bicause it should be the more substancially done the said ffisher sent his owne man therw^th who tarried at Kenelworth till the comyng of Sr John hubond wch was about one of the clok in thafternone that Saturday the xxi^t of July at whose returne he deliverid the lre to him who first reading the same ymediatly theruppon deliverid it to the said Brooks & to John Jeffreys to puse And theruppon willid the messinger to make as good spede as he could home to his master & will him to cause Mr Bailief & him to mete the said Sr J. hubond at the Shire hall in Warwik assone as they could for he woold be there assone as the messinger wth wch message the messinger returned And Mr Bailief the said John ffisher Mr hudson Mr Townsend Mr Powell & Mr ffrekulton spedely reped to the shire hall to expect the comyng of the said Sr John hubond who about three of the clock cam thither acompanyed wth Mr George Turvile Mr henry Besbich the said Brookes & Jeffreys and after some straunge kind of g^rtulons entrid into the matter as herafter shalbe shewed.

Joh. hubond herewith the lre to Brookes and Jefreys

ayes freendes desire lres from Mr Balif to the Mr of Requests

But whiles thes things were thus in doing The frends of Raye having intelligence of the former lre come from Mr Sekford desired lres to the said Mr Sekford to advertise him of the behavior of the other parties supposing veryly to bring further order to the bailief for his pceding to thexecucion of the comission the rather for twoo causes one bicause they had not bene made privy that the Mr of Requests wolde deale therin. And other bicause the hand of Mr Seckford subscribed to the decree did much vary wherby also some zelosy entred into Mr Bailiefs & other officers heades towching that matter, wherin they desired to deale so as they might in tyme to come aunswer their doings and therfore so much the willinger to write to Mr Sekford at the request of Willm Worcetor & Robart Sheldon who both promised to travell therin, and therfore wrote as followith, wch was done before sight of the lre only upon the report of John Grene seing the lre in Ric. Brooks hand.

the copie of Mr Balifs first lre to Mr Sekford

Our humble dueties premised. It may please yor wo'shipp to be advrtised that on tuesday last being the xvijth of this instant moneth July Mr Bailief of this borough of Warwik receivd comission under the quenes ma^{tys} privy seale to the Shereff of the County of Warr & to him the said bailief addressed. wherby it was comaundid That proclamacion of Rebellion should be made against Richerd Brooke defendant in a Sute brought (folio 147) against him by one John Ray for the title of a Burgage & certen tuithes in Warwik and also for the aprehenen of the said Brook where & when he may be found. And wthall to kepe & maynteyne the said John Rey in quiet possession of the said Tuithes and to ymprison such p'on as would or should go about & dispossess the said Ray therof and also to kepe such persones offending untill her hieghnes pleasure might be signified for their further ponishmt. By vertue wherof and for the further & better knoleig of her ma^{ts} pleasure in this behalf I the said Balief wth the ayde of my bretherne & assistants of the same borough did the said xvijth daie cause the said proclamacion to be published according to the said comission & comaundment And further uppon complemt made the next daye after that certen light persones had taken uppon them to gather part of the said tuithes namely certen cockes of heye or gresse fallen & set furth as tuithes w'hin the said fields of Myton, caused the said proclamacion again there to be openly red & withall chardgid that no man or person should be so hardie as to meddle wth the said tuithes, but only the said Raye or his assignes uppon the perill specified in the said proclamacion All which notw'tstonding the said light fellowes namely Richerd Brookes of Warwik aforesaid Tanner and James Richerdson Shomaker did most manifestly contempning the said pclamacion contynewe the gathering of the said haye or gresse tuithes which they said they were comaundid did & would doo for & to the use of one Thomas Oldnall sonne in lawe to the said Brook proclamed and were there maynteyned in open showe by Marye the wief of the said Brook pclamed & by Thomas Brooke brother to the said Richerd and so to dispossesse the said Raye & such as he had apointid his assignes. ffrom which their doings they wold in nowise be restrained by any gentle meane or speche, but rather chose & offred themselfs to trye their Maisters title by force w*t* the hassard of their lives (according to their pmises before made) (as they said) then to depart & leave their intendid purpose. Wherupon I the said Bailief being personally present w*th* such officers & other honest assistants as I thought necessary procedid in thexecucion of the said comission & caused the weapons of the said twoo evill doers to be taken from them And comitted them to warde the comon gaole there to remayne untill further order should be taken acording to the order of the said comission. Sithens which tyme the said Thomas Oldnall is come in persone & chalengith the Title to be his & not Brookes & that the persones comyttid bee his srunts & wrongfully ponishid withall giving out many great woordes that he & such frendes as he will make will kepe & have the said possession threatening further that the said officers & assistants in this behalf shall knowe that they have doon wrong in those their procedings & shall receve acordingly litle esteming (as it may seme) the auctorytie alredy recevid to the great discomfort of the good & obedient subiects but greater to the incoragement of other malefactors. Besides all this the said Brookes pclamed, affirmith that yo*r* worshipp being Judge of the Court from whence this comission is sent have by yo*r* lre required that the said comaundm*t* or comission shall not be psecutid or executid before the first day of August what tyme you will tak further order betwene the said Brooke & Raye for pmisses which lre, if any be, the said Brook kepith w*th* himself without delivering the same to the said Bailief or other officer reconing the said Bailief unworthie to be of sufficient trust to have that lre whereof he can tak no knoleig bicause he never sawe the same and thinkith that yo*r* wisdome having grauntid out yo*r* proces in such orderly meanes will not by yo*r* private writing calle back the same for better understanding wherof the said Bailief hath examined the said Ray & his freends whither they be privy that yo*r* wo*r*ship intendith about the first of August to deale w*th* them and the other parties for that matter who make playn aunswer that they were never movid therunto neither doo think you will deale therin but by ordynary proces & in yo*r* court Wherupon the said Bailief & assistants being somewhat acquayntid with the conyng devises of the said Brook in other cases gave the lesse creadite to that hath bene reportid towching that lre And therfore my humble sute & request to yor wrshipp is not only to have some spedy order for the further ponishmt or delivery of the said Richerd Brook Tanner & James Richerdsonne but also that all such officers as according to their dueties are prest & willing to execute her maties comissions & comanndmts may be mayntenyd in their honest behaviors without checkes or tauntes of so light persones and also that such proces as come from that yor honorable counsaill & court may be better estemid of and besides that that it may like youe to give order wth as great spede as may be in this matter which if shall long depend in case as it doth We doo greatly feare what wilbe the end of thes daungerous attemptes wherin many yong heades are more forwarde than advised ones the rather therfore eftsones we besech yor good pleasure to be spedyly knowen unto us And so most humbly take or leaves at Warwik the xixth of July 1576. Yor wrships to comaund J.R b w.h. R.T. J.f w.ff. T.P.

Thes lres were sent away as before is remembrid before & orever that Brook had sent Mr Sackfords lre to Mr Bailief and before that any lre was writen to Sr Jo. hubond for at the writing therof it was not well knowen that Sr John hubond was come from the court &c. But the same lre so gone and Sr John writen unto as before he came to Warwik on saturday the xxjth of July as before is said And there began (folio 148) to say thes or like woordes in maner folowing.

Sr Jo. hubond his spech at Warwik to the Balif & others

Mr Bailief I receuid lres from youe on thursday last wherein ye come to me for my assistance in a matter betwene Mr Brookes & one Raye for certen tuithes and that you had recevid a comission against Mr Brooks. but sent me not the comission wherfore I could not tell what advise to give you & therfore desired yor company & such other of yor bretherne as you thought metest to conferre about that matter And it was promised by ffrekulton that was yor messinger that you woold come to me that daye by twoo of the clock to Kenelworth or at the least yf you could not come that then you woold send such comission as you had to thend that I might the better understand the same having then wth me some such learned men as if I or you doubtid of any point we might be resoled by them. And for that cause yone

made me tarrye there all that daye & a great part of the next day almost untill
night to wait yor comyng but you have had other determinacion amongs yor selfs
nor so much as sent unto me, wherin what you ment I knowe not except you
think me not worthie to be aunswerid again. And I believe never a gentleman in
this Shire woold so have dealt w^t me first to desire myne ayd or advise And
apointid me a tyme to come to me causing me to set apart other matters of some
ymportance to abide yor coming and then neither to come nor give me knowleidge
to the contrary Wherin you shewe yor selves either very ignorant or otherwise,
I can not tell what, so lightly to esteme of me yor neighbo^r & a gentleman as you
all know I doubt not And surely if you or any of you had requyred my coming
so farre as from Kenelworth to Warwik It is like I should either have doone it
(if great cause had not letted) or at the least to give you aunswer that I could
not or woold not, which if you had done I might have aplied myself otherwise.
But it is no matter padventure you think me not a man to pleasure you. Nor
that you are to be drawen out of yor corpacion by so meane a man as myself
wherein ye may stand in yor owne opinions as you list. ye shall not offend me so
to think. neither will I take my occasion to think further of the matter then it is,
neither will I seek to recompence you w^t any unkindnes or displeasure if I were
hable as I am not And yet in some trust as an officer emongs you for both my
lordes therles of Warwik & leicester whose Steward I am you all knowe, But let
that passe I am now uppon a second sending unto come to know yor myndes and
can not long tarry I pray youe therfore let me understand the cause & specially
of this trowble ye write of And yet before we enter into the matter you write
that great force is used if you do think that any present danger of quarrell be, let
me know for then I will goo myself to the place to appease the same, the rather

fishers aunswer for that ye say my men be there. To that it was aunswerid by
John fisher it is not like that any present perill is in hand though yor servants
be in dede there wth unmete weapons to gather tuithe. And the cause that makith
us so to think is for that contrary to the comission recevid & the rather for
keaping of the peace & comon quiet of this towne partly bicause the cause
towchid a man of yo^{rs} Mr Bailief hath given chardg that neither Ray nor none

for him shall offer to doo that he might. to gather or stirre the tuithes nor to have any nomb^r there more than one man to see the ordering of things, untill further order should be taken. Which we think both Raye & his freends will observe And now Sir as towching that youe before spake. It may please you to conceive otherwise of Mr Bailief & us than it semith by the progress of yor speche, and to examyne the doings & circumstances therof and then to think of us as cause shall requyre. And therein first as towching Mr Bailief & our comyng to you to Kenelworth. uppon knowleig from you. We can not denye but o^r messinger M^r ffrekulton here stonding did bring us woord from yor worship that yor pleasure was that we should come to youe that daye. Yee & that within twoo howres after he had bene w^t you orells yor busines was such as you could not tarry, ffor as he thought you went that night back again to the court or to Grafton and that you would rest at Kenelworth the heate of the daye & ride about three of the clock & so make yor iourney in the cool evening. And it was past twoo of the clock before the messinger came to us againe. whom when we heard & believid It was thought then to late to make o^r selfes readye to come to you having neither horses nor any other thing prepared to come upon that so len. And as towching the sending of the comission unto you. neither did the said messinger mak any relacions to us therof ffor if he had it had bene very like that ye should have had the same sent you or at least a copie wherby ye might have understood the effect therof And therfore if any such promise was made by the messinger it was more than he had comission from us or did in any wise report from you to us for as towching that comission we had no spech therof after his returne more than that he said of himself. That if he had had the comission wth him at his first comyng to you the matter had bene endid and when he was so pemptory of yor spedy depture from thens We thought it would have bene vayne to send to Kenelworth whan you had bene gone. And so much towching Mr Bailief not coming or sending that day to you whom we veryly believid to have bene gone towards the court agayne that day. untill the morrowe after (folio 149) what tyme Willm Edmonds riding thorough Warwik it was askid whan Sr John hubond woold be agayn at Kenel who aunswerid that he was presently there.

Wheruppon a lre was writen to you & a messinger namely Oliver Brook dispachid therwith who meting twoo of yo' servants in Kenelworth lane was told by them that you were gone to colshill an hower before and that you woold not be at Kenel untill this day who so returned to M' Bailief who sent another messinger towards colshill after you And he was aunswerid at Kenelworth that for certen youe were not gone to Colshill, but you were riden an other way whither they could not tell. but veryly you would be this day agayne at Kenel in the morning. Wherupon being not in good case to travaile I was bold to write my mynd. Well

S' Jo Imbond / the comission shewid to S'r Jo saith S' John. What comission is it that you speak of, out of what court cometh it and where is it. Let me see it. Therwith M' bailief drewe out the commission under seale and shewid it

S' Jo habotts opynion of that comission unto S' John who reading the same over said that there were in it woordes both hard & sharpe but yet a matter of course not to be taken or executid according to the lre. And albeit that M' Bailief had such comission yet he might very well have forborne such hastie execucion as he put in use and therw'th askid when the said comission was delivered to the Bailief & it was told him on the tuesday before. Than S' Jo said ye are very sharpe to deale this hastely to peede against one of yo' owne company in this extreme sort as to pclame him a Rebell & that w'thin twoo dayes after the recept of this comission a thing not often sene ffor though proces came out w'th extreme woords & comaundment Yet Sheriffes & other officers of experience doo take tyme & deliberacion in executing them & so might you have done M' Bailief very well.

Jo fisher To that Jo. ffisher aunswerid S' it is a kinde of proces that is neither comon nor so ordynary as you make it. but rather extraordynary and that to mete w'th extraordynary persones ffor as it may appeare by the circumstance of the pces their have bene many reasonable & ordinary sentences & proces sent furth & as it semith litle regardid but rather manifestly contempned an offence in myne owne opinion deserving as much reformacion as may be for where obedience is not & especially to the quenes comaundments & processes there is small token of subiection, and take away auctorytye, take away government & of good order. And surely S' it greveth not only M' Bailief but also all of us to more than I think it doth the ptie to think or know that we have any such disordered pson emongs us whose doings shall deserve such declaracion. But yet being so if he were a great deale nerer unto us I for my part woolde advise M{r} Bailief as I have done to do his duetie to her ma{tie} and to be forward in execucion of such her hieghnes comaundements and to speak of the man & of the offence. Surely it is a very great offence in myne opynion both towching her ma{ties} prehemynence & auctoritie & a perillous example to others, w{ch} being so is greater in that man that is rekoned resonable & hath had government of other than in a rude or ignorant body of no understanding. And this man against whom this proces is nowe sent is not only rekonid wise, but also hath had the governement of many & bene in auctoritye as a Justice of peace for the tyme of his government w{th}in this towne and therfore it aptenid that he should have more care of his creadite than to give occasion of such proces, w{ch} being brought to M{r} Bailief on the market day was required to be publishid acordingly, as he woold aunswer for the contrary W{ch} being often & earnestly urged it was thought mete & very convenient by such assistants as M{r} Bailief made privy that the same should be publishid acordingly, as a meane wherby wilfull persones ignorant of such order being moved therunto might be staid from executing such unlawfull actes as before were or might be devised. As on the otherside reasonable people having knowleidg therof might the rather be encoraged to assist the said M{r} Bailiet in such cases as required his presence or assistance. And yet M{r} Bailief had such consideracion to the partie who was towchid That it was twoo of the clok & past & the market in effect done, and not many straungers left whan the

S{r} Jo. hubond — same was pclamed. Well said S{r} Jo. hubond besides that yo{r} spedy pclaming him a Rebell. Some of youe said that any man might kill him, and that he was a man not worthy to live and that his goodes might be spoilid & that ye devised to cease his yards, speeches very unmete & such as shewid neither indifferency nor wisdome, nor very tolerable or in any wise to be allowed.

Jo. fisher — Towching such speches in part they are true saith ffisher & in part untrue & false. And if you will credit all that he saith or tellith youe he will fynd you somewhat to do, but to the matter It is true that I sayed that Brookes stonding in this case reputid in her ma^ty opynion a Rebell & so out of her ma^ty pteccion, if any man killid him, he or his freends had the mending in their hands, wch I spake lamenting the case that any of Brookes his calling should fall into so daungerous a case as to be reputid out of her (folio 150) ma^ty proteccion & good governement But in that ye saye it was devised that his goodes should be seasid is very untrue for their was no such devise nor ymaginacion therof wch if had bene entendid some thing would have bene doone to shewe that meaning, but as theire was no such intencion So say I nowe more than I have sayd That if M^r balif had taken his goods & seasid them I think he might have so done lawfully

S^r Jo. h   & kept them so untill he were reconciled. Say you so saith S^r Jo hubond, think you those mete speches to be used to a multitude. Nay. There is no wise man nor man of auctorytie that will allowe them. And if you spak them I knowe where, you woold be made to aunswer them, I warrant you, ffor

ff.   the aunswering them before any man in Englond I do nothing fear, but where you say I to speak them in a multitude if I did, I might well do it, but I have not spoke them in any place but here, where no great multitude are, and the rather I speak them to thend the party hearing my woords may knowe what opinion I have of his daungerous state, wherof it semith he hath

Brokes   litle regard. Well said Brookes I knowe yor malice well enough

ff.   for all that is doone is by yor counsell & meanes. Surely said ffisher my counsell hath bene redy to advise Mr Bailief. I can not denye & yet without malice for if I had borne the malice I might, I could have given other counsell than I have done, to yor greater hurt, but let that goo, And sithens the case on yor side is so ill as it is, Yt were good for you to seek some way for yor

S^r Jo. h.   helpe. I remember said S^r Jo. hubond that Sir George Throkmrton in his tyme when he heard of controversy betwene his neighbors, woold call the matter before him, and what order he took in any matter his woord stood & was taken for leave & none of the pties woold or durst break any

ff.   jote of it. Yf you have sene that Experience said ffisher I pray you followe that example & take you some paynes we beseche you to order this

S^r Jo. h.   cause for otherwise I doubt this man will not be ordered. Nay saith Sr John hubond in that tyme I spek of their were not so many lawyers nor the lawe so knowen but now euery Raskall will tak uppon to knowe the law aswell as the best gentleman & will not be ruled but at his owne pleasure, but than if Sr George had spoken it they durst aswell have bene hangid as gaynsaid him, or broken his order. But the tyme nowe goeth on & I can not tarry. What order doo you think is best to give to & for this matter towching thes tuithes. You wrote to me ffisher that they might be indifferently ynned till the matter

fi. might be tryed. Sir said ffisher I wrote unto youe myne opynion that it was good to have the tuithes indifferently ynned and that if both parties might be brought to consent to forbeare the taking of them till a further order were, it woold avoide a great deale of trowble & discord that otherwise might followe & that I wrote was to pcure quietnes & conservacion of the peace.

Sr Jo. h. Where is Raye saith Sr John hubond or Rayes frends that we

fi. may talk wth him. That we knowe not said ffisher But as I think this speciall frend Willm Worcetor who is the greatest doer in this matter is gone to the Court to attend the Mr of Requet for his further order, to whom Mr Bailief & we have writen what hath bene doone before their going upp. and therfore what consent to have I doubt untill his comyng agayne, but before his going he was content upon some pswacion to agree that the hey might be ynned indifferently & laid in an indifferent place untill further order were taken, but that order than took none effect bicause there was none to consent for Mr Brookes

Brokes disclamith who than was not or woold not be knowen to be at home. The matter said brookes towchith not me but my sonne Oldnalle and he it is that stondith in his right & I think will doo, & ye have therfore doone more than I think you may in comytting his men to the gaole for you have no such comission & for my part I medle not wh the matter for I have delivered over myne estate

Sr Jo hubond testi- to Thomas Oldnall long sithens as it is well knowen. It is true
fieth Oldnalles said Sr John huboud I knowe that Thomas Oldnall hath the
tytle said tuithe sett over to him, and he paid well for it for he took them for a good some of mony for his legacyes due to him, and that he had conveyance therof twoo yeres ago, and therfore howe this comission towchith him

I cannot see. It is marvaill said ffisher that Thomas Oldnall should have his title so long sithens seing that Richerd Brookes being callid in question & sute for it hath pleadid in his owne name within lesse than two yeres, and the decree sett downe purportith that Brooks was party & was present at the setting downe of the same decree wch bereth date in ffebruary last whan the said brookes alleagid nothing to the contrary wch is like he woold have spoken of if any former bargayn had bene passid betwene them but as for that we have not to examyne whither it were or not But Mr Bailief is comaundid to ayde & maynteyne the possession of Ray against all others. And so Thomas Oldnall disquieting his possession is brought w'thin the comission of that decree, & his men to if they were his men as it is well knowen that they are not his men but Brookes men for so they have confessid. And saith ffisher if oldnall have (folio 151) come so derely by it as youe speak of his bargen is the worse, and I am the more sorry that he should be so decevid to pay dearly for a thing of small or no value, but I have not to doo therwith nor will not medle w^thall untill a more convenient tyme wch is not to be long unto that thes quarrels in hand may tak end betwene Brookes & Ray assuring you that wch of them shall have the leace shall have the worse bargayn.

S^r Jo. h. Than said Sr John hubond I will send for my man Oldnall out of the field and therwith began to ask in what field or what part of the towne thes tuithes ley wch being declared Thomas Oldnall was come into the Shire hall before any messinger had his arrant and shewing himself w^t a courageous mynd before his Mr Sr John said unto him Oldnall youe are here greatly complaned of to be a disturber of the peace wth divers of yor fellowes about the possession of c'ten tuithes within this towne and that youe give Mr Bailief here very unfitting tearmes & behavio^r and that you use great force therfore I woold see what you can say to aunswer them. Sir saith he I kepe no possession but myne owne and that I will kepe of my tuithes of Myton, which as yor worship knoweth I have had thes twoo yeres and I will kepe them yf I can & so told Mr Bailief who came into the field & woold have dischardgid me & brought w^t him a great nombr who woold have put me out of possession & therfore shewed a thing come out of the court of requests towching

thomas oldnall affirm-
ith the tuythes to
be his

my father, w^t wch I have not to doo nor his hath nothing to do w^t me bicause that wch I doo is in myne owne right & not for my father. And therfore I willid Mr Bailief to be advised how he cam & what he did for if he cam to dispossess me he should come at his perill, and told him that he might goo home for there was none that ment to break the peace except it were he & his company. And that I spak saith Oldnall was bicause the Bailief willid Rayes men to go their
M^r baylif work & to gather the tuithes & so did enough brak the peax That is not so said Mr Bailief I did nothing to break the peace for I came downe but w^t my litle whit staf in my hand & accompanyed w^t constables & other honest men who had no weapons but only the constables had their constables staves to shewe to be officers And when we cam to you we bad you good spede & praid you to kepe the peace. And then you said in dede as nowe youe doo that you myndid not to brek the peace if no man came against you or to let you, but if any man did he should come at his perill & should find as hot as he brought, and that you were in yor owne possession and that you would kepe or dye for it. And then I told you it semith straunge that you should be in yor owne right & possession for within twoo dayes before they that were there said they were in the possession of Mr Brookes, and howe it should be yo^{rs} so sodenly or in so short a tyme it was marvelous, but that is not the cause of my comyng for I am comaunded to ayde & assist John Raye & his assignes in the possession of the said tuithes & so I mynd to do & whither the title be yo^{rs} or M^r brooks I must doo as I am comaundid And bicause ye may the better understand of myne auctorytie, I have brought it wth me & youe shall both see & here it And therwith I drewe the comission & proclamacion and red so much therof as aptenid to the matter so as both you & all that were there did here it wherof youe made light regard, as of a thing of no great auctorytie and said it came but from Mr Sekford and he should not order anything of yo^{rs} And further youe did tell me that I had done more than I might doo. and that I should aunswer it, which I told youe I woold doo. And whiles that I was talking w^t youe & some others of yor company Rayes man woold have turned some of the gresse there left for tithes & you & others cam to him, & thrust him away & offred matter enough of strokes, if other men had

come as rash as yor self. And besides that yor company said that if I cam to do anything there my coate should be torne first from my back & that I should be sent whom agayne & asmany as I could bring Wherunto it was aunswerid by some that came wth me that those were but woordes ffor if I woold I might bring enough of the towne to aprehend that company & to use them at my ples^r to which it was again sayd that if the bailief brought fourty they (meading Oldnall & his company) might & woold brink iiij^{or}xx And if the bailief brought one hundred they would bring cc. And so if the bailief brought three hundred they could & would bring five hundred they were so well apointid, and knew where they were wch be great brags & unmete for such a one as youe to stand uppon. I

Oldnall said not so saith Oldnall I doo not chardge you said the bailief
baylif but they were spoken by some of yor company & in yor quarrell wch words though I heard not yet there be present here divers honest men that
Sir Jo h. did here them. Than said S^r Jo. hubond, Oldnall what nombr
Oldnall of yor fellowes were w^t you. mary said he there was dick cook &
S^r J one or twoo others. It is told me that there was v or vj of my
oldnall men w^t you. no S^r said Oldnall there was but three of my fellowes beside myself & two others that I apointid to gather the tuithes & they
B.ilif had but pikeforks & no other weapons. That is not so said M^r bailief, their was v w^t swords & bucklers & one w^ta long pikid staff, besides the
oldnall pikeforks. there was not said oldnall & brookes Than said ffisher
fi. I can not tell howe many of yor felowes had swords & bucklers in the field But I remember very well yor comyng up at night to yor freend hickes and there I sawe youe & yor boye w^t swordes & bucklers walking the streets in great bravery as though some quarrell were in hand & besides them twoo others of yor fellowes dwelling in this towne came to you but had no weapons. Who
Sr J. h. were they said Sr John hubond, I can not believe that for I brought downe but seven w^t me from the court and three of them were still w^t me and ffulwood went home to his owne house to Tanworth And therfore there
fi. could not be so many. S^r said flisher that I sawe I (folio 152) doo testifie & it is true for divers others sawe them as well as I and they were in

yor livery sixe besides Thomas Oldnalls boye and besides yor twoo men that
<small>S^r Jo. h.</small> dwell in this towne. I have no men dwelling in this towne said
S^r Jo. to my knowleidg but I pray you name those that you say you sawe for it
is strange to me that so many of my men should be here & brought so fewe w^t
<small>ffi.</small> me, S^r said ffisher it were hard for me to name yor men being
not acquaintid wth them for some of them be such as I never sawe before But
bicause ye shall be the more satisfied I will gesse at their names. And first for
m^r ffulwood he was not there that night. But there was Thoms Olnall Dick cook
or Smyth one ( ) Barnaby one ( ) Keane & an other that I knowe not,
and besides them there cam to them John the horserider sometyme brookes man
& Baker a takerer both which dwell in this towne & we take them to be yor men.
and besides thes Thomas Oldnall had a lacky wayting uppon w^t a sword &
buckler walking the strectes betwene ix & ten of the clok in the night a straunge
<small>Sir J h.</small> sight wth us quiet men of this towne. I marvail of that said S^r
John for I took two w^t me to lapworth & I left Kene at Kenelworth. But M^r
Bailief said Sr John hubond which of my men said they woold pluck of yor cote
<small>baylif</small> over yor eares or bring such company as you spek of S^r said M^r
bailief they be here that told it me, for I did not here it my self. And therwith
Anthony clemens & William Stevins were callid who iustified that the cook spake
<small>Sr J. h</small> the wordes to Richerd Smith pewterer Then Sr John callid for
the cook but he woold not be found, then he askid what keane or the other did,
then M^r bailief said asfor kene. I can not chardge him w^t any woords nor other
matter other than that he was there and that he cam galloping so fast & in so
<small>ffi.</small> great hast as he woold be partaker of the matter. Then said
ffisher this I heard of Keane that he cam galloping as fast as he could into the
fields And as he rode at the bridg end he should say Gods bloud I doubt I doo
come to late adding many othes as though it lay him greatly uppon to be at the
matter, wch may seme rather he desired to be at the fray or bickerment if any
<small>oldnall</small> were then otherwise. Well said Thomas Oldnall you can not
charge him w^t any thing he did for he did but come to me as his fellowe to see
how I did, and I am the more to thank him for it, for it stood me uppon to have

	some freends at nede So it aperid said M^r bailief for you told

b.lif   some freends at nede So it aperid said M^r bailief for you told me that you woold carry both the corne & hey or that you woold lie in the dust.

Oldnall   I said so said oldnall & so I will doo. Will you said Sir John

Sr J. h   you are a proper man to doo so and to stand against such a multitude you well shewe yor self in that speche doo you knowe howe long you are at yor owne pleasure. I am sure that you apoint to go w^t me whan I goo & so all yor fellowes. and neither I nor youe did know whan I should be sent for. And if I had bene sent for yesterday as I veryly looked for doo you not think I wold have had my fells w^t me. And then who should have plaid this part for you, are you of that power to stand against a whole towne. Surely this being time ye should have doone well Mr Bailief if youe had set them all by the heles, And if you had so done & sent me word I woold not have mislikid but thankid you for as I woold be redy to pleasur my man in his honest cause asfarre as I may if my man misbeheave himself to any officer or in any such owtrage I will well allowe of his correction & ponishm^t And nowe Sir said S^r Jo. to oldnall what company

oldnall   have you in the field None said Oldnall saving one or twoo that

S^r Jo. h.   gather the tuithes. Where be yor fellowes said Sr John S^r said

fi.   he they be come up into the towne. It may be so now said ffisher for we are enformed that they have carried the hey home to Brookes his

oldnall   barne. nay it is to my barne said oldnall. Then said Sr John M^r

Sr J. h   Bailief ye see that this matter towchith a man of myne who hath entrid into it as I told you & as I took it laufully and that a good whiles sithens, and what that will prove to I can not tell. And I see that the Maisters of Requests have set downe an award but that award aperith not. Where is that

fi.   award. that we knowe not said ffisher. But I think both Ray &

Sr J. h.   Brookes have it. if we might see it said Sr John padventure we should see more, but forsomuch as it towchith my man, and that you requyre myne ayde for keping of the peace, I will chardg my men that they shall do so, & so I chardge both you Oldnall & all yor fellowes doo. but for the hey I could consent that it might be laid in some indifferent place untill the M^r of Requests might set downe their order (wch they have pmised to do as aperith by their lre very shortly. And yet howe that may be without my mans prejudiice towching his possession I can not tell. And I woold be lothe to deale so as he or his freinds should say that by my doings he should be left in worse case than I found him, and therfore howe to sett an order I am doubtfull, To that said ffisher S^r you see what comission Mr Bailief hath recevid, & I doo assure you that he is earnestly urged in thexecucion therof. And therfore is forced to do more than he willingly woold And as towching Thomas Oldnalls title such as it is either good or otherwise can not be empared by sequestring the possession of that wch is to be gathered, bicause he hath alredy entred & carryed away some of the tuithes though not fully made. And surely it were very convenient that some good order were set downe both for their quietnes & also for the value & goodnes of the thing ffor if no order be set downe than the one on the one side & the other on the other side will be snatching and will carry what they can either in hey or gresse & most likist before it be thoroughly made & so in thend the thing litle or nothing worth. & yet padventure (folio 153) not w^thout blowes or bloodshed or worse. And therfore if it might please youe to advise yor man to some resonable end I think it woold be best & most for both their quietnes. And in my poore opinion if some honest men were apointid to gather & make the haye & cause the same to be carried into the tuith barne where is a convenient rome & metest place for it to lie untill some direction were had from the Maister of the request it woold avoid a great deale of trowble supflous chardg And we of the towne wishe it the rather bicause we knowe howe hard a thing it is to restrayne wilfull stomackes earnestly bent wherof we have had no litle care thes twoo dayes past wherin all that we could do was litle enough to deteyne such as woold willingly have bene there. Than

S^r Jo. h   said Sr John howe may we growe to end w^thout Raye or his freends, dare any of you take uppon you that Ray shall not medle further wth the

fi.   possession untill the maister of Requests have orderid it. To that ffisher aunswerid. whan Ray & his freends was here, & Brooks away he was by pswacion contentid that the hey should be ynned indifferently and so remayne

motion to ynne the hey by an Indifferent man untill &c   untill the M^r of Requests should set an order if he woold do it before the first or second of August. but that consent than took none effect bicause none was to undertake for brookes. who nowe disclamith & turnith it upon yor man. And what yor man will do I knowe not. But this me thinkith I might be bold to saye for Ray & his freends for quietnes sake, that they will stand to asmuch as they have pmised & I dare be bound so if Brookes & Thomas Oldnall wilbe likewise bound not to meddle wth it but suffer it to remayne where it shalbe agreid to be laid untill further direction

S. Jo.   be given from the Mr of the Requests. Will you so said Sr John, howe saye you Oldnall can you be content to have the tuith hey gathered by an Indifferent man & laid in the tuith barne there to remayne untill the matter may

Oldnall consentith   be further ordered. Wherunto after much adoo & some con-

Brokes desirith that Mr J. Grene might be apointid to se the laiyng therof   ferrence wt his father Brokes he consentid & so Brokes moved that John Grene of the crowne might be apointid as an indifferent man & to see the gathering & ordering of the said haye for the tyme. wch was not mislikid And so it was agreid &

consentid unto as aforesaid. And further that Rey for him might have one man, & Oldnall for him another man to walk in the fields to see that such as were apointid to the labor did their duetyes truely & diligently but should not medle therwth And that Mr Bailief should speak wth the said John Grene & tell him

the order taken   that order & desire his travell therin for quietnes sake And so that matter for that tyme was thus ordered & Sr John hubond deptid freandly from the bailief & company & went that Saturday night to Kenelworth and the next day towards the court. And that Sonday after Servise the said Mr Bailief & flisher spake wth the said Grene in the church & relatid the order to him who

J. Grene takith uppon him the oversight   after some speche took it uppon him, and travellid so as that week brought ( ) loades of hey & laid them into the tuith barne and hangid a lock uppon the doores.

In this meane tyme William Worcetor & Robert Sheldon travelling to london to Mr Sekford wth the lres writen from the bailief of Warwik & his bretherne sped them so as on Sonday night they returned to Warwik wth other lres to the bailief addressid from Mr Sekford. The tenor wherof ensuith.

lres fro Mr Sekford to the balif.

I have receuid yor lres of the date of the xixth of this moneth wherby ye advertise me of yor doings towching a comission awardid unto youe out of the Court of Requests against Richerd Brook & all others who clamyng under the title of the same Brookes have disobeid an order made in the said court for Raye pl. against the said Brook deff. I doo very well allowe of yor doings herin. And as towching the pties arrestid, if they will put in surety in resonable somes of monye as the some of xx li a man psonally to appeare in the court of Requestes the second Returne of the next terme and not to depart from thence untill they be licensed by the said court, and in the meane tyme to be of good behavior Then ye may deliver them. Yf not, then I pray youe send them upp to me to London to my house wth spe le wt   of their lewde speches of me. And as towching lres to be sent by me for the staye of the execucion of the said comission, true it is that at the request of Sr John hibbotts, I have directid such lres as ye write of thinking then that her mats woold have bene at Grafton the first of August next but within one howre after I had intelligence of her mats progresse an otherwaye, and therfore sent for the messinger to have recevid the same lres againe, but he was not to be founde. And bicause her hieghnes comith not to the place, these lres be of no force. And thus much I have thought good to signifie unto you. ffrom the cot this xxjth of July 1576

Yor assured frend

Tho. Sekford

endorsed To my very frend the bailief of the towne of Warr. geve thes. delivered

Wm Worcetor requireth the possession of the hey

to Mr bailief the xxijt of July by Willm Worcetor who was than very desirous that the hey might be restored from brookes or oldnall to his frend Raye. and that Ray might be investid acording to the first comission. Wherin Mr Bailief & ffisher desired to be advised especially for so much as Sr John hubond had by their consent in their absence

fishers perswasions   set downe such resonable order as they thought very comodious for the said Raye and as good in a maner as if the possession were in Ray.

R

Worcetor & Raye consent to forbeare untill the Justices of Asises might be moved

Which they did also the rather bicause they desired to be advised by the lord chief Justice dyer & Mr Srjant Barham Justices of Assises who woold be at Warwik on the next thursday night, & for that also the said Robert Sheldon & Willm Worcetor had informed the said Mr Bailief & ffisher That Mr Sekford had writen to the said L. chief Justice to have some dealing in this matter untill whose comyng they desired that the order taken might stand. Wherunto in thend they agreid & so did John Rey. And in the meane tyme the said Wm Worcetor sent the lre from Mr Sekford to my l chief Justice to Northampton wth such solicitacion as he thought mete. Wheruppon the said Lord chief Justice awarded furth a writ of capias to bring the bodies of James Richerdson & Richerd Brook Tanner before him to aunswere to such matters as should be chardgid against them. The tenor of wch writte ensuith.

my L chief Justice of the comon place being Justice of Asise sendith proces for Richerdson & Brokes tanner

the copy of the proces (folio 154) Elizabeth dei grā Angl. ffraunc hibnie Regina fidei defensor &c Balliuo ville n̄re Warwic saltm precipm tibi qd capias Ricm brook et Jacobum Richerdson si vivent fuerint in balliua tua et eos salue custe Ita qd heas corpora eor coram Iustic nros ad Assis ad gaolam nram ville Warwic de prisonibus in ea existen deliberand assigd ad prox generalem gaole deliberacoem in com Warr tenand scilt die veneris vicesimo septimo die Julii prox futur respondend nob de & sup. hijs que ex parte n̄ra tunc ibm eis obijcientr Et heas ibi hoc bre S. Ja dyer apud Northampton xxiijo die Julij anno rī decimo octavo

Balliuo ville n̄re Warr attach vrs. Ricm Brookes Tanner et Jacobum Richerdson essend. coram Justic nros ad assis vicesimo septimo die Julij instant.*

---

* See Appendix c.

Thes twoo James Richerdson & Richerd Brookes tanner had before bene taken by the bailief & sent to the gaole by vertue of the first comission for resisting the possession of Ray & standing the title of oldnalles as before is said. and being in Gaole it was orderid also by Sr Jo hubond at his being at Warwik at the Request of oldnall that the said Richerdson & Brooks should delyverid out of the gaole uppon the undertaking of the first named Richerd Brook who before the said Sr John & the said Bailief did undertak that the said Richerd Brook tanner & James Richerdson should come furth appere & yeld themselfes whan they should be callid for. And so were delivered for the tyme. Nowe on thursday night being xxvj^th of July this writt being brought to him Mr bailief callid for the said Richerd Brookes tanner & Richerdson who cam not furth. Whereuppon the said Mr Bailief being carefull of his comaundm^ts the next day being frydaye & the first day of Assises caused his Serjaunt & other officers to seek to apprehend the said Brookes tanner & Richerdson. And found & attachid the said Brookes tanner. but Richerdson could not be had. wherof the other Richerd Brook hearing that Brookes tanner was taken againe & that Richerdson was lookid for gatt Richerdson home into his howse & there kept him doubting what woold ensue understanding also that Mr bailief acompanied w^t half a doosen of his Assistants had the thursday night bene w^t the Judge about that matter as true it was the said Mr Bailief & officers knowing the malicious practizes of brook, where he could by any meanes spie advauntage & weing howe diligently he attendid Sr John hubond in this case & as many other as might doo him pleasure, nothing doubting but if oportunytie & tyme woll hereafter serve he will call thes doings in question for Revenge of himself to the hurt of never so many he careth not his condicions being such as to delight in the hurt of a multitude & the more the losse is the more is his ioy. And the said Bailief being not acquayntid w^t such comissions pces or courts desired for their better instruccion & upright dealing thadvise of the said Judge & Justices of Assise who at good length hearing their request or peticion and the whole state of the matter reading over both the

Mr Balif callith for Brookes tanner & Richerdson. who be not brought furth

Brookes tanner attachid

Mr Balif desireth the opynyon of the Justices of Assise.

the Judges opinions return'd by S James Dyer Knight L chief Justice of the Comon pleas & Mr barham S'jant at lawe Justices of Assises in this Countie

comission & lres on both sides & understanding maturely the full accions towching thexecucion therof deliberately advised themselves And than gave aunswer to the bailief that he had doone well in making proclamacion & pceding as had bene done by vertue of that comission. which assuring as her ma^{ts} ordynary proces under her privy seale the seale assigned for that court was his sufficient warraunt, to wch all good subiects & officers must & ought to have duetifull regard & to obey or execute as to euery man shall properly apteyne. without making question of the validity & Auctorytie of the court or officers therof ffor as the court hath bene many yeres sithens erected by the Prynces comaundm' for speciall causes & so from tyme to tyme by kings & quenes Prynces of this land establishid & confirmed as an ordynary meane to execute their speall comaundm' or pleasure by, it was not by any good subiect to be either contempned or derogatid in such maner as hath bene of late reportid of. And therfore Mr Bailief being the officer for those purposes is to execute acordingly uppon receipt of such warraunt. And albeit the M^r of the Requests be in degree not of so great calling as some or the most of other Judges of the lawes of this land be yet in his Court he is a Judge & of auctorytie to determyne & decree as the cause shall requyre, which determynacion ordered shall stand & be as a Judgm' to bind the persones in accion. And therby provided for as other Judges are towching matters of slanders, And yet in their private writings to be estemyd no further of than private persones. wherin Mr Bailief ye are tunderstand that the private lre of Mr Seckford is not sufficient warrant or supsedeas or dischardge of the sentence or pces sent out by him as Judge of the court under seale Wherin yet it is not my mind utterly to disalowe the private lres of him or any other Judge in like cases who uppon reasonable or newe causes may sometymes write privately for the stay of their owne former doings. Yet I say those lres no warraunt to be pleadid in such doings. And as towching this matter ye move us of we see not but ye both may & ought to followe yor first comission which we take to be sufficient warraunt for yor doings. And M Sekford hath writen unto me to examyne c^rten speaches that should be uttered by some psones against him & his auctoryty And the dygnity of that court. wherin albeit we understand that we shall have great busines for the quene other wayes, yet if ye can bring any such psones before us, we will take some tyme therin either on Saturday or Sonday. for I doo pceve the gentleman myndith to have it further examyned before the lords. And so I think it very mete, for if her ma^{ts} courts & Judges shalbe so spoken of & her ma^{ts} proces of no better estimacion It shalbe in vayne to have either law or Judges w^c is so necessary as in all tymes hath bene w^t the good of great estimacion. As by the lawe of god appereth where S pawle writing to Titus chardgith him that he suffer not himself nor his ministry to be evill spoken of. And so in o^r comon weale here in Englond great men & men of Auctorytie be pvidid for by statuts & lawes very penall that their creadits & auctorities be not towched by any slander As by the statute of scandalarū magnatū all Judges are includid. And thus have you o^r opinion wch both my lord dyer & Mr Barham in their sevrall arguments confirmed. Wherby both Mr Bailief & the rest of the hearers were more resolutely satisfied & theruppon myndid to

the cause why the balif suffrid Wm Worcetor to carry the hay

procede acordingly. And therfore yeldid to the earnest desire of Willm Worceto^r that he might be suffered to enter in to the barne & carry away the haye. and so to the rest of the tuithes as they should happen. wch the said Willm Worcetor did that Saturday night the rather that if any resistance should be made, the Judges being present in the towne might be advertised. And at the tyme of carrieng away the hay neither Ric Brook nor Thomas Oldnall nor any for them shewed to interrupt them, saving only Tho. Brok Ric brother who came thither weaponed all in great woords & othes & would nedes take the names of such persons as were there but in vayne bicause they were all or the most part straungers & dwellers out of the towne. Whiles (folio 155) thes were in doing Richerd Brook

Ri. Brookes ridith up to the Court & submyttith himself to Mr Sekford

pclamed acompanied w^t James Richerdson a man of like mould & a redy instrument for such a woorkman ride that Saturday to Sr John hubond at the courte. w^t what grievouse tale or complaynt I knowe not but gesse by the sequell. And so by Sr John hubonds meanes pcured Sir James croftes comptroller of the quenes houshold to be his Spokesman to Mr Sekford for his favor or at the lest to forbere his displeasure. And theruppon Brooke submittith himself to his order either by ymprisonment or otherwise And that not only himself but also Thomas Oldnall & all other clamying by him shall stond to his direction & decree for the said tuithes And became bound in cc^marks aswell to appeare in the court of Requests the second returne of the next terme as also to suffer the corne & heye to be ynned into the barne & not to be meddlid wth by them or any of them & also to stand to what order shalbe pnounced wheruppon Mr Seckford wrote an other lre to Mr bailief of Warwik the tenor wherof ensuith.

Mr Sekfordes lre signifieng the yelding of Brookes

Mr Bailief Sr John hibbert Knight hath brought unto me Richerd Brooke to yelde his bodie to the prison of the fleet for the breche of the decree made against him for the mater betwene him & Ray. Nevertheles bicause the said Sr John hibborts enformeth me that he took order at his last being at Warwik by the consent of the freends of the said Raye That all the haye & corne belonging to the personage in varryance betwene the said parties should remayne sequestred in the handes of one John Grene. And for that also the said Richerd Brooke stondith bound in CC^li to appere in the court.

referrith the choyse to Mr Bailif to ioyne an other w' Jo. Grene for the Innyng of the tuithes

of requests the second returne of the next terme and not to depart thens w'hout speciall licens of the said court. I have thought good to suffer him in the meane tyme to goo at lardge. But if you shall think good to ioyne any other wth the said Grene for the more indifferent sequestracion of the said corne and the more suretie of the said Raye. Than I pray you apoint such other psone wth the said Grene as you shall think good. Also the said Sr John hibborts declared unto me that no informacion was given unto him of any slaunderous speches uttered of me (as the bringr of yor lre enformed) ffor he saith yf he had harde of any such thing he woold have taken order for their sharpe ponishement. Yf any remayne wth you in prison for this cause, youe may uppon boundes to appeare the day abovesaid set him or them at libty. I tender the case of the said Raye and I take the order abovesaid to be most beneficiall for him. Thus farre ye well from the court at Westm this xxxth of July 1576.

Yo^r loving frend
Thoms Sekford

endorsed To the wo^rshipfull my loving frend the bailief of the towne of Warwik geve thes.

<small>Rychard Bettes disturbith the possession of Raye.</small>

But before the comyng of this lre one Richerd Bett being srunt to the said Brooks goeth into myton fields And there some haye being made readie for the cariage. And Rayes folkes or Worceto^{rs} coming to carry the same. The said Bett woold not suffer the same hey to be lodid but stonding uppon the hey said that he woold lye in the dust before it should be taken from him. Wheruppon Rayes freends having in comaundm^t to kepe the peace came upp to Mr Balief who apointid c'ten persons to apprehend the said Betts & bring him to him, which was doone w^t quietnes acordingly. who being before Mr Bailief & the Stuard was askid what comission he had to stand in defence against John Rey or his srunts for the hey in Myton or in whose title he did it. To that he aunswerid that he was Mr Brookes hired srunt & had mete drink & wages of him. But he kept the hey in the title & right of Mr Thoms Oldnall, for so he was comaundid by his said maister. Wheruppon he was willid to be advised of his aunswere bicause there was a comission directid to M^r bailief to maynteyne the possession of John Rey and for quietnes sake some order was taken that Mr Grene of the crowne should have the ynning of the hey for a tyme and therfor padventure he was apointid by Mr Grene To that he said he had heard of the comission wch was against his Mr Mr Brookes. But he was comaundid to be there in the right of Mr Oldnall And that Mt Grene had given him no comaundm^t or comission to do any thing but Mr Grene comyng on a tyme thorough the fields saw him this betts there and bad him god spede, and there

<small>Bettes Confesith himself to be brokes hired servant and to kepe posesion for Oldnall.</small>

<small>denyeth to be apointid by Mr Grene</small>

<small>Mr Balifes speche to Betts</small>

was all that Mr Grene said unto him. Well said Mr Baylief you do not well having knowleig of the quenes comission to let the possession of Ray & you are like to aunswere. Sir saith betts that I did was in the title of Mr Oldnall & to maynteyne his possession and I did therin what I could, & more woold have done if I had bene more hable and I doubt not but Mr Oldnall will beare me out. Then was it told him that it were good for him to be better advised remebr himself, who apointid him there To that he said I have told you who apointid me, and what I have done And I say if it were to do again I woold do it & more to if I were hable. Theruppon Mr Bailief told him for his so doing he must go to warde if he had not any frend to be bound for him To that he said I have no frends I am content to go to warde for I knowe I shalbe fetchid out agayne. Wheruppon he was comyttid to prison for his contempt And theruppon Mr Bailief wrote to the M^r of Requests to advertise him, the teno^r wherof ensuith.

his answer

Mr Balif wriuth to Mr Sekford signifieng the ymprisoning of Brookes tanner & Bettes

My duety pmised to yor worship. the same may please tunderstand that acording to yor last lres of the xxith of July there is in the gaole here at Warwik one Richerd Brookes Tanner before that tyme taken & arrestid for resisting the possession of John Rey of the tuithes of Myton, against whom there is no great proof made of any lewde speches of yor worshippe Therfore I have spared to send him uppe untill further matter be proved & have in the meane tyme comitted him to the comon gaole. And w^t him there is an other named Richerd Bett s^runt to Richerd Brook named in the decree which Bett on Saturdaie last being the xxviijth of this July resistid such persones as for John Rey woold & did carry the tuith hey of Myton aforesaid. And the said Bett did therin use all the force he coulde as well to dispossesse the said Raye as also to mayntayne the estate & possession of one Thomas Olnall in whose right he affirmith he will do what by any possible meanes he may acording to his maisters comaundm^t wherin he offred violence but being taken is now ymprisoned acording to her ma^{ts} comission. And nowe I am humbly to desire yor pleasure to be shewed what shalbe further done w^t the said pties now ymprisoned, which signified shalbe performed acordingly As know^th thalmighty who prosper you wth thincrease of wo^rshippe. At Warwik this last day of July 1576. Yo^r w^rships to comaund

J. Ridgeley balif

the former lre of Mr Sekfordes brought Not many dayes after this last reportid lre dispatchid, The former lre sent from Mr Sekford was postid downe by Thomas Oldnalls lackey, but Brooks tarried behind to come wth Sr John hubond. And so the same lre (folio 156) being unsealid was brought up to M^r bailief by *Thomas Brookes speche to the balif* Thomas Broke the last daie of July at night, who using some licensious speches other than became him requyred to know where Betts & Ric. Brookes was, who told him that they were in the Gaole & that ye knowe it well enough. Then said Thoms Brookes to the Bailief ye have done the better, I doubt not but you shall answere it. To that said M^r bailief I will aunswer any of my doings doubt you not. And so ye shall said the *the manner of the delivering out of prison of Brookes tanner & Bettes* other and so went his waye. within a while after Smalley the under Gaoler cometh upp the strete w^t Brookes Tanner & Bettes, and in the street betwene Thoms. Cooks doore & Willm Sadlers stall John Grene of the crowne met them, where having a fewe words togither the said brooks & Bett were delivered from Smalley & went home *Mr Balif sendith for Willm Worcetor to give him knoleige of Mr Sekfords lre* to Rycherd Brokes house. all which this writer sitting at the crosse did see & therfore reportith acordingly, for some causes moving him. Then Mr Bailief having recevid the lre from Mr Seckford & making the Stuard privy therunto they sent for Robart Sheldon and wrote their lre to Wm Worcetor & Robert Sheldon cam acordingly. And Mr Bailief having assemblid divers of his company for their advise there they openid the contents of the lre to the said Willm Worcetor & Robart Sheldon to knowe whither they for John Ray woold agree to that order aswell for the hey as for the corne wherin some direction must be orells the corne being nowe in a maner ready might take losse & hurt, and the peace also

W. Woorcetor & Robart Sheldon come conferences & speches touching the sequestracion of the corne

likly to be broken. To that William Worcetoᴿ aunswerid the cause was not his but his freends & whither he wold agree to that order or not he knewe not, nor he did not understand that any order was agreid uppon for the ynning of the corne other than that was sett downe by the court for which Mr bailief had comission to maynteyne John Rey in his quiet possession, and he trustid he woold so doo, and not to hinder the poore man so much as to kepe him out of his possession of all his living wᶜʰ the court ordered unto him. To that it was told him that if Ray & his frends could agree to have the corne indifferently ynned it were not any loss to him more than a forbering untill the begynnyng of the terme, and that was not long unto. And the corne woold not be the worse but the better for lieng. To that Worcetoᴿ allegid that the poore man & his wief had nothing ells to live uppon. And therfore could not spare it so long and therfore besought Mr bailief that he woold execute his auctorytie given him by comission under seale To that it was aunswerid that Mr Sekford being Mr of the court from whence it came hath writen his private lres as might appeare And it semid to him as it did to the present to be but a resonable mocion seing it shalbe sequestred for a tyme. Than saith Willm Worcetoᴿ this is like to come of it whan it is brought into the barne. Brookes will by some meanes get the same into his handes. As he did about two yeres ago whan a like order was taken for the said tuithes, And whan he did see the matter should passe against him he brake the barne doores, & took out the corne contrary to his promise, as ye all knowe. Than

Jo. Grene defendid

saith John Grene Mr Brookes did no more than you did nowe. Whan it was agreid that I should see the hey layd into the barne, wᶜʰ I did, and it was promised & undertaken that it should lie there untill the matter might be tryed. And yet you brak the barne doores & carryed away the hey wherein I was greatly abused to my great discredit. There was no such order that I knewe of said Willm Worcetoᴿ Yes that there was saith John Grene for so both Mr bailief & Mr ffisher told me when they came to me in the church to entret me to see it gatherid & laid in wᶜʰ I refusid to do untill Mr ffisher told me that he had undertaken for John Rey & woold be bound that neither he nor none for him should medle w^t it. As towching that said ffisher in dede Mr Bailief & I cam to the church & there entretid you so farre as as you say to take some travell for the Innyng therof and I confesse that I did say I had undertaken that John Raye nor non for him should medle w^t it untill some further order were taken. And I kept my promise, for no pson medled w^t it untill Saturday last before wch tyme Mr Sekford had writen again to M^r bailief to maynteyne John Reys possession Wheruppon the former order was dischargid And yet I tell you truly that was doone was doone w^thout my privytie or advise But you were wth us whan you heard my l dyers opinion towching the comission & lres and so did or might understand the det^rminacn of that agream^t. Then seth Wm Worceto^r you kno Mr Grene that I sent to you for the key of the barne. and you woold not send it me but said that Brooks had it. And therfore I had iust cause to do as I did & not to think you indifferent to deliver the key to Brooks. I said so said John Grene but indede I had the key at that tyme & yet have. And I think myself not well handled in it. Well said ffisher let us growe to some end. Are you content Mr Worceto^r that the corne may be ordered as this lre purportith, And if you so be and will undertake for John Ray. We will desire Mr Townesend to ioyne w^t Mr Grene and desire them to take some paynes therin. Nay said Mr Grene I wold be loth to medle further to my discredit to be mockid as I have bene and they say I am not indifferent. And yet in these matters that I tak in hand I wilbe as indifferent & honest as Mr Worceto^r & so began to growe to some heate which being hushed they desired to growe to an end. And it was said to Mr Grene that inasmuch as Sr John hubond & the M^r of Requests had thought it a resonable way for quietnes And also bicause he might therby be a meane of quietnes in his comon weale they desired him to take some paynes & so Mr Townesend likewise which in thend they woold be content so as both sides & parties woold be bound to suffer the corne to lie quietly &c. And that was not grauntid bicause neither Brookes nor Raye were to be spoken wth. Wheruppon Willm Worceto^r said he woold ride to Mr Sekford agayn and therfore desired the company that they wold write their lre to signify the trueth to him that there

W. Worcetor

J. f.

Jo. Grene

Willm Worcetor
desireth another
lre to Mr Sekford

was no order agreid uppon for the corne whan Sr John hubond was at Warwik nor for any thing but the hey only and that Sr John hubond had therin enformed more than trueth. To that it was aunswerid that they had writen so many lres & found so many determynacions set at large or revoked that they were almost weary to write, and as to write so much to reprove Sr John hubond they ment it not, though they must confess & will at all tymes testify That there was no speche of corne at his being at Warwik. And that they woold testify where & when they should be callid uppon their othes. but thought it not convenient (folio 157) to write any thing wherby to set gentlemen in displesure or to bring trowble in this case wherin they have bene so much trowblid alredy as they be altogither wery of yt. Then said William Worceto^r if you will not write I trust then that you will execute the first comission. Neither is that request in myne opinion said ffisher whan you are offred so resonable an order wch if you acept I doo verely belive that Brookes for his part will not brek, being alredy bound before the M^r of Requests as ye see by Mr Sekfords lre. I doo not knowe said Willm Worceto^r howe he is bound And therfore if I might have yor lre Mr Bailief I woold bestowe my labo^r to the court And so urged Mr Bailief to write. Than said ffisher if you will nedes have Mr Bailiefs lre (if it please him to graunt it) I will tell you before hand what I advise M^r bailief to write & that shalbe that he is wery of thes countermaunds & to desire to be rid of thes inc^{er}ten travells. I am content said Willm Worceto^r so as I may have a lre to signify that I come from hens. And then Mr Bailief grauntid to write & so did all the whole company. Which was theruppon done the teno^r wherof ensuith

the answer

Worcetor requirith execucion of the first comission

ti. answer

Worcetor urgeth M^r balif to write

it is graunted

the tenour of the lre to Mr Sekford

Maye it please yor wo^rshippe to be advertised that I have receuid your lre of the xxxth of July Wherby it aperith that youe have taken bond for thapparance of Brookes and so pmittid him to go at libtie. But as towching any other pretending title ye set downe no order neither what shalbe doone wth any but such as used evill speches of yor wo^rshippe & yor

auctorytie. Wherin as yo{r} w{r}shipp hath bene enformed w{t}hout o{r} lres, so we trust ye will expect the proof therof at those mouthes that have enformed the same. And as towching an order for sequestracion of the corne by consent, the said Brookes is not yet come home, And therfore we knowe not whither he will agree of the same order or not likeas on the other side wee fynde no great willingnes therunto the causes wherof this bring{r} will declare unto youe. And therfore neither John Grene as ye write of nor any other to be ioynid w{th} him perceving the form{r} practizes will not w{t} any good liking take travell to see the corne in safegard onles both or all the parties wilbe bounde to suffer the corne to he & be in the place where it may be ynned untill some further order by yo{r} court may bee under seale set furth for the delivery therof to such as the court shall adiudge. To which poynt it semith that the parties be very unwilling to be bound. And as it is to be wished that an end of thes trowbles might be even so both I & all my brethern & assistants woold be glad to be at some certen staie howe to behave our selves in this matter especially for the comon quiet of o{r} people & countrey who have us in no small question for so often chaunging our doings. As sometyme to execute the proces under Seale w{th} effect, & sometyme to followe the course of yo{r} lres. for staie therof Wherin although we be resolved which is o{r} warraunt, Yet the multitude will not be satisfied but offer unto us many meanes of reproche And therfore humbly besech youe, that what we shall heare further from yo{r} worshippe & have to doo, in this matter may be by writing under Seale autentique & of auctorite, as a sure warrant for our defence, & meane of o{r} better aunswering o{r} doings whan we shalbe chardgid, which is grevously threatened to the overthrowe of our poor estate, which o{r} dutie is carefully to defend preserve & provide for as we may. And so humbly we take o{r} leave. At Warwick this first of August 1576. Thes lres were well likid And taken in hand to be delivered by Willm Worceto{r}, who travellid w{t} the same. But not long after, and before the returne

S{r} Jo hubond sendith for M{r} Balif to come to Kenelworth

of the said W{m} Worceto{r} Sir John hubond is returnid from the court to Kenelworth on fridaie the (   ) day of August from whence he writith to M{r} Bailief requiring him to come to Kenel & to bring w{t} him M{r} hudson M{r} ffisher W{m} ffrekulton & such other of his company as was at the last order taken betwene his very frend Mr Brookes & Ray at his last being at Warwik & also to bring Robart Sheldon wth him and to be their either by vij of the clock in the morning or by three of the clok in the after none, And to send him woord what howre they woold come, Wheruppon the said Mr Bailief & his company namely Jo Ridgeley Bailief Willm huddisdon Richerd Townesend John ffisher Willm ffrekulton Thoms. Powell apointid to go in the next morning And took wth them John Grene & Robert Sheldon, All wch went so much the rather in the morning bicause it was market daye, and came thither before vij of the clock And wth the said Mr Bailief & company rode Mr George Turvile to spek to Sr John about busines of my L of Warwik, And by the way as they rode they might perceve ij^o or iij^o footemen going before w^t long staves in the necks on foote wch when they were discreid were James Richerdson Richerd Brook Tanner & Ric. Bett. And after the Bailief & his company postith galloping Richerd Brook qui interturbat omnia The Undersherif named John Lynyacres & Thomas Oldenall all on horseback & Thomas Oldnall his lackye on foot. wch passing by the said Bailief & his company looking earnestly uppon them said no woord but only to Mr Turvile to whom the said Brokes & the Undersheriff did speak but made more hast to Kenel to speke w^t S John before the said bailef. And so they did ffor so sone as they were come they wet let in to Sr John being in bed and there were wth him twoo long howres before the bailief might be admittid to presence. So about ix of the clok or after Sr John being risen & made readie the bailief & his company were callid for & let into his chambr Where Sr John being set in a chaire, and the bailief & his company stonding before him Sr John hubond began to saye thes or like woords.

M^r balif & his company goo to Kenel

S^r Jo hubondes speche

Mr Bailief I did yesternight send for you & yor company such as were in the order taken by me at Warwik towching my frend Mr Brookes. And nowe you are come I am not nowe to use you here as if I were at Warwik for as you all knowe I am yor countryman & neighbo^r a poore gentleman of yor country and yor officer under my good Lordes the Earles of Warwik & Leicester and though I could not do you pleasure, yet have bene willing therunto in such sutes & causes as you have had to do wth their Lordshippes And so of late redy wth my best advise at yor request in a matter doubtfull wherin to plesure you I was content to set aside other busines which I had to doo for my lord of leycester here & to come to you for wch my good will you have well rewardid me to seek my discredit asmuch (folio 158) as youe can, and have contrary to all reason gone from your owne promises & agreaments and besides that cease not to execute yor auctorytie to the uttermost in mayntening of quarrells when before youe have complaned therof as matter daungerous, and therfore desired myne ayde for the appeasing of the same wherin when I by yor consent had taken resonable order for pacifieng of trowbles and such as both sides were contentid w^t youe have notw^tstonding

balif   altered the same to the wrong of the one part To that said Mr Bailief I trust I have done nothing sir to the breking of yor order. No saith S^r

S^r Jo. h.   John hubond have not youe sithens my being at Warwik ymprisoned men of my man olnolls, and wheras it was agreid betwene us the hey & corne of Myton should be ynned by John Grene you have delivered the hey to Ray contrary to the order & have comyttid such to warde as the said Grene apointid to gather the heye And besides that you have sought to towch me in this matter but you might have been better occupied a great deal and I will not bere it at any of yor handes for if you deale w^t me otherwise than well I will make you to aunswer it, doubt you not & if you were a better man a great deale

fi.   than you are. Sir said ffisher It may please you tunderstand the trouthe & then you shall find no such cause in Mr Bailief or any of us all But it semith that you have bene greatly abusid in some informacion And they are not honest that so have doone ffor s^r Mr Bailief hath not doone any thing more than he may well do & will aunswer And it is much that he shalbe chardgid so farre

brokes   & no proof made Therfore wilbe proof enough said brookes Yea
fi.   said ffisher if all were proof that you speak but I think Sr John hath had experience of youe yf he have not if he followe yor devises he shall have

S^r Jo. h.   I doubt not shortly. Whie M^r ffisher said Sr John hubond youe nede not to tak the matter in such doogen I doo tell you you have not done well to do as you have done And I pray you what comission have you to sift me or my doings. On what warrant have you to come into any mans house & to fetch him out as a cutpurse & comyt him to warde or what reason have you to break the barnedores & take away the hey that was laid there by consent Sir saith ffisher

ffi.   herin it appɐrith howe much youe are decevid. There wilbe none of this proved And I say againe Mr Bailief hath doone nothing but that he hath warrant for & may doo & should do if it were to do again And I dare take uppon me to answer for his doings and specially for yor self that he never ment to sift you or any yor doings nor hath no plesure to towch yor men neither nor woold not medle w^t any matter towching them, if he might otherwise do & that he hath doone hath bene in dischardge of his duty & office to kepe the quenes peace. No

S^r Jo. h   saith Sr John have you done nothing ells And therwth openeth a shete of paper wch he had in his hand. And began to reade c'ten articles wch bylike had bene delivered him by Brookes wch this writer so supposith bicause theruppon brookes steppith to the said Sr John & directith him to the points. Did you then Bailief & ffisher & Sheldon send for divers psons of yor towne and examyne them whither I were privy to the entry of my man Oldnall, & whither

ffi.   I send my servants & bad them stand to it wth force. No said
brookes   ffisher it is utterly false, & he is a lyar that so enformed. No sir said Brookes to Sr John I think M^r ffisher was not at yt. But the Bailief & Sheldon sent for divers into Sheldons house & did examyne it & put it in w^rting

baliff. Sheldon   It is untrue said both Mr Bailief & Robart Sheldon. It is true
brookes   said Brooks & it shalbe proved. Let it be proved said Sheldon,
S^r Jo. h.   but no proof was made, did not you M^r bailief said Sr John come in forcible maner wth a nomb^r to breke downe the barne doores & to deliver the hey laid theire to Wo^rceto^r wthout the consent of Mr Grene who had the chardge therof and contrary to yor promise, what comission had you so to do.

balif   I did not said Mr Bailief. You did said Brookes & it shalbe
brokes   proved and I think you can not deny but the hey is gone & was
ffi   carryed in yor sight. It is true indede said ffisher that the hey is gone, & that I think some was carried in M^r baliefs sight & yet neither the

order nor any promise broken. howe so said Sr John. Marry said ffisher the order was that Mr Grene should have the care & chardge of ynning the hey to be laid into the barne there to rest untill further order were given. And sithens that tyme further order is given by the M^r of Requests who hath not only callid back his first lre but also apointid the comission to be in force And theruppon Worceto^r in the behalf of Raye hath made his entry & gotten the possession of the heye & I think carried it away. I think w'hout the knowleige either of my self I am sure or Mr Bailief either ffor as I have heard Mr Bailief knewe not that he was carrieng the hey untill Thomas Brooks cam up to him & told him of it enforming that there was thirty or a great nombr in the barne in a riotous

Balif   maner, & that there woold be some mischief done, wheruppon the bailief went downe & took wth him some of his officers as constables to kepe the peace. and what company he found he can report. I cam to the barne said M^r bailief w^t iiij^{or} or vj honest men w^t me. And there I found in the barne not past three persones loding the hey And in the backside of the barne in the close were foure or five more & not passing wch were occupieng in turning & making hey. And I sawe no other misdemeano^r. And whan I cam I bad them god spede And asked whose men they were & the said John Rayes & Willm Worceto^{rs} And I found there none of Mr Brookes or Mr Oldnalls side more than Thomas Brookes, who was writing the names of others, & this was all the misdemeano^r that I sawe. And indede they lodid & carried away the hey and I peevid none to w^tstond

S^r Jo. h.   them. Where is that order saith Sr John that you say the M^r of Requests set downe to take away the hey, or to put the comission in execucion.

Balif   here it is said Mr Bailief & therwith drwe out the lre, which S^r
S^r Jo. h   John reading over & often pusing said here be but slender woords to warrant yor doings for any thing that I see and the chiefest matter is that he cometh not to Grafton & therfore takith not that order as he ment. And this takith not (folio 159) away the agreement before me at Warwik for that that I

Jo. Grene   can peeve. Than steppith furth John Grene & saith S^r I think myself not well delt withall neither in creadit nor honesty ffor I was intretid by

s

Mr bailief & Mr ffisher to bestowe my labor & travell to see the tuithes gotten made & laid in the barne. Wherof when they spak unto me I told them that I woold be loth to medle therin for I doubtid the one or the other either Mr Brooks or John Rey or some of their s'unts woolde at some tyme play some such part as before had bene done that is to take the hay away w'hout my knowleidg or consent and so bring my creadit in question to which Mr ffisher & Mr bailief aunswerid me I should not nede to doubt therof for Mr Brookes & Thoms Oldnall had undertaken before yor worship that they nor none of them should medle w'hall. And that Mr ffisher had undertaken for the other side that Ray nor Wo'ceto' nor none for them should medle w'hall untill further order were taken or untill the first day of August And theruppon I yelded to bestowe my labor and have done for them as for myself. and have caused the hey to be laid in the barne & lockid the dores & yet for all thes promises the hey is carryed away wherby I am greatly discreditid. And I can chardge non so much as Mr bailief &

balif
fisher

Mr ffisher. To that aunswerid Mr Bailief. It is true we did so say to you. And so said ffisher. And yet no such unkindnes to be taken nor no such discredit to you as you speke of ffor first the order was that it should be suffred to lie there untill further order were sent downe by the Mr of Requests wch was brought to Mr Bailief three or foure dayes before it was take away. Besides Willm Worceto' cam to you from Mr Bailief for the key of the barne, and you woold not deliver it to him, but aunswerid that Brooks had it wherin by yor leave you shewed not yor self indifferent to deliver the key to Brooks being a party & that was contrary to the order. Brooks had it not said Grene. You said so said ffisher. Besides that said ffisher you were by whan we movid the Judges in this matter, who made us aunswere & advised Mr Bailief to have regard to the comission under seale, & not to respect private lres. That saith

Grene

fi.

Grene was after the hey was carried. I confesse said ffisher. But yet & you remember you & I standing at the crosse on the thursday night before the hey was carryed I told you that Mr bailief had then recevid a dischardg of the lre brought by Richerd Brook and you thought much

Grene

that you could not be made privy to it aswell as some others.

Nay said Grene it was after but me thinks It had bene as mete for me to have known it as any other considering I was put in trust above other. I finde said Sʳ John hubond no woord in this he wherby ye are warrantid to deliver the hey. But said ffisher there be woordes wherby Mʳ Sekford signifieth his mynd that he woold have the comission executid & that is that Rayes possession may be mayntenyd & to call back his former apointment to here the matter the first of August Me thinkith said Grene that Mʳ Bailief did not well in ymprisoning such as I apointid to gather the hey whiles I had to do wᵗ it. There was no such thing done said ffisher. Yes said Grene you sent Bett to warde. True it is said ffisher Mʳ Bailief did so & I think he could do no lesse. ffor when he was askid whose man he was & in whose right he was there & who apointid him to be there he said he was brokes hired sᵘᵃⁿᵗ and was apointid by his Mʳ to be there in the right & possession of Thomˢ Oldnall, and denyed that you had apointid him. I appointid him saith Grene even as I appointid pardy, and that was of either side one. Nay said Thomˢ. powell & Mʳ Bailief he denyed that you apointid him but said that when you saw him in the field you bad him god spede & look well to his busines & there was all. Than said Sʳ John you ymprisoned one Brooks a tanner contrary to yoʳ pmise before me. howe will you aunswer that. I have warrant for that said Mʳ bailief. That is straunge said Sʳ John what warrant can you have against yoʳ own pmise. and it is more straunge to mak serche for a man in his owne house, as for a thief or fellon. I did not so said the Bailief. Yes said Brookes you serched his house and said you sought for a cutpurse & that is litle worse than a thief. I was not in his house said Mʳ bailief but sent myne officers. Whie said ffisher what if Mʳ Bailief had bene in his house & said so to had it bene of any matter. I think verely he might have done it. Yea saith Sʳ John if you will chardge him wᵗ felony orells padventure you may be made to aunswer it. I think not so said ffisher. But Sʳ to satisfie you in that, Brooks that you spoke of was not ymprisoned nor taken for

Mr Balif shewith to Sr Jo. h. the writ wherby Brookes tanner was arestid	that matter but by a speciall proces & comaundmt, and he is so light a fellow as hardly to be found, and therfore Mr Bailief did well in myne opinion to do as he did. Why what proces have you against him. You shall see said Mr Bailief & therwith
Sr J. h	shewid furth the writt, wch whan Sr John & Ric. Brooks had long considerid of & pused. they said here is no cause shewid against him.
fi.	Therfore said flisher more severely to be executid for if the cause were open as comonly they are. it were the lesse matter but whan it is secret to the Judge & unknowen to the officer the more considerately to be
Sr J. h.	handlid. And what the matter is I do not yet knowe. Whie said
fi.	Sr John what did you with him we kept him said flisher untill we had made my lord chief Justice privy. who having not tyme to talk wt him willid him to be comittid to prison untill he should or wold put in such surety as to answer when he shalbe callid. And theruppon Mr Bailief comyttid him to the Gaole but where he is now we know not for he is set at libtie & so is the other
Sr Jo h	Bett to. Well said Sr John I do peeve that there is more affeccion borne to the one side more then to the other, And I had thought it a good order that was agreid uppon at my being at Warwik to have both the hey & corne laid into the barne & to be indifferently kept untill further order might be given, wherof I told the Mr of Requests who allowed very well therof. As for
fi.	affection said flisher I think there is none borne (folio 160) to either party more than for execucion of Justice & that is on executing that which is comaundid. And therin we think Brookes to be a subiect & so to be delt wth. And as towching the order for sequestring the corne under yor correction I think that at yor being at Warwik there was no order taken for the corne for that came not then in question but the hay only for if you remembr Mr Sekfords first lre was but to spare execucion untill the first of August. And their was no corne readie that tyme. And so we took yor meaning to extend no farther. It is true said
townesend	Richerd Townesend and I faith Mr Brookes I woold you woold
Brookes	not doo the poore man soch wrong. Youe are a trym man said Brookes what wrong do you him whan you have one of the best things that he

townesend	hath for nothing & yet you can hold it. I have nothing said Townesend but that w*ch* I paid truly for & more than it is worth, but it is a shame for you for xl*li* to take a leace worth xxx*li* by yere & better, what
S*r* Jo. h.	conscience is that, worth xxx*li* by yere said S*t* John, Yea said
ffrekulton	ffrekulton I will give so for it above the rent. Nay said Robert
Sheldon	Sheldon where M*r* Townesend saith it was xl*li* It is to be proved that he never had of you above xviij*li* in mony at the first for w*ch* yone took Interest and would come to no reconing untill w*th* the Interest it cam to xl*li* And then you made writings betwene you & for that xl*li* he paid you sixe pounds yerely so long as youe had in Interest for that xl*li* or rather for that xviij*li* xlj*li*. And yet youe seke to undoo the poore man to tak the forfeit of the leace contrary to yo*r* owne pmise by lre w*ch* we have to shewe. And this is yo*r* consciens And as you deale w*t* him so you have done w*t* poore Tibotts to undoo him, & take away his land & kepe him in prison Wherof ye may be ashamed. What a lie is this
Brookes	said Brookes ffor it is knowen that Ray oweth me above nij*xxli*.
Sheldon	It is no lye said Sheldon for you lent him no more mony than xviij*li*. And the rest of the debt growing unto you was for Interest & for a lame Jade & such other things as he took of you, which he took of your owne price, and paid foure tymes so much for them as they were worth, And yet you might have had yo*r* mony long sithens if ye woold of Willm Worceto*r* But you woold take nothing but only the leace, w*ch* is the only living of the poore man. William
brookes	Worceto*r* never offred me my mony said Brooks untill the leace
townesend	was forfeit unto me nor then neither all my mony. Will you say so said Townesend was not I often tymes w*th* you from William Worceto*r* sent to desire you to knowe what John Ray did owe you. w*ch* you woold never be acknowen of nor never woold come to reconing but alwayes shifted of aunswering that John Ray & youe woold agree well enough. and so woold never let it be knowen for if you had I knowe when Willm Worceto*r* had brought so much mony
brookes	to the towne as woold have paid you yo*r* duety & more to. Ye say not truly said brooks So you said that S*t* John hubond woold have set his men by the heles & that he callid them villans & knaves. & that he had none but

rascalles and that he woold use them as varletts whan there was never such a
woord. did I sayd Townesend Ye saye not truly I spake no such
woords, But said that Sr John said to the Bailief That if he had ponished his
men he had srvid them well enough. And he woold not be offendid wt it. Orells
I never spake of Sr John or his men. Yes you are very lusty in yor speches
against me said Sr John as I am enformed But look to yt I will
not take it at yor hands to be so said off and to be so searchid ffor if youe medle
wth my doings or sift me I will mete wth you & teach you howe to deale wt a
gentleman for all yor corporacions. And Brookes if you have delt this hardly to
the poore man you have not done well. I have not Sr said he. Yf it may be true
said ffisher that you lent him at the first but xviij li & took so
much ynterest. And stond uppon the advantage of his leace, youe may be
ashamed of it for you borrowed xxt marks of that mony that you lent Ray of me
to redeme the leace out of my handes. which leace lay to me for xvli and was to
be redemyd on midsomer day. And on midsomer even you sent to me to borrowe
xxt marks wch I sent you wthout either scrippe or stroo. And bicause I had then
no other store I sent you the most part in gold. And the self same gold That you
borrowed of me the daye before I recevid of Ray the next day after to fetch the
leace out my hand. And then to take ynterest for that mony wch you borrowed &
had of me frely was but hard dealing. Well said Brookes I do
not remember that nor I can not tell whither it were so or otherwise. Well said Sr
John. Brookes I woold advise you to fall to some end And let
the poore man be considered. You knowe it hath bene my pswacion often And so
I say agayne let some of yor freends & his comon of it. That
said Sheldon and ples yor wo'ship hath bene done often but he will no end but
such as plesith himself. As you say said brooks. I say trueth
said Sheldon. And there be here that can tell that you have had
great reson offred you but nothing will please you but the leace. Sheldon saith
Sr John you told the Maister of Requests That many lewde
speches had bene given out against him & against the auctorytie of the court of
Requests. What be they. for nether you nor no man ells did ever tell me of them

whan I was at Warwik for if I had heard of them I wold have sene them reformed & ponished. It is true Sr said Sheldon. I told Mr Sekford so. What be the speches said Sr John Such said Sheldon as be not to be borne What be they said Sr John or who spake them. Ye shall   me therof Said Sheldon they are to be proved And shalbe whan tyme shall serve, but I will not spek them here. It is strange said Sr John that you will enforme the Mr of Requests & will not tell what they are. you may tell them openly for he hath told them me aledy. I knowe not that said Sheldon but I will open them when & where I see tyme. And where the pties shall aunswer them I doubt not. You will do many things said Brooks, I pray you Mr Bailief shew yor comission wherby you & Sheldon did tak uppon you to examyn men & to send for them home to Sheldons house to say what you woold have them against Sr John. It is not true said the bailief that youe do report (folio 161) I did not send for any to examyne them of Sr Johns doings And what I did I have doone & will aunswere. The cause that movid Mr Bailief said ffisher to heare what some could say was by comaundm' from the Judges who not only advised but also desired Mr balif to examyne such lewde langwage as had been given out against thauctorytie of the co'rt of requests wherin Mr Bailiet hath not bene so busy as brookes informith you neither had Mr Bailief any meaning to towche yor wo'shippe & creadite at all, nor none of us neither but woold be glad of yor favor & frendshipp as one whom we acknoleidg hath doone us good & whose frendshipp we much desire & besech. wherof we shall stond in some doubt so long as we shall peeve that yor wo'shipp will give creadit to eury private Informacion of this man. And therfore we humbly beseche you to examyne his & or doings And as cause shall requyre to iudge equally of us. I am said Sr John not weddid to any man one more than another, but mr brokes being my freend I woold be glad to pleasure him in his honest cause as I might. But Richerd Brook put this matter to order so I have often advised And I think you shall find that the best end. It were good so said ffisher ffor this I say as I have often told him the lease that he sueth

Sheldon
Sr Jo. h.
Sheldon
Sr Jo h.

Brokes

Balif

fi.

Sr Jo. h.

fi.

for is not worth one peny. but is void. And as I have told him so have I told the other side also. And though twoo strive for it It is the towne that suffreth the wrong. As shall appere assone as thes two are at end. Say you so said S'r John then It were good for them both to be at end So emongs you I pray you helpe to bring it to an end And nowe M'r Bailief & my maisters said S'r John I thank you for yo'r paynes taking to come so farre to me. and I will do asmuch for you at any tyme. And bicause I have some busines of my lords I will not trowble you any long'r at this tyme. M'r Edmonds I pray you have them to the Buttry & seller & make them drink of my lords beare & wyne And so w't thanks M'r Bailief & his company deptid from the said S'r John frends as apperid.

<small>S'r J h.</small>

<small>the writers mynd declared Why he writeth so much of this cause</small>

Of this matter this writer bestowth his labo'r the more for divers causes him moving but chiefly for that he knowith the disposicion of Brooks. he thinkith this matter may come in question in tyme to come whan he may spie a mete tyme to use his malicious mynde w'ch this writer thinkith can not be restraned w'th wordes of frendship nor bandes of love nor yoke of othe. All w'ch he hath before this tyme broken and taken in hand the lose lynes of libtie And therof to give a tast. It is not unknowen howe subtilly he hath dealt w't this simple sowle under colo'r of faithfull frendshipp most like a suttle serpent to supplant him both of goods & living wherof being his owne he will make the lesse report neither is yet forgotten howe manifestly he bestowed an othe to profit himself. Swering solemply uppon the testament That he had paid a debt of xv^{li} which he before had borrowed from M'r Whateley of coventry And which afterwards the said M'r Whateley set over to this town as good mony pcell of fieftie pounds to be lent yerely to the poore for which the said Brook had made him a bill which bill M'r Whateley delivered to M'r Yong then balief to recover the said xv^{li} of the said brook who for a yere or more confessid the bill & promissed the payment of the debt But afterward uppon a covetous mynd thinking to defraud the towne therof said That he had paid the said xv^{li} to John Hisher who never had the bill nor any comission to receve the mony nor ever made any bill of recept therof nor other dischardge to the said brook nor never recevid or had the same of Brook and yet uppon his false othe yeldid to satisfied so much to the towne & did so besides that The said Brookes being bailief & burges of this borough had the recept of the Rents due to the borough & the payment of such dueties as the towne should & ought to aunswer And uppon his acompt demaundid allowance of vj^{li} xiij^s iiij^d as paid for the tenthes of the corpacion. Where he can not pve that he paid it As apperith by a demaund of the same for the quene v yeres after or more at what tyme the towne was forced to pay the same in theschequyre. Besides that some doo think that he stretchid his consciens in the tyme of his baliwik And more his unhonest dealing wth all such wo^{r}shipful & honest as have put him in trust is manifest the end wherof is his casting of. The circumstaunce of his uncharitable & yet most crafty practizes to wyn Tybotts land from him may be better set fourth by some other that knowe more than this writer who understandith yet this farre that he sekith & hath gotten the possession of the poore mans land & kepith the poore man like a slav in the marshalsie or kings bench. When the land hath aunswerid him more mony than ever he laid out & yet upon a fraudulent bargayne his owne neighbo^{rs} & paroshions of saint nicolas parishe knowe to well what trowble he puttith them unto by conyng compassing of a leace of peall of the church lands by a false & most fowle practize as they say. And howe he applieth himself to serve euery tyme turning from one to an other is not hidden neither is it doubtid what he will not doo to have his will or private profit and to conclude this writers opinion is that he tarrieth expecting a fit tyme for his purpose to doo what he can for the overthrowe of this state supposing therby to gayn him credit though it be to the undoing of many hundreds & the perill of his soule which God defend & make him a better membr or none at all of this quiet comon weale Amen

the progresse of Brokes devises in this matter

After the things thus orderid for the tyme, John Ridgeley being out of his office of Baliwik and John Grene occupieng that office John Raye by his freends peured out of the Court of Requests an Iniuncion directid to John Grene nowe Bailief and Richerd townesend for the delivery of the corne sequestrid to be deliverid to John Raye according to a second decree made in Michilmas terme 1576 uppon a newe hearing of the cause before the maisters of requestes, at the great sute & Labor of Brookes. But before that Inuincion a copie of the decree was brought to the said John Grene & Richerd Townesend who bicause it was not under seale nor yet directid to them thought it not sufficient warrant for them to deliver the corne by. The, the rather for that the same corne was in the meane tyme seasid uppon & taken into the custodye of the Undersherif by colo^r of an extent brought against the said Brookes for debt due to Sr John Throkmton to whom it was supposid Brooks should owe v^{cli} uppon a statute & therfore nowe extendid, though colourably as afterward shall appere. The copie of the second order or decree made by the Maisters of requests uppon a newe & second hearing followith. viz

      Septimo die Novembr Anno regni Regine
      Elizabeth &c decimo octavo

the copye of the seconde decree in the Court of Requests for the tithes of Myton

Wheras in the matter in varyance depending in the quenes ma^{ts} honorable Courte of Requestes betwene John Raye complainant & Richarde Brooke defendant At the speciall Request of the said defendant, All the tuythe corne hey & other proffites of the fieldes of Myton in the parish of Saint Nicolas in the countie of Warr. Sithens the terme of the holy Trynytie last past were by the speciall order & commaundement of the quenes ma^{ts} counsaill of this said Courte sequestred taken & ynned into the handes & safe custody of one (folio 162) Richarde Townesend and of John Grene nowe Bailief of the towne of Warwik So to remayne to the use of such of the said parties playntif or defendant as uppon the further hearing of the same cause shoulde be adiudgid by the same counsaill to have right therunto And forasmuch nowe as uppon the full & deliberate hearyng and debatyng of the same matter in the presence of both the said pties and of theire counsell learned It appeareth unto the quenes ma^{ts} said counsaill of the said courte That the said defendent neither had or cowlde shewe or proove any other

sufficient or better matter in the mayntenaunce of his pretendid right & tytle in
& to the premises than heretofore he hath doone Therefore it is nowe the daye &
yere first abovewriten by the quenes maies^ts said counsaill of the said courte
ordered That the said Rycherd Townesend & John Grene in whose custodie the
said Tuythes nowe remayne in sequestracion as is aforesaid shall presently uppon
the sight or knolege of this order deliver or cause to be delivered unto the said
complaunt to his owne use all the said tuithes of corne hey & other the proffites
of the said fieldes of myton And that the decree heretofore made in the same
cause by the said cownsaill of the said courte shall stande & contynewe in full
force towching the possession of the said Tuythes to be contynewed in the said
Playntiff

concordat cū Regro — { Thomas Sekford
{ Ry Oseley

This copie of decree or order subscribid w^t Mr Sekfords hand & Mr Ostleys
was brought to the said John Grene by (   ) the (   ) day of November
1575 and shewed unto him wherby the said (   ) requyred the delivery &
possession of the said Tuyth corne & hey acording to the said order. Wherunto
the said John Grene aunswered (as this writer is enformed) That before the
comyng of that order the said Tuyth corne & hey were taken out of his hands, &
seasid uppon by the Undersherif into the quenes handes by vertue of an extent
pcured & sued out against Rycherd Brookes by Sr John Throkmorton unto whom
the said Brookes was indeptid in five hundreth poundes as appeared by the said
writt of Extent. ffor aunswering wherof the leace of the tuythes of Myton and
the corne in the barne emongs other the goods & landes of the said brookes was
extendid, and the said leace was valued at xl^li and so seasid uppon & taken for
the quene into the handes of John Lynakers Undersherif to Willm Boughton
Esquire hiegh Sherif of the county of Warr. which Lynakres was then gone to
returne the said writt or extent at the terme So as he the said John Grene or

Rycherd Townesend could not deliver the said corne without further warrant. But that notw'stonding the said John Grene at the ymportunate request of the freندes of the said Raye promised this much to do to staie the corne nowe in the barne for sixe dayes, And that in the meane tyme neyther the Sheriff nor any other should carry away the same although he brought a liberate for the same And that if within the said Sixe dayes the said Raye or his freendes could & did procure sufficient warrant to him the said John Grene & Ric Townesend for the delivery of the said corne & hey. Notw'stonding the former seasure & extent within sixe dayes after that daye They woolde deliver yt accordingly. Wheruppon the freندes of the said Ray desyred the said Mr Bailief & Mr Townesend to signify their knolege or understanding towching that extent to Mr Sekford Mr of Requests which they did by their lres delivered to (   ) the (   ) day of the said Novembr Wheruppon the said Ray travelled to london to the saide Mr of Requests who theruppon sent furth the quenes ma^{ty} proces under the privie Seale in forme following That is to saye

hitheranto upon reports made to this writer

By the Quene

the copye of the Iniunction Comaunding the delyuery of the corne & hey to Ray

We wille & in most straight wise charge comaunde & enioyne youe Richarde Townesend & you John Grene nowe Balief of o^r towne of Warwik & either of you uppon payne of cc^li to be levied of yor landes tenements goodes & cattells in o^r Eschequyre to o^r use That ymediatly uppon the Receipt Sight or knoleige herof you furthw^th deliver or cause to be delivered unto o^r Subiect John Raye or to his assigne all such Tuyth corne hey & other profits & comodities of the fieldes of Myton in the parish of St Nicolas in o^r countie of Warr. as remayne sequestred in yor safe custodie by order & comandem^t heretofore made by o^r counsaill of o^r court of Requestes which said tuyth corne hey & other proffites & comodoties of the said fieldes of Myton are sithens the said Sequestracion ordered by o^r said counsaille unto the said Raye. As by the said order bearing date the Seventh day of Novembr last past appeareth. According to the effect of which order Our good pleasure is and eftsone wee comaunde & enioyne youe & either of you uppon the payne aforesaid. That ye make present delivery of the said tuyth corne hey & other pfits acordingly. Gyven under our privy Seale at oʳ honoʳ of hampton cowrte the xxiᵗʰ daie of Novembr in the xixᵗʰ yere of oʳ reigne

        Subscribid. Ry. Oseley

 directid upon a labell

      To Rychard Townesend gent and John Grene nowe Balief of oʳ towne of Warwik & to eyther of them

Rey delynereth the Iniunction to Grene — With this Iniuncion & comaundement John Raye wᵗʰ William Worcetoʳ cristofer knight & others came on Monday night being the xxvjᵗʰ daie of Novembr about six of the clock at night to the said John Grene Bailief into his house in Warwik and delivered to him the said Iniuncion under the privy Seale, there being present George Turville William Huddisdon John ffisher gent & others ready to goo to supper which processe the said John Grene in humble maner recevid & reading the same considered of the contents therof And desired that he might have tyme till the next mornyng to take advise in that matter Wheruppon he woolde reasonably aunswere them. Wherwᵗʰ Willm Worcetoʳ semid to be contentid. But bothe the said Worcetoʳ &

Knolege given to the Balif that Brookes sernunts were in the barne — Ray said that wheras the said Mʳ Bailief had promised to kepe the corne saffe untill the comyng of this warrant they understood that the Servaunts of Brookes or some for him had gotten into the barne & layen there (folio 163) keaping possession ever since And therfore doubtid lest the corne were or shortly should be carried away.

Grenes aunswere — To which the said Mʳ Bailief aunswerid That was untrue There had not bene any for Brookes or for any other euer sithens, And if any bodye be there nowe yt is more than I knowe ffor you knowe well that I took the chardge uppon me but for six dayes and they bee expyred three or ffowre dayes past.

And in that meane tyme there laye no body there any night. But on Wensday night certen fellowes were gotten into the barne without my knowleige wherw^t I mislikid assone as I hearde therof. And theruppon went downe myself about ix of the clock and put them out and so none laye there so long as my promise or undertaking contynewed But what hath bene done sithens I knowe not for whan you came not w^t any warrant nor I hearde not from you in those sixe dayes I had the lesse care therof. Wth this answere after some other woordes to litle purpose the said Raye & Wo^rceto^r w^t their company deptid. Wheruppon Mr Balif sent ymediately to warne all his assistants the principall burgesses to be at the court house the next mornyng by seven of the clock. where mett first the said Mr Bailief M^r hudson Richard ffisher Ric Townesend Richerd Roo John ffisher Willm ffrekulton Thomas Jenkes humfrey crane John Rydgeley & John Dyche. And there & then the said Mr Bailief signified to the said Mr Townesend & the rest of the company what processe he had recevid by Jonn Raye & Willm Worceto^r And bicause the matter was of some ymportance & principally towchid himself & Mr Townesend, and so might also towch the state of the whole towne (if any owtrage might or should happen emongs light persones wilfully bent in this case he desired their advise & counsell what was best to be done in this matter both for there & all theire discharges (for he thought & heard say that there woold be some standing in this matter) And which way in their opynions he & Mr Townesend might work their discharg Wheruppon it was thought convenient by the most of the assistants that this last proces or Iniuncion being under the quenes seale, nowe lastly brought shoulde be executid and that the corne should be delivered to Raye or his assignes. but than the maner howe the same shoulde or might be executid without slaughter or bloodshed grewe in question. for it was informed that in the barne there were not so fewe as a dozen apointid & furnisshid wth divers kindes of warlike weapons to kepe the possession against all men. And that some of them were so desperate that they woolde fight it out, and kyll or be killed before they departed. And therfore howe the corne may be taken & quietly delivered semith very harde And

the Bailif assemblith Assistants to consult what was best to be doone

resolued to execute the comaundment

Consideracion howe

saith M{r} balif though this Iniuncion be come to me on the payne of cc{li} I had rather for myne owne part hassard the losse of cc{li} than any man should be slayne for yf that should happen I see no warrant to defend me. To that the

<small>the deuise</small>

most agreid. And then fell to devise of the maner of the enterprise. Wheruppon it was concludid. That the constable & the Thirdborough of that warde, namely John hynman constable & (   ) thirdborough shoulde goo to the barne sent from M{r} Balif to knowe what company & nombr was in the barne & who they were. And w{th}all to comaund them in the quenes mat{s} name

<small>the constable and thirdborough sent for the Rioters</small>

from M{r} Balif to come furth of the barne to speak w{th} M{r} Balif about such matters as he lately had recevid comission to deale in. And with this message the said constable & Thirdborough went to the said barne. And there callid to those that were within to come to talk w{t} them. Wheruppon James Richardson and Richard Brookes tanner came

<small>there annswere</small>

to the gates of the barne being lockid & barred to knowe what they woolde have. Wheruppon the said constable & thirdborough desyred to know the names of all such as were within the barne and further tolde them their message from M{r} Bailief To which the said Brookes & Richerdson annswered

<small>the answer returned</small>

that they should not knowe the names of any that were there, and that there were no more but they twoo, And they woold tarry there & not come to M{r} Bailief at that tyme for they had nothing to doo w{t} him nor would not come at hym. With this message or answere the constable & Thirdborough returned & tolde M{r} Balif what they had doone, and what annswere they recevid at Brookes & Richerdsons mouth, and that they did see no more but they heard divers others speaking within the barne, as they thought to the nombr of half a dozen or above. emongs whom they thought George Hulshurst & some other of M{r} Brookes howse were there. Then was it advised & concludid that M{r} balif &

<small>a second deuise</small>

M{r} Townesend taking w{t} them some resonable nombr of staid & honest quiet men shoulde goo thither for the delivery of the said corne. and bicause the peace might the better be kept It was thought good & resolued that M{r} Balif should comaund the constables to attend uppon him thither for his ayde. And that euery constable should bring or take with him his constables staff and no other weapon for himself, and also that every constable should tak w{t} him one man of his warde being well weaponed and yet the most staid & metest man to kepe the peace & give assistance as cause shoulde requyre. And to thende that mete men should be apoyntid to that service. It was thought good that eleccion shold presently be made by M{r} Balif & his Assistants of such as should be callid which was doone. And thes were apoyntid. William Loson constable of the hieh pavement[a] to bring Richard Bromley, William Stevins constable of the Market place to bring Olyver Brook, Willm Sharples constable of the Jury to bring henry Chaplyn Richard Blik constable of the castel street to bring William Hodgekins Hugh Elkyns constable of the West strete to bring Oliver Griffyn William Ives constable of the Saltesford to bring (   ) hopkins the Shomaker Leonerd holmes constable of Smith street to bring Raffe Martyn wherof neither constable nor man were at home but Cristofer Knight supplied the constables place & brought others w{th} him. As for any man beyond bridge (folio 164) yt was not thought mete to calle more than the constable yet John hopkins husbondman & others did come, herof the constables being sent for were warned & comaundid to be ready w{t} their men apointid to attend on M{r} Bailief at the crosse by one of the clock. And then M{r} Balif desired for his better assistance That all the pryncipall Burgesses present woolde take the paynes to accompany him to & at the place bothe w{t} their aide & counsaill. w{ch} was grauntid & parformed. And it was thought mete & directid that twoo of the principall Burgesses & twoo of the constables shoulde stonde uppon the bridge to staye all others saving such as were apoyntid, And to suffer none other to goo after or follow M{r} Balif to the place. ffor it was forseen, that whan the comoners shoulde perceve M{r} Balif & his bretherne to goo so accompanied, Many uncallid woolde followe, And so the nombr encrease farre beyond their direction and whan a

the names of the men callid to assist the Bant

the principall Burgesses required to assist the Balif

---

[a] A Court Leet is held annually in Warwick in the month of October, at which the Court Leet Jury among other appointments, appoint a resident in each of the wards as constable of his ward for the next twelve months. On Court Leet day the Corporation are called "Lords of the Leet."

multitude of rash heades be togither especially about such a matter & in a cause towching such a persone as this did, daungerous discordes might have risen contrary to their meanyng Therefore it was apoyntid that Mr Roo & Mr Dyche shoulde stonde & kepe the bridge, and wt them the constables of the west strete & Saltesford. This being so determyned John Raye & William Worcetor were warned to attend on Mr Balif & Mr Townesend by one of the clock about what tyme they yntendid to deliver them the corne acording to the Iniuncion, if they might by any meanes reasonable which they gladly hearkened unto And so at the tyme apoyntid, or rather something before Mr Balif & Mr Townesend the constables others & apointid mett at the crosse & so took their Journey towardes the tythe barne⁽ᵃ⁾ beyond the bridge In which barne the corne lay, and on the bridge stayde a great nombr of others that woolde have gone & so leving there such as had charge to staie the followers) Mr Balif & his company kept on theire way, and comyng to the farther end of the bridge, he sawe Thomas Brookes (brother to Richarde) whom Mr Balif callid to him & tolde him what comission or Iniuncion he & Mr Townesend had recevid, and what he entendid to doo, willing hym that if his brother had any srvnts or freindes in the barne (as he harde say) there were) That he woolde procure them to come away & not to resist the auctoryte. Thomas Brookes answerid that he had not to doo in the matter, nor his brother neither as he thought, but the Sheriff who had apoyntid eten persones to kepe the corne & the barne, And he thought they woolde so doo. Mr bahf said unto him. It were better otherwise And the other wt many woordes aunswerid the contrary, advising Mr balif to take hede what he did least he shoulde aunswer yt and so wt many more stout woordes & indecent behavyor the said Thomas Brookes kept way wt Mr Balif to the barne whither Mr Bahf & his company being come Mr Bailif knocking at the gates softely wt his white staffe, askid who was within and by & by comith to the gates being fast lockid Rycharde Brookes tanner & James Richerdson wt their bowes

Rey and Mr Worcetor apointid to be redy to receve the corne

the Balif &c goo to the barne

Coicacion betwene the Balif and Tho. Brookes

the behauyor of the Balif at the barne

(a) There are no remains of this barn.

T

bent & arrowes or boltes in theire bowes and askid who was there and what woodde you have. Than said Mr balif I John Grene & Richarde Townesend are here and have receyvd comission to deliver away the corne in the barne, and therfore are wee come. Open the dores therfore & suffer us to come in. Naye saye *he is denied to enter* Richardson & brookes you come not here, nor we will open no dores, for we are apoyntid to kepe possession here & so will we doo. Who apoyntid you so to doo saith Mr Balif. That did Mr Sheriff said they, and that you knowe well enough. Than said Mr Bailief but I have here the quenes comission which shalbe your & my dischardges. We will take no such discharge said they, & wt that a greater noyse than of twoo was hearde in the barne. Then was it askid of them Who or howe many other persons were there wtin, and they *others in the barne* said no more but wee twoo. That is not so said John ffisher for *shewe themselves* I hearde nijor or v more And therwt steppith into the ffore within the barne Thomas Oldenall sonne in lawe to Richarde Brookes & George ffulshurst brother in lawe to the said Brookes either of them having a qualiver of harquebuz in their handes & matches burnyng, and saide, Yea marye here be more And what woodde you wt them. Yee Mr Oldnall are you there said John ffisher, I am sorye to see yone & Mr ffulshurst there. I wisshe yone bothe awaye. It is no matter said they, here we are, & here we wyll bee doo what you can. *the Balif spekith to* Than Mr Bailif spake to them, saing. Mr Oldenall & Mr ffulshurst, *them &* and all that bee wthin heare I pray you what I saie, here Mr Townesend & I have the quenes mats processe & comission under her seale to deliver the tythes of Myton felde & the proffits therof to John Ray or his assignes and to that end are we come. And bicause you may the better believe us, here is the comission, as yone may see, & shall heare yt red, harken unto yt. *the comaundem' or* And theruppon a great silence was made. And Mr Bailif openly *Injunction red* in sight & hearing of all that were there, red the proces verbatim *heard openly* which being red & seene of many that were in the barne Mr Balif said I trust that all you that be in the barne have hearde the comission. Yea sayt they, wt one voyce wee have hearde it, Youe understand therby saith Mr balif that Mr Townesend & I bee comaundid to deliver the corne. Wee pray you therfore come furth & suffer us to execute the comission. Wee knowe the Comission well enough say Oldnall & ffulshurst, and what it is, but you shall deliver no corne here, nor come in neyther, nor wee will not come furth for all that comission Yf you will not come furth saith M{r} Balif wee must use youe otherwise than wee woolde, And assure yo{r} selves you shalbe fetched (folio 165) furth before wee goo. And therfore I pray you w{t} gentlenes laye aside yo{r} weapons & departe quietly, and so no man shall offer you any vyolence. Nay say they ye can not get us furth, nor no man shall come in here. Yf any man doo, let him take yt for a warnyng, & stond at his owne perill, for we will dye before wee leave the possession and he that offreth to come in shall dye for yt. Well said M{r} Balif, I trust that you wilbe better advised, you knowe what it is to shede blood, and ye knowe what will come of yt, yt any man be slayne, and therfore I chardge you in the quenes name to lay aside yo{r} weapons & to keape the peace, and to come quietly furth, and suffer us to do that we are comaundid. Nay M{r} Balif saith Oldenall I charge you to kepe the peace & see that no hurte be doone, for if any thing happen you shall aunswer for yt. Than said John ffisher I am sorry to see you M{r} Oldenall & M{r} ffulshurst that shoulde have discrecion & knowe what daunger you stond in, that you will stand so obstinately against the quenes offycer & her comission & auctorytie. And therfore I hartely pray you give over thes daungerous attempts and come furth where you may be very well assured bee yo{r} freindes, and will see that you shall tak no harme. Otherwise M{r} Balief must doo that he is comaundid and so you may be further towchid than you woolde or any of us desire, And be you well assured that you can not long resist the officer who hathe power enough here as you may see to pluck the house downe uppon you, and to handle you more straightly than in any wise he myndeth, if reason may leave any swaye w{t} youe. It is no matter for that saith Oldnall here wee are in possession and here we will live & dye, and if any man goo about to enter, let him come at his perill. with thes and many such frivolose aunsweres the tyme was spent more than half an howre. Then was it thought good and advised that a proclacion shoulde be made to this end that

marginalia: they w{ch} resist — many persuacions used — thes stick to their possesion bicause it was not knowen howe many was in the barne and so if they were the nombr of xij or above, that the statute of Riot Routs & unlaufull assemblies being remembrid unto them the proclamacion made acording to the said statute might

<small>proclamacion was made</small> terrifie them, and so cause them to disperse their company & to depart within one howre least they shoulde fall into the doomgies pvided by that Statute. Wheruppon Mr Balif, The Stuarde or Towneclerk & the Serianut at mace aproching nere the dore, proclamacion was made in forme following viz first three noyces or oyes. then were they in the barne & all other callid to give eare & heare the proclamacion, & so after silens made. It was openly publishid wt thes or very nere the woordes following. Mr Bailief of this borough of Warwik being Justice of pece w'in the same borrowe & libties therof accompanyed wt the constables & other officers of the same borrough dooth in the quenes mats name straitly charge & comaund all maner of persone & persones unlaufully assemblid & being within this tuith barne to laye away their armoure weapones forse & furnyture and quietly & peaceably to goo furth & departe from the same barne w'out further contynewing or comytting any further Ryott Rowt unlaufull act or unlaufull assembly as they will aunswer their doings & avoide the perille & paynes provided by the statutes made against Riotts Rowts & unlaufull assemblies. And god save the quene. After this proclamacion made & publishid by the Stuarde & Serjant, Mr Bailief & Mr Stuard spake to them that were w'in and saide Sirs you that bee within you have hearde the proclamacion, and they annswer that they have hearde yt. Then saith Mr Bailief & the Stuarde

<small>other persuesion</small> you knowe what dannger is nere of you doo contynewe togither in this unlaufull maner the space of one howre after this proclamacion made being that nombr which wee think you to bee xij you are to annswer yt as in case of felonye. wherof wee warne youe & desire you to have respect to yor selves,

<small>they still resist</small> and come furth peaceably & quietly and no force or harme shalbe offred you. Oldenall & ffulshurst annswerid, wee care not wee are determyned, and therfore bee content, youe come not here. Than Mr Bailief & the rest peeving their stubbornes and that they were wilfully bent to persevere their ntendid purpose doubtid what woolde or might come of yt, and consaling on the

matter feared the hassarding of any mans lief or blood, & on thother side regarding the quenes comission & auctorytie, and waying what an example this might bee to other like misdoers to contempne auctorytie yf this should be so given over, resolued by the grace of god to break into many partes of the barne at once, having company enough so to doo by meanes wherof the company within the barne shoulde have cause to defend many places at ones and so the weaklyer and so to give the adventure to enter & execute that comission And yet spared to use that force so long as might bee the rather in hope that the tyme of daunger woolde have wrought better consideracion emongs the Rioters, using in the meane tyme many freindly offers to be bound to annswer the Indempnytie to Richerd Brookes if by Lawe in this doing he were wrongid, But all to no purpose though M{r} Bailief forbare to execute any force more than an howre & a quarter after proclamacion In which meane tyme hee & the wyser sorte travellid from place to place about the barne speaking to the Ryoters, who showed themselves to the nombre of ten in warlik maner weaponed at dyvers loopeholes, But neyther faire promises nor any entrety, nor the remembrance of the ymynent daunger & perille coulde any thing move them.

the Balif agayne consultith what is to be doone

resolued to enter

So at the last (folio 166) twoo fyre hookes & other great poles being fetchid to pluck downe & beate downe the dores & walles by consent of John Ray & William Worceto{r} and the houre & a quarter & more after proclamacion being spent and withall the evening drawing on It was thought good after an other admonyshement given to execute the attempte But no persuasion could take place, but they within woolde kill or bee killed, & leave their carcases there before they left the possession And what tyme by many loope holes or watch holes they in the barne had percevid the fyre hookes to be brought & other engynes prepared to beat downe the walles They (thinking as it may be supposed) to terryfie the Bailif & his companye) dischargid a shott of a gonne callid a qualiver or harbuz, and shott out of barne some arrowes & boltes but yet in such maner as hurt no man (God be

Ray & Woorcetor consent to have the barne walles and dores to be broken

preparacion thereunto

the Rioter discharge a gonne

thankid) But whan the crack of the goonne was hearde and the comon sort willed to set their handes to the hookes & poles to break downe the gates & walles most men without very willingly showed their good willes, and so the hookes were hoised to the barne doores the poles shoved against the walles the stakes beat downe the lome & roddes on the outside And they within shott out sheff arrowes & boltes good plenty wherwith they did hurt some assalants but not greatly Others within with long piked staves thrust at such as came neare the walles & others within with long rapiers & swoords & one buckler cast many pricks & thrusts and some within having forrest billes strake at them without so fiercely that they brak twoo forrest billes others threwe great pible stones at the assalants all wch force they without defendid as the might and withall brak downe the walles on bothe sides so as they might have entrid though w^t perill; and therin so well behavid themselves that after a quarter of an houres conflict The Ryoters within cryed out & desyred to holde and that they might speak w^t Mr Bailif wheruppon the assaulte was stayed, And M^r balif came to the walle. Then they within desired to speak secretly with him, and that therfore he alone might come yn to them a matter very perillous in so furious a tyme yet he went unto them alone without any weapon, and the commed w^t hym And ffulshurst & Oldnall offred to Mr Bailif that upon condicion that Ray should not be put in possession, and upon his former offers to be bound to answere brooks indempnitie. And that the corne might be suffred to lye there vii dayes and that Mr Balif woolde undertak that the corne should not be removid w^tin that tyme uppon thes condicions they woolde depart Mr Balif answerid that he could not graunt any thing of himself but he woolde speak w^t Mr Townesend & the rest of his bretherne & theruppon give them answere In the meane tyme no man shoulde come into the barne nor give any further attempt So this conflict stonde And Mr Balif talkid of the matter w^t his assistants who remembrid unto him that his commission was to deliver the corne to John Rey without condicion and to that end was he come and in so much as they within had withstood him

[marginal notes: the manner of the conflict / The Ryoters cryed hold desired to speke w^t the Balif / the Balif goeth in to them they comen together / the cometh forth and cometh w^t his assistants / Resolucions]

& showed their force which nowe was at an ende It wolde be greatly to his discredit to yeld to such condycions And because there shoulde no further harme bee done It was devised that such psones as John Ray or Willm Worcester had

th'expedicion

there & which were a dozen well apointed should be readie to enter & thrust in themselves assone as Mr Balif was gone into the barne to give them answere which was expeditid & quickly done to the great grief of the Ryoters companye who than were so matched and kept upp as had no Roome to strike, though they made great semblance And so being that way overmatched they were content to leave the place & resort to their Refuges, part wherof namely ffulshurst & some others to & thorough John Jeffreys house The Rest to Richard Brooks whose quarell only this is thought to be and there were receivd of Mary his mischevous & malicious mate. The Riotous offenders were thes

the name of the Rioters

namely Thomas Oldenall who first showed himself w^t a goonne & after fought w^t swoorde & buckler George ffulshurst first w^t a goonne, & after fought w^t a long staf w^t twoo pikes & a swoord & dagger. James Richerdson with bowe & arrowes & did shoote, Richerd Brookes tanner w^t bowe & arrowes & did shoote, Richerd Bettes w^t bowe & arrowes & did shoote ( ) Carpinter or Smyth w^t a forrest bill strake lustely Clement hill threwe stones & offred to strike w^t Oldenall's Rapier Three straungers whose names be not knowen having long staves swoordes & daggers ( ) a lackey of Thomas Oldenalls who w^t sword or Rappier thrust very desperately & daungerously through the wall many thrusts And Thomas Brooks in the Intermission whiles Mr Balif was in coⁿcacion w^t his bretherne gat into the barne where finding a gilt halberd took it in his hand bending the same as though he woolde have striken or thrust at Mr Townesend coming in w^t Mr Balif the second tyme using w^tall very cruell &

persones hurt in the conflict

furious woords. Thes persones were hurt on the balifs part, though not daungerously God be thankid therfore Henry Chaplin hurt in the brest w^t an arrowe or bolt shott Willm Hynce boocher hurt on the head w^t a bolte Richerd Lytle hurt on the head w^t a staf & on the body w^t a bolt John Fisher hurt on the thomb w^t what he knowith not.

In thend all things fynishid the Ryoters were suffred to depart. And M{r} Balif & M{r} Townesend putting all other persones out of the barne saving John Raye, took a handfull of barley in the strawe & their delivered him that & all the rest, and so executid their comission leaving him in his possession of the barne & corne who there acknolegid himself possessed & satisfyed acording to the order of the court, & so callid to him Willm Worcetor & such other company as they had provided for his ayde & assistance. who the next day carryed the same corne awaye to the great grief of Ric. Brookes & his complices, namely John Jeffreys & John Lynacres who fumed at the hearing therof & showid their affections for Jeffreys & Lynacres comyng from london & hearing herof by the way. Jeffreys being clerk of the peax showed his good nature & wisshid that some had bene slayne. of which part he had not cared. Lynacres being undersherif wisshid he had bene there for than some of them should have dyed for it &c.

Ray put in possession

Joh. Lynacres John Jeffreys good desire

(folio 167) Nowe towching the collusion & colorable handling of this matter.

setten notes showing collusion emonges Brookes Lynacres Jeffreys

ffirst it is to be remembrid that before this tyme Richerd Brookes had disclamed in that tythe affirming the right to be in his Sonne Oldnall. which was also confessid the yere before by Oldnall & affirmed also by S{r} John Hubond. And so the leace being not the goods of Brooks nor the pfits therof rising could not be liable to the debt owyng by Brooks & so not to be executid to S{r} Jo Throkmton.

Secondly. The extent was not taken out nor sitten uppon untill the M{r} & counsaill of the court of Requests had sett down their second order against Brookes for the possession to Ray.

Thirdly the Sheriff being brookes one hand returned none to be of the Jury to fynd the extent saving only the freends of Brooks & such as he apoyntid, who also dyned at Brookes house the day of their verdyte & appeared uppon one nights warning.

ffourthly the Jurats knowing & seing that brookes had many other goodes & catalles in their sight or within the libties of the borough as not so fewe as vj^c shepe on the backside his house xx^ty kyne besides oxen & horses. the leace of the tuythes of harbury the leace of the mylles of Bereford the leace of his ferme of the temple which things wold better have satisfied the debt, woold not fynd none of thes, but found only the leace of Myton & the corne in the barne wch wold not annswer the vj^th part of the debt

ffivethly after the Inquysicion sithen uppon Sir John Throkmton being earnestly labored unto by Brookes & his freends woold not consent that any liberate should be taken out for the execucion But confessid in dede that he was otherwise satisfied. And yet woold very gladly have pleasured Brookes so farre as his creadite might suffer.

Sixtely those that were in the barne in that Riotose maner were nerely allyed or household srunts or haugers on & hirelings of Brookes. as for example Oldnall his sonne in lawe ffulshurst his own brother. clement hill his warde. (   ) Carpinter his hired srunt Betts also his hired srunt, Ric. Brookes his kinsman & relivid only by him, Rycherdson his comon carror, the Lackey being Oldnalls boy, & all the rest hired by Brooks. wch he woold not do in any other mans right.

Seventhly. after this doone and the corne delivered. Brookes exhibitid a bill of complaynt into the starre chambr against Richerd Townesend & xx^ty others that he supposed were at the delivery of the corne. wherin he complaned that he the said Brookes being possessid of the said tuith barne & the said corne the xxvij^t day of Novembr (being the day of the delyvery) as in his owne right and having bene therof possessid many yeres. The said Rycherd Townesend & the nombr of xx^ty aforesaid & many others had ryotosly w^t stafes &c dispossed him therof & so confessith the right in himself. All wch things consideridd & many others doth manifest give presumpcions of collusion & very collusion itself.

Brookes conyng to avoyd ponishm. in the Court of requests

Now towching his conyng in avoyding the ponishm^t for disobeing the order of the court of Requests being before the second hearing bound to stand to what order should be made. After that the Maister of Requests sent out many processes to apprehend him which could not be served and many messingers or pursevants to catch him at last he was found by a pursevant who wolde have brought him into the court of Requests but was lettid by the under Sheriff of Midlesex whose name is Yardley a great freend of Brookes. This undersherif woold not suffer the pursevant to have him from him bicause as he said Brookes was his prisoner. The maner howe was. Brookes thinking to shift the order of the court of requests procured himself to be arrestid by the Sherif of Middlesex being his freend (& before that his Attorney) for a debt owing by Brookes to Mr Richard Cook esquyre in whose debt in dede he was as afterward Mr Cook confessid to the M^r of Requests being Mr Sekford, who was not a litle movid against Brookes for this & many other his practizes used for the defacing & as it were the disanulling & overthrowing of the auctoryte of the court. wch Brokes practized by all the meanes & devises he could have or use, and so protestid in divers places where he thought he might be bolde So as nowe being under arrest & in warde of the Sherif of Middlesex by proces out of the quenes bench he was not to come into the court of Requests untill the Sute there had his full determinacion which brookes was content to protract as long as might be, and therfore was content to lye in that Sherifs warde all hyllary terme, and that terme endid he was licensid by the said undersherif to come downe into the countrey unto his owne house but w^t a keaper, such a one as Brookes himself likid to chose, w^t this keper he walkid upp & downe London Westm & into the countrey & in the countrey many tymes ten myles from his keper, herof the M^r of Requests being advertised contynewed his proces aswell by attachements to the Sherif of Warwikshire as pursevants into London, but all to litle purpose for what w^t frendship of the Undersherifs & free speche of his purse he still passid the pikes untill Easter terme. Whan Easter terme was come and than acording to his composicion he must yeld himself to the undersherif of Middlesex, he came w^t his keper to London wherof the M^r of Requests being advertised & cryed uppon by Ray & his frends the court & counsaill of Requests made an order that the undersherif of midd should bring in the body of brookes under a certen payne and that order they sent by a pursevant to the said undersherif of Midd w't comaundm't to come himself & bring in the said Brookes. Wheruppon the said Yardley being undersherif of Midd came into the court of Requests and there avowed that brokes was his prisoner arrested for the debt of M'r Cook before any pces was sent out of the court of Requests And bicause he could not put him in sufficient suretyes or speciall bayle into the court of quenes bench he remane'd in his warde as by order of lawe he must doo. Then M'r & counsell of the court of Requests made an order and enioyned the said undersherif that so sone as the cause now laid against Brooks by M'r Cook was determyned or orderid That he the said undersherif should deliver the body of the said brookes into that court of Requests w'thout any collusion or serving of other proces. and so the said undersherif was for that tyme dismissed wherof he was not a litle glad. But see the further practize of Brookes. before this arrest at (folio 168) M'r Cooke his sute, he having bene collecto'r of the second payment of the subsidy of part of warrshire in the xiiij't yere of the quenes ma'ty had gotten one C'h to be stallid for c'ten yeres to be paid by xx'li the yere and those payments being not out he procured a wryt of privilege out of theschequyre supposing him to be accomptant & indebtid to the quenes ma'ty there and therfore not to be sued ells where, and this privelege was showid to the M'r of Requests. who finding the thwarting of him by Brookes went into the Excheq'r and declaring the circumstance of all things & Brookes his practises procured the dissolving of that privilege & so was referred to the order of the other courtes and so brookes his labo'r & cost Lost in that behalf. But nowe all easter terme he

the Court of requestes send out contynually proces

contynewed in the warde of the undersherif of middlesex & the next vacacion & so all Trynyty terme. In the meane tyme proces was contynewed to the Sherif of warrshire & to the balif of Warwik for the Apprehending of Brooks but he could not be found there. And in trynytye terme John Ray & his frends prosecuting their sute in the court of Requests obteynid out of the same court a processe or warrannt directid to the hiegh Sherif of the county of Warr & to the bailif of the borrough of Warwik comaunding them or either of them not only to mak proclamacion of Rebellion against Richerd Brooks for his disobedience. but also to aphend him whersoever he might be found, & to bring him before the counsaill of the court of Requests to annswer his misdemeano'. but also to ayde assist & maynteyne John Ray & his assignes in the possession of the tuythes of myton w' the profits aptenances and also to apprehend & comyt to warde all such persones as should interrupt let or disturb the possession of Ray or his assignes & theruppon to send up the psons or c'tifye the court that further order may be taken for their ponishm' which comaundm' was in order & forme as is set furth the last yere in the tyme of John Rigeleys bailiwik. This proces was brought to John Grene balif of Warwik & delivered to him after Trynytie terme & was urgid by the freends of Ray to be pclamed w'th spede. But bicause the Assises was not long after the delivery therof. the Balif thought good to spare the pclamacion untill he might have the opinion of the Judges. And so forbare till that tyme the rather bicause neither corne nor hey wold be redy before that tyme of Assises (& also padventure for some other secret causes him moving) So at the comyng of the Justices of Assises. M' Bailif requiring the company of M' hudson M' Townesend & John ffisher on the thursday night after supper attendid on my L dyer Lord chief Justice of the comon plees & M' Wyndham electid S'jant at lawe then Justice of Assises of Warrshire, and impartid unto them what comission or proces was come unto him, and what daunger was like to happen, and therfore desired their opynions what the Balief might or was best to doo in that matter & whether the comission might be his warrant. And also whither the possession of the said tuythes might be mayntenid for Ray insomuch as the said Balif was enformed & did understand that the same were lately sithens the comyng of this comission extendid as the goods of Brookes for a c'ten debt of CC'li owing by Brookes to John Jeffreys. herof my L chief Justice & M' Wyndham conferrid together a litle while before the gave any answere. But not long after my L chief Justice sayd. What meane

proclamacion of Rebellion attachment

the proces delyverid to the Balif

he spareth till he may bee advised by the Juges

the Justices of assises opinion desired

you to trowble us w{t} thes matters as though we were counsalers. I have bene twoo or three tymes movid in this matter for myne opinion. I tell you truly I am wery of yt. Wee come downe as Judges & not to give Counsell And why should you trowble us w{t} yt, and so semid to be somewhat movid. Then John flisher besought his L not to be offendid for the cause in hand being doubtfull & stonding uppon a question of value & auctorytie of a court & the quenes proces as they took yt being many wayes impugned by trowblesome men, they were bolde to move the question to their Lordships as Judges to tell them what became them to doo. for otherwise being of themselfs ignoraunt in such a cause knewe not howe to behave themselfs as they woold most gladly for the discharge of their duetyes. Why saith my L chief Justyce you may goo to counsaill as here is M{r} Buk who stod by & was ptely made privy to the cause by Robert Sheldon or by some other, w{t} that M{r} buck steppith in & began to   the cause wherw{t}. my L more mislikid & swinged away. Than saith M{r} Wyndham is not this brookes one that dwellith at the townes end. Yes said flisher. That fellowe saith M{r} Wyndham mett us a myle or two hence, and askid me dyvers questions. the one was whither he being arrestid by the undersherif of the Shire & in his ward, might be afterward arrestid by an other proces by the balif of the libtye. And I told him myne opynion was no so long as he was in the Sherifs ward. And then he rememored unto me howe I was of his counsell in a matter betwene him & Ray and that I had both bene in the court of Requests for him & bene meane to my lord keaper for him. Which I then well remembrid & so calling the matter therby the better to memory I advised him to fall to some end, for though he might shift it for a tyme yet in thend he must be glad to yeld. Uppon thes woords of M{r} Wyndehams John flisher took occasion the rather to enlarge his talk to the said M{r} Windham both declaring the condicions of brookes & his practizes. and what his ayders were especially Jo. Jeffreys clerk of the peace who may be reconid qui intertubat omnia for sithens his comyng into the towne more discencion hath growen emongs neighbors than was in xx{ty} yeres before. And therw{t} John Jeffreys cam

my L chief Justice unwilling to give his opynyon

M{r} Wyndam confessith that Brookes had bene in hand w{t} him by & maide an errand to speke wt Mr Redford clerk of the assises & so passid by into the further part of the garden. Then Mr Balif desired secretly of Mr Wyndham his opynion whither he might mak the proclamacion against brookes & what he may doo towching (folio 169) the rest of the comission who told him that he might make proclamacion whan he thought good, and for the rest he might ayde & assist Ray in his possession so farre as in anywise he forsee that no Ryot be comyttid by & therfore advised him in such case not to tak many wt him whan he went about that matter and towching the arresting of brokes showed his opinion betwene them two. This being orderid Mr Balif the next day being fryday & day of Assises spake wt Mr humfrey fferrers hiegh Sherif & told him what comission he had recevid directid aswell to him as to him, and theruppon showed the comission to Mr Sherif who desired to have yt all night to consider uppon and so he had and the next day delivered the same agayn to the Balif, saying it is a matter as I understannd towching tythes lieng w'in yor libtye and therfore by yon to be dealt in, and I will not medle wtall. Theruppon the balif recevid the comission agayn. And being urged therunto on the Saturday during the tyme of Assises in the tyme of open market & in the market place he made proclamacion of Rebellion against brookes, and sayd further that he woold arrest him, if he might catch him. But Brookes kept himself for the tyme in and had freends enough abrode to harken to his causes. Nowe behold an other shift to save him from arresting by the Bailief Brookes peured a Latitat to the Sherif of Warrshire for the arresting of himself at the sute of one ( ) marchant of London for a debt supposing to be owing to him and heruppon the undersherif named John Lord who lay at Willm hicks howse (I will not say wt his wief) being Sister to Richerd Brookes (Such a brother such a Sister) arrestid Brookes suffring him nevertheles to go & be at his owne house & in his owne groundes, & appointid him a keper by deputacion one Richerd Brooks tanner his owne kinsman & of his houshold and he should have the keping of brookes as a prisoner whithersoever he should goo. And this was done to thend

Mr Wyndeham sheweth his opynyon

the Baili sheweth the proces to the hiegh Sherif who refereth the execucion therof to the Baili

the Baili maketh proclamacion

an other shift of Brookes

he should not be arrestid within the towne. Nowe let the Reader judge whither this be playne or cleanly dealing or otherwise. And so Richerd Brookes walked abrode in the fields & about his owne house under the keaping of Richerd brookes but yet not without other espialls to view the coste ne forte &c This went so on for a season untill a privie sessions was afterward procured as shall afterward be declared. But first it is not ymptement to shewe the originall cause of that Sessions, wch was a conyng devise if it may be so honestly be termed. But this was the matter. The said Richerd Brookes being, or not being in debt to John Jeffreys in CC^{li} suffred an extent to be brought against him at the sute of the said Jeffreys for CC^{li} uppon the forfeyture of statute. And this extent must nedes be sitten uppon at the howse of Willm hickes in a soller or hiegh chambr whereunto must enter none but only the undersherif John Jeffreys & the Jurats being of their owne piking & were freends to Brookes, wherof some of them labored & sent to by Brookes w^t Request thas as they lovid him they woold appere. this warning by brookes owne srunt given at the howses of some of them by five of the clock in the morning was sufficient to cause them to appere by ix of the clock. Some of which pformed his request. others did not but have confessid that they were so earnestly desired by brookes as they woold if great busynes had had not lettid them. Whan the howre was come none but xij of the Jury & the said undersherif & Jeffreys must be suffred to heare any thing, no not so much as the Balif of the hundred that warned them And dyvers psones hearing that an Inquysicion should be, fearing least the matter might towch them pressid & desired to be admyttid, but it was annswerid that no man should come in for yt was a matter for the quene & therfore none but the Jury to be pryvy nor none should be pryvy. So they peedid and Jeffreys being clerk of the peax & having a meany of his freends on the Jury shewid his statute & urged the debt requyred that he might by their meanes be recompenced w^t the fruytes of the tythes of Myton wch was the goods of Brookes & w^t the tuythes of Snyterfeld being also Brooks. This Jeffreys being next neighbo^r & dwelling nere to brooks, did every day walk brokes

an other shift

Jo Jeffreys bringeth an extent against Brooks

the maner of finding this extent

Jefreys desire of speciall thinges being in sute

groundes where he sawe cattell worth twise his debt, & knewe other leaces & land that brooks had of better value. But yet none to his liking so much as this which he knewe to be in sute of Lawe ready to be iudgid from Brooks. and to helpe Brokes tythe as may appere would have some colo' of interest. Than Thomas Staunton th'elder being broks great frend being forman of the Jury testifyed that Brokes was in possession of the tythes of Myton in the xvijth yere of the quenes ma^{ts} reigne and for Sniterfeld Jeffreys declared that Brookes had a clere title therin. But some of the Jury knowing that Robert Sheldon had tryed w^t brookes & was uppon a further triall for Sniterfeld woold not fynd the same. wch grevid Jeffreys gretly & so I think brooks. So in the end being kept togither three or foure houres & not suffred to dept untill they were agreid they founde the proffits of the tuythes of Myton for Jeffreys & c'ten houses or cotages to aunswer his debt. Which if be a good debt of CC^{li} woll not be resd of those things in xl^{ty} yere. And whether this be like to be a collusion or no let the Reader iudge. ffor it is manifest that Brookes goods at that tyme in open shewe was more woorth than v$^{c\ li}$ besides thes things But all this was practized to ympeche the tytle of John Ray in myton tuyth. and so therby to wyn the matter from him by Liberate uppon returne of this Inquisicion or to bring the matter to the comon lawe, Orells (which this writer doth think was chief pretendid) to bring some slaughter or extreme accion wherby the libties & charters of this borough might be infringid or forfaytid ffor let the Reader well note the circumstaunce and it will in maner shewe itself. Such is the fidelity & faithfull othe of the prinner Brookes and such be his practizes that if he can neither gayne ne save yet it pleasureth him to hurt others & that without any remorse or conscience. he was bailif of this towne & then sworne (folio 170) maynteyne susteyne & uphold the libtyes & privileges thereof to the uttermost of his power & howe he doth it behold he causith undersherifs & other meaner officers to infringe the same by their arrests of divers psones, he settith discord & debate betwene neighbors Yea he pcureth quarrells & those so daungerouse as most likely to growe to slaughter. he subornith straungers to take out copyes of ch'res & Evidencs

quere

Brookes had other goodes in open sight worth much more than this debt

Brookes disposicion

to encounter the good orders of the towne & to thwart asmuch as may be the orderly procedings of officers. Thes be the fruytes of such a membr as wold if it lay in him overthrow the whole to glory of part, what should I say more. my pen is weary and I am most sory to wryte, if otherwise it might bee, that any hope of goodnes might be expectid. but it is past. non est timor domini ante oculos eius. and so I end for this tyme.

(folios 170 to 179. Part taken up with the arrangements between Warwick and Banbury re Oken's gift (see ante pages 161 to 165), part with a copy of Mr. Tooley's feoffment: the remainder blank.)

The Rectory of Budbrook.

towching the grannt-ing of a leace of the Rectory of Bud-brook

(folio 179) It ys to be remembrid That after the death of Thomas Butler and his late wyef marryed agayne to unthrifty Warner Sute being made by Mr Raphe hubond and his freendes to o^r good Lord the right honorable Earle of Leycest^r. It pleasid his lordshippe to wryte a lre on the behalf of the said M^r hubond to the Baliet and his bretherne the Burgesses of Warwik. The Teno^r of wch lre ensueth. & first endorsed

To my very loving freendes The Bailief & his brethern and the rest of the corporacion of the towne of Warwik

a lre from my L therle of Leycester for a leace to be grauntid to Mr Raf. hubond

Budbrook

v

After my hartie comendacions, where you have to demyse certen Tuythes belonging to yor corporacion which were lately in the tenure & occupacion of one Butler. I veary hartely and earnestly pray youe that you will nowe lett the same to my very freend Raphe hubond give therfore as any others resonably wille, Wherin yf at this my request the rather you wille pleasure him, I will thank you for yt And not be unmyndfull to requyte yt you any wayes I can. fare ye well. from the courte the xxth of ffebr. 1580

Yo^r very loving freend
R. Leycester

This lre was not delivered untill the xixth day of May And then was it delivered to John ffisher Balief who woold not break open the same nor look into yt untill the rest of the principall Burgesses might meet togither wch at Mr Richard Brookes request was apoyntid to be at the cowrt house nere the crosse the xxiij^t day of the same moneth. Where met the said Jo. ffisher, Balief Richard ffisher, Richard Townesend Richard Roo, Richard Brookes, Willm ffrekulton, Thomas Powell, Thomas Jenkes humfrey crane & John Rigeley principall Burgesses. Where the said lre was openly publishid And considered but not resolued uppon for any direct annswere But Mr Ric Brookes thought it convenyent to give some certen answere at that tyme, wch yet was not agreed unto But yt was agreid that M^r hubond should have woord to resort to the said balif and his bretherne the xxixth day of the same moneth And then they woold use further conferrens of that matter And so for that tyme that cause restid.

On the xxiijth day of the said moneth, Raph Wagstaff a S^rvannt of the said honorable Earle brought an other lre from his hono^r to the said Bailief, requyring on my said L behalf an answere therof. The teno^r ensuith. endorsed

To my very loving freends the Bailief and masters of the Towne of Warwik

a lre from therle of Leycester for a leave to be graunted to Mr W. Beynham

Budbrook

After my very hartie comendacions, Wheras I am geven tunderstand that yor granntes of the Rectorye of Budbrook and Tythes lieng in the towneships & fieldes of Budbrook hampton and Norton Lynsey and Norton Curley made to my late Servant John Butler decessid is voydable and of no force in Lawe And that for my sake you tolerated the use therof in his sonne Thomas Butler also decessid. Sithens whose death the said voyde grauntes (as I am enformed) are come to the custodye of a straungier who dwelling farre from you hathe not deserved any gratytude at yo' handes. My earnest request to youe is that youe will make a sufficient grannt and leace of the said Rectorye and tithes to my loving freende Willm Beynham Esquire for the terme of xxi yeres reserving the accustomed Rent and for such reasonable ffyne as your selves shall think him woorthie to paye taking uppon him the casualtie & charge of the Sute (if any shalbe) wherin what favo^r & frendely consideracion you shall shewe unto him for my sake, I wille take the same doone unto me, and will not forgett to gratifie the same with any good I may doo yor towne or any of youe furthering this requeste And so bid you farewell.

Yo^r loving freend
R. Leycester

This letter was made knowen also to the principall burgesses who thought good to deferre any resolucion untill their next meting wch was before appoyntid to bee on the xxixth of the same moneth And the said bringer so answerid was dismissid.

On the said xxixth of May 1580 the said Bailief and Burgesses namely John ffisher Bailief Richard ffisher Richard Townesend Richard Roo Richard Brookes William ffrekulton Thomas powell Thomas Jenkes humfrey crane John Rigeley and John Dyche being come togither in their said house, & conferring of both thes lres and what annswere were mete to be made to satisfie our said good Lord A messinger came to desire Richard Brookes to come to M^r hubond to Willm hicks house who went unto him but tarried not long away but returned to his place. And whiles the Bailief & Burgesses were thinking howe to satisfie my lord An other lre was brought from his L by a footeman of Mr Beynham. The teno^r of which ensueth endorsed

To my very loving freendes & neighbors the Balief and masters of the towne of Warwik.

a second lre from therle of Leycester on the behalf of Mr Beynham Budbrook

After my veary harty comendacions where of late I wrote unto you on the behalf of my veary good freende Mr William Beynham that you woolde the rather at my request grannt unto him for the terme of xxi yeres the Rectorye or personage of Budbrook for such reasonable fyne or Incom as you should think meet. Sithens the wryting wherof I have heard nothing from you of yor peedings therin. And being nowe further enformed that there is earnest sute made unto you for the same Leas aswell by Warnr that married Butlers wief as others that they might have yor consents for the lik graunt to be made unto them. I am therfore earnestly to pray you to graunt yor good willes & consents to Mr Beynham that he may for such resonable ffyne as he & you can agree have the same assured unto him for xxi yeres. I knowe yt is a thing that lieth very neare to Grove park very necessarye for him mynding to lie there, he shall give you for a ffyne more than any other, And will think himself beholding to you. And so shall you finde him a thankfull man. And I my self wille thank youe asmuch for yt as though ye had doone yt to my self And will not bee unmyndefull therof towardes you and your Towne as occasion shall serve. And this not doubting of yor good willes herin notw'standing any former lres to the contrary. I bid you hartely farewell. the coll xxvijtℎ May 1581

Yor loving freend
R. Leycester

Uppon the sudden receving of thes last lres the company was much appalled, and knewe not by what resonable meanes to satisfie the nest desire of Mr hubond & his good frends requesting earnestly for him namely Sr Thomas Lucy Sr ffulke Grevill Mr George Digby & others for whose sakes the rather they were well enclyned to have yeldid consent to Mr hubond but this second & earnest request of my Lord put the matter to a gret staye. And after they had made Mr hubond privye to my Lords other lres. They agreed to wryte to my said lorde to put him in remembrance of his first & second lres. The methode wherof was devised by Richard Brook who yet restid in hope of my said lords speciall choice of M{r} hubond by meane of his frends about my L. And therupon it was concludid that a lre should presently be writen and sent to my Lord to referre the choise to his L. The tenor ensuith, endorsed

      To the right honorable o{r} singuler good Lord, the Earl of Leycester M{r} of the horse to the quenes ma{tie} and one of her ma{ts} most honorable privy counsell.

the annswere to my L of Leycester Budbrook

Our duetie most humbly pmised to yo{r} good L. It may like the same tunderstand that wee recevid divers yo{r} honorable lres for the grannting of a Leace of the Rectory of Budbrook the first on the behalf of M{r} Raphe hubond brother to S{r} John on whose behalf wee have bene earnestly requested by divers woo{r}shipfull namely S{r} Thomas Lucy S{r} ffulke Grevill knights. Sithens which also other lres on the behalf of M{r} Will{m} Beynham for the same thing. And sithens the delivery of those lres the most part of us are served with proces out of the chauncery tannswer Symon Warner & his wief for the same Rectory as it is said, And so so much as some of us are in doubt to fall into Lappes of Lawe if wee shoulde grannt any leace of the thing being nowe in sute, wee most humbly doo beseach yo{r} honor to respitt our resolute annswere therin untill by learned counsell wee may be further advysed what wee may lawfully doo, which wee mynde to seek w{th} all the spede wee may And then will doo what shall become us to gratifie such of them as (folio 180) your good Lordshipp shall appoynt according to yo{r} honorable requests.

23º Eliz.

And so most humbly take o{r} Leaves at Warwik this xxix{th} of May 1581.

Yo{r} most honorable L at Comanndm{t} John ffisher Balif. Richard ffisher Richard Townesend, Richard Roo Richard Brooke Will{m} ffiekulton. Thomas Powell Thomas Jenks humfrey crane John Rigeley John Diche

Theffect of this lre was made knowen to M⁽ʳ⁾ hubonde who semed to be thankfull for the same hoping well that my L woolde prefere his sute. But it fell out otherwise for after this lre was delivred to o⁽ʳ⁾ said good Lord. The balif and foure or five of the company having occasion to goo to London in Trinytie terme following to annswere Warner in the chauncery Our said good lorde being aduertised of their being there sent for the said Balif and as many of his company as could be found to come to the court lieng then at the Whitehall to knowe his pleasure, wheruppon the said Bailief and Thomas Powell William ffrekulton (   ) attendid his L good pleasure where at the last none being left in his bedchambr but the L north and M⁽ʳ⁾ Beynham his L said that the cause of o⁽ʳ⁾ sending for was to signify his mynde unto us & by us unto the rest of the company towching his requests for the psonage of Budbrook for w⁽ᶜʰ⁾ he gave his harty thanks for his very freend there M⁽ʳ⁾ Beynham to whom he desired us & the rest of o⁽ʳ⁾ company to pforme the said grannt & mak him a leace for w⁽ᶜʰ⁾ he should not bee unthankfull and his L said he woold take yt doone to himself and wold be redy to requite it acordingly And willid us so to say to the rest of o⁽ʳ⁾ company w⁽ᵗʰ⁾ his harty comendacions & thanks. And yt pleased his L further to say that he woold consider Raph hubond in some other thing to his good liking. This message was delivered by M⁽ʳ⁾ Bailief & those that were w⁽ᵗ⁾ him to the rest after their homecomyng. Yet was there no hast made in sealing of the Leace. untill afterwards That my said L therle wrote agayne the tenor wherof ensueth. endorsed

the Earle of Leycester sendith for the Balif and others and signifieth his pleasure for the grannt and leace to bee made to M⁽ʳ⁾ Beynham

Budbrook

To my very loving freends the Bailif and Burgesses of the towne of Warwik

After my veary harty comendacions, Where I have before this tyme twyse wrytten unto you on the behalf of my very good freende M⁽ʳ⁾ Willm Beynham for the having a grannt by Leas from you of the Rectory of Budbrook for such reasonable fyne as you shall think mete. Sithens the wryting therof I receuid

therle of Leycesters third lre on the behalf of M⁽ʳ⁾ Beynham

Budbrook

aunswere from you Mr Balie and tenne of the burgesses by writing under yor hands that I had also wrytten to you in the behalf of Mr Raph hubond for the same thing And that you were well contentid the leas should be made to such of them both as I shold grannt my good wille unto And then within some short tyme after you Mr Balif and some of the Burgesses came to me to the courte to knowe my mynde & pleasure therin, to whome I did then declare that my desire & request was that you shoulde grannt the same to the said Mr Beynham and willed that the reste of yor company might understand by you my full mynd therin And so I did think the same had byn fully endid ere this, Nevertheles I am furthr enformed the same remaneth still unfinishid wherfore I am ones agayne to pray you to pcede to an end therof wth asmuch convenyent speede as you may, not doubting of all yor furtherannce therin in such sort as I shall have cause to give you thanks, for yt is for one I wishe well unto, And if any emongs you shall happen to be wilfull or froward not agreable to the rest of the company, then I doubt not but you wille procede wth the consent of the greater nombr acording to yor anncient order & customes. And that I may understand of yor pcedings herin wth all convenyent spede, And so shall you fynde me myndfull of yor good willes as occasion shall serve The court xvth July 1581

        Yor loving frend
         R. Leycester

the grannting & making the leace to Mr Beynham

Uppon the Receipt of thes last lres the Bailief and principall Burgesses mett agayne and agreid to make a leace to Mr Beynham for the terme of xxi yeres for the yerely Rent of xiijli vjs viijd where before the rent was but xli xiijs iiijd And also all tithes of wedgenok park & other Tythes lieng in Warwik at Lynnen felds & the others were resruid from the said Mr Beynham, and his ffyne agreid upon for the said

Budbrook

Leace was Ch to all which Mr Beynham agreid And theruppon a leace was drawen & sent up to him wt a clause of forfeiture & reentry for none payment of rent, wch he likid not, but agreid to have a clause pene of iijli vjs viijd for none paymt and so yt was agreid uppon and the leace engrossid as afterward may appere wch Leace was uppon the comyng of Mr Beynham wch was on the Wensday the (   ) day of August sealid by all the Bailief and principall Burgesses namely John ffisher balief Richard ffisher, Richard Townesend Richard Roo Willm ffickulton Thomas powell Robart Phillippes, Thomas Jenks humfrey crane John Rigeley John Grene and John Dyche in the place in the churche where the chest stoudith and ymediately uppon the sealing of the leace there was also sealid a lre of Attorney made to Mr Willm Skynner to deliver the Leace uppon some part of the grauntid premisses And those things being doone the said Bailief and principall Burgesses came from the church to the signe of the swan being then the bailief his dwelling house where Mr Beynham & Mr Skynner were then psent. And so they all togither went to dynner And after dynner Mr Beynham told them the cause of his comyng wch was to desire them to pforme their grannt made to my l therle of Leyct^r and him towching the Rectory of Budbrook wch he trustid they had made ready like as he was come to pforme that wch by him was to be doone wth most harty thanks. And theruppon the leace being sealid and the counterpayne being not sealid were redd and theruppon Mr Beynham sealid & signed the said counterpayne And then drewe out a bag wherin was gold wch he powred uppon the table saing here is my fyne and desired the balief to tell yt. But the balief desired some other of the company to tell it and see whither yt were good Theruppon John Grene took the matter in hand and told yt & found it to be iust C^li and allowed of the goodnes of the gold. Wheruppon the Bailief in the name of himself & the rest of the burgesses delivered to Mr Beynham the said Indenture or leace sealid by them And the other pte of the said Indenture Mr Beynham delivered as his dede to the said Balief for the use of the Balief and burgesses of Warr. And theruppon the said Bailief taking agayne the said grauntid leace & the lre of Attorney delivered them both to Mr Skynner auctorizing him to enter into some part of the said Rectory and to deliver the leace and possession of the said Rectory grauntid to the said Mr Beynham or his assignes. W^ch doone the monye was put up into a bag & delivered to the bailief to the use of the borough. And so theruppon the company deptid. After the

John Fisher dwelled at the signe of the Swan

sealing of the former Leace some doubt grew of varriance in a woord betwene the Leace and the lre of Attorney. and theruppon M{r} Beynham desired that the Leace being written up agayne & the lre of Attorney also newe written up & emendid might be newely sealid which was doone in the tyme of Babwik of M{r} Tho. powell as by the date of the said Leace may appear. And so they were both agayn sealid at w{ch} were psent humfrey crane balief Richard ffisher Richard Townesend Richard Roo Willm ffrekulton Thomas Jenks John Rigeley John Dyche and John ffisher. The said John ffisher being weak & not hable to goo up the steares to the place where the seale lieth, staid in the vestry w{th} whom also staid John Grene who woold not give his consent to this newe leace but to all other leaces besides then also sealid he gave his consent and both he and the said John ffisher sent up their keys to come to the seale.

The Corporation charged with misgovernment.

Brookes ioyneth w{t} Symon Warner

Budbrook

(folio 181) After the sealing of this Leace for Budbrook Richard Brook ioyned earnestly w{th} Warner and did asmuch as in him lay to psecute the sute in the chauncery. And more than that he was contynually in hand w{th} Warner to buy his title in the said Rectory which afterwards he brought to passe for Warner having comyttid a burglary in Staffordshire came to Brooks and comoned for those Leases and so in thend they bargained for them. And Brooks entrid & took the proffits of the glebe & after that of the tithes as they fell. And so drave M{r} Beynham to sute w{ch} yet

Brookes becometh open enemye

contynueth betwene them for the said Rectory. Brookes not content w{t} the Bailief & burgesses making the Leace to M{r} Beynham and w{t}hall for his expulsion & putting out of the company of Burgesses[a] becometh an open Enemye and voweth the overthrow and breking

---

[a] Brookes does not appear to have been formally expelled untill 1582, as is shewn by the account of his expulsion.

the neck of the corporation wch he puttith in vre to the uttermost of his power And beginneth first to creape in creadite w^t some gentlemen about my Lord of Leycester. Then enformeth my lord that dyvers things be misgoverned by the Balif & burgesses. namely in that they kepe grete stocks of monye given by good men to the use of poore occupiers in the towne & convert yt to their owne gayne Than that they wast the yerely revenues rising of lands & tenements given to fynd mynisters and yt to their private advantage. Then that they tak no accompts or recongs howe the monye is bestowed. And that the Bailiffes are and have bene unduly & not laufully chosen &c. Wheruppon he obteynith L^res from the said honorable Earl of Leycester & after from his noble brother Therle of Warwik both to the towne & also to divers gentlemen in the county to examyne thes misdemeano^rs As by the l^res following shall more manyfestly appere. And first having practized three or foure such as himself he & they exhibit a supplicacion to the right honorable Therle of Warwik. The teno^r wherof ensueth

Brooke, Olney Philips and Yardley exhibite supplicacion to therle of Warwik

To the right honorable Ambrose Earle of Warwik Baron Lisley of the noble order of the garter knight master of her ma^ts ordynannce and one of her hieghnes most honorable pryvie counsaill

Humbly complanyng showeth unto yor good L yor humble and dayly Orato^rs the poore Inhabitants of the towne of Warwik in the county of Warr. That wheras Willm Willington Late of Barcheston in the countie of Warr aforesaid Esquire decessid Thomas Whateley late of the Cytie of Coventry in the said county of Coventry marchant And Thomas Oken Late of Warwik aforesaid in the said County of Warr yoman likewise decessid did in their lief tymes by their sevrall Last willes and testaments in wryting under ther sevrall handes & seales devise and bequeath unto the said Towne of Warwik thes sevrall somes of monye herafter named That is to saye The said William Willington^(a) the Some of ffowrescore poundes of

(a) This Charity has now no existence: it is either lapsed, or in time past been joined to some other similar Charity.

like lawfull mony of Englond The said Thomas Wheteley[a] the some of flieftie poundes of like lawfull mony of Englond And the said Thomas Oken the some of one hundred powndes of lyke lawfull mony of Englond to the yntent that the same seuerall somes of mony should be distributid and lent out to certen poore Occupyers of the same Towne of Warwik by the discrecion of the Baliff and principall Burgesses of the same towne to be ymployd by the said poore Occupiers to theyre best Advanntage & comodytie and for the benefit and Relief of the poore and Impotent w^{tm} the same Towne. So yt is right honorable That the Balief and principall Burgesses of the said Towne having recevid and gotten into theyr handes & possession the forsaid sevrall somes of monye have not only contrary to the seuerall last Willes before mentyoned and contrary to all equytye and good consciens, not ymployd or lent out the forsaid seuerall somes of monye acording to the good yntents and charitable meenyngs aforesaid by the space of ffowre yeres nowe last past or therabouts to the great damage and hinderance of the said poore Inhabitants, And by all the same tyme have and yet doo ymploye and use the same or the most part therof to their owne private proflittes and comodyties without any consideracion to yor said poore Orators by them had at all for the same But also have contrary to all good concionable dealing refused to make Accompt yerely of the ymploying of the said severall somes of monye as before tyme was accustomed and as they ought to doo. ffor that they woold not have yt knowen in whose handes the said severall somes of monye doo remayne, And forasmuch as by the meanes of thes & the like extreme & unconcionable dealings The said Towne groweth into great Infamy and slaunder. Your said poore suppliants knowing yor Lordship greatly to tender the good estate and comonwelth of the same. doo flye unto yor hono^r as their chief patrone and defender against such grevous oppressions and Iniuryes Beseching yor Lordship of yor accustomed goodnes & favo^r towards such poore and humble Suppliants to procure a comission out of her ma^{ts} hiegh court of chauncery to be dyrectid to Sr Thomas Lucy Knight S^r ffulke Grevill knight Sr John hubond knight George

---

[a] This Charity was absorbed in the King's Schools Foundation, under the new Scheme for the Management of the King's School of 1875.

Digby Edward Boughton and Clement ffisher Esquires auctorising and comannding them therby or any fowre of them to heare & examyne the trothe of the pmisses And to take such order towching the same as to there wisdomes shall seme to stond wth equytie & good consciens And yor said poore suppliants shall daylie pray for yor L long lief in health wth perpetuall happynes

Yo^r honors most humble suppliants in the behalf of the Inhabitants of the said Towne Thomas Olney Richard Brooks Robart Phelips John Yardley

Uppon exhibiting the said supplicacion yt pleased the said honorable Earle of Warwik to wryte his Lres as follow^th.   endorsed

To my very loving freends the Balie & Burgesses of the towne of Warwik

the Earle of Warwik wriuth his lres to the Balif & Burgessis

After my hartie comendacions, where sondry somes of monye hath bene given to that towne by divers well disposed psons & good Benefactors to be ymploid & usid to good purposes which somes was given under very streight condicions that if it can bee pued the money not to be bestowed acording to the good meanyng of those benefactors but translatid to other private purposes, that then the somes of money so bestowed should returne to thexecutors of the said benefactors, and the towne utterly to loose the benefit of so great benevolence. And where I am enformed the said somes of money have bene well ymploid untill nowe of late, and that the consciens of divers men being put in trust to the same welbestowed according to the good meanyng of the Benefactors are towched for that they see the monye neither well employd nor the good meanyng of the benefactors pformed because the same is nowe in private mens handes Who maks to themselves a peculier gayne without any Regard had to the good entent of the benefactors Thes are therfore to will you Mr Balie and the rest of yor bretherne (having a speciall regarde to see such good purposes not abused the rather to encorage others to be beneficiall herafter and for the speciall love I beare to that towne and the Inhabitants therof) to call a (folio 182) halle and assemble the Burgesses togither and make diligent inquirye

towching stockes of money not ymploid

howe & in what maner those severall somes of money haue bene of Late employd. and in whom the fault especiall restith ffor yt is pittie to suffer so liberall benevolence to be turned to abuse and the honest & good meaning of the benefacto^{rs} no better pformed w^{t}hout due reformacion This hoping you will not faile but aduertise me w^t spede the trueth of this matter, I bid you all hartely welto fare.

At the Court this xxixth of Novemb^r 1579

Yo^r loving freend

Amb. Warwik

This lre was brought down by Robart Phillippes & deliuerid to Mr Richard Roo. balief the said day that we met to giue our voyces to Mr Digby to be knight of the Shire viz on Sr Tho. day before xremas following the date

After that tyme an other hall was callid for the purpose aforesaid and to examyn the matter & for annswering of the said noble Earle of Warwik And that was the answer following devised and made up to be sent to the said Earle in lre. endorsed

To the right honorable o^r singuler good lord Lord Ambrose Earle of Warwick master of the quenes ma^{ts} ordynannce and one of her ma^{ts} most honorable pnvy counsell.

the Balif and Burgesses doo annswer therle of Warwiks lres

All duetie most humbly remembrid unto yor most honorable L. It maie please the same to be aduertised That wee & other our Bretherne having had sondry meatings & conferrences and therin made diligent examynacions of the Enormyties supposed by yor honorable lre of the xxixth of Novembr last. doo fynde That albeyt things bee not in the best sort ordered, yet not so farre amisse as semith reaportid to yo' hono' neither may that compl as executo' take such benefit to the hinderance of the Towne as he hath pretendid, Wherunto nevertheles herafter wee will acording our dueties have speciall Regarde. holding our selves greatly bound to your hono' for that it pleasid the same texpresse yo' honorable and loving care towards the comon weale therof by so favorable exhortacions.

And bycause it is confessid by Robart Phillippes That this compleint is come not onely to yo' good L. but also before the Q ma^tie by his speciall meanes (being otherwise in great Sutes in lawe wth this bringer Jo. ffisher) The said ffisher takith that informacion to be chiefly ment tempeach his credit wth yo' hono' and that Phillippes myndeth to pcure yo' L ayde for staying such trialles as shortly by order of Lawe are to come betwene them, and yet nevertheles to procede in thexecucion of this cause before the Masters of Requests before whom the said Phillippes hath conventid the said ffisher tappere at a day assigned by a doquet delivered in o' presens Wherin the said ffisher thinkith himself badly dealt w^thall, and therfore desired us to signifie o' opinions of him.

And forasmuch as wee have sought by all meanes devised by Phillippes which waye to charg the said ffisher and fynde nothing prooved against him, wee humbly besech yo' hono' to contynewe good lord towards the said ffisher and to conceive no woorse opynyon of him then before Who with us rest bound to praie to god for yo' good L prosperous estate tencrease wth everlasting felicitie. At Warwick this xxvj^th of January 1579

Yo' hono^rs humble to comannd

Ric Roo Balif Ric ffisher

humfrey crane. John Rigeley

At the tyme of writing of this lre neither the Balief or burgesses or ffisher did understand of the supplicacion exhibited to my Lord of Warwik but supposid it had bene enformed by only Phillipps Executor to Oken. and therfore the annswere was made as before recited. But whan ffisher came up to London & could not speak wth my L of Warwik bicause of his Infirmytie he caused the said annswer to be deliuerid to my said L by M^r ffenton then my Lords Secretarye by whose meanes he understood of and got a copie of the said supplicacion exhibited to my Lord as before is remembrid. But besides that Phillippes had exhibitid a bill of complent against the said ffisher & Ric Townesend to the masters of requests in the names of himself as executo^r & three of the overseers of the will of Thomas Oken, the copie wherof followith viz.

<small>Robt phillipes in his own name and Jo. Grene Th. powell W^m frekelton exhibit a bill against John ffisher Ric Townesend Ric ffisher Ry Roo in the court of Requests</small>

To the Quenes most excellent ma^{tie} Humbly complaning showeth to yor ma^{tie} yor faithfull Subiectes & daly suppliants Robart Phillippes Burges of the towne of Warr in the countie of Warr. Lynnen Draper one of thexecutors of the last Wille & testament of one Thomas Oken of Warwik aforesaid decessid and John Grene Thomas Powell and William ffrecleton Burgesses of the same towne of Warwik and three of the Overseers of the said last Wille and testament of the said Thomas Oken. That whereas one (   ) Wyllington of Barston in the countie of Worceto^r esquire myndyng encrease of the good & prosperous estate of the said towne of Warwik by his last Wille & testament did geve unto the said Towne of Warwik about xx^{tie} yeres last past the some of fourescore powndes of lawfull english monye to bee distributid by way of Lone to such Artificers in the said towne of Warwik as shoulde newely begyn to trade and set up in their profession or misterye, they to have & use the same emongs them for and during certen yeres uppon good assurance of repayment to the Bailief and Burgesses of the said towne of Warwik at the order appoyntment and discression of the said Balief and Burgesses which said some of money was by the Balief and Burgesses for that tyme being recevid and taken and afterwards for and during divers yeres well truly and godly ymployd & bestowed to the said use and purpose to the great helpe succo^r & advancem^t of all the said towne of Warwik And wheras one (   ) Whateley of the cyttye of Coventrye grocer in lyke sort about tenne yeres last past did give unto the said towne of Warr the some of fiefty^e powndes of lawfull english monye to be ymploid to the lyke use and purpose as by the said (   ) Willington before that tyme was Lymytted & appoyntid, which said some of flieftie powndes was likewise recevid, and for a certen tyme likewise most pollitiquely & godly bestowed according to the good and godly entent of the said Whateley.

And wheras moreover by the good example and precident of the said Willington and Whateley and of the good and godly use of the said severall somes of mony by them so bestowed and most orderly & comodiosly ymploid accordinglie The said Thomas Oken late of the said towne of Warr mercer by his last wille and testament made 1570 did give & bequeth unto the said towne of Warwik One hundreth powndes of Lawfull english mony to thintent therwth to buye some pyece of grounde for ever to Laye to the encrease of the comons of the said towne and relief of the poore and needye people there dwelling And if such pyece of grounde coulde not be bought then that the same hundreth powndes should be emploid either to tenne honest comoners of the said towne of Warwik euery of them to have x^{li} a piece orells to five honest comoners euery of them to have xx^{li} a piece for & during foure or five yeres at the discrecyon of the said Bailief and of his bretherne and such as shoulde bee put in trust for to see the due disposition of the same Yelding and paying yerely for the use of euery pounde eighte penie to be ymploid in manner & forme following that is to saye foure pence yerely to the relief of the poore people of the said towne of Warwik and the other foure pence to the said Balif and his bretherne for that tyme being to mak merry w^{t}all once euery yere as they should think good in such manner and sorte as by the said testament most playnely dooth appeare. Not long after which said Testament made the said Thomas Oken died at Warwik aforesaid after whose death the said Robart Phillippes one of yor Suppliants did well & truly pay the said some of one hundreth powndes unto the said balief and Burgesses of the said towne of Warwik then for the tyme being according to the true Intent of the said testament which said some for & during certen yeres was well & truly ymplond to the great benefite of certen comoners in the said Towne according to thintent and true meanyng of the said last will & testament of the said Oken fforasmuch as there was then no pyece of lande to be bought to the said towne to thincrease of the comens of the said towne. Nowe so yt ys yf it may please yor hieghnes that all & singuler the said severall somes of monye geven & bestowed to & uppon the said Towne of Warwik by the said Wyllington Whateley & Oken in (folio 183) godly zeale to necessary & fruytfull uses as is aforesaid about twoo yeres last past in the tyme that one Richard Townesend Burges of the towne of Warwik aforesaid was Bailief of the said Towne weare gathered & recevid into the handes of the said Richard Townesend and one John ffisher towneclark of Warwik aforesaid, and the same nowe remayne and bee still either ymployd to theyr owne use & gayne w^{tout} any consideracion or proffitt to the towne, orells are lent or bestowed to such persons as them pleasith, nothing making privie the Burgesses of the said towne howe in what maner or to what psones the said severall somes of mony be delivered or bestowed, or what benefite cometh to the said towne by the use therof Wheras before that tyme the said Burgesses were alwayes accustomed (as in reason they shoulde) to be made privie yerely to the ymployng and bestowing therof & of euery parte therof. And the trueth is for yor said Supplyants have conferred in manner w^t all the Burgesses of the said towne of Warwik and also w^t the rest of the comonalty of the said towne that if all & singuler the said severall somes of monye there is not ymployd above the some of twentie or thirtye powndes to such godly uses as by the good zeale of the Benefactors and donors was purposed & intendid, and in right equitie & good conscyens ought to be ymploid or bestowed. Wherfore forasmuch as your said suppliants being burgesses of the said towne and also charged in consciens with the oversight & due execucion of the said last Wille & testament of the said Thomas Oken have divers & sondrye tymes most earnestly requyred the said Townesend and ffisher to declare & showe to yor said Suppliants & to the rest of the Burgesses of the said Towne howe & in what mann^r the said seuerall somes of monye were bestowed & ymploid since the tyme that they came & weare recevid into the handes of the said Townesend and ffisher which to doo the said Townesend and ffisher have altogither refused

w

& denyed and still do refuse & denye. And forasmuch as also one Richard ffisher late Balif of the said towne & brother to the said Jo. ffisher and also one Richard Roo now psently Baliff of the said towne by reason of the speciall favo^r which they bere to the said Jo. ffisher have not nor will not as they ought to doo calle or cause an assembly of the said Burgesses and comonaltie to be made to thintent to knowe howe & in what manner the said seuerall somes of money bee bestowed or ymploid yor said suppliants and the rest of the Burgesses & coraltie of the said Towne be altogither without remedye to come by or attayn to the said seuerall somes of monye or to see or cause the same to be bestowed according to the true intent & meanyng of the said benefactors & donors And moreover the Artificers of the said Towne bee greatly defraudid of the use of the said monye, And lastly the povertie & poore people of the said towne are most pittifully berevid of the woork and Relieff comyng dayly by reason of such monye and therby the whole towne greatly chargid for the necessary sustenance of the said poore people, Maye it please yor hieghnesse to graunt yor ma^{ty} most g^{r}cious writt of privie seale to be directid to the said John ffisher Richard Townesend Richard ffiysher & Richard Roo them & euery of them comannding at a c^{r}ten day & under a c^{r}ten payne therin to be lymyttid personally to appeare before your hieghnesse in the hiegh court of Requests Then & there to annsweare to the p^{r}misses And to abyde such further order as shall seme consonant to reason & equitie, And yor said Suppliants and also the whole bodye politique of the said Towne shall & will dayly praye for the p^{r}servacion of yor ma^{ty} in long lief & prosperytie.

This bill of compleynt being put into the court of Requests Phillippes took out pces of privy seale against all the said Jo ffisher Ric Townesend Richard

<small>John ffisher only served w^t processe</small>

ffisher & Richerd Roo and w^t a doquet made out of the said processe servid Jo. ffisher only before the said Ric. Roo Balif Ric ffisher & the most of the principall Burgesses assemblid for thes purposes & shewid the seale of the said proces to ffisher but woold not suffer him or any of the rest to see the pcesse or the Labell wheruppon at the day appointid being hillary terme A" (   ) Elizabeth The said Jo. ffisher went to London appeared tooke out a copy of the said bill of compleynt woold have annswerid it and therfore drewe his annswer redy to be put into the court But the courte being moved and made pryvie that the processe was taken out against all the said Jo. ffisher Ric Townesend Ric ffisher & Ric. Roo and that Phillips one of the compl be conversant and also in company w*t* them all after the pces awarded and yet served but John ffisher onely, And for that also the said Jo. ffisher was in the said compleint chargid w*t* matter concernyng the corpacion and not in respect of any matter towching his owne pson The court awardid that the said Jo ffisher should be dismissed w*t* some costs And so that matter cessid without any further psenting. So also my L of Warwik was satisfied as towching the said Jo. ffisher.

fisher appereth is dismissed

Libelles caste abrode After thes things so handled Brookes and some of the forenamed compleyners finding no ways to woork their willes devised or caused to be devised (as this wryter veryly thinkith) matter to sett the worst sort on woork either to mak some notable ryott styrre or mischief not only against the said Jo. ffisher but also rebellion against the Balief & his Assistants and that under a pretence of pittifull peticion. And therfore divers libelles were devised wrytten cast abrode some at the Assises in the Shire hall some left in open wayes & stretes & one left at the hiegh crosse in Warwik. w*ch* libells conteyned matter of great slannder to divers psones by name & others covertely wherof one of the libells being left at the crosse was thought to be Laid there by clement hill a pupill of Richard Brooks w*ch* hill was seene at the crosse before three of the clock in the morning, and by foure of the clok the said Libell was founde & brought to M*r* Balief. The Teno*r* wherof ensuith

To the wo*r*shipfull Thomas Powell Balif of the Borough of Warwik and to the rest of the capital Burgesses of the same borough that have any care of their conscience and beare good will to the same towne & coralty therof.

the tenor of the Labelles

In most humble wise complaneth unto yor wo^r ships yor poore and needye neighbo^rs of the borough & towne of Warr. who most humbly beseche you to have regard to the voyce & groning lamentacion of such as bee poore & nedely distressed on whome to take pittye & compassion yor hartes (as wee hope) are movid ffor miserable are wee & swallowed up (as you see & peeve) in mysery it self, but bycause this o^r p^rsent myserye hath had Issue from the frowardnesse of some of yor owne company as Mr John ffisher and Mr Townesend, and not altogethers of o'selves ffirst for that the monye geven by Mr Willington Mr Whateley & Mr Oken to this towne aswell to have bene ymploid towards the furtheraunce & helpe of yong begynners w^thin this towne as also for the setting of us the poore people on woork was by the said Jo. ffisher & Richard Townesend most uncharitably in the tyme that the said M Townesend was Balief of this borough (as all yor wo^rshippes well know) deteyned & kept in their owne handes to their owne use & benefitt, and as yet a great part therof is remanyng in their handes contrary to the will & good meanings of the givers therof and contrary to the good order taken before that tyme by yo selves for the good using and ymployng of the same for the benefit of the yong occupiers and of (folio 184) the poore of this towne, by meane wherof since that tyme there have bene a great nomber of us constrened most myserably to begge o^r bred from dore to dore that might have bene hable to have gotten o^r livings w^t the woork of o^r handes, which wold have bene greatly to the comfort & relief of o^r selves & of o^r poore children yf the same monye had bene ymploid in setting the poore on woork as yt should have byn, And yet the said M^r ffisher not so contented wth the abusing of the towne hynderaunce of the yong Occupiers deceving of the poore A thing most horryble to god & man, to the no litle slaunder to the towne & corporacion But hath nowe wth this ffortnight further to encrease our penuryes persuaded a newe order to be taken wth this towne, that none of the poore Lame olde nor Impotent people shall goe abrode in the towne to gather the good & charytable devocion of good people but must be constrayned to live of that which is apointid to bee paid weekly at the church, wch is so smalle that yt suffiseth not to relive them that are allowed to have the almes, And besides a great meany of us that have as great nede as the reste have no Relief at all. So that yf spedy redresse bee not had herin a nombr of us are like to perish wth famyn, a thing most Lamentable to bee hard of emongs Cristians, Howebeit when wee did cast our eyes of consideracion uppon you seuerally and when wee examyned in o^r secrete conscience yor anctority to be greater then those that have & doo offer thes manyfest wrongs & abuses to the towne & coraltye therof, and that it restith onely in yor selves to calle them to accompt and cause them to restore & emend that which is amysse, And that you be bounde in consciens so to doo, Wee have wth the more boldenesse of spirit and confidence, made supplicacion to yor wo^rshippes. Sithens wee can not nor dare not psonally appeare in yor presens, wth a lamenting voyce & in writing witnessing the woo of o^r wretchednes wee calle uppon you to be comfortid, and to you wee mak o^r moane most humbly beseching you, ffirst that the monye may bee gotten out of their handes, and ymploid for the benefit of the Inhabitants of this towne, as yt ought to be, Next that better order may bee taken for the relief of the poore lame olde and ympotent people wch will bee a way & meane to defend and kepe a many honest psones from becomyng bankerupts & beggers and the poore & Impotent shalbe the better relieved, The Lord god almightye so enclyne & turne yor hartes to pitty for the behoofe & availe of this towne & of us yor poore suppliants nowe in this great distres as that the thing wch w^t such earnestnes is desired may in semblable maner be atteynid The lord grannt you long heves & p^rserve you in pp^etuall happines

vox clamantis

Blessid is he that considereth the nedye & the poore in the evill day the Lord shall deliver him, psal 41

An other of thes was dyrectid to the wo^rshipfull Mr Richard Brookes & Mr John Grene and that was let fall on the bridge by Mr Brooks himself as it was thought, for he comyng over the bridge and no other pson after him or with him, Untill the wief of James Richerdson who a farre of followed him. She found yt & took yt up, and come streight weys to Willm hicks house where the said Brookes was talking w^t John Jeffreys and there she delivered yt to him And he w^{t}out looking on yt delivered yt to Mr Jeffreys and willid him to see what gere was found, and presently they both laughid at yt.

An other was directid to the worshipfull M^r ffrekulton Mr Phillips & Mr Jenks and that being lappid upp in an other paper & bound about w^t a threed was lost in the shire halle at the assises or lent and being taken up was brought to Mr Powell Balief.

Wth thes both Mr Balief for the tyme being & the most of the company but manely Jo. ffisher & Townesend were much moved and did what they could to fynd out the writer and so the deviser, but could not do it though they suspectid divers, & yet doo some in the towne. They examyned the most of the comoners and almost all the poore people whither they were grevid w^t any such matters & desired them to utter such griefs as they had and none was found to complayne or might be towchid w^t this devise.

And so the matter being openly spoken of in the next leet & request made that evry man should utter his grief if they had any, nothing was spoken of by the comoners & poore who openly denyed to be privy to any such complaynt And so for that tyme the matter was laid in water.

<small>practize betwene Brookes & Olney by compleynt in the Chauncery</small>
This practise taking not theffect it was ment for, wch belik was rebellion, or some notorious murmuracn against the Magistrats Brooks practizeth an other way to vex the Balief and his company and to sett division in the whole towne. And to bring it the better to passe he first begynneth w^t a mate like himself one Thomas Olney or Onley of Tachebrook and fyndith the meanes that the said Olney should tak uppon him the care of the decaid state of the towne, and poore comoners And that he should be a complaner therof in the name of the rest and that he should put in a bill of compleint into the chauncery to compleyn of

Brooks for keping the townes stocks in his hand & wasting the same at his pleasure. And then Brooks woold be defendant & discharge himself & charge others (folio 185) To this the said Olney was easyly woonne uppon condicion that he should beare no part of the charges either of sute or other things and w'hall they devised howe to bring to passe that some of the principall Burgesses might be removed and that they & others of their faction might be placed wch was all undertaken by brookes so as onley wold be the complaner. Theruppon they agreid. A bill was framed in the name of Thomas Olney & the Inhabitants of Warwik against Richard Brook supposing him to have all the foremembrid somes in his hands that he had ioyned w^t the balif and principall Burgesses and had made such choyce of Balief & principall Burgesses as agreid not w^t their ch^{rs} had taken no accompts of the rents & Revenues for many yeres past & such fals untruethes many. Brooks becam defendent to this bill, annswerith that he hath done none of thes things, but that the Balief & Burgesses have done all things without his consent. They grow to comission Sr Thomas Lucy Mr Thomas Leigh & others are apointid comissioners. The Interrogatoryes be drawen the comission sitten uppon at hicks his house subpenas taken out to serve the balief & principall Burgesses to testify & appere as Witnesses before the comissioners. Clark the Atto^rney made the clark other of broks his fraternyty brought furth to testify (and all this at Brooks only charge and no part therof borne by Olney. The principall Burgesses being sodenly callid doo refuse to swer Such as be brought furth by Brookes are recevid namely John Grene William Avery Richard Griffin Anthony clements, divers other sruid w^t ticketts or doquets as though subpenas had bene awardid brookes after the comission sitten uppon sendith for subpenas antedatid. his lre is interceptid complaint is made to the L Channcelo^r who pmissith execucion of the cause, my L of Warwik hering of the cause desireth to have the trueth found, the matter by order in the channcery is found to be fraudulently

Marginal notes:
- Olney takith uppon him the name
- Brookes becometh Defend^t bearith all the charge
- Interrogatories devised by Brookes
- the comission sitten uppon the whole charges Borne by Brookes
- the principall Burgesses serued w^t tyketts or subpe^s to testifie refuse
- the matter moved in the channcery is thought to be fraudulent

devised theruppon it is ordered that the examynacions should be suppressid Otherwise the piuries of brooks Grene Griffin Avery clements Staunton & donghill by the subornacion of brooks had bene sifted. The maner forme & circumstance of all wch foreremembrid pceedings being in other papers very tedious & long are therfore spared to be writen here, and therfore the reader referrid to coppyes of the said bill answer Interrogatories deposicions brooks lres for subpena, & maner of satisfieng my L of Warwik by orders in the chauncery

asmuch as should ympeche the Charter is quasshed by order

All this can not satisfy Brooks who to kepe his credit wt such as woold the disframchesing of this borough sekith a newe devise by compleynt to the right honorable Earle of Leycestr about whom he fyndith freends to further his ppse and after long attendance & great sute, obteyneth so much favor as to speak wt my said Lord. Enformeth his honor of many manyfest untruethes movith his honor to comiserans towards the towne &c to give ayde to reformacion of misdemeanor besechith his Lres aswell to the Balief & Burgesses as to divers men of wor shipp of the county of Warr to conferre & devies wayes of reformacion pmseth the prayer of thowsands &c Theruppon & uppon what other sinister & privy speaches unknown yt pleasid the said honorable Earle of Leycester to wryte in forme following

Brookes exciteth the Erle of Leycester against the towne

To my loving freends the Balief and principall Burgesses of the towne of Warwik

After my right harty comendacions being given to understand that you have not employd 230li of monye bequethed to godly & charitable uses according to the last willes of Wyllington Whateley & Oken the givers therof, As also that you have not made due accompt for the rentes of yor towne for thes five yeres last past, nor chosen yor bailief & principall Burgesses acording to yor charters, The matters towching yor creadites & the state of or towne. I have thought it not amisse to pray some of myne & yor freends therabouts as Sr ffoulk Grevill Sr Thomas Lucy Mr Thomas Leigh Mr Edward Boughton or three

therle of Leycester lres towching not ymploying of money not making of Accompts not making due election of Balif of them to come and talk w^t you in those cases and either to sett downe some order in that they shall fynd amisse Orells to aduertise me wherin the defalt shalbe Wherin I hartely pray you to shew yo^rselves readye and conformable when they shall repayre unto you. And so I bid you farewell from the Court the last of June 1583

      Yo^r very loving frend
        R. Leycester

Thes lres so obteyned Brookes kept w^t him from the date of the same lres untill he had labored the said gentlemen and peured their comyng to the towne wch was in July after, And on the vijth of July he brought other lres from the said S^r ffulk Grevill Mr Boughton & Mr Leigh wch wth the lres before last remembrid he delivered to humfrey crane then balief. the teno^r of wch lres from the said gentlemen ensuith. viz.

      To our loving freends M^r humfrey Crane Balief of
      Warwik and to the rest of the capitall Burgesses of the
      same borowe give thes

Lres from S^r ffulk Grevill Mr Boughton Mr Leigh to appere before them

After o^r hartie comendacions, wheras wee have receyvid lres from the right honorable therle of Leycester for the examynying & ordering of some causes depending in question betwene the Inhabitants of the borough of Warwik & some of you, for hearing of which matter we have apointid to mete at yor towne of Warr uppon Seterday next, willing you not to faile to be before us at the Shere hall by eight of the clock in the mornyng of the same day as you will annswere to the contrary Kenelworth this vij of July 1583

      Yo^r Loving frendes
       ffulk Grevill. Ed Boughton. Tho Leigh

This lre & the former were deliuerid to the balif on thursday the ( ) of July wheruppon the Balif making the principall Burgesses privy therunto. they thought good to send for their Recorder Mr Aglionby and Mr Buck for their aides to annswere such matters as might come in question (folio 186) about the charter and the eleccion of the Balif. Both which came And they and the Balif & the principall Burgesses all save Mr Sheldon prepared themselves to attend the said gentlemen that Saturday morning. But so fell it out that before the said Saturday the Lady Grevill decessid which was some Lett that S^r ffulk could not come. And Mr Leigh having intelligence therof did not come. Onely Mr Boughton came who at the swanne comonyng w^t Mr Balif Mr Aglionby and the others of the towne, uppon the poynts of the charter, a copy wherof brokes did there deliver him, some question & doubts semid to him, wch he then woold not seme to bee hable to decide and so after dynner the said Mr Boughton deptid from the said M^r balif & his brethern, somewhat misliking w^t his fellowes in comission that woold not give him knowlege of their not comyng. And so for that tyme the matter restid. But Brookes not satisfied pcureth other lres from Sr Tho Lucy Mr Boughton & Mr Leigh the teno^r wherof ensueth viz.

Mr Boughton onely cometh at the day apointid

other lres from Sr Tho Lucy Mr Boughton Mr Leigh

To o^r loving frends the Balif & Burgesses of the towne of Warwik

After o^r hartie comendacions wee have apointid to meet at yor towne of Warr uppon Thursday being the eight day of August next at the Shire hall by nyne of the clock in the mornyng where we requyre you to mete us that wee may procede acording to o^r directions from the right honorable therle of leycest^r for the hearing & appeasing of such matters as are in question emongs you and so praying you not to faile to be ready at that tyme & place aforesaid wee bid you farewell.

charlecot this xxvth of July 1583

Yo^r loving frendes

Tho. Lucy. Ed Boughton. Tho. Leigh

the maner of sending the lres

This lre being kept open was showed to as many of Brookes freends as he thought good & great brags made that that thursday the old Burgesses should be displaced And that the gentlemen woold choose newe in their places, and therfore Brookes Olney & other of their faccions warned asmany as woold take part wt them & in any newe choice to be at the Shire hall that thursday by nyne of the clock when they should heare howe shamfully the old Burgesses had decevid the towne. They kept that lre from the date therof untill yt was the Sonday before the day apointid And than Thomas Olney cometh to the Bailief namely Mr Crane & delivereth yt unto him comannding him in the quenes name to appere before the said gentlemen that next thursday And that day was appoyntid by Brookes meanes bycause about that tyme one Mr Atkinson a Lawyer & subtill Sophister being alwayes of Brooks counsell woold bee in this countrey, whom he & John Greyne pcured to come to the day & place apointid, wherof Mr Bailief and the prncipall Burgesses secretly hearing did think mete to have some man towards the Lawe to be redy to annswer by Lawe uppon such poynts in difference as might come in question And theruppon they devised to send for Mr Pagett being of counsell wt the towne and dwelling at Rowley in Northamptonshire who uppon short warnyng very frendly came on wensday night to Warwik and also Mr Recorder Aglionby was sent for & came, but the tyme being so short that they could have neither instruccions nor conferrens, were not so well pvidid as othewise was wishid.

Sr Tho. Lucy Mr Boughton Mr Leigh come to Warwik to Examyn &c

That thursday the viijth of August the forenamed gentlemen came & lightid at the swanne, whither the Balif & principall Burgesses went unto them & movid them That forsomuch as their comyng was to conferre wt the said Balif & principall Burgesses howe to put things in good order. The said Balif & Burgesses thought that the Shire hall was no convenyent place for conferrence, bicause yt was a place very publike. and where all maner of psons both of the towne and countrey woold thrust uppon them. And therfore desired of the said Sr Thoms and other gentlemen to come into the towne hall or court house or any other honest & convenyent house where they might be more quiet & private, wherunto they rather movid them, bycause one branch or article concrneth the Accompts of the towne, wch to mak publik to all straungers or Tounesmen was thought neither convenyent nor to be the meaning of my said Lord. To this Sr Tho Lucy & Mr Leigh agreed but Mr Boughton woold have it in the shire hall & no place ells and where all comers might heare. There was no remedy yt must be so, and therunto M{r} Balif & his company saving this writer yeldid, But he could not lik of it M{r} Sheldon had taken occasion that day to be from home. There was no remedy, but to the hall the gentlemen woold and theruppon yt was thought by some that yf the balif & his brethern woold not there appere some grevous informacion woold be made to my Lord. Theruppon & w{t} many other devises this writer was drawen the rather knowing that the matter was specially sought against him and knowing himself clere & hable to annswer his doings, he yeldid. To the Shire hall the gentlemen went where were assemblid of countrey people about C besides a nombr of Townesmen having nothing to doo in the cause. The gentlemen took w{t} them M{r} Rafe Griffin preacher, And those that is to say S{r} Tho. Lucy M{r} Boughton M{r} Leigh & M{r} Griffin took their place uppon the Bench to whom M{r} Aglionby the Recorder & the Bailief ioyned themselves & sate w{t} them. But the rest of the principall Burgesses must stand at the Barre belowe as men ready to come to arraynem{t} only M{r} Pagett & John ffisher were allowid to come w{th} the cheker to lay out their books & sitt the rather bicause ffisher was both lame & sick & weak at that tyme.

<small>the manner of handling this matter</small>

The gentlemen being sett they signified that they were come to this place uppon request of o{r} very good Lord Therle of Leycest{r} who being informed of many disorders & disagreings in the towne had comiseracion therof And for the good will he bare the towne & townesmen & their well doings, had requyred them to come & conferre w{t} M{r} Balif & Burgesses and to examyn things amisse and to give their helpe for the appeising & mending of them. At whose pleasure & comaund they were come acordingly And therw{t} caused the L{re} writen by my L to them to be red w{ch} did in sence & effect agree w{t} that written to the towne saving in their lre Brookes & Grene were named to have given thinformacion, and were therfore required to be present at this meting further to instruct them of such things as they knowe to be misgoverned And theruppon both Brookes & Grene & as many as they could name to say anything were admyttid to come in who came

<small>Ric Brookes and Jo Grene named in the lres writen to the gentlemen to bee the Informers</small>

to the right hand of (folio 187) the long table in the chequer in the Shire hall.

<small>Mr Atkinson a subtill sophister pledith against the Balif and Burgesses</small> Than Mr Atkinson before remembrid being a fyne and fayre spoken man began to shewe what good dedes had bene done to the proffoting of the more of this towne men by weldisposed givers. Namely Mr Willington a man of wo'ship & so tendering the psperity of this towne that he gave iiij^{xx}li Mr Whateley L^{li} and Mr Oken an hundred all to the use of yong beginners & occupiers wch having for a tyme bene very orderly used acording to the mynds of the givers had doone much good & pfitid many. But of late a fewe ildisposed men taken uppon them auctorytie had convertid the good use therof into their owne pvate comodytye. and either kept the mony in their owne handes orells had spent the same to maynteyn their wickid willes. And settith furth this matter w^t such eloquence rhetericall woordes that almost all men present were fully of his mynde And after he had showid the wickidnes of such ill magistrats concludith that for their so abusing the trust & place they tak uppon them they ought not only presently to be displacid but comyttid to some place where they might receve further ponishm^t untill further order might be taken w^t them to thexample of all the woorld. Then after he had bestowed above an howres speche in thes pswacions & exhortacions to the Gentlemen, whom he said had auctorytie to place & displace & to give order & correction he than being urged to goo to the pticularities of the cause and to mak pfe. ffirst began w^t those somes of mony and first as towching the inj^{xx}li given by Willington that yt was not nor   any part of it put out but kept in the hands of twoo or three of them that callid them principall Burgesses. To that

<small>Jo ffisher annswereth some obiections</small> point Jo. ffisher annswerid That he thought himself to be notid in that nombr of those twoo or three And therfore first for himself denyed that the saing of Mr Atkinson and such as had told him so to be true both for himself & for others, Therto Atkinson replied that it was true that he was one of those that had the mony and twoo other more namely Townesend and Powell. yt is utterly untrue said ffisher, and therwith pve yt said he to Atkinson. Then Atkinson callid Mr Brooks & Mr Grene Who said yt is true for the mony was paid to yor hands. That is also untrue said ffisher there was none

paid to my hands and therfore prove you yt. howe can he prove it said brooks & Grene seing you kepe all the bonds & wrytings. I doo so said ffisher and so mynd to doo still whatsoever either of you say. Then Townesend and powell being callid They denyed the having of the mony or any part therof Then said the gentlemen namely Sr Tho. Lucy. M^r ffisher if you have the keping of the bonds you shall doo well to shewe them. In dede said ffisher I have the bonds and could be content to shewe them to you that bee in this comission either nowe or sone or when yor pleasure shalbe. But to shewe them openly or to thes untrue accusers I think it not either requysite or resonable, they having not to doo w^t the matter. And me thinkith them very busy bodyes that will meddle so much in that they have not to doo. Then said Mr Boughton yf you be cleare and that there be no mony in yor hand, and yf it be put out as it ought to be yt woold be a good declaracion for you to shewe the bonds openly that all that be here may peeve that you are wrong said of and yt shall satisfie them much. To this Mr Pagett agreid that it can not be amisse to shewe the bonds. Theruppon ffisher taking the bonds out of a fosser shewing them. then the gentlemen desired to have them in their hands pmising safely to redeliver them. Wheruppon they were delivered into their hands. Then Mr Boughton Looking on the first said here is one Bykar where is the man, who aunswerid here. Theruppon he examyned him whether he had any of Mr Willingtons mony in lone howe much when he had it deliveryd and a nombr of other questions to wch he annswerid truely. and that he had had it many yeres, and that he recevid it last the very day of the date of his obligacion. Then Mr Boughton turned over to an other bond and so from one to an other over all and callid the parties who all or the most part apperid and confessid the having of the mony acording to the bonds, & delt very strickly in thexamynacions but it fell out truely that the mony was all put out acording as it ought to be much contrary to their expectacions. Then Mr Boughton caused one to take a note of the names of them that said they had the mony and of their somes & kept it w^t him.

Marginalia:
- first for Mr Willington's monye
- the bondes shewed to proove that the monye was out.
- notes taken of the names of them that had the mony and the somes

second for Mr Whateleys mony

Then they came to Whateleys mony and examyned likewise how that was bestowed. To that ffisher denyed That any such some of ffiefty pounds was ever given and delivered by Whateley to the towne (as was untruely enformed) Yea said Brookes wooll you deny that. Yea that I doo said ffisher & Let me see howe you will prove yt. w^t that Brooks showed furth a coppy of the condicion of an obligacion wherin ffisher & others had bene bound twoo yeres before to bring in ffieftie pounds to Whateleys executors but neither showid the bond nor the copy of the bond, what pvith this said ffisher. Yf you think that I have not brought in such mony as I ought to doo, the executors have to charge me & not you. but I owne neither them nor you any grote and therfore I take this to be no great evidence against me.

Loke for more of this in the 206

(The writer has made the above note at the end of folio 187. The account is continued on the second half of folio 206. Instead therefore of taking the folios in consecutive order I have here gone on to folio 206 in order to keep the narrative of these proceedings together.)

the gentlemen suspect fisher denyeng the having of L^li of Whateley

(folio 206) Then the gentlemen began to whisper and thought something woold fall out not well w^t ffisher bicause he denyed the giveng of the mony by Whateleys will And therfore said. had you not L^li given by Whateleys will. to that ffisher annswrid I denye not the giving of so much, but I deny the having or receving of so much, Yea said Brooks you will deny anything. I deny that said ffisher & will you to prove yt. Woold you have a better pfe saith Atkynson then yor owne bond.

Grene sheweth a paper the copy of the condicion of a bond put in to the exec of Whateley

Shewe that said ffisher and yt will suffice. here is a copye of it said grene & I will depose that I recevid yt from one of the masters of coventry said John Grene. Depose then said ffisher that is a true coppy. But admyt it to be as it is not a copy of my bond, what say you then. Then said Atkinson that will prove that you had

L^{li} of Whateley. I deny that said ffisher. Whye said the gent will you deny that Mr Whateley gave not L^{li}. I deny it not said ffisher, but deny the receving of yt. But nowe to satisfy yor worships and bycause this earnest gentleman (meaning Mr Atkinson wold nedes have him thrust out & ponishd that doth defraud the good meanyng of the giver. You shall understand That Mr Whateley had divers debtors dwelling in this towne some very poore & some others emongs whom this man Richard Brook was one, who psuading Mr Whateley that he woold help him to a good wief & gentlewoman very rich & honest, borrowed xv^{li} of the said Mr Whateley & gave his bill for yt and pmised payment at a c^{r}ten day long before Whateley died. And when he had the mony he did & woold have helpid him to one M^{rs} meystye a woman knowen to be nothing worth nor of the best fame Whateley misliking the choice gave over w^t some cost was often in hand w^t Brooks for his mony who pmised to pay it but deferrid from tyme to tyme, wch Mr Whateley pceving and mynding to doo some good to the poore of this towne, was content to sett over that xv^{li} and ix or x more of such debts to the balif & burgesses of this towne and to mak upp the some of L^{li} which he woold have to be put furth yerely & yerely brought in to coventry. And this man Mr Brookes being then one of the principall burgesses dyd acknowleig befor the said Mr Whate and the then balif of this towne that he ought Mr Whateley xv^{li} and pmised the paym^t to him or whom he woold appoint And theruppon Mr Whateley deliuerid over the said bill of debt yn Lewe of xv^{li} as pcell of the said L^{li} to Symon yong then balif of Warwik unto whom the said Mr Brookes promised the payment of the said xv^{li} dyvers tymes after. But at the Last after that Mr Yong was dead, he Mr Brookes said that he had paid yt to one who never recevid yt nor had auctority to receve yt. so as that xv^{li} yet remaneth in M^r brooks hands and therfore by the Judgem^t of this gentleman Mr Atkinson he is to be ponished for yt. Then said Brooks I paid yt to you by (folio 207) Anthony Richmond the S^{r}jant when I was balif

ffisher sheweth howe the mony given by Whateley was reised

y^t Brookes ought xv^{li} parcell of the fiefty

brokes bill for that xv^{li} deliuered over by Whateley to Symon yong Balif

brookes yeldid to pay the mony to yong

said he had paid yt to fisher

fisher never receued It nor the bill

the xv^{li} yet due by Brookes

youe sent it never to me said ffisher nor I never receeved or demaunded yt of you, for the bill was in Mr Yongs keping and I had never occasion to receve yt of you nor never did of you nor any other Nevertheles bycause you wickedly did swere uppon a testament that you had paid yt to me I was content to beare so much yerely out of myne owne purse, bycause the poore should not be defrauded. Then said Brookes to ffisher swere here uppon a book before thes gentlemen that you

<small>ffisher chargeth Brookes to owe that and other somes also to the towne</small>

never had it and I will pay yt And will not swere said ffisher but affirm yt uppon conseyens that I never had yt. And said ffisher yt were more mete for you to be put to yor othe for yt then I bycause you are to prove yt. But I am afraid to charge yor consciens so farre having experience of you otherwise. ffor besides this you say you do owe nothing to the towne here is a note to prove that you owe very nere an C^{li} to the towne wherof xxxij^{li} for Rent of Myton tithes & almost Lx^{li} for arrerages of xl^s a yere resuid uppon yor leaces unpaid for many yeres, besides that you being Balif of this towne in the viij^t yere of the Q ma^{ty} that nowe is

<small>that Brookes hathe not yet made his accompt for his Balywik being almost xx^{ty} yeres past.</small>

have not yet made yor acompt for that Baliwik And besides that when you were burges you askid allowance of vj^{li} xiij^s iiij^d paid for the rent resruid of the lands belonging to the towne, & paid it not but suffred proces to come out of thexcheq^r for it and therby the towne was forced to pay it into thexcheq^r and you alwayes deferrid the answering of it agayn trusting to fynd an acquitans of my brother Tho. ffishers land or of Gardeners And this being almost xx^{ty} yeres ago you can not yet bring furth the acquitans. So as by Mr Atkinsons Judgem^t you are to tak open ponishm^t in example of others. you saie truth said brooks but I paid both that xx^{ty} nobles & the xv^{li} to. And for my acompt for my Baliwik you knowe I owe nothing to the towne for yf I did you would have calld me to accompt before this tyme. And as for your rents I owe none. Well said the

<small>bondes for Whateleys mony shewed</small>

Gentlemen then it semith there should bee L^{li} of Mr Whateleys Lent out and you say there is not xv^{li} of it brought in What is become of the rest of that L^{li} ys that put furth. Yea said ffisher yt ys not said

Brooks & Grene, pve that said ffisher. Nay say the gentlemen to ffisher, you must make proof of that. Nay said ffisher by yor Licens he that hath enformed is to prove his informacion. Nevertheles bycause you shall see that they have untruly reportid to my Lord, & to yor worshippes, here bee other bondes wch will testify that the mony is out, and so shewid turth the bondes taken for the L^li of Whateleys monye. Wheruppon the partyes were callid & the most of them appered & confessid the having the mony emongs wch was Edward Browne debto^r for x^li John Townesend for x^li Mighell herriett for x^li & Willm hopkins for x^li the rest at xl^s a piece. thes x^lis was much mislikid & thought to bee some counterfeit dealing and therfore those psons were more severely examyned Who all confessid the having of the mony & making of the bonds, wch mony in dede they had of Mr Townesend by reason of an order in the chancery uppon confession there of the said Mr Townesend in Easter terme before this compleint exhibitid to my L of Leyc^r as in his place shalbe shewed There was much wispering emongs the gentlemen uppon those bands and they veryly ymagyned that the mony was not put furth. And taking notes of these obligacions & the names of the psones bound, secretly requyred Mr Griffin to send for every one of the psons named to have the mony and to examyn them privately of their consciences & trueth of the matter, wch Mr Griffin afterwards did, and yet could not fynd that they lookid for.

the debtors depely examyned

notes of bondes taken

third Mr Okens mony

ffisher chargith Jo Grene with the keping of x^li parcell of Okens mony

Then came they to the C^li given by Oken towching wch ffisher said this gentleman (meaning Mr Atkinson) is very ernest in sentence against such as withold any of the monye wch should be in comon uses and wold have them displacid out of there offices. As towching this C^li I must confesse is not to be well handled as it ought, for this man Jo. Grene being one of the Informers hath x^li in his hand & hath had thes vij or eight yeres and will not pay yt, ys it yor mynd Mr Atkinson that he shall towche of yor sentence. Nay said Grene I have not the monye but was surety for x^li deliuered out to Porter and porter being dead I must see yt repaid but I am suer I must pay viij^li of it of myne owne purse, so you may said ffisher for the comon saying is that you had asmuch goods of Porters as came to x^{li} & above but yet you have not paid yt for here is yor obligacion for it, I confesse said Grene my hand is there, but there is other to pay more of that C^{li} aswell as I. Yea said ffisher the more the worse, and I think you are the cause that some other doo not pay that wch is due by them, and you may bee ashamed to kepe the monye & yet to complayne felsely as you doo. And said ffisher here is twoo other obligacions for parcell of the said C^{li} viz for xx^{li} yet in the hands of a poore widdow one Reynolds wief and x^{li} in the hands of henry ffoster whose tyme of repayment are not yet come and therfore the mony not to be requyred of them, though in dede the same (folio 208) somes

the hundred poundes given by Oken made out and paid for land bought — be by other meanes made out And that C^{li} paid for land bought to the land to the comons acording to Okens will. howe doth that appere saith the gentlemen that any Land should be bought or is bought. It appereth saith ffisher by the will of Oken that he woold have land bought wth the said C^{li} and for that ppse specially he gave yt And that yt is bought shall appere also though wee think no cause to make all this pryvy that be here, bycause the matter conc^{r}nith not them. But

the dede showed — that you may see that Land is bought here is a dede of p'chase from M^r S^{r}jaunt Puckering who recevid iiij^{xxli} xiij^s vj^d for Land for this purpose. And so the dede was showed furth wch dede was made to foure psons only namely to humfrey crane Thomas Powell Robart Sheldon & John Rigeley wch dede also had relacions to Okens will & mony and the use yt should be put

the deed cavilled wth by Atkinson — unto. But bicause the deed was made but to foure yt was much cavellid w^t by Mr Atkinson & others of that faccion M^r dafferne M^r brooks Mr Grene &c as though those fowre will convert it to their owne uses

the gentlemen leaned — & not to the uses of the comens. And surely the gentlemen leaned greatly to all the reasons made against the townes men & their truste having speciall suspicion & entencion against some of the principall Burgesses.

then cometh the second poynt for taking of accomptes — Thes things falling out otherwise then was expectid The gentlemen fell then to the next article of their lre, that was that we had not taken accompt in five yeres before. Therfore requyred to see the accompts of the balifs & such as had the trust and receving of the mony for those tymes & a yere or twoo before. In which poynt this writer was very unwilling to shewe thaccompts contenyng many matters of allowance aswell for publique as private causes openly before such a multitude both of the towne that had not to doo w^t the taking of accompts, as other a great nombr of srningmen & countrymen, and was hardly drawen to the shew^g of those Accompts, but by p̃suacion of M^r balif & his counsell, he yeldid. Wherin he first took uppon him the auctoryty of his office of Auditor of this borough claimyng therfore power to tak accompt w^tout the privytie of others either Balief or burgesses And said he had so doone, and theruppon showed furth a book wherin all the accompts taken in his tyme were entrid according to his skill, which auctorytie was earnestly ympechid by argum^t of Mr Atkinson untill he shewid furth a patent of the said office under the towne seale. wch yet woold not serve, bycause yt was thought mete that accompts for a corialty ought to be heard publikely by the Inhabitants at least by the head officers & principall Burgesses so it semed litle

the Accompte must nedes be seen credit to be given to those accompts writen into the book bycause they were as was then thought doon of speciall favo^r of one private man to an other to the conceilment of the Revenues & Rents belonging to the multitude. nevertheles the Audito^r was of mynd not to shew any

they are showed other. But Mr Balif and his counsall urging At last he shewed furth Accompts taken the very same which were also writen into the book before showed, And to thes Accompts the hands of such Baliefs & Burgesses as before whom the same were declared were subscribed. And comyng to the Accompts of

Brookes and Grene their handes to some of those accomptes the tyme p̃scribed in my Lords lre that is to say for five Last yeres before yt appered as yet it doth that to one of those Accompts of those five yeres. both Richard Brookes & John Grenes hand were subscribed to an other of those v yeres John

Grene had also subscribid The third yere was for Richard Roos charge who in his lief tyme had p̃titid thaccompt but yt was not declared the fourth was for the tyme of Thomas powell who had not fynishid a piece of woork begoñe in his baliwik but yet in doing so as no accompt could be p̃fitly set down and the vth

yere wᶜʰ was the tyme of humfrey cranes baliwik who could not accompt bycause his yere was not expired. Thes accompts seen and both Brooks & Grene in this case thus reproved the gentlemen lookid one uppon an other yet much pyering was for the order of those accompts and that they would by Brooks his meanes have cavillid of the allowance, and one thing was specially lookid for in the Accompts, that was for the hundred pounds receviḍ of Mʳ Beynham for his leace of Budbrook, which was said to have bene put up into Jo. ffishers purse & spent by him but yt append otherwise. Then they cavillid uppon the hearers of the Accompts Saying the accompts were taken by such psons as pcially favored the Accomptants. So as nothing was left un-spoken that might empeach the credit of the Balif & Burgesses.

the fyne for the personage of Budbrook lookid for

Cavillacions against the takers of Accompts

the thirde poynt

touching election

After thes things they come to the principall matter uppon wᶜʰ said Mʳ Atkyns the whole corpacion stood to be forfeitid by reason of misusing And that was thelleccion of the balief on Michilmas day yerely⁽ᵃ⁾ and thelleccion of the principall Burgesses⁽ᵇ⁾ both which saith Mʳ

(a) The Charter of Philip and Mary, dated 12th November, 1554, provided that there should be a Bailiff and 12 principal Burgesses, and that these might appoint assistants according to their discretion (tantos alios Burgenses de Inhabitantibus phioribus Burgi illius in Burgenses ejusdem Burgi facere constituere et admittere possint de tempore in tempus juxta discretionem suam. For the election of Bailiff, the Bailiff and principall burgesses were directed to meet at their Court House annually on Michaelmas Day, and choose two of their number in the presence of the Assistants and such of the inhabitants who were in attendance, and submit such two to those inhabitants for their choice. (nominare et assignare valeant et possint duos homines tunc existentes de principalib ejusdem Burgi coram aliis illius Burgi Inhabitantes ad tunc ibm psentib ad intentionem qd alii homines et Inhabitantes Burgi illius ad tunc et ibm psentes aut major Pars eorundem eligant et eligere valeant et possint unū ex illis duob Burgensib. sic nominatis et assignatis nominandis et assignandis ad officiū Ballivi &c). The Baliff thus chosen entered upon office and took the oath on All Saints day following.

(b) As regards the election of principal burgesses the poor Bailiff and his bretheren seem to have been unjustly and unnecessarily harrassed by the Earls of Warwick and Leycester, in their repeated statements that the principal burgesses were improperly chosen. The Earls appear to have misread the Charter, or to have been wrongly advised. The Charter provides that in case of the death of a principal burgess or his removal from some other cause the Baliff and principal burgesses shall fill up the vacancy within eight days. (liceat et licebit Ballio et Burgensibus illius Burgi p. tempore existentib infra octo dies px sequentes morte sive amotione dci nominare et eligere unū aut plures alias psonas tunc inhabitanten dci Burgi &c).

Atkinson ought to be doone by the whole multytude. And nowe of late saith he a fewe sometymes not past six or seven clamyng the whole power to themselves have made eleccions not onely of the balif yerely but also of the principall Burgesses when any happen to dye. And more than that they take uppon most iniuriosly & unlaufull to displace honest & good Burgesses and place such as favo^r their owne affections directly contrary to the charter wherby they have desruid to have the charter taken from them & the burrow to be disfranchised, a lamentable thing and worthy due reformacion at the least spedye displacing of such as have bene the causes theof.

this matter was much ympugned by Mr Atkinson

to that (folio 209) poynt Mr Pagett spak and said That the King and Quene graunters of that ch^r had set downe in the same Charters howe those eleccions should be made and according to those orders & directions he is informed thellecions have bene usually made both in the tymes prescribid in the places & in the maner & forme And for that cause showed furth the maner of the eleccion on Michilmas of the Balif, wch was done in this maner, first twoo of the twelve principall Burgesses were by the balif & principall burgesses named to stand in eleccion and their twoo names delivered to the other burgesses & Inhtants pnt. The other burgesses & Inhitants psent assigned one of those twoo, and he who was so assigned was chosen Balif and at Alhollowday following took his othe before all that woold come that day wch he took to be a good ellection & directid by the charter. W^{ch} was denyed by Mr Atkinson who that thelleccion ought to be by the whole multytude of thinhabitants being all Burgesses, And also that the pncpall Burgesses ought to be chosen by the multitude being all Burgesses. wch Mr Pagett also denyed. But Mr Boughton he thought no eleccion could be made w^tout consent of the whole multitude and urged Mr Balief and his bretherne to yeld to such election. And so doing although things had bene doone amisse for lack padventure of knowleig or understanding. yet they might now and from hensfurth be better ordered. Mr Balif and some of his company was willing to yeld. But Jo.

annswered by M^r pagyt

Mr Atkinson holdeth that every Inhabitant is a Burges and elector both of Balif & principall Burges affirmed stifly

M^r paget of an other opinion

Mr Boughton urgeth the consent of the multytude

fisher utterly denyeth

ffisher stonding up said the manner of eleccions nowe of late usid was prescribed by the quenes learned counsell & other learned counsell at or some uppon the begynnyng of this borough by vertue of this charter And hath bene so contynueed untill now that some thinking to bread trowble have practized to put all in hazard by new devises and what ynnovacions may doo, yo{r} worshippes may conceve and specially in so waughty cause as this, call you this innovacion saith M{r} Boughton to mend that is a mysse & taking a better course in yo{r} ellections. I take not you for no competent Judge in this case said ffisher bycause the poynts in difference stand uppon matters of Lawe & Judgm{t} of Judges and therfore I can in no wise agree to any other order of ellection than that w{ch} hath bene used, Am I no competent Judge said M{r} Boughton. and theruppon grewe somewhat more passionate in affection as this wryter thinkith. But M{r} Atkinson & M{r} Pagett differid in divers points of the charter howe the woords should be understood So as spending long tyme about a litle the Gentlemen arrose and went to the Swanne where at the charge of the towne they dyned. After dynner they fell agayn to psuacion to have eleccions by the multitude. But yt could not be grauntid. Then in fyne after they had entreatid M{r} Griffin to examyn strikly such as were said to be bound for the somes of mony before specified They psuadid agreament emongs all. and said that they woold signifye to the right honorable Erle what they had done & found, and so deptid for that tyme leaving all things as they found yt.

M{r} Boughton takith hold of a word spoken by ffisher

M{r} Raph Griffin required to make secret inquisicion of the debtors

the Balif desireth the gentlemen to certify

At the quarter Sessions following w{ch} was tuesday after michilmas day all the forenamed gentlemen mett, on whom the Balief & burgesses attending to knowe their pleasures towching the certificate to my Lord of Leycest{r} w{ch} if it pleasid the gentlemen to wryte upp the Balif promised to send yt presently to o{r} said good Lord. To that M{r} Boughton annswerid that he woold shortly go up to my Lord himself and then my L should be certified of their proceadings.

The next day being Wensday all the rest of the Justices of peace being gone saving M{r} Boughton & M{r} Aglionby, M{r} Griffin as yt semed made reaport of what he had found by pticuler exacion of such as were bounde, And withall moved those twoo gentlemen to move the Bailief & Burgesses and M{r} Ric Brookes to some bringing this & many other trowbles to end. Wheruppon M{r} Balif & his bretherne were sent for to come to the swanne where M{r} Boughton & M{r} Aglionby & M{r} Griffin being togither M{r} Boughton agayne moved the Balif & his company to yeld to election by the multitude. And w{th}all to end of all sutes betwene them & the townesmen. The mocyon broching the genrallytie in eleccion was thought to be very daungerous and therfore not to be yeldid unto without good advice of learned counsaill. Than said M{r} Boughton can you bee content then in avoyding of great charges, to name twoo, and M{r} Brookes other twoo either Judges or Lawyers to end thes matters and to iudge of the matters in differens, and then from henceforth to followe their directions. M{r} Brook said he could so as my Lordes of Warwik & Leycest{r} might appoynt the Judges. Then was yt said by this wryter And I will advise M{r} Balief and can consent that either twoo may be chosen on either side as yo{r} wo{r}ship spak of, Or twoo to be indifferently chosen by o{r} said good Lords, & sett downe their opynions & directions uppon the matters in question. I agree to yt said Brooks. And so do wee said M{r} Balif and such of the principall Burgesses as were p{r}sent. Then said this wryter, yt ys then very convenyent first to sett downe the points in differens in wryting and deliver them to such as shalbe appointid by the Lordes, and also copies of the charters. Wheruppon they may bee advised. Every man p{r}sent thought it convenyent so to be. Then said this wryter to M{r} Brooks you finde yo{r} self grevid therfore you downe the poynts. The poynts be short saith Brooks, and that is who ought to choose the principall Burgesses, and who ought to take the Accompts. thes be all, will you rest uppon thes twoo said this writer. Yea said brookes. Those be said M{r} Boughton the poynts you differre uppon I think And therfore saith he to

A motion made for the ending of thies controuerses.

the Balif sent for

offer of a meane for quiet ending

the examynacion and explanacion of the meaning of the Charter by twoo indifferent Lawers.

the differens consistith only in twoo poyntes

the poyntes

John Fisher the writer of this Booke	this wryter M^r ffisher you can best do yt. I pray youe sett them downe psently before wee goo or assone as may be if not before I go so as I may have them under all yor handes before my going from Kenelworth where I will tarye twoo or (folio 210) three dayes and yf youe send yt me thither I will take yt up wth me whan I goo to London and move my Lordes in yt and then yt were good for some of you of the towne to be there to attend those that shalbe assigned by the Lordes, to that it was pmised that some should be there if they might know the tyme. Then said Mr Boughton I mynd to be there w^tin twoo or three dayes after alhalowday and then if any of you come to me I will speak to my Lords for you Theruppon the articles were set downe in writing the next day after and showed to Mr Griffin who said that they were acording to the agreament. The teno^r wherof ensueth.
the matter agreed uppon set downe in writing	Be yt remembrid That on Wensday the second of October 1583 in the xxvth yere of the reigne of o^r souereigne Lady Quene Elizabeth &c Mr Edward Boughton Mr Edward Aglionby Esquires and Mr Rafe Griffin preacher psuadid a freendly end & cessing of trowbles & sutes betwene Richard Brook & John Grene on the one side complanants against the Balif & principall Burgesses of the borough of Warwik on the other side where were p^rsent humfrey Crane Balif and John ffisher Thoms Powell & John Rigeley principall Burgesses of the same borough, and also the said Richard Brook & John Grene, Wheruppon it was by all the said psones agreed & acordid That the matters in varryance towching the corpacion of the said towne should be set downe in wryting and should be deliuered under the handes of all the partyes, that is to say the Baliff and principall Burgesses, and the said Richard Brook and John Grene, and also subscribed by the said Mr Griffyn, and by him sent to the said Mr Boughton to the Intent & purpose, that the said Mr Boughton should choose one or twoo Lawyers of Judgem^t such as by his discrecion should bee thought well hable and yndifferent men to judge & determyn of the causes in question, which also shalbe such as have not bene feed or reteyned of counsell in those cases with or for any of the said persones. To

whose Judgement determynacion and order bothe and all of the said parties have & doo promise to submytt themselves from thenceforth to parforme the same, which matters in question are onely twoo and no more, that is to saye, The flirst wheather by the true sense or meanyng of the woordes in the charter towching the election placing & displacing of any those principall Burgesses of the said borough, the persone who shalbe electid to bee a principall Burges should or ought to be named chosen & placed by the Balieff and principall Burgesses of that borough or the greater nombr of them onely, Or by the said Baliff principall burgesses and the rest of the Inhabitants of the said Borough or the greater nombr of them only.

Item the Second, whether by their Judgem^t dete'iacion and order The Balief and principall Burgesses or the greater nombr of them onely or such psone or psones as they shall auctorise in wryting under their comon seale shall or ought to take the Accompts and geve the charge and make allowanes of all such thinges and allowanes and to all such persones as shall have the receaving payment or Layng out of the Rentes Issues and other dueties belonging to the said Borough in use or right of the said borough. Or whither all the Inhabitants wth the same borough or the chiefest of the honest of the said Inhabitants ought or should be present and doo the same.

And yt ys further agreed & accordid That all processes complents and sutes for those cawses and matters towching the corporacion shalbe forborne and no further followed renewed or executed (Savyng that the parties themselves & euery of them may be present or may have their solicitors or counsaillors to open & declare their said causes & circumstancs therof before the said one or twoo indifferent Lawyers for their better informacion and understanding, And yt is also agreed and consentid unto That all former Eleccions putting out of monyes takings of Accompts and other matters towching the said Corporacion before this tyme doone, shall stand remayne & bee as they weare & have bene doone, without any further compleint controlling or Revocacion. And all unkyndenesse about those matters to bee no more spoken of in gryef, but utterly to be quenched, Nevertheles yt ys not ment nor prohibited but that the partyes or any of theme eyther in right of the Towne or any of themselves, maye prosecute any other their laufull Tytles claymes demaundes or Sutes one against an other by order of Lawe quyetly & reasonably, Any thing before agreed or consentid unto notw'stonding, In witnes of which consents and agreaments wee have hereunto put o^r handes.

<small>shewid to Mr Griffin allowed of by him</small>

This Agreament put in writing was first shewid to Mr Griffin who confessid that yt was the true meanyng of all parties as he thought, and substance of the speches agreid uppon before the gentlemen & him, And therfore willid that the same might be subscribed &

<small>subscribed by the Balif & Burgesses</small>

assigned unto as was pmised. Wheruppon The Balief and Burgesses all saving Grene & Phillippes did put their handes

<small>sent downe to Brookes who detenyth the same</small>

unto the same wrytten upp, and having so doone sent yt downe to Rychard Brook for him to put his hand & to get John Grenes hand to yt, to thend that they being put to, yt may be delivered to Mr Griffin to put his hand & by him to be sent to Mr Boughton acording to pmise. Brooks recevid the same writing subscribed by the Balief and principall Burgesses but desired respit to be advised before he put his hand to yt, and so kept it w^t him & wold neither subscribe nor send it back, which being peevid to

<small>a copy therof subscribed delyuered to Mr Boughton</small>

the Balif & Burgesses The caused an other coppy to be writen upp. and put their handes to yt and sent it the next day by this wryter to Mr Boughton at Kenelworth where he delivred yt to

<small>the tyme of going to London apoyntid</small>

Mr Boughton w^t the answer that Brooks had sent to the balief. And Mr Boughton receving yt willid that some of the

<small>afterward deferrid</small>

towne might be at London w^tin twoo or three dayes after alhoulow day for then he wold be there and wold move my

<small>Mr Boughton writith to give knowlege</small>

Lords for us. But afterward that is to say uppon Alhoulouday Mr Boughton wrote a lre to the balif signifieng that he could not be at London so sone, the tenor of (folio 211) his lre ensueth

Being this day ready to take my Journey towards London, I have recevid Lres from my Lorde, wherin he earnestly requyreth me to ryde presently to Denbigh for despatch of some busynes of weight, wch I meane god willing to p'forme and therfore must differ my Journey to London till the xx^th of this moneth when god willing I wilbe theire Readye to doo what I can in your cause wisshing that before that tyme youe doo not appoint yor iourney to London for that p'pose. So wisshing you as my self I take my leave in haste from Canson the first of November

Yo^r loving freend
Ed. Boughton

Jo. fisher & Jo. Rigeley appoyntid to goo to London to attend for resolucion

they goo up to fishers gret charge

Mr Boughton moveth the Earles of Warwik and Leycester who doo assigne Mr Owen of Lincolnes Inne only to be the man to give opinion

Mr Boughton signifieth so much to Mr Owen

he promiseth his paynes

fisher & Rigeley attend Mr Owen and so doth Brookes

Uppon receipt of thes Lre the Journey to London was staid untill the xx^th day of Novembr And then John ffisher and John Rigeley twoo of the principall Burgesses were appointid & sent up to attend such as should have the Judgem^t of thes differencs. When they came upp they attendid first Mr Boughton who lay at Leycester house, but my lords busynesse were such no tyme could be spred convenyent for Mr Boughton to move his L untill about a sevenight after then Mr Boughton signified to the said ffisher & Rigeley that the pleasures of my Ls therles of Warwik & Leyc^r were that Mr Owen of Lyncolnes yn only should be the man to puse the charters and to satisfie their Lordships and that therefore wee should attend uppon him for that purpose, and that he had message from therles to the said Mr Owen for that purpose ffisher & Rigeley thankid Mr Boughton and then gave there attendance on Mr Owen who could not be at Leasure untill foure or five dayes after the terme After attendance and some Leasure sruing it plesid Mr Owen to tak the copies of both the charters pmising his labo^r therin and that wee should resort agayn to him w^t in three or foure dayes. We

Brookes fisher & Rigeley hope for annswer of Mr Owen	did so and ones or twise. wee for the towne, & Brookes for himself met before Mr Owen, Who examyned both sides the causes moving the doubts. In thend both Brooks and wee were desirous to knowe his opynyon which he woold not utter but annswerid that he wold deliver his opynyon to therles of Warr & Leycr as he was required or to one of them. ffor wch purpose he did dyvers dayes & tymes come to Leycestr house but could not be heard by reason of greater causes then in hand. So the said ffisher and Rigeley danncing attendance there from the xxijth of Novembr untill Christmas even spent xxli and came downe without any resolucions Wheruppon the matter restid for a tyme.
his annswer was that he woold delyuer his opynion to the earles	
he attendid for that prpose but he could have no hearing	
Brookes fisher Rigeley come away wtout Resolucion	

(Here follows this note.)

the matters that followe next after this before written should have come in before in the accions of former tyme. and doo depend uppon a subtill practise put in use betwixt Brookes and Olney by a compleynt in the Chancery. But is rather insertid here bycause it may the better appere where the mony was, and also that there was no cause of compleynt, when the Earle of Leycester wrote his lre.

(Then follow copies of Brooke's letter for Subpœnas and Chancery orders.)

the copye of Ri. Brooke his lre for subpenas with ante dates	To his very freend Mr Thomas Gille Servannt to Mr Cordoll his howse in ffletestrete or at his chamber in channcery lane a little from the Roles d Hinse delur this lre wt yor owne hand that you may go for annswer

I am hartely to prey you to send me a subpena for thes psones underwritten to testify in a matter betwixt Thomas Oldne pl and Rychard Brooks defd Let it bere teste of the last terme in any case, they comissioners before whome they are to appere are Sr Thomas lucy Knight S^r ffulk grevill knight Thomas Leigh and Jobe Throkmrton esquires, the names of them that are to appear Rychard Townesend, Thomas Allen, Cristofer Knight henry Chaplyn Roger hurlebutt John Brook, I pre youe put in thes fyne for this once and I will requit hyt, yf you will nedes leave out anye leave John Brook, I pre you send yt so sone as you may, there is a freende of myne will Resorte unto you for it apon monday comesenight, I pre you let it be closed upp in a lre, I woold not have yt sene, this in hast I comyt you to god warr. the xvth of March

Yo^r loving frend Ry Brook

A copy of an order in Chancery ordering Interrogatories

(folio 212) A copy of a certificate to the Earl of Warwick that the Bailif & Burgesses had properly applied the money left

A copy of an order in Chancery for discharge of the matter touching the Corporation.

(Then follows this note)

thies before written orders in the channcery and the certificat to my L of Warr and Brookes Lre for subpena woold come more aptly after the sute in the Channcery Betwene Olney and Brookes. But bicause those bookes be long to write and also bycause it may appeare what followed the said sute I have thought good to place them here. the rather also bycause the same came to my hand at such tyme as I coulde not enter them in a place more conveynyent.

Brookes malice miti-gated for a tyme

But begynneth agayn in Mr Sheldons Baliwik

(folio 213) It is nowe to be remembrid That after the being of John ffisher and Jo Rigeley attending at London for some resolucion Richard ffisher then being Balief. Brookes psecutid not any further during the said Baliwik. But Mr Robart Sheldon succeding in that office of Baliwik. Brooks began the trowbles agayne, as towching ellections of Burgesses. And obteyned lres from both the forenamed Earles of Warwik and Leycester. The Tenor wherof ensueth viz.

To o{r} loving freends the Balif and Burgesses of Warwik

the Earles of Leycester and Warwiks lres for election of principall Burgesses

some Burgesis chosen contrary to the Charter

very unfit men

discredit the borough iniury the Inhabitants give occasion to calle the Charter in question

the l love to the place their desire to doo good

After o{r} hartie comendacions, wee have written unto you heretofore towching thimployment of the towne monye according to the true meanyng of the givers, and also for the orderly eleccion of the Balieffs & principall Burgesses there, as the woordes in yo{r} Charter doo ymport. And albeyt wee understand that uppon the receipt of o{r} lres, you haue w{th} care made good choyce of yo{r} balifs Yet the due reformacion in thelleccion of the said principall Burgesses hathe bene hitherto neglectid, ffor as wee bee credibly enformed) some be chosen not only contrary to yo{r} Charter, but also very unfitt men, for divers respects to supplie the same place, wherby you doo greatly discreadit the borough, Iniury the Inhabitants, and offer occasion to calle yo{r} Charter in question, Therfore being moued aswell by the speciall affection wee beare to the place, as also w{th} the earnest desire wee haue to doo the towne & the Inhabitants therof that good wee maye, Wee have thought good once againe to put you in mynde of o{r} former Letters towching an advised consideracion, orderly pcedings and the good government wee wisshe to finde in yo{r} corporacion.

opynyons of the best learned towching ellections

request to make a newe choyce

And for the order of the eleccion of yo{r} principall burgesses wee haue receiud the Opynyons of diuers of the best learned in the Lawes of this Realme, that by yo{r} charter you ought to choose them by the voyces of the Burgesses of the whole Burrough or the greatest part of them, ffor which good & waightie respects wee doo earnestly praye & requyre youe to assemble yo{r} selves togither, and to make a newe choyce of the said principall Burgesses by the generall voyces according to the construction & meaning of yo{r} charter, wherin wee doo not doubt but you wilbe very circumspect & carefull to preserve & make choyce of fitt, wise & discreete men, to the said Romes. And to thend that this o{r} request might sorte to better effect wee haue desired o{r} very freendes S{r} Thomas Lucy Knight Edward Boughton & Thomas Leigh Esquires yo{r} neighbors or some one of them to assiste you in the same newe election at such convenyent opportunytie as you shall have notyce of them or any of them, to nomynate a tyme certen for that purpose, wherof wee pray you not to faile, as youe will either further the comon comoditie & creadit of yo{r} borough, Or allowe & respect our earnest requestes made unto you for the good of the Towne and in the favo{r} of youe all, So wee bid you farewell. At the Court the xij{th} of March 1584

Yo{r} loving freendes

R. Leycester   A. Warwik

Marginal notes: to be carefull to choose fytt wyse & discrete men / That S{r} Tho. Lucy M{r} Ed. Boughton M{r} Tho. Leigh or some of them to assist the election

This lre was kept w{t} M{r} Brookes untill the xxij{th} daye of Aprell 1585 and then about ix of the clock at night brooks deliuered the same to M{r} Sheldon then Balief in Willm hicks house, saing here is a lre for you. This lre so written kept & deliuered M{r} Sheldon openid and myndid to have made the principall Burgesses privie to it on the Sonday following, But on fryday being the morrowe after the delivery M{r} Boughton cam to the towne to mete w{th} others of my l of Warr officers sitting at W{m} hicks house about the setting of my L landes. And on Saturday morning M{r} balif being sent for to them M{r} Boughton askid him whither he had not receuid Lres from the Lordes, w{ch} he said he had receiud on thursday night late, but his company being from home, he could not mak them privy to it. Nay said Brooks being present you mynd not to doo yt for you regard it not when it was deliuerid you, M{r} Boughton annswerid and said M{r} Balief my lords both are enformed that yo{r} eleccons of yo{r} burgesses bee not as they ought to bee and that you have hassarded yo{r} charter for yo{r} misdoings w{ch} they have

Marginal notes: M{r} Boughton cometh the next day after the deliuery of the lre / offreth him self

care over. And therfore have earnestly spoken to me that I should come to you & see a newe choice of such as be mete men & also in due order by voyces of all or the greater part of the townesmen for so the Lords are advertised by the best lerned in England yt ought to bee. And I thought you wold have had more care of their lres and that I should have found you redy to their so good & godly desires being for the comodytie of yor whole towne and for that cause I came purposely to be here this day. To that Mr Balif annswerid that both he & the rest of the principall Burgesses doo acknowledge themselfs greatly bound to their lordshippes and wolbe redy to doo any thing mete & reasonable comanded by their hono^{rs} but as yet he hath not made them privy to the lres, for there is not past iiij^{or} or v of them at home. And although they were all at home yet yt wolld ask long tyme to call all the Inhabitants togither wch could not be doone in a day or twoo or sevenight. Nevertheles his mynd was to have had a hall on sonday being the next morrow and uppon conferrens w^t his bretherne the principall Burgesses, his wo^rship should have heard from them but in so short a tyme as a day it is not possible to warne them. That is not so said Brooks they might have bene callid togither by the officers in an howre or twoo, and I dare tak uppon me yet yf you will so That you may have enowe for this purpose w^tin this houre. wch brooks might the more boldly speak for he had of his owne auctorytie that fryday before labored & procured to be labored not so fewe as fourtye to come to the crosse & to be there that saturday morning by eight of the clock to mak this eleccion part of wch were his old adherents and the greater part men of no value estimacion or understanding such as in dede have nothing to meddle in those matters As wilkyns his neighbo^r & poore Stinter Richard Brook tanner & such like, who in dede were redy by the houre apointid and playd the Loyterers all that morning Looking for that wch might not bee. But agayn to come to Mr Boughton he annswerid (folio 214) Mr Balief that uppon the Lords speciall comanndm^t he was there and if the eleccion might be made according to their desires he would be with him that day which

Marginal notes:
- to be at a new choise of mete men and in due order.
- by voyces of all
- Mr Baliefes Annswer
- Brooke replyeth
- Brookes and his frendes procure his colleges to be ready to give their voyces in ellection
- Mr Boughtons offer agayn

Y

was the day appointid for yt. And if it could not be that day, he could not come agayn for he had busynes for my L of Leicester in Wales whither he must goo on monday or tuesday following, and could not return untill after michilmas therfore if any thing shalbe doon that day he could be w^t them otherwise not, Mr Balif

Mr Balifs annswere — annswerid that it was not possible to call the people togither that day and besides he had not made his company privy, And therfore besought his wo^rshipp to give them tyme to annswer untill monday or tuesday, and in the meane tyme he woold call a hall, and theruppon his wo^rshipp should hear from them. Well saith he I see you little regard yor owne benefit or the lords writings and so for that tyme deptid.

the Balif Burgesses and many Comoners mete to consider of thes lres — On the morrowe being sonday Mr Balif appointid a hall whither came the most part of the principall Burgesses and there the L^{re} was redd to them wheruppon it was thought very daungerous & very inconvenyent to have any such ellection untill the towne might be advised by their Lerned counsell Nevertheles yt was agreid that a nombr of the most honest & best sort of thinhabitants should be callid togither to feele their myndes howe they were affectid towards the principall burgesses & whither they were desirous of any newe choice or displacing of those put. And theruppon Mr Balif sending for the constables & such w^tin every ward as he thought mete there came togither to the nombr of iiij^{xx} or more unto whom the matters being openid & they willid to speak their mynds freely.

the Answere of the Comoners — they w^t one voyce said that they had good liking both of Mr Balief & all the principall Burgesses nowe being & knewe no cause whie they should think otherwise, and so desired them all to think of them. Then the Lords lres were redd and they all semid to mislike w^t him that was the pmer and thought no reason to have such maner of ellection trusting that Mr Balif & his company had dooue and wold doo acording to the charter.

Mr Boughton cometh agayn comoned w^t Mr Balief — On the tuesday following Mr Boughton having appointid a court baron to be kept in the Castell for my l of Warr Tenaunts, the rather bicause he was lately made Steward of my

L lands and had kept no court there before that tyme, he came to Warwik into the Castell, And there after a while he talkid agayne w{th} M{r} Balief where then was present John flisher & divers of the principall Burgesses And then he said to M{r} balif I lookid to have heard from you towching my Lords l{re}s for you told me that you woold have a hall and then send me word when I should come to yo{r}

M{r} Balif's annswere ellection, S{r} said M{r} Balief I did promise yone that I woold have a hall & make my company p{r}ivye to my lords l{re}s, and that you should bee advertised from us whither their should be election or otherwise But you also sayd that you must goo out of the Countrey and except their might be ellection that Saturday you could not tarry. And I have callid my bretherne togither & a good nombr of the honest comoners and considered of my L{rs} requests and I fynd them not willing to have any newe choice and somuch I would have synified unto you if I had knowen yo{r} wo{r}ship had bene at home, but I thought that you

M{r} Boughton replieth had bene gone towards Wales. Well said M{r} Boughton it appeareth howe litle you regard of yo{r} estate, and of the good favo{r} the Lords beare unto you aswell by this as by the maner of receving of their L{re}s but it is no matter for if you will have no more care for yo{r} owne good & comon wealth you shall see what will come of it. But my lords shall understand that I have bene here redy to doo that they have comanndid. Then was it annswerid that it is ment that my Lords shalbe annswerid and of the mynde of the townesmen so as wee trust there good L{rs} shalbe satisfied. Well agods name saith M{r} Boughton but if you write to them I pray youe Let them know that I was redy to have done my duety. Yes said M{r} Balief, that shalbe done, and so for that day an end.

the Lordes l{re}s annsuerid Hereuppon yt was thought good that the Lords l{re}s should be annswerid wherby either they might be satisfied or quetid for the tyme. And therfore a L{re} was devised the tenor wherof ensueth.

To the most honorable Lords Robart Earle of Leycester Lord Steward of the quenes ma{tes} most honorable household, And Ambrose, Earle of Warwik twoo of her ma{ts} most honorable privy counsaill

The copye of the lres of the Balif and Burgess to the former lres rec from th erles of Warr and Leyc

    Our bounden dueties most humbly pmised It may like yor most noble lls tunderstand That yor honorable Lres of the xij^t of March were deliverid here at Warwik on thursday night the xxijth of Aprell instant, The which were made knowen unto some of us by Mr Balif the morrowe after being fryday. On which day also Mr Edward Boughton came to Warwik expecting a newe ellection of the principall Burgesses of the same towne But for that the tyme was so soden & short, as the thing could not be considerately doone as yor desires is and also for that divers of the company were then absent, and for other great consideracions, such as wee trust wilbe allowid of by yor noble wisdomes, wee did forbeare to procede therin untill wee might satisfie yor honorable lls otherwise whan yor good pleasures may be to grannt us favorable Audyence, which wee most humbly & hartely beseche w^t such convenient celeritie as to yor most grave wisdomes shalbe thought metest. In the meane tyme acknoleging o^r selves most bounden for yor g^rcious care towardes the good estate of the said poore towne & the contynuance therof wee rest in dayly prayers to almightie god to blesse all yor most noble accions. Warwik the xxvjth of Aprell 1585

    Yo^r hono^{rs} most humble at comanndm^t

nota.   the cause whie therle of Leycester was herin placed before his elder Brother was in respect of dignity of office, being for the tyme of Parliament L steward.

Mr Sheldon Bailief and others ride to London to satisfie the lordes

(folio 215) In Easter terme following it was thought mete to send upp some of the company bothe to conferre w^t counsaill lernid and also to satisfie the said Lordes wheruppon it was agreid that some of the principall Burgesses should goo upp and also some of the second company & other honest comoners. Of the principall Burgesses it was appointid that Mr Sheldon Balif should goo. John ffisher Willm ffrekulton & John Rigeley besides them Mr Richard ffisher Richard Townesend Thomas Powell having busynes of their owne there did promise to ayd the Bailief

& rest the best they could of the comoners Mr Worcetor henry chaplen Willm Loson Leonard holmes, yt fell so out that John ffisher was taken wt his disseas that he could not goo. But Mr Balief & the rest went upp, though scatteringly and the most of them being there applied their owne businesse so as Mr Balief said he had litle help of them more then of Mr Rigeley Mr ffrekulton & Mr Loson. Long it was erre Mr Balief might speak wt either of the Lordes for Therle of Warwik was very sick, & not to be trowblid wt any busynesse, my L of Leycester greatly occupied in matters of state & came seldome abrode. Therfore it semid good to Mr Balief & such as were wt him to prepare a supplicacion, and so to move the cause to my Lords wch Mr Sheldon drew. The copy wherof ensuith

To the right honorable or very good lordes The Earles of Warwik & Leicester

A Copie of a supplicacion exhibitid by Mr Sheldon to therle of Leycester

Our humble dueties to yor honors remembrid wt our contynuall & daylie prayers for the good estate of yor Lordshippes being next under god and her matie or speciall Patrones and defenders. Wee have recevid yor honorable Lres purporting on Informacion to yor honors that by or negligence oure principall Burgesses of your towne of Warwik should be chosen contrary to or charter but also very unfitt men for divers respectes appointid to supplie those places, with yor honors further admonicion towching an advised consideracion & orderly proceading in the Eleccion of the said principall Burgesses, and the good government of or said corporacion, ffor which yor honorable & favorable Lres As wee acknolege our selves greatly bound to yor lls for the same. So wee protest wee never had purpose or wille to infringe or said charter or doo anything to mislike either of yor honors. And if any thing have passid contrary to or charter, or to yor lls mislike, wee assure yor lls it hathe pceded of ignorance & not of will. But forasmuch as wee are informed by or Learned Counsell that wee have made choice of or principall Burgesses according to Lawe and the poynts of or Charter wee most humbly beseche yor honors to comytt the hearing and examynacion of our doings herein and the consideracion of or Charter to Mr Srjannt Cawdye Mr Sergeant Puckering and Mr Solicitor or any twoo of them or to such others learned in the lawes as yo' lls shall lyke uppon whose reaport wee shalbe ready to parforme what soever hath bene mistaken through ignorannce with the contynuall prayers of us and all the Inhabitants of yo' said Towne of Warwik for the long & prosperous estate of yo' good lls

      Yo' honors humble Orators The Balif and Burgesses of the Borough of Warwik .

my L therle of Leyor usith divers speches to M' Sheldon   This supplicacion was deliured to therle of Leycester by M' Robart Sheldon Balif & M' John Rigeley in Leycester garden at London on ffryday before Whitsonday 1585, where my lord gave some hard speches to M' Balief nevertheles afterwardes more gentlier willid him to come to the court to him where he should knowe his further pleasure, and appointid him to be there on the sonday following, where they attendid and after long wayting yt pleasid my lord to use very honorable & favorable countennce & speche towards both him & the towne & then referrid untill an other tyme But in thend it pleased my Lord to send them woord by M' Moore his barbo' that they should no longer attend but goo whome & Look to the good government of his charge, And he woold stand good Lord unto them in what they had nede to use him, and that he was satisfied.

my l therle of Leyer semed to be satisfied

Brookes procureth other Lres from my L therle of Warwick.   This notw'stonding could not stop Brookes his malice, but he peeving that my lord therle of Leicester grewe werye of thes idle accusacions, goeth to one M' Stanley Audito' to therle of Warwik and settith him on against the towne and peureth him to get my L of Warwiks hand to an other Lre. The tenor wherof ensueth

    To the Balief and Burgesses of Warwik give thes.

the copye of my L of Warwiks lre   Having heretofore togither wth my brother written unto you severall Lres touching the orderly Imployments of the towne money according to the true meaning of the gevers of the same, and also concerning the due ellection of the principall burgesses there according to the charter w{ch} of long tyme in that poynt hath bene by the frowardnesse of some of you much abused. And in the same other lres to thend yo{r} newe election might tak better effect, wee did lett you knowe, that we had desyred S{r} Thomas Lucy, Edward Boughton & Thomas Leigh Esquires yo{r} neighbo{rs} to be present at the same. Wherin wee now finde by good advertisement that you have doone nothing, neither regarding o{r} form{r} lres nor respecting the creadit of yo{r} selves, nor the comon comodytie of the Borough, But making light reconing of o{r} earnest request, & of M{r} Boughtons offer to be present at yo{r} ellection as he was required by us. Wherby albeyt you have given us sufficient cause to think that such men as delight in mysdoing, and denyeng o{r} earnest desire to doo the towne good, and offer us occasion to bring you to good order by other meanes then by requestes w{ch} (if this may serve) wee are lothe to attempt, I therfore yet once againe in former sorte requyre you, that you assemble yo{r} selves togither, and make a right choyce of yo{r} principall Burgesses by the generall or more parte of the voyces of the burgesses of the whole Borough as the Lawe doth warrannt & appoynt youe by yo{r} charter to doo. At which ellection ones againe I desire & require youe that the said Ed. Boughton may bee present, by whose meanes it may tak the better effect, And that also he may appoint & give notice unto you of the tyme when the same shalbee, wherof you will not faile (folio 216) if youe make accompt of my favo{r} or bee desirous of good government of the towne, Of which I will be carefull and bring youe to reforme yo{r} mysordered doings if herin youe bee negligent. ffare ye well from Northall the x{th} of July 1585

       Yo{r} Loving freend
        A. Warwik

  This lre M{r} Boughton sent to M{r} Robart Sheldon by Richard Griffin the xx{th} day of July, M{r} Boughton himself & other therles officers being presently in the towne.(a)

  (a) What was the end of this matter does not appear, as there are no further entries with regard to it in the Black Book. Perhaps, as on a former occasion M{r} Fisher's pen was weary, or perhaps the recurrence of the sickness to which he was subject, prevented him from continuing the narrative.

Counsel's Opinion on the Charter.

The Copye of the opynyon of divers lerned Lawyers whervnto they have subscribed touching the poynt in question

Warwick Burgh

Domini 1585
Octauo Augusti Anno Re Eliz 27

Uppon consideracion of the charter of Corporacion of the Balieff and Burgesses of the Borough of Warwik, wee thynk that the principall Burgesses are to be chosen by the greater part of the comen counsell of the said Borough which comen counsell are the Balieff and the principall Burgesses for the tyme being who by the Charter have (as wee think) the onely auctorytie for all Actes and Ordynannces, for the better direction & ordering of the men, the cawses, the thinges, & the affayres of the said Borough (except onely concerning such matters wherin by speciall woordes of the same charter any other are mencioned to entermeddle) as in the clause of the choice of the Bailief is mencioned that the other men & Inhabitants of the borrough may make the eleccion, But for the choyce of the principall Burgesses wee fynde in the charter no mencyon of any other to entermeddle therwth. In which o^r opynyon wee are the better confirmed for that wee are advertised, That at all tymes since the making of the charter, the principall Burgesses have bene so electid. And wee thinke that if they shoulde make theire election otherwise, yt woolde be danngerous unto the Corporacion, And many Inconveniences might arryse therof

        Thomas pagytt
        Edward heron
        ffranc morgan

Thes abovenamed gentlemen and others having bene of counsell w^t the towne did alwayes encorage the Balief and Burgesses that thellection of principall Burgesses was to be doone by the comon counsell for the tyme wch bee only the principall Burgesses wth the Balief And that they have power to make Leaces &c, wch made the Balief & Burgesses to forbeare any newe ellections at the Lordes requests. And of that opynion also was Mr Egerton the quenes

Solicitor Mr Owen before Remembrid Mr harrys of the Inner Temple, who argued that point before Mr Sute & Mr Gawdye Justices of Assises as herafter shalbe remembrid. And uppon hearing of a triall for the tuithes of Budbrook in thescheqr the Lord chief Baron Sr Roger Manwood uttered his opinyon acordingly, and sins that tyme Mr Beaumond hath so thought also. And to the foreremembrid note did Mr Thomas Walnest Sergeant Mr Richard Shuttleworth Srjant & Mr Cristofer Yelverton subscribe as may appere by the said note

(folio 217) Bond dated 27th of June 1591 from Ralph Hockenhull of Chalfont St Peter in the County of Bucks Esq. to the Bailiff and Burgesses of Warwick the condition of which was that if the said Ralph Hockenhull should pay to the Bailiff and Burgesses such sums of money as Sir Henry Goodier Knight and John Puckering should assess to be due from Richard Brook to the Bailiff and Burgesses then the obligation should be void otherwise of full force.

Then follows this memorandum.

Md that this was deliued by Mr Horkenhull to Mr Sergeat Puckering to the use of ye Bayliue and burgesses of Warr as an escrowe to be his deed & soe to be deliued as his deed to ye saide Bayliue and burgesses when there shalbe any lease or leases passed under the great Seale of England of the Castell mylles and Temple farme in Warr by any meanes consent or pcuremt of the said Mr Hockenhull or Richard Brook or anie other in theire or eithr of theire behalfe.[a]

John Fisher's last speeches.

(On folio 189 is the following memorandum)

Memorand that Mr Jhon ffisher in the laste speaches wch ever he delivered unto mee towchinge temporall affaires uttered these words, The Q: is to have 26s 8d out of the friers for that the lande was given to the L. of warwicke the towne to receaue 3s 4d in respecte of the tithe yearlie

W. Spicer

[a] Some proceedings in Chancery seem, according to the above, to have been going on between the Town and Richard Brook, but there is nothing to shew whether they arose from or had any connection with the matters previously related.

THOMAS STAUNTON OF LONGBRIDGE.

Thomas Staunton his practise towching the tyth acre in Bareford meadowe

(folio 190) Be yt remembrid That uppon complaynt made by the tennts of longbridge namely Richard ffysher Tenaunt of the Earle of Warwiks ferme and demanes Thomas Saunders a freeholder Willm Boyes a tennt to Mr Bewfoo (   ) Wylmor tennt to Thomas Saunders And John Bykar one of the fermors of the tithes of corne & hey in longbridge ffor that Thomas Stanton of Longbridge aforesaid had more than a yere sithens digged upp a meere stone stonding in the meadowe callid Bareford(a) meadowe being parcell of the Lordship of Warwik which stone had bene pitched many yeres sithens as a meare to limytt and bounde the meadowe then the freehold of Mr Clement Throkmorton esquire from the meadowe being the freeholde of the Balief and Burgesses of Warwik in the said Bareford meadowe callid the tithe acre and that the said Thomas Staunton having prchasid the said pcell of meadowe sometyme Mr Throkmortons had removed the said stone out of his right place to the great preiudice of the freeholders & occupiers of the said meadowe And nowe presently that the said Thomas Stanton had privately without calling any of the freeholders or their tennts measured out & lottid euery tennts doles or porcions as plesid him without their knoweleidges and also had caused the gresse of part of the said tithe acre to be mowed downe by his owne moyers as his owne and apointid the tithe acre to lie in an other place by his assignt to the dishenheriting of the said Balief & Burgesses and their successours and to the no litle trowble & disorder of all other Tenaunts there. This mondaye being the ixth daye of Julye 1582 in the xxiiijth yere of the reigne of our souereigne Ladye Quene Elizabeth Thomas Powell nowe Balief of the said Borough of Warwik and also being Balief & Reeve of the right honorable Lord Ambrose Earle of Warwik John ffisher Stewarde of the said Borough of Warwik calling unto them Richard Townesend Thomas Jenkes John Ridgeley & Roger hurlebut principall Burgesses of the said borough and also henry Chaplen Robart west Tho. Chapman assistants to the said principall Burgesses went into the said meadowe callid Barford meadowe Whither the said Thomas Stanton Richard ffysher

(a) Barford is a large village three miles to the South of Warwick.

Thomas Saunders & (   ) wilmore being sent for & present but Wm Boyes was absent The said Bailief & Burgesses & others did see the stone being in length about five foot by estimacion, lieng uppon the grounde distant from the hole wherin hit before had bene stonding And there the said Thomas Staunton being demaundid whither he had diggid upp and removed the same stone or not he confessid that he had diggid yt up and Laid yt there And being demaundid whie he so had doone transgressing not onely the Lawe of this land but also goddes Lawe he aunswerid that he had doone nothing but what was lawfull for him to doo And being said unto that yt was not Lawfull for any man to remove a meare stone & landmark he aunswered that stone should be no meare stone for yt stoode within his owne grounde & freeholde And that being denied by all the neighbours & tenaunts there all they affirmed that yt was a meare stone sett there about xviij yeres passid by the comaundement & apointmt of Mr Clement Throkmorton then being surveyo^r genall of all the quenes ma^ts lands in Warwikshire and then being also owner and tenaunt of that piece or peell of meadowe which nowe the said Tho. Stanton hathe, and the said stone was theire pitched & sett to be a meare betwene the said Mr Throkmorton & the Balief & Burgesses of Warwik who have lieng next to the said parcell of meadowe one acre of meadowe callid the tithe acre And the said tithe acre dooth conteyne in bredth foure poles and so by that messure abuttith right against the dich that cometh downe from Longbridge ward. But the said Tho. Staunton confessing that the said Balief and Burgesses ought to have an acre thereabouts denieth that it should come westward in bredth so farre as to the hole where the stone had stood but said that it ought to be from the place where the stone nowe lieth and so to have foure pooles forward estward in Bredth And affirmed that somuch they nowe have allowed them by this last messuring set furth But all the rest of the freeholders Tenants & neighbo^rs there affirmed that it ought to bee from the hole or place where the stone had stood forward toward the east and so to ioyne to the lott of meadowe of my lord of Warwik nowe in the tenure of Richard ffisher hereuppon the comon poole of Longbridge by which all theire medowes were mesured was sent for, And being laid at the myddes of the hole wherin the stone had stood, the said poole reachid estward iust to the middell part of the nether end of the said stone as nowe it lieth, wherin was notid some fraudulent devise of the said staunton to gett a pole of meadowe to his other pcell of meadowe wherw^{th} the said Staunton being burthened aunswerid that he had done nothing but what was lawfull for him to doo, ffor he had taken no more then his owne & that he woold keape And being demaunded whie hee woold say yt to be his owne sethens he had purchasid no more then that Mr Throkmorton had and Mr Throkmorton never had nor required any more or further then to the said hole where the stone had bene pitchid he aunswered that Mr Throkmorton was a gentleman and might doo with his owne as pleasid him and might loose some of his owne if he woold but he woold not so doo for he knewe it was his owne & he woold have yt To that it was aunswerid that Mr Throkmorton was (folio 191) a gentleman in deed but yet such a good husbond as woold not lose any part of his freeholde besides that he had sufficient knowleige by the bookes of survey & other auncient recordes to knowe howe farre his owne stretchid And withall he was a man of sufficient creadit & auctorytie a Justice of peace and of great living and therefore hable to defend his right and therto knowen to have a will to hold his owne and therfore it cold not be thought but that he had apointid the merestone to be placid to his owne comoditie & others without any such preiudice to himself. And as to that that the said Stanton said he woold have yt It was afirmed there that the fermors of the tithes of the balief and Burgesses of Warwik ever hitherto so farre as any man can remembr had the said acre in bredth from the said hole foure pole eastward And that being so it was no reason That they should be put from or dishenheritid which the said stanton denied to goo about but said that they should have their full measure still but it must be where he had apointid Emongs other speches It was said that there is or had bene of late an other mere stone lieng at the nether end of the said meadowe next unto Avon side which had bene sett many yeres past without memory of man which woold be some rule to the rest which stone being diligently lookid for could not be nowe found And all the tenaunts there afirmed that it had bene stonding there & seene within twoo yeres past and said that it was a great stone and Richerd ffisher affirmed that he had often sitten downe uppon it to rest him, this stone can not be found And Thomas Saunders said that he thought that he that had removed the one had taken the other away also To that Staunton aunswered he had not taken it away but bad them goo lock it if they woold have yt And being demaundid howe he thought it should be gone the said Staunton said it might be that some anglers comyng by Avon side should pluck it up to look for woormes under yt orells he knewe not what should be come of yt which was taken to be but a weak reason. But after much tyme spent & many frivolous woordes the said Stanton said this is long of Mr Ric. ffisher & his neighbo^r Saunders who could never hold themselfes contentid and yet they did as much wrong as he did and had as much for their porcions as he had, & so grewe to further speaches wherin as well the said Tho. Stanton as M^r ffisher & Tho. Saunders confessid that there was in that callid Bareford meadowe a certen overplus of mesure more than the c^{r}tenty of their tenures lymittid which overplus had bene used to be devidid emongs those three viz M^r ffisher Tho Stanton & Tho. Saunders and the said Stanton said that he had in his last deviding and mesuring laid out the parts of the said M^r ffisher & Tho. Saunders and had taken this pole lieng next to himself for his overplus which he thought to be more comodiose for him and no losse to any other neither to Mr Balief & the towne But yt was aunswered by John ffisher that removing must nedes be losse & in thend dishenheriting of the Balief & Burgesses And therfore by consent of Mr Balief & others present the said ffisher willid John Bikar being the fermo^r of the tithe acre to gather the gresse mowed by Th. Stanton his moyers from the hole eastward in such maner as before he had used to doo and not to meddle any further Estward then the bredth of the acre And the said bredth was mesured at bothe the endes & withie boughes stickid downe. And then the said Staunton demaundid howe he should be allowed his part of the overplus. And that was left to be taken as before it had bene used Wherunto Mr Powell on the behalf of my lord of Warwik said yt was the lords & that he woold take a leace of yt. And Mr Ric. ffisher fermo^r to the Lord said that the overplus of measure was promised to him by my Lords surveyo^{rs} But in the end they both were contentid that for this tyme it should goo as before it had bene used And thereuppon Thomas Staunton yeldid to the said John bykar the gresse fallen from the said hole And the moyers of the said Stanton being mowing uppon the said Staunton's piece & uppon part of the said tithe acre clamed by the said Stanton were dischargid & willid not to fall the gresse stonding toward Aven side uppon the said tithe acre, nor that they should mowe any further then to the uttermost part of the said Th. Stauntons piece as it was then of newe troden out. But awhile after the said Staunton contrary to that he had before pmised said that he woold fall the rest of the gresse & tak it as his owne so farre in bredth as he had begonne unles that the rest of the tenuts of that meadowe woold come to him to see the meadowe that day mesured agayne and that his porcion for the overplus might be laid out & apointid to him and that being promised he promised agayne that the said John Biker should quietly enioy the tithe acre where it had bene used And his promise was made to Jo. Biker by the said Stanton in the hearyng of John ffisher Richerd Townesend Roger hurlebut Robart west Thomas Saunders.

Yf this maner of leyng out by Th. Stauntons mesure & alotmᵗ had bene suffered Then the tithe acre should have bene laid on part of my lord of Warwiks lond And my lord of Warwik should have bene laid uppon Tho. Saunders lond & so Tho. Saunders agayn laid uppon my lord of warr. And so brought all out of order & cᵗtenty to all their great detryments and the comoditie only to the said Stanton wynnyng the fourth part of an acre ioynid to his freehold.

folio 192) And further yt is to be remembrid That albeit that the said Thomas Staunton had made his promyse as before is remembrid and that he had suffred John Bykar to mowe downe the gresse left stonding uppon the said Tuithe acre yet the said Staunton ymediately after the same gresse was mowed downe by William Boyes by the apointmᵗ of the said Bikar the next morning being tuesday the Xᵗʰ of July the said Staunton raked away the gresse newe fallen and leid it emongs his owne to the dishenheriting of the towne if it be suffrid.

(No further reference is made to this matter.)

Copy of lease of a messuage and land at Ilmingdon to William Lewes 8th Oct., 1585.

(folio 193) Copy of lease to Humfrey Crane of a close at Hatton, 1st Oct., 1582.

(folio 194) Copy of lease to Matthew Blik of a tenement and land at Norton Linsey, 1st Oct., 1582.

(folio 195) Copy Composition between William Barkeswell, Dean of the College of St. Mary, and William Orme, Vicar of Budbrook, 12th July, 1467. (Latin.)

THE PRINCIPAL BURGESSES EXPELL ONE OF THEIR BODY.

Richerd Brooke put out of the office of Burges

(folio 197) Be yt remembred That this xviijth daye of June 1.5.8.2. in the xxiiijth yere of the reign of our souereign Ladye Quene Elizabeth &c uppon great & urgent causes by Informacion made to Mr Bailief of this borough and the principall Burgesses of the same borough of the mysdemeano^r of Richarde Brook late one of the pryncipall Burgesses of the said borough It is nowe agreid consentid & ordered that the said Richard Brook shalbe from hensfurth none of the said corpacion But is this present day by the voyces & deedes of thes undernamed and whose handes are under subscribed denounced declared & putt out of their felowshipp and companye of Bailief & Burgesses of this borough And shalbe no more used callid or taken as any of the said corpacion. And that the said Richard Brook from hensfurth shall not have any voyce or consent as any of the said corpacion. And yt is also agreid that Accions and Sutes by lawe shalbe brought and comensed against the said Richard Brook for such debts and duetyes as bee by him due to the said towne or borough. In witnes wherof wee have hereunto put o^r handes.

Th. Powell Balief Ric ffisher Ric Townesend John ffisher Willm ffreculton humfrey crane John Rigeley Robart Phillippes Thomas Jenks John Dyche Robart Sheldon

M{d} that after the amoving & putting out of the above named Richard Brook from the company of principall Burgesses The Bailief and principall Burgesses above named did elect & choose into their said companye and felowshipp of principall Burgesses Roger Hurlebutt in the Rome & place of the said Richard Brook And the said Roger Hurlebutt was sworne a principall Burges the said xviij{th} day of June 1582.

And the said Roger Hurlebutt being sworne They all abovesaid Bailief & principall Burgesses did elect & choose William Jenks into their felloweshipp of twelve assistants of the said borough which William Jenkes being sent for was sworne one of the said Assistants in the place of the said Roger hurlebutt the said xviij{th} daie of June 1582.

In the name of god

speciall causes of the putting out of R. Brookes

Bycause in all determynacions & decrees. Nothing can bee doone so exactly But that Question may rise whie the same ys or shoulde so bee decreed & determyned. And then A reason to be yeldid for the doing therof. It is not unfitt to remembr the consideracions whiche moved the Bailief and principall Burgesses of the borough of Warwik to depose and displace Richarde Brook from theire socyetie companye & counsaille, as A man unmete to remayne in that feloweshipp. Emongs whome good orders & lawes being orderid for the more establishing of euery sort of people in the due and reuerend seruice of god, duetie to the Quenes ma{tie}, comfortable concord emongs themselves, & good example to others, (unto w{ch} aswell the subiect as the magistrate ought to bee obedient) fforells It is truely said y{t}, That comonwealth must nedes dekay, where the magistrate ruleth the lawe, and the lawe not the magistrate, And therefore magistrates & officers ought to bee circumspect, least (they fayling in their dueties) shall suffer themselves to bee seduced by Ambicion & hawtie Aspiracion, and so should lett slipp Justice, Equitie, & conscionable dealing, the veary groundwoork & foundacion of all Honestye (As this Rychard Brook dooth) who forgetting that magistrates ought to bee of synceare lyving & lovers of vertue, and to bee directid in their doings by the rule of cyvile order, hathe (not only) chosen to be countid A connyng companyon, in querelous causes (unfitt for an honest magistrate, And preferrid his pryvate profite before the publique comoditye, But also, (contempning all duetie of humanytye) hath most unnaturally practised to perturbe the quyet peace & unanymyty of the weale publique, wherof he was a membr, and ought to have beene a father & defender. And all this cometh of his selfliking & resolute opynyon, ruled by the loose lynes of Lybertye, without respect or regard of the Lawe of God or man. (As may perticulerly appeare by his accions, not fully emblasid, but as yt were a litle towchid, in the true discourse following. And therin first to begynne wth such lawes & orders as himself hath in tymes past ratified by subscribing unto them. It is to bee knowen, that certen politike constitucyons, have been agreid uppon by & emongs the Balief and principall Burgesses of Warwik (the said Brooke being then one of them) Emongs which is sett downe & orderid As followth viz.

4. That the Balief & principall Burgesses shall every sonday bee at their parishe church all the tymes of divyne servyce aswell in the morning as in the Evening. And at all Sermons &c.

5. (folio 198) And that euery of the principall Burgesses shall have A gowne of black cloth faced with some semely lyning or furre which gowne shalbe made after the cytie fasshon And also shall have a coate or Jacket of black cloth or other thing of black or sad coolo^r his dowblett hose & cappe to be black. And the same shall use & weare when any assembly or meting is apointid by the Balief And the same shall weare to the churche, to the halle, and to & in such other places, as hee shalbe apointid to acompany the said Balief.

6. And that every of the principall Burgesses shalbee obedyent & attending at the comandement of the Balief for the tyme beyng in all resonable causes, and shall come & acompanye the said Balief at all tymes when he shalbe apointid, and shall not refuse to doo any resonable or mete thing, which they or any of them shalbe apointid unto.

z

7. And that euery of the principall Burgesses shalbe readye & attend on the Balief for the tyme being yerely on Michilmas day & on Alhalloudaye by nyne of the clock in the morning at the halle & theire give theire voyces for the eleccion of A newe Balief acording to the charter.

8. And that euery of the principall Burgesses being in the towne, and having no lawfull lett shall attend on the Balief at euery fayre to make the proclamacion acording to the lawdable order, and also when any spiall proclamacion is to be made for the quenes ma^tie

9. And that euery of the said Burgesses, that shall heare the Balief or any other of the principall Burgesses reviled slanndered or evill said of in his absens, especially by any dwelling within the said borough, Shall geve the Balief or him so reportid of or slanndered knowlege therof.

10. And if any quarrell afray or brawle happen to bee in any streat of this borough The pryncipall Burges dwelling nere the place & knowing therof shall doo what in him lieth to appease the same, and to cause the offenders to bee taken & carryed to the Balief or to warde untill such tyme as the Bailief may tak further order w^t thoffenders.

11 And to the end that unytye & concorde might be therby better encreased It ys ordered that euery of the principall Burgesses shall calle the rest of the company of principall Burgesses by the name of Brother

30. And that neyther the Bailief nor any of the principall Burgesses shall utter or Reveale any comunycacion counsaill agreament or advise had or spoken in the counsaill howse of matters towching the said borough or corporacion, or the charters libties landes or possessions of the same, neither shall yterate or report the same agayne to any persone not being of the same howse & companye

31. And that neither the Balief nor any of the principall Burgesses shall practise wth any others of the Burgesses to yelde to or graunt theire good willes or consent to any matter or cause towching the said borough or the libties of the same, or towching the grannting of any landes Tenements Tithes Advowsons &c

or towching noiacion election or choise of any balief burges or officer, out of their counsaill howse or place of assembly. neither shall any grannt his owne will out of the saide place.

32. And that yf the Balief or any of the principall Burgesses shall at any tyme herafter, wittingly & willingly, devise procure consent, or doo any thing to overthrowe frustrate or make voyde, Or doo promise or yelde to surrender or give upp the charters of corpacions or any of them or any libertie or franchise or any landes or tents Tithes pronage or possessions alredy grannted or herafter to be grannted unto the Balief & Burgesses of the said Borough, Every such whither hee bee bailief or burgesse so doing devising or consenting, shall ymedietely bee displaced of his place & Roome, & shall suffer such further ponishmet As by the Balief and Sixe of the principall burgesses shall be laid uppon him. Saving that they may assent to sell or exchannge any theire Landes or Tenements for good p'poses and to the better comoditie of the said Borough.

Thies above remembrid orders & constitucions Richard Brook hathe not observed, But hath broken them.

4. ffor he hathe not come to his parysh churche euery sondaye at tymes of divyne sruice & sermons, but hathe absentid himself very often, a moneth & more together, And many tymes being at or about home in the sruice & simon tymes, hath frequented such company as have not resortid to the church, nor come at sermons nor recevid the sacrament in many yeres together wherby some doubtes have & doo rise of his Religion.

5. (folio 199) And whan the said Brook hath come to any conferens by the apointement or sending for of the Balief for the tyme being, hee hath many tymes come in garments unsemely for the tyme & place. As sometyme in a cloke and in other undecent apparell, and that of light or whitish colo^r, betokening him rather to be a miller then a magistrate

6. 7. 8. And veary often he knowing the tymes of metings, and having been sent for, hathe not come to accompanye or attend the Balief, As at faires & other

metings Insomuch as being sent for & invited to accompanye the Balief & principall Burgesses, at M{r} Okens day of dynner & accompts: and for such other causes & conferrences that the said Balief & principall Burgesses had to doo for the benefit of the said borough He hathe refusid to come. and hath answerid that he reckonid himself none of them. Nor woold have to doo w{th} them. but as a straunger to defend his owne sutes & causes against the towne. And willed the said annswere to be reportid to the Balief.

9. And wheras he should not suffer to heare the Balief and principall Burgesses to bee slanndered or evill reportid, He hathe not onely suffered that to bee doone. But also hath offendid therin himself And also hath bene causer of others to doo the like and to use themselves veary outragiously in woordes & evill behavio{r} to the officers as well behind their backs as to their faces. As for example. his owne wief: & Sonne in Lawe, his owne brother. & inferio{r} sruntes. And also he himself hath made both slannderous & also untrue reaports of sondry baliefs in the tyme of theire offices, namely of M{r} Rigeley in the tyme of his baliwik afirmyng divers untruethes of him to S{r} John hubond. And also to M{r} Peyto hee accused M{r} Townesend in the tyme of his baliwik as a thief for stealing corne. Insomuch as he procured both the said baliefs to bee sent for by p{r}cept out of the libties of this borough during their Baliwik to bee examyned by Justices of the peace of the shire, wherby also he caused the libties & franchises of this borough to bee infringed.

10. And as towching his disposicion to quietnes & appesing of quarrells yt is manyfest That he hath bene a breeder of many trowbles and procurer of great outrages. And therfore hath and yet dooth maynteyne & susteyne divers masterlesse men. brawlers and fighters. namely ffranncys Bybbe Richard Brookes James Richardson (when he livid) and divers others unknowen encowraging them to mak quarrells frayes & Bloodshedde aswell w{th} the libties of this borough as for example in myton feilds against John Rey, and in the barne A notable Riott, As also in other places abrode. As in the feilds of Snyterfeld against Robart Sheldon & others to the hassard of some of theire lives.

11. And in stede of the name of brother he and his have callid some of the principall Burgesses gorballied choorles. gowtye wretches. craftye knaves, & other names as best likid him

30. And as towching his secrecye in keping counsaill he hath not onely reaportid such things as he hath heard secretely But also procured divers psones not being of the same house to derogate & resist the resolucions & determyacions there sett downe & agreed upon, Insomuch as some mutynyes & murmurs have theruppon risen by his & his complices especiall labo^r & procurement.

31. And he hath contrary to his promyse & subscribing yeldid his good will without the counsell house to grannt parcell of the lands and tithes of this borough. And more then that he hath procured a gentleman to procure lres from a nobleman & great estate of this land namely my lord the Erle of leicester directid to the Balief and burgesses to grannt the psonage & tithes of Budbrook to Mr Raffe hubond.

32. And yt is not to be forgotten That he bothe wittingly & willingly, hath practized by devises to have the liberties and franchises of this borough to be forfeited & seasid And therefore devised & procured That Thomas Olnoll George ffullshurst James Richerdson Richard Brooks tanner Richerd Bettes carpenter or Smyth clement hill and three or foure other desperate psones set on by him chiefly & with entendid p'pose to resist the officers namely Richard Townesend balief of this borough and John Grene a principall burges having speciall comission under the quenes ma^{ts} privie seale to deliver the tuith corn to John Rey by decree ordered unto him. and so furnished the said outragious psones wth gonnes bowes billes & warlik weapons & comfortid (folio 200) them wth meat drink & monye so that therby he encoraged them most riotosly to enter into the tuith barne of myton But also most rebelliously as yt may bee saied to kepe the same against the quenes comissioners. Insomuch as by the malice force & other disorder of the said Rioters divers of the company assisting the said Bailief & Grene in the execucion of their comission, were by the said Rioters woundid & danngerously hurt. Wherof knowleige being brought to the said Brookes. he

utterid his mynd. Saing that he was sorrye that none were slayne. but wished that some had bene killed on the one side or on the other, wherin he manifestid his secret mischevous malice & meanyng desirous that by those practises the franchises of this borough might have bene forfeitid or brought in question by the bloodshedding & death of any were yt his owne sonne in Lawe or other deare freend whosoever he cared not

And thes be matters thought worthye his displacing. But wheare the feare of God is wanting, there humayne societie is not to be expectid

And therfore the said Brook neither regarding the penalties of mans lawe nor the ponishment threatened by gods lawe, hath broken his othe solemply taken when he entrid into the office of Balief of this borough, In which emongs other things. Hee did sweare to make a true iust and parfitt acompt of all such monye & other thinges which should come to his handes to the use of the said Borough during the tyme of his baliwik And shoulde in due tyme pay & discharge all fees & fermes due in discharge of the said borough. And should not demand or take any allowance of any monye or other thing but such as was or should bee iust & true, And also did sweare that he woold to the uttermost of his habilytie knowleig & power maynteyne the privelegies libties right & franchises of the said Borough. Which othe not regarding hee hath not payd vj^{li} xiij^s iiij^d due to the quenes ma^{tie} within the tyme of his Acompt for a tenth or Rent resrued of certen Landes tenements personages & hereditaments granntid by the worthye prince of famose memory King henry the eight to this borough but coruptly of wickid purpose kept the same in his handes to the great preiudice of the said borough, and yet uppon the declaracion of his Acompt of Burges asked and took allowance therof as matter dischargid, contrary to his said othe. And besides that he owing xv^{li} to Thomas Whateley sometyme of Coventrye by a bill of debt subscribed wth the said Brook his hande. which bill the said Whateley delivered over in liewe & value of the said xv^{li} to bee requyred & recevid of the said broks by Symon Yong then balif of Warwik to be lent to the use of the poore of the said borough And the said Brook confessing the said Bill to be true and the debt to be due wth

his promise to Yong for paymet therof Afterwardes the said Brook being requyred to pay the said xv^{li} in discharge of the said debt & bille He voluntaryly of his owne mocyon did tak into his hand a testament and willingly & corruptly did swere by the contents therof That he had paid the said xv^{li} to John ffisher, a man that had neither warrant nor comission to receve or demannde the same debt. nor never had or recevid the same of the said Brook which foreremembrid things may shewe a sufficient cause of his unworthinesse. But yf his condycions conversacion & behavio^r bee further examyned, yt may bee thought that he is a companyon unmete to bee matched wth quiet & playne meanyng men. ffor hee, to have his folly floorishe leaveth no unkind parte unpractised, nor any subtille slye or craftie devise unacomplishid. wherby he maye eyther acquyre to himself comoditie, or extorqnate any thing bee it never so smalle value from his quiet neighbo^r Or craftely convey himself in or out of trowblesome tytles to the hurte of others. ffor Example, his crafty connyng to solicite John Rey to fall into his dannger, a matter for the length therof not to be written here, bycause yt hathe appeared most manyfestly by his owne lres and the decrees of courtes in that behalf. his great & servile keaping of the said Rey to the said Rey his undoyng (folio 201) his subtill shiftes for keaping of his owne bodye out of arreste lieng many moneths bothe at London abrode & at home in his owne howse secretly under the gard of the undersherif of middlesex to defraud his credytors His procuring & prosecuting of sutes in the hiegh court of Starrechamber and other chargeable place against his honest neighbo^{rs} not offending him, but doing their dueties in assisting officers in the execucion of their comission, his denyeng and renouncing of his title & clayme to the tuythes & leaces of Myton entyteling Thomas Oldnall to the same. his exaccions of monye from ynnocent & honest neighbo^{rs} by colo^r of proces dispensing w^t some for their apparancs for bribes. his malicious practise in pleading that the moytie of the tuithes of Myton are not belonging to thies corporacions of Warwik, his witholding the monye due for the rent of the said tithes from the chamber & use of this borough spending the same in sutes of Lawe against the balief & Burgesses for requyring there owne, that is to saye, xx^{li} xiij^s iiij^d for twoo yeres rent due in the yeres that Richard ffysher &

Richard Townesend were last Baliefes, and for Lx^{li} due for arrerages therof He devise to hinder the towne of xl^s by yere reserued by expresse woordes uppon the leaces of the tithes of Myton, His connyng knack in sending for Edmond Wright being put in trust to receve the rent of the tuithes of Myton at the last day of the moneth after the feast of the Annunciacion of saint Mary last past, pswading the said wryght to say that he had recevid the said Rent, and yet tendered the same at the tuith barne at the last howre wherby most manyfestly doth appeare his fraudulent practise to withold the same untill sute should compell him to pay yt and wth the same money to defend such sutes as should be brought against him for such his wrong doyngs, And in the end to defraude not onely the said Borough of all their dueties but also all others with whome he hath had to doo for matters of monye by a connyng devise (as it is thought in making a dede of gifte of all his goods & chattells to his secret freends. his faithlesse promise made to Sr Thomas Lucye & Sr John hubond to stond to the Judgem^t and apynion of the Lord Dyer and Mr Justice Meade towching the validitie of his long leace of Myton tithes and yet in the meane season, or before that promise made, hee had conveid his tytle therof to John Jeffreys his neighbo^r whoo took out a liberate uppon an extent of the said leaces & tithes, By which liberatie Mr Jeffereys recovered & had of Willm Wo^{r}ceto^r being surety for John Rey xxviij^{li} for one of those yeres for which the rent is yet behinde.

This Richard Brook in the Baliwik of Richard ffisher hearing of a gelding come into this libertie, as a streve and taken upp by the officers in the bridge end. cawsed the said gelding to be kept in his pasture many weekes or moneths without making the Balief privie therof and delivered the same gelding awaye at his pleasure w^{t}out annswering any thing to the use of the borowe for the same gelding.

This Brookes hearing of the pursuyt of a Robbery doon by taking of monye from a woman in the feildes nere Charlecote, enquyred out the woman and offred
fulshurst to agree & satisfie her for her losse And so stopped her from any pursuyt and yt was thought that the offender was herbored in Brooks howse.

In the tyme of baliwik of Richard Townesend, this Brook having no auctorytie or comission, but of his owne head without knoweleig of the then Balief did stay or take into examynacion, a straunger supposed to be a cutpurse, and drawing him into M{r} Phillipps howse fell into such examynacion that he caused the suspectes cloke to bee conveid from him, which afterwards (as some saye) fell to Brooke his owne share without any acompt made therefore.

(folio 202) This Brooke solicited & procured John ffisher being Balief and the rest of the principall burgesses of this borough the last yere, not only to grannt but also to write to my lorde the Earle of Leicest{r} to make a lease of the personage of Budbrook to such pson as it should like his L to appoynt. And therin not only devised the forme & draft of that lre, but also put his hand therunto of speciall entencion & p{r}pose to overthrowe the title of Symon Warner & his wieff in the said tithes. And yet sithens that tyme (bycause my lord of Leyc{r} yeldid his good wille for that leace from him whom Brookes hath procured to sue for yt) The said Brookes sithens (as it is saide) bought the olde leace of Warner and stondith in defence therof, soliciting and prosecuting earnest sute in the Chauncery in the name of Warner & his wieff against the Balief and all the rest of the principall Burgesses in the same Title, to theire great charges & no small vexacion, Affirming publikely that the Leace made at the request of my lord of Leycester was corruptly doone & against consciens forgetting that himself was the first stirrer therin, hee hath procured greevous compleintes to bee exhibitid to the Lordes of the quenes ma{ts} most honorable privy counsaill against the Balief & Burgesses of this borough most slannderosly enforcing dyvers untruethes to the great slannder of the Balief & Burgesses and to the great detryment of their creadite corpacion & auctorytie and sekith asmuch as in him lieth the Ruyne therof, And therin spareth no labo{r} nor cost to send for divers unworthye Inhabitants of the said borough perswading alluring & procuring them w{th} swete woordes & dissembling dayntys to put their handes to his develisshe devises and to the uttermost of his skill and power aydeth them that followe those sutes. hee hathe ioyned w{t} them which have devised libelles

to bee writen & cast about in divers places of this borough (wth a mynde as it may seme) to stirre up light & lewde heades to mutynye & uproure against the officers of this borough. Generally there hath not bene any g^t sute trowble or unquietnes emongs neighbours & Inhabitants of this towne wherin hee hath not bene a practizer or partaker (if not the chief onely or whole causer).
hee obeith no orders of courtes or leetes nor will suffer other to doo. But pswadith his dearlings to resist the same. Examples of Thomas Howe, who by his setting on & pswasion most manifestly contempnith the comendable custome & most proffitable order of the leete in resruing pasture for their laboring oxen. which the said howe by synister & wicked counsaille of the said Brookes eatith up wth his kyen to the great hurte not only of the said howe but of all his neighbo^rs also.

And all thies & many more mischefes he puttith in ure to stirre up matter of discord & discencion therby to sett on ffyre the willes of the lewdly disposed to comitt some outrage wherby the libtyes of this borough might bee drawen in question of seasing.

And bicause he can not have his wickid will by thies devises hee hath sought an other meane promising to make leaces the next yere of divers things belonging to this borough therby to allure his confederates to make him Balief, which office hee so affectith that he hath not lett to saye that he will Rule the next yere as pleaseth him, which (if should bee suffred) woolde bee most tyranycally and uncharitably no doubt. if he might aspire unto that place wherin he might under colo^r of regiment rule by will. And therfore to prevent his premeditatid purpose. It is most iustly agreed that he shalbee none of this society or felowshippe.[a]

[a] Richard Brooks seems to have been a miller and large farmer, occupying the Temple farm, and probably the Castle mill; he also seems to have been one of the Churchwardens of St. Nicholas, in 1579 and 1580, as a Mr. Richard Brooks is mentioned in the accounts for those years, as one of the wardens presenting them. In the account for 1618, there is an item of the receipt of 4d , great bell money for Richard Brookes. If this was the same man as the Richard Brooks, who was expelled from the Corporation, he must have reached an advanced age before he ceased from troubling.

(folio 203) Election of Roger Hurlebutt as Bailiff on 29th September, 1585.

Election of Henry Chaplen as a principal Burgess on the 3rd of March, 1586.

Election of Thomas Saunders as an Assistant Burgess on the 15th of March, 1586.

Election of John Hickes as a principal Burgess on the 8th of October, 1586, and on the same day election of Alexander Rogers and William Roo as assistant Burgesses.

election of Willm hudson to be balif

(folio 204) xxix September anno xix R^e Eliz. John Grene Balief Richard ffisher Richard Townesend Richard Roo John ffisher William ffrekulton Thomas Powell Thomas Jenkes humfrey Crane John Rigeley and John Dyche principall Burgesses did name Willm hudson and Richard Townesend to stand in election to be balief for the year to come

And Robart Sheldon Roger hurlebut Oliver Brooke Phillipp Coo John Griffin John Bikar Roger Weale henry Chaplen cristofer Knight Thomas chapman & John hickes comoners did elect Willm hudson to be balif

Willm hudson absentith himself

And on alholouday the said M^r hudson being callid to bee sworne & take the office uppon him absentid himself. Wheruppon the bailief & principall Burgesses viz John Greene Balif Richard ffysher Ric Townesend Richard Roo John ffysher Willm ffrekulton Thoms Powell humfrey crane John Rigeley & John Diche did name Richard Townesend and John Dyche to stand in ellection to be bailif for the yere to come

Richard Townsend electid baliff and sworn.

And Robart Sheldon Phillipp coo Oliver Brook John Griffin Roger hurlebut John Bykar henry Chaplyn Roger Weale Tho Chapman John hickes and Leonard holmes in the psence of the whole multitude assemblid did elect & name Richard Townesend to be Balif &c who was sworne that day &c

On 29th September, 1578, Richard Roo was elected Bailiff, but refused office, and so on All Saints' Day following, Richard Fisher was chosen and sworn.

On the 29th September, 1579, Richard Roo was elected and took office.

John ffysher electiō Balif refuseth for a tyme afterwards is sworn

M^d that on the xxix^th day of Septembr being Michilmas day in the xxij^th yere of quene Elizabeth Richard Roo balief Richard ffisher Richard Townesend Richard Brookes John ffisher Willm ffrekulton Thomas Powell Robart Phillippes Thomas Jenks humfry Crane John Rigeley John Grene and John Dyche did name John ffisher and Thomas Powell to stand in ellection to be balif for the yere to come.

And Robart Sheldon Oliver Brook Roger hurlebutt henry Chaplen John Byker Roger Weale Tho Chapman John hickes Leonard holmes cristofer Knight and John Gryffin did elect name & choose John ffisher to bee Balif for the yere to come. But on alhollouday the said ffisher being before the Balif and principall Burgesses and many other of the towne refusid to tak the offyce uppon him. and desired them therfore to pcede to a newe elleccon, and sparing him at that tyme, he woold give the towne x^li which in a bagg he did cast downe on the table before them. But the said Bailief and principall Burgesses & the others stonding by woold not goo to any other eleccion. But ernestly entretid the said ffisher to take the offyce uppon him & pmised him many things And his brother & other frendes being ymportune & earnest w^t him he determynately answerid that he woold not that day take it uppon him bycause he had sworne the contrary. but offred at their Requests that if Mr Roo woold contynue the office but twoo or three dayes lenger, he woold bee content then to take yt and be swoorne. Wherunto Mr Roo wth a heavy mynd yeldid unto. And on the thursday following the said John ffisher came into the hall and there before the said Old Balif & most part of the principall Burgesses & many other Inhabitants he was sworne and took the office uppon him

(folio 205) Election of Thomas Powell as Bailiff
on the 29th of September, 1581.

xxix" September a° xxiiij^th Eliz

Humfrey Crane electid Baliff

Be yt remembrid that on Michilmas day in the xxiiij^th yere of Quene Elizabeth Thomas Powell Balief Richard ffisher Rychard Townesend John ffysher William ffrekulton Robart Phillippes humfrey Crane John Rigeley John Dyche Robart Sheldon & Roger hurlebutt principall Burgesses assemblid in the Shire hall in Warwik being that tyme their hall for election accompanyed w^t their inferio^r Assistants That is to say Oliver Brooke John Bykar henry Chaplen Leonard holmes cristofer Knight Thomas Chapman John hickes Barnabee holbage Robart West Richard ffisher the yong^r Willm Jenks and Thomas Grene And there being allso a nombr of other Inhabitants (then follow these words which have been scored through, "wherof many procured by Richard Brookes And the same brooks having bene before that tyme displaced out of the company of principall burgesses yet cam thither as an Inhabitant of the borough And began to psuade that bycause some question was growen of the chosing the Balifs before tyme That no choyce should be that day made But the Baliff and principall Burgesses aforenamed knowing his malice allowed not of that psuacion But went to thellection ") And the said Balif and principall Burgesses named humfrey Crane & Thomas Jenks to stand in ellection to be bailief And the others inferio^r assistants before all the rest did name ellect and choose humfrey crane to be Balif for the yere to come who at halloutide after took the office uppon him.

xxix" September A° xxv^th Eliz.

Richard ffisher electid balif the fiveth tyme

Humfrey Crane Balif Richard ffisher Richard Townesend John ffisher Willm ffrekulton Thomas Powell John Rigeley John Dyche Robart Sheldon and Roger hurlebutt principall Burgesses named Richard ffisher and John Rigeley to stand in ellection to be balif the yere to come

And the multytude being present electid and named Richard flisher to be balif for the yere to come. Who at holloutide after uppon much entreaty took the office uppon him But John Weale glasier did name Richard Brooks on michas day but his single voyce took litle effect.

Election of Robert Sheldon as Bailiff on 29th of September, 1584

Election of Roger Hurlebutt as Bailiff on the 29th of September, 1585

Election of Richard Fisher as Bailiff on the 29th September, 1586

Election of William Woster as a principal burgess on the 29th of December, 1586

Election of William Woster as Bailiff on the 29th of September, 1587

Election of master James Dyer Recorder
M^d that the said xxixth of Septembr Anno xxix^o R^e Elizabeth The said bailief and principall burgesses and John flisher w^t the consent of Richard Townsend Robart Phillippes and William Woster principall Burgesses did elect & choose James Dyer Esquire to be Recorder for the said borough in the Roome and place of Edward Aglionby esquire late Recorder of the said borough who bycause of his great age & ympotency to travell & faling of sight and some other causes him moving was content & desirous to leave the said Roome & office yelding very good will & consent to have the said Mr Dyer to bee placed in the same Roome who being also greatly & worthilie recomendid to the balif and pryncipall burgesses by Sr John Harington Knight did also in very frendly maner come and accept the said election & took the place & was solemplie sworne & setled into the said office the vth daie of october next folowing being the daie of the Leete holden for the said borough. And that day did both give the chardge both consortable & learnedly wth en adsum to the great reioysing of very many & not w^{t}out murmuracion of a fewe mutynous companions of Brooks whose olde malice continewng blasted out buddes that pued not brannches.

Uppon w{ch} placing & settling of the said M{r} Dyer Recorder Therle of Warwik was enformed who allowid very well of that choice & doings. and to shewe the same. and better acceptans of the gentleman, it pleasid him to write his frendlie lres The teno{r} wherof ensueth viz

    To my very loving frends the balief & principall Burgesses
    of the Towne of Warr.

After my hartie comendacions Being given tunderstand That upon the surrender of M{r} Eglionbie of his office & Roome of Recordershipp of the borough of Warwik you have electid & chosen one James Dyer Esquire to the same, who for his better creadit & countenannce in that place hath earnestly craved my favour & good liking thereto, as also that I should signifie the same unto you, fforasmuch as I am creadiblie informed, he is a man in all poyntes very meet for the Roome, and like to proove a good member amongs you, have thought good hereby to declare my good opinion of yo{r} proceadings in that behalf as also to request you the rather for my sake to encreas your affections towards him, wherin I shall think my self in his behalf beholding unto you, And thus comytt you to god, from my lodging this xiiij{th} of Novembr 1587
      Yo{r} loving freend
        A. Warwik

the death of M{r} James Dyer Recorder

the electing of M{r} Sergeaunt Puckering to bee Recorder

(folio 206) M{d} that on Sonday morning callid Loo sonday being the xxvj{th} day of Apriell and in the xxxij yere of Quene Elizabeth It pleasid god to call to his mercy out of this lief M{r} James Dyer Recorder of this borough After whose decesse & buriall that is to say on thursday following being the last day of Apriell in the said Twoo and Thirtieth yere of Q. El. John Townesend Bailieff Richerd ffisher John ffisher Thomas Powell John Ridgeley John Grene Robart Sheldon Roger hurlebutt Willm Woster John hicks cristofer Knight William harmer & Rafe Townesend pryncipall Burgesses of the borough of Warwik did assemble them selves & mett togither in the court house here the crosse being then their hall & counsaill house and after dyvers opynions shewed & men named the Balief & greater part of the said principall Burgesses did elect name & apoynt the right worshipfull M{r} John Puckering being then the quenes Sergeant att lawe to bee the Recorder of the said Borough to w{ch} choyce the fewe other of the principall burgesses w{ch} before had named other did agree And thereuppon the said M{r} Balief & x others of them went to the said M{r} Sergeaunt signifieng their election and earnestly entreating him to tak the said office uppon him who accepting theire good willes thankid them hieghly for that it pleasid them to think so well of his neighborhood assuring them withall that if the Recordershipp of london w{th} the fee thereof being foureskore poundes yerely besides other good gifts had bene offred him, hee woold have refusid it But seing that his good neighbers had liking & made choice of him to that place so freendly, hee was content to accept their offer (though it bee but foure nobles by yere) most thankfully promising to stand them & the whole towne in what steede he coolde And so the night growing on his othe was deferid till the next day which was fryday the last of Apriell And on that fryday he was sworne and red the othe in his owne pson acording to the former order of the othe writen in the book for that ppose apointid And there were present at the said othe John Townesend balief John ffysher Willm Woster Roger hurlebutt John Rigeley & Willm harmer & others.(a)

post 266. a. He made M{r} Gregory Town-clerk

The said Sergeant Puckering was afterwards Lord Keeper of the great Seale of England And dyed y{e} last of Aprill 38. Eliz 1596

(a) The office of Recorder appears to have been much sought after as is shewn by the following extract from one of the old books before mentioned:—"And shortly after the said Robte Lord Brooke his being Recorder the Warres and trobells betwixt the Kinge and Parliament began and the said Lord Brooke goeinge to raise the seige at Litchfeild was there slaine and then the said M{r} Bryan became an agent suddenly and secretly to the Corporacion to make choice of Willm Earle of Bedford to be their Recorder." The Earl of Bedford was appointed, and subsequently the office was held successively by most of the Lords Brooke and Earls of Warwick until the passing of the Municipal Corporations Act of 1835.

(folios 217 to 237) (These pages contain copies of Leases and Indentures, and also of Interrogatories and depositions in Olney's case, beautifully engrossed. A great many pages are blank.)

An election difficulty.

(folio 238) Be yt Remembrid That on fryday the Seventh day of October in the xxviij^th yere of Quene Elizabeth Roger hurlebutt Balif Richard ffysher Richard Townesend John ffisher Thomas powell John Rigeley Thomas Jenkes Robart Sheldon & Willm Worcestor principall burgesses of the borough of Warwik assemblid in the court house at the crosse in Warwik being then their comen halle And then & there did elect name & chose John hickes to be a principall Burgesse of the said borough in place & Rome of henry Chaplin Lately decessid which said John hickes being sent for & psent was sworne & placed a principall Burges of the said Borough

After wch done the second company of the assistants being sent for yt was given them tunderstand that their company being weakened by taking away twoo of them namely John hicks & Leonerd holmes It was thought mete by Mr Balif & the principall burgesses (folio 239) to choose and ioyne twoo other unto them to make up their nombr of xij and therfore Mr Balif & his company had made choice of twoo as they thought bothe honest & mete men for those places namely Alexander Rogers and Richard Smyth powterer. To wch Thomas Grene aunswered & said they so chosen were honest men but yet in his & some other mens opynyons there were other might rather be placed and named divers but chiefly he Barnabee holbech & others of that company desired instantly to have William Roo to be plaiced for one of those twoo And so at their speciall Instance Mr Balif & principall Burgesses chose William Roo & Alexander Rogers who both being sent for did come & after excusing themselfs of sufficency desired to be spared But their desires were not grauntid And so in thend they bothe were sworne in the second companye of assistants to the Balif & principall Burgesses

After thies things orderid Mr Balif openyd to them all present That where there was a parliamt somoned & newe elections to be made of Burgesses for this borough. He had herd say That dyvers of that company & many others of the towne had grauntid their voyces to Mr Job Throkmorton to be one of the burgesses for this towne wch if they had done was not well, nor according to Lawe or good order ffor as yet he hath recevid no writt precept or comaundemt to make any choyce and therfore to mak chose before warraunt was not well Besides that the statutes made & apointing the maner howe & by whom and what psones should be chose doth manifestly shewe that they ought to be Townesmen & Burgesses & free that should be chosen wch Mr Throkmorton is not & therfore can not be chosen besides that or good Lord therle of Warwik hath writen his lres in recomendacion of Mr Thomas dudley a gentleman & kinsman of his who before this tyme hath srued the place of one of or Burgesses and the quenes pleasure is also signified aswell by the said Earle of Warwik as other of her hieghnes privy counsull That her maiestye pleasure is that such Burgesses as have servid before in other parliaments being well affectid to the state should be contynewed & have their places again if they be not otherwise ymployd So as yt is very mete & necessary that my L of Warwiks request be grauntid for Mr Thomas dudley for one And then for the other doubtith not but they bee of mynd That it is most expedyent That he be a Townesman & dwelling within the Borough and such a one as may be trusty & faithfull and also hable to annswer for the towne as cause shall requyre and therfore trustith That they will have due regard herof & not to be hasty wt their voyces untill they may somewhat understand the mynd of their Balif and principall Burgesses in that matter To that Thomas Grene said That in dede he for his part had given pmise of his voyce for Mr Throkmorton not knowing but he might so doo for none other had requested him and he knoweth not of any statute or lawe agaynst yt and he thinkith that Mr Throkmorton is an honest & worshipfull gentleman neighbour to the towne & thinkith that he Lovith the towne well and woold be or freend in any thing he may doo

Theruppon it was thought good that the statutes should be red unto them, and so the Statute made A⁰ primo of H the fiveth & that of xxiij^{tie} of Henry the sixt were redd wch prove that he that should be chose burges of the parliament ought to be a burgesse free & resiant w^{t}in the borough And also that the chosers must be burgesses & free & none other. To that Tho. Grene aunswerid that if he had knowen so much before he wold have bene advised of his graunt Than barnaby holbech said that in deed Mr Throkmorton had desired his voyce and he had grauntid bicause he knewe nothing of to the contrary So the rest psent said that they were glad they had heard the statute for they wilbe better advised and many of them said That they had bene spoken unto for their voyces to Mr Throkmorton but had resrvid them untill they knewe Mr Balif and the rest of the companyes mynd

Theruppon was red unto them the Earle of Warwik's lre written on the behalf of M^{r} dudley as folowith

the tenor of my l of Warwik his lre for Mr Dudley to be burges of the parliament 1586.

After my hartie comendacions wheras it hath pleasid her mat^{y} to calle a newe parliament for very weyghty affayres and to dissolue the olde bycause the newe is to begynne soner then the tyme of prorogacion of the olde Wherby wryttes be dyrectid for the election of Knightes & Burgesses acordingly. But her ma^{ties} pleasure being that such as have alredy served in those places of whose good zeale towardes her hieghnes and the state there hath bene good proofe should be contynewed in their places as many of them as may attend the same. I have thought good to recomend unto you my very good freend and kynesman Mr Thomas dudley to be placed agayne for one of yor Burgesses his sufficiencye is so well knowen unto you as I neede not to wryte therof for that besides his well discharging of the place I have in my former lres in his behalf to this effect very fully advertised you of his good partes very earnestly prayng and requyring you to mak yor eleccion of him into one of yor Burgesses Romes who I am well assured is hable many wayes as occasion shalbe offred to stand yor towne in good steede wherfore as heretofore uppon my Recomendacion you have affordid him the place, so making no doubte of yor lyk good wille towardes mee I doo expect at this present the lyke effect of my request which I shall most thankfully accept And so bid you farewell from the court the xviijth of Septembr 1586

       Yo^r very loving frend
        A. Warwik

To my very loving
freends the Balif of Warwik
his brethern and the
Burgesses there

(folio 240) The former lre was brought to Warwik by M^r henry Bestoich on wensday the xxviij^t of Septembr being mich^s even and was delivered to Mr Roger hurlebutt Balif in the psens of the most of the principall Burgesses But before the comyng of that lre the said Balief and principall Burgesses had written to my said Lorde the Earle of Warwik and sent the same by Evan Morys.

  The tenor wherof ensueth

the copie of a lre written to my L therle of Warwik offring to choose Mr John Goodman or others whom the said Erle should recomend to bee one of the Burgesses for the parliament

Right honorable o^r very good L wheras somons is given for a newe parliament to begynne very shortely Wee having receuid no Request from yor good L towching the placing of any for this borough, have hitherunto forborne to make any election. Neverthelesse yf it maie stand wth yor L good liking wee could be very well contentid to offer the place of one of o^r Burgesses to Mr John Goodman yor L servaunt or any other meet man whom yor L will recomend unto us Wherof wee humbly beseche yor good L to signifie yor honorable pleasure wth such celerytie as may bee and so humbly take o^r Leave Warwik this xxvjth of Septembr 1586

       Yo^r good L to command

To the right honorable o^r singler
good lord Therle of Warwik one
of the quenes ma^{ts} most honorable
privie counsell his good L

The said Evans being dyrectid to the court then at Wyndsore went thither but founde not my said Lord there and therefore followed after and found my said L at melchborough in his iourney towards ffodringay & there delivered the lre To wch it pleasid the said Earle to annswer as followith

To my very loving freends the Balief and Burgesses of Warwik

the Earle of Warwik's answere to the former lre

After my hartie comendacions wheras I understand by you lres that you have differred the choyce of Burgesses for yor towne for this next parliament till such tyme as you might further knowe from me whither I was resolued to comend any unto you for those places I doo think my best beholding unto you for the care you have of pferring such psons to doo her ma^ties s^ruyce herin that may bee of such sufficiency as may best stand wth my liking. And therefore I have thought good to recomend unto youe my coosen Mr Thomas dudley whom I wold not in any sorte to be disapoyntid of the one place and the other I doo very willingly & freely leave to yor owne libertye to choose whom you shall best like of. Wheryn I doo nothing doubt but you will have that good care & consideracion of the sufficiency & honestie of the man as shalbe nedefull in this case and as I shall have cause also to thank you for yt And so I bid you all hartely farewell. ffrom melchborough this vj^t of October 1586

Yo^r very loving frend
A. Warwik

Whiles thies thinges were in doing and no precept yet delivered to the Balif from the Sheriff for any election Mr Job Throkmorton made very great labo^r to many of the Inhabitants of this borough for their voyces to choose him for one of the burgesses of pliam^t wherin being much assistid by the Busie Richard Brooke and his complices namely Thomas Brooks, Roger Saunders, Nicolas Smith Willm Lane Rafe martyn & others of the meaner sort They prevalid so much w^t the husbondmen in the brige end & west strete & others that had little to doo in that matter as M{r} Throkmorton was put in good hope to have the voyce of the multitude to chose him where in dede the Balif and principall Burgesses verely purposed uppon due consideracion to have one of the principall burgesses to serve that Rome But M{r} Throkmorton encoraged in his enterprise came to Warwik to gratulate his welwillers and at the swanne made a solempne dynner whither were brought unto him by Brooks & the other facto{rs} pcurement Lx or nere Lxxx of the meanest Inhabitants of this borough. Who for the good cheare sak the rather yeldid to be redy to yeld to his request Besides them the said M{r} Throkmorton had pcured S{r} ffulk Grevill and other gentlemen of great creadit to labo{r} divers of the principall Burgesses for their good willes for the said M{r} Throkmorton who (as they said) did not graunt otherwise Then that if therle of Warwik wold write for him to be the one in place of M{r} dudley But M{r} Throkmorton took their pmisses and affirmed it to be absolute Wherby was like to grow much inconvenyence by reason of the dissencion emongs the townesmen namely betwene the Balif & Burgesses on the one side & other Comoners on the other side Bicause the Balif & Burgesses purposed to have electid either John ffisher who semed to be unwilling therunto or M{r} John Rigeley To which meaning the most part of the honester sort of comoners agreid And the election could not be made bicause M{r} Sheriff so handled the matter by M{r} Brooks meanes That the pcept for election was not delivered untill (   ) dayes after the day of pliament assigned only to thend that M{r} Throkmorton might mak his part so much the greter And before the election and before that any precept could be delivred S{r} John harrington S{r} ffulk Grevill & others had obteyned pmise of M{r} Roger hurlebutt then balif of Warwik that proclamacion should be made twoo dayes at least before the election when the election should be wherby also grewe some inconvenience ffor where the Balif and principall Burgesses w{t} the greatest part of other the Burgesses & honest townesmen did fully resolve to choose one of the principall Burgesses And a meating of the Balif and principall Burgesses apointid for that purpose to prepare their resolucion on some one of them by name And the said Balif and principall Burgesses resting uppon the election of John Rigeley theldr to be named at the tyme of election And the said M{r} Rigeley yelding and preparing himself for that purpose sodenly in an evening M`r` Robart Sheldon being one of the said company of principal Burgesses who before had refused to yeld to be electid movid with what I know not sent for Roger Saunders one of M`r` Throkmorton's practizers, and said unto him that if M`r` Throkmorton wold not stand for it himself he desired the said M`r` Throkmorton to give his voyces (folio 241) to him for he woold stand for it if M`r` Throkmorton woold not, this being brought to M`r` Throkmorton eare having before somewhat qualid in hope was hereby newely encouraged to thrust in when he saw that the balif and his company were devidid Theruppon more & more earnest sute was made for voyces to M`r` Throkmorton & many unfrendly & speches passid betwene divers of the townesmen and further querells were likely to have followed w`th` being pcevid by the balif & principall burgesses the most part of them saving M`r` Sheldon who absented himself thought to send to M`r` Throkmorton and to psuade him to forbeare labo`r` unduely and to have regard to the pill (peril) that otherwise might ensue Therfore they wrote to M`r` Throkmorton requireing him to come to speak w`t` them Who annswered them fir`t` by lre afterwards came. The tenor of his lre is as folow`th` viz

I can by no meanes come to you so early as you request me by the reason of my mothers & brothers riding there way at ix of the clok But if my comyng to you about x or xj of the clok may any thing satisfie youe & yo`r` bretherne I will willingly come twice as farre to you as Warwik to doo any of you good. ffor the Burgesshipp I may safely say it is a thing that I have not affectid my self But being drawen therunto by the best in the Shire & by your leave by some of yo`r` owne companye w`th` such a nomber of the Inhabitants arguyng their better liking of me than I can any waye deserve I rather think some Iniurye offred mee to be thus crossed without cause, than that I do you any iniury by yelding to that wherw`th` I was pressed by my betters. Whether I have it or have it not all is one to my self. But to be defeatid of it by uniust slaunders as that I am an Enemye of yo`r` corpacion &c is I think in the hardest degree of measure that you can requite yo' poore neighbo' & freende wth. Yf it please you to trye me Then you shall see whither I bee an honest man or no. Yf not, yet condempne me not before ye have tried me And so I leave the whole to yo' best discrecion

Haseley in all scribelid hast this thursday at night 1586
Yo' loving freend
J. Thokmton

When he was come bringing wth him his brother Mr Lane M^r harvye finding ready assemblid Roger hurlebut Balif Ric. ffisher Ric. Townesend John ffisher Thomas powell Thomas Jenks John Rigeley Willm Worcesto' & John hicks yt was told Mr Throk^t that as Mr Balif was given tunderstand, he had greatly sought by undue meanes to be placed the one of their Burgesses for the parliament wherby was like to happen very perillous division & disencion emongs the townes men praid him therfore to have due consideracion of his doings and to   that he should not be occasion of greater mischief then might afterwards be well remedyed and Mr Balif and his brethern marvealid not a litle That he being a gentleman of worship and wise woold offer to intrud himself into such a perill he placed in of the whole corpacion and therfore desired him to forbeare any further travell in a matter nothing concernyng hym ffor (it was also said to him) that this eleccion of Burgesses for this borough did nothing towch him being a gentleman & no burges of the towne nor having any Interest in any matters or causes of the towne nor any colo' of freehold in the towne. Therefore he in no case chargeable or to be trowblid w^t the cares of the towne. being also dwelling out of the towne and as he was not to be chargid wth the cares & doings and especially in this point of elections for burgesses of the parliament So was he not in any wise to take uppon him that place if he were electid ffor neither may Mr Balif and Burgesses of this borough elect him dwelling out of the borough & being not of the corpacion Bycause the election must be made acording to the Lawe which by expresse woordes saith That it must be dooue by freemen &

1. H. 5 cap 1. that ye Citizens & Burgesses of y{e} Cities & Boroughs be chosen men Citizens & Burgesses resiant dwelling & free in the same Cities & Boroughs & not other in any wise

burgesses inhabiting the same borough also hee that is to be chosen a burges for the parliament must be a free burges & dwelling w'in the borough at the tyme of election Orells the election is not good and the chief officers of the borough subiect to greevous fyne Therfore and forasmuch also as this borough is not w'hout enemyes (as he well knoweth) and besides that many occasions are redye to be offred wherin the Burgesses helpes is necessary the said Mr Balief & his brethern have thought it a matter of great necessitie to mak choice of one of them selves for this tyme And therfore doo frendly praye him to forbeare any further travel in this case Wherby they should be quietid of such a broile as likely is to happen much to their grief by reason of some froward & unreasonable behavio^r of the worst sort of the Inhabitants, who in deed have no Interest in this matter wherof (they trustid) it woold please him to have due consideracion. To this Mr Throkm^{r}ton answered in maner as he had written that he of himself had not sought the place but it was offred unto him by some of this towne and even by some of those that were psent & others of the same company who had grauntid their good willes unto him and therwth chargid Mr Townesend Mr Rigeley & others Mr Grene being absent who had to divers his good freends some knights & the Rest Justices of the peace & Esquires labored on his behalf onely M^r balif Mr R. ffisher Mr J. ffisher Mr Worceto^r had not grauntid but all the Rest both to S^r ffulk Grevill Mr Verney & others of like wo^{r}ship who had ernestly excitid him to doo that he did wherunto it semed also that many of the honest Inhabitants had agreid by that at his late being here there were w^t him not so fewe as iiij^{xx} or hundred to whome he thinkith himself so beholden for their good willes That he myndeth to put it to the Jurye by election trusting that Mr Balief will doo as before he had pmissed to make publik proclamacion of the place & tyme twoo dayes before the election and in so doing he should think himself well delt wth and then if it were not given him he woold not have any great care but he woold not have this matter huddled upp in a corner as the most of yor matters bee amongs yor selfs and not in publik. Besides he answered that although he were not dwelling in the boorough nor a burgesse emong you yet he had as great privelege as other the quenes subiects that have had the same Romes as namely his father M^r clement Throkmorton who had bene burges for the towne and M^r dudley whom they had often and nowe agayn (as it is said) had the same place And then he being a gentleman & their neighbo^r might be aswell allowed of if it pleasid (folio 242) Mr Balif and his company and he trustid that he had given no cause to the contrary To that it was annswerid That as towching the ellection of Mr Thomas dudley they had therin observed the order of the Lawe for he had bene sworne a burges of the towne before he was electid for the pliam^t and as for M^r clement Throkmton when he was chosen he was not onely a good freeholder in the towne & dwellid there and kept house there many yeres and so also made a burges of the towne, and therfore might & did Lawfully serve the place But the case stondith not so w^t yor Mr Throkmorton nowe for to o^r knowelege you have no maner of habitacion within this borough nether doo you desire to be a burgesse of the Towne, but for the Parliament where peradventure some freends of yo^{rs} may have some causes in handeling And evenso peradventure this borough may have some cause there pferrid by them that be adversaryes and then howe much it behoveth the towne to have such as they may trust and wilbe both faithfull & painfull for them youe may consider. Like as Mr Balief & his companye doothe and therfore pray you to desist and not to offer any further wthdrawing of those townesmen which if you have their voyces can stand you in no steede though the nomber may be greater than wee think for wch if should happen so as part taking should breead any unlawfull act You might haply breed us that wee woold not nor yo^rself and padventure afterward repent youe. I meane not any disorder (said Mr Throkm^{ton}) but surely sins I find myself so farre beholden to many my good neighbours of this towne that have pmised me I will put it to the question. And if I faile them of yt, Yet Mr Rigeley I meane to meet you at the Parliam^t dore to trye the title betwene you & me. Well (said M^r hardye) Brother Throkmorton I pceve that Mr Balief & his company are in doubt least they may have some thing for the towne to be done in the parliament and therfore they woold look to have suche as they send thither sworne & assured to them and they have reason so to doo (as farre as I pceve) and therfore I could wisshe that you woold shortely assure yor self unto them as farre as reason may require. So I will said Mr Throkmorton, and if there be no other matter I will doo any thing shalbe thought resonable or meete and may stand w^t duety of cristian Religion Yee & if it be by othe, though I trust to behave my self so as they shall not have iust cause to mistrust me. To that it was annswered To have you swere or tak an othe is not all, for if it should stand uppon that point, an othe w^thout trustie trueth were but a meane of further mischief But Lett us understand truely & faithfully yor mynde how you stand affectid towards the good of this borough & the comon weale therof and setting apart the matter of election for the parliament can you be well content to become a burgesse of this borrowe and be sworne to the good therof and to beare a faithfull & freendly affection to the mayntenance of the state therof, and to be ready to advannce the same to the best of yor power. Yea surely (said Mr Throkmton) so farre as shall become a good & true subiect w^t duety to god & my prynce. Wth thies speeches the most of the hearers were much pleasid and some said you are a good gentleman, and we trust you will doo for this towne as yor father did for he lovid yt and so we trust you will &c. Then was it annswered agayn You say you wilbe content to binde yor self w^t an othe to the good of this towne and to the mayntenance of the comon weale & proffit therof (And w^t that John ffisher drewe out a paper) & said Bicause you have so frankly offred I doo consent that you may be made a Burges of the towne & be sworne as a burges. And bicause youe may the better consider therof before ye be sworne here is the teno^r of an othe Wherof I pray you consider and then resolue w^t yourself & us whither ye will swere or no, Let mee see it saith Mr Throkm^rton and tooke it in his hand & red it And pusing it twice or thries over said I will sweare all that is heare saving my duety to god & my prince, Be well advised of it, said Jo. ffisher and if you fynd anything therin worthy reformacion shewe yor mynde and either it shalbe emendid orells ye shall be resonably annswered of yor doubt to yor liking wee trust. wth that Mr Throkmorton annswered agayne I like the othe well adding some fewe woords of saving as before Wheruppon was delivered unto him pen & Ink & he was desired to add what he woold wheruppon taking the pen Ink & paper w^t his owne hand he wrote on the last end one lyne conteyning thies woordes viz. that are not derogatorye to the service of god and her ma^{tie} so help me god. And theruppon said agayne give me a book, & I will sweare willingly wch his willingnes was greatly pleasing to the most of the company. And theruppon a service book was brought & laid uppon the boords before them all. And Mr Throkm^{r}ton laing his hand on the book did openly reade the othe wch conteyned thies woordes following viz. I Jobe Throkmorton shall faithfull & true bee to the quenes ma^{tie} Elizabeth quene of England and to her heires & lawfull Successors Kings & Quenes of Englond, And to this borough of Warwik And the ffranchises previleges libties and good orders of the same borough will keep maynteyn susteyne and defend to the uttermost of my power & skille And I wilbe assisting ayding comforting and helping to the Bailief & principall Burgesses of this borough wth the best of my power witte & skille for the good governm^t and benefitting of the same borough liberties & franchises and the people of the same, And I will not have any consent or agreament wth any person to the hurt of the same borough or to the dymynishing of the ffranchises & priveleges of the same but the same shall ayde and defend as one of the Burgesses of this borough to the uttermost of my power in all thinges that are not derogatory to the servyce of god & her ma^{tie} So help me god, and kissed the book. The company thankid him, and prayd god to give him grace to kepe it Then said Mr Throkmorton, Mr Balief & Mr All nowe that I am sworne and that you have made me a burges of yor borough, I hartely thank you and doo promise by gods grace faithfully to doo that I have pmised by (folio 243) my othe And so woold have you think of me orells not to be countid a cristien. And nowe I saye & offer unto you that if it will please youe that I may w^t yor good willes bee one of the Burgesses for this parliament I will wth all my hart thank you and on the other side if you like not to chose me but rest uppon some one of yor company to serve the place I will be well content also ffor I woold youe shoulde think that I seek not the place for myne owne gayne, neither woold I serve there w^{t}out yor

Mr Job Throckmorton takes the oath of a Burges of Warwicke

good willes and therfore advise yoʳ selves And if you think me an honest man & woorthy the trust and may have the place wᵗ yoʳ good favoʳˢ I will doo the best that is in me for both yoʳ & my discharge though haply not so well as you hope in other.

This spech after the other movid the company much to yeld their consents to Mʳ Throkmʳton, wᶜʰ being peevid, John ffisher said Mʳ Throkmʳton albeit that you have by yoʳ othe (wᶜʰ wee tak the most assured band) tied yourself to the good of the towne yet you knowe it is not that theruppon you shalbe oʳ burges for the parliament wᶜʰ nevertheles wee could the soner have yeldid unto if soner wee had knowen yoʳ good will & affection towardes the towne, as howe wee doo belive it But I must let you knowe, that yoʳ so seking the place wᵗʰout or as I may saye against oʳ good willes, I meane Mʳ Balief & principall Burgesses & other burgesses who have iustly have most Interest in thies accions, did not a litle trowble us, and made us to doubt of yoʳ frendshipp, and so much the more that wee peevid yoʳ famyliarity wᵗ Richard Brooke, and his diligent laboring of those that be redy to ronne headlong into any loosenesse Besides that I myself think my self not a litle iniured in that I should be thrust out of that place wherin to my no litle charge I have spent bothe tyme & yeres not so fewe as xvj or xviij and I trust behavid myself so as howe soever myne owne causes. Yet them of the towne have bene carefully lookid unto And more then that me thinkith that my Interest should be pferid to that place by the quene oʳ soueigne Ladyes consent.

(This is a somewhat abrupt termination of minutes of these proceedings)

(folio 243 to 252) (some records of Leases; most of the pages blank.)

(folio 252) Mᵈ That on wensdaie the xxvᵗʰ of Septembr in the Thirtieth yere of oʳ Souereigne Lady Quene Elizabeth. Mʳ henry Bestoich Servaunt to the Ladye counties of Essex & Leycester widowe brought from the right honorable Lorde Ambrose Earle of Warwik a lre directid to the Balieff & Burgesses of Warwik requesting that Tho. dudley Esquire might bee electid one of theire burgesses for the Parliament for the said towne. The tenoʳ of which lre ensueth. viz.

To my very loving freends the Balief & Burgesses of Warwik

After my hartie comendacions Wheras you are nowe to make choice of the Burgesses of the parliament for yor towne I have thought good to recomende unto you my kinsman Thomas Dudley to bee used in that place for you. hee is a man who hath heretofore servid in the same place, and of that sufficiencye every waye as I knowe not wch way you might better be spedde, and therfore I woolde entreat you to make present choice of him and Lett me understand of the same by yor lres I woolde be lothe he should be preventid by any other mans sute unto you. And therfore I desire yor expedicion herein wch I will take in very good part, and thank you all in his behalf So I bid you hartely farewell. ffrom London this xxj^th of September 1588.

Yo^r assured loving freend
A. Warwik

This lre was deliuered by the said Mr Bestoich to John ffisher in thabsence of Mr William Worster Balief And the said Mr Bestoich further said That my L of Warwiks spciall desire was to have annswere ymediately to wch speche the said ffisher annswered that the lre being directid to Mr Balief and the burgesses It became not him to open the said lre untill the balief might be present, who woold be at home this night As the said ffisher did think And if it might please Mr Bestoich to tarry for answer he woold send for Mr Balief to make his spedye returne. To that Mr Bestoich replied that he had very earnest busines to be this day dispached at kenel. wch must be doone w^t all spede and having ocasion to send a messinger the same night to my L of Warwik he did instantly desire to have annswere sent to his howse the lodge in kenelworth park this night by ix or x of the clock and he woold pay the messinger but he could not tarye Wher-

The Earle of Leic. newly dead   uppon the said ffisher using some other speaches tunderstond whither the funerall of therle of Leycest^r(a) should be here at

---

(a) The Earl of Leycester died on the 4th of September, at Cornbury Park, Oxfordshire, of a fever which he took while journeying to Kenilworth: his body was brought to Warwick, and buried in the Beauchamp Chapel.

Warwik & whan the same should bee, he pmised to move M{r} Balief & the principall Burgesses for their annswere and to returne the same to him that night w{ch} was doone acordingly. And the annswer by lre as followth viz

>To the right honorable o{r} very good L Therle of Warwik his good Lordship

Oure dutie in most humble maner pmised to yo{r} good L The same maie please to be advertised That uppon receipt of your honorable lres this daie towching thellection of M{r} Thomas dudley to bee one of the burgesses for the parliam{t} for this Towne. Wee are readye & most willing to satisfie yo{r} L request so farre as in us Lieth Neverthelesse untill some warraunt come under her ma{ties} great seale thellection can not be perfitid Yelding unto yo{r} hono{r} all dutifull gratuitie as becometh us in this & all things ells. At Warwik this xxv{th} Septembr 1588

>Yo{r} most honorable L to comaund
>W{m} Worster balief Richard flisher Richerd Townesend John flisher Tho. Powell Jo Rigeley Jo. Grene. Ro. Sheldon. Roger hurlebutt Jo hicks cristofer knight. Jo. Townesend.

(folio 253 to 267) (Most of the pages blank; the remainder contain some records of leases, among which are in the year 1593, a lease to Thomas Beufoe Esquire and Ursula his wife of the Churchyard of St. Mary's and the Shire Hall Garden, at the yearly rent of 30/-, and a lease to Mr. Thomas Powell of a "shoppe or roome under the southeast end of the schole in the markett place" for the yearly rent of 6s. 8d.)

(On folio 263 there is the following)

"Uppon Wensdaie beeinge the xij{th} daie of December 1593 the Balliue and Burgesses did after the deathe of Humphrey Weeringe clarke vicar of the pishe churche in S{t} Nicholas in Warwick p{r}sente to the saide churche one Hercules Marrell"

(On folio 266 in a report of a meeting held on the 4th of December 1594 there is the following)

Mr Tho. Hall schoolem^r makes 2 requests

On that instant daie in the same place Mr Thomas Hall⁽ᵃ⁾ Scholem^r did move to Mr Bailiue and the rest of the Burgesses twoo requests being both reasonable and therefore doubtid not of the grant The one was that hee might bee disburdened and eased of the charge and troble of readinge comon praier in the churche. The reasons inducing him hereunto was not his owne labor wch or greater hee would most willinglie susteine for them and the whole congregation but that hee was in dutie bond to attend another office the fruichon whereof was by this meanes in some measure hindered yet not soe much neglected as the mallice of some harts did conceive, or the spight of some loose toungs reporte the wch that hee might the better sstane hee wholie would imploy himself whereunto hee was called. The other petition hee made not for his owne gaine although some perhapps would censure him covetous of the wch vice hee frelie clearde himself but for the avoydance of some misconvenience wch might ensue,

The multiplicity of Schoolemaisters complaynd of

(a) The name of this minister is not included in the list of Vicars given in Dugdale. In the list Andrew Bordman is mentioned as having been appointed in 1590, and next to him Richard Venour in 1639. The place on the list for Thomas Hall is therefore between these two. This Vicar seems to be have given some trouble to the Corporation, for in the minute book referred to on p. 224, I find the following minute made at a meeting on November 6th, 1618. "That Mr Bayliffe and twoo of his company talke wth Mr Hall about his invective sermons and reprochfull & scandolous speeches against the Baylife & Burgesses & if uppon their motion he will not reconcyle himselfe and be peaceable then articles to be exhibited against him to the highe Comissioners." Again on the 10th of August, 1631, there is a record of the Corporation having added to Mr Hall's stipend, and of his dissatisfaction coupled with a threat of legal proceedings: the minute states that "he spareth not disgracefully to reproach us retorninge evill for good," they therefore decided, until he withdrew his threat to give him no more than they were bound by the Charter to give. The matter was amicably settled, for on the 7th of October, 1631, there is a minute that the Bailiff and Burgesses "takeing into their consideracon the request made by Mr Thomas Hall Viccar of St Maries for some increase of his mayntennce, and weighinge well his great chardge and paynes taken in the execution of his ministeriall ffunction in the visitacon and comfortinge of sicke psons his hospitallity and Charitye in reliuing the poore and that the said Mr Hall is now aged and hath more cause of expence then heretofore haue therefore thought fitt and soe agreed to paye unto him in increase of his stipend the benefitt and pfitt of the Easter booke yearly or x^{li} in money in lewe thereof, which the said Mr Hall doth thankfully accept &c.

that the nomber of teachers and scholem^rs might bee w'thin this borough abated The toleration of whom impugned comon law of the realme, imposed penaltie uppon the corporacion insured diversitie of opinion, and p'rjudiced the good education of yonge schollers. To the first his continuance in the place untill suche time as they were convenientlie furnished wth some other sufficient was desired whereunto hee consented for the later necessarie reformacion wth equall and indyfferent favor was pmised.

30th Sept. 1595. Copy of bond entered into by Edmund Gregory on his being appointed Town Clerk by Sir John Puckering Knight, Lord Keeper of the great seal of England and Recorder of Warwick.

(folio 267) It is also by generall consent of Mr Bailiue and the greater part of the principall Burgesses this instant daie agreid that Widow Dungon should be dispossessid of the seate wherein shee sittith in the pishe church of St Maries in Warwick, and that the wife of Willm Spicer and Thomas Ichinor togither wth the twoo daughters of Isabell ffisher widow deceased shall there be placed

(The following is an order for certain poor not belonging to the town to remove out of it)

ffebruary 20th
1604

(folio 268) Wheras manie inconveniences have accrued to the estate of this boroughe by receavinge straungers of the poorer sorte heere to inhabite and tolleratinge an excessive multitude of Innemates bothe doth threaten ioynchlie a sodeane desolation unlesse providence by execution of good orders in that behalfe pvent the iminent danger It is this daie orderid that these psons undernamed shall avoyde suche tenemts as they have harboored by suche time as is unto them assigned

BB

Markett pl. ward.
    tollerated. Edmonde Linstrey
    tollerated James Norton respighted onelie untill the feaste of St John Baptiste at the farthist.
    Simon holliocke
    Jhon Knight
        Grafton appoynted to giue securitie for dischardge of ye boroughe before the next Leete

West street wa: Richarde ffisher inioyned to remove his undertenaunts at the feaste of the annunciation of the blessed virgin marie next.

Richard marshall appoyncted to avoyde his Innemate at the same time Thomas Venables, undertaken by George clerke yt hee shalbee removed at that time.
Jhon ffreeman
Thomas Rogers
Henrie Bishopp required to giue securitie for dischardge at the next Leete
Jhon Griffin
Stephen Arlethrope

Saltesford ward Jhon Thompson
    tollerated Richard hardinge
    Richard Tandie appoyncted to remove Beniamin Dale before the feast of the annunciation of o^r ladie next
    Richard upcote
    tollerated Jhon cater
    Jhon Large
    tollerated Jhon Adkins

George clerke undertaketh after the deathe or depture of the psent tenaunts not to admitt anie other in his newe erected cotags.

castle street wa: Samuell Jarvys
Mr Ridgeley

Smith street wa: Baldwin Loyndon
Richard Poors inioyned to avoyde his tennts before the feast of St Jhon Baptist
Widowe Shottiswell limited the same time for the like
Peter Proffitt respighted untill the feast of S^t michaell.
michaell harriott pmisethe after the death or depture of the p'sent tenaunts not to place anie other in his newe erected cotags.
Widowe Nicholas
Jhon Lee
Jhon wiggs

(folio 269) Jurie street wa. Thomas Savage to remove his Innemate before the feast of St Jhon Baptist to give securitie for good behavior and dischardge &c.

Bridgende wa: henrie Patston

tollerated christian hemings

tollerated Thomas cater
henrie ffurnishe
Jhon Shenston
Jhon Sloughe either to bring securitie at the next Leete for (   ) Addo or else to remove him before the feaste of S^t michaell
Richard woodward.

February 27 1604 2 Jac.

M{r} Baliue havinge assembled unto him in the courte house at the shire hall the greatest pte of the principall Burgesses and divers of the burgesses assistantes did then signifie what exceedinge chardges did accrue by the necessarie reliefe of the visited psons w{th} the planige and howe all the somes of money w{ch} had beene collected either by waie of taxation gifte or lawe either from companies or private psons was disbursed and that some meanes must presentlie bee made for supplie of their wante, whereuppon they findinge that the companies of masons and tilers carpenters and ioygners, Bakers, Sheremen and Dyers Sadlers and whelewrights had not allowed anie contribution It was ordered that those severall companies shoulde bee required either to giue or lende a certenie some to that charitable use, or otherwise warrants to bee sente according to lawe for the assessinge of the pticuler psons of the said companies. Then did this writer[a] intimate unto M{r} Baliue and the rest that usuallie at the enteraunce of his office the commendable orders made for the more civill and politacke order and governemente of this boroughe were accustomed to bee redd that eache instructed shoulde bee readie to pforme duetie and none throughe ignorance shoulde excuse his neglecte the w{ch} hitherto had beene forborne in regarde there had beene none opportunitie offred of soe convenient an assemblie: uppon w{ch} mocon they were publicklie redd muche commended, but never observed, In readinge whereof some of the Burgesses assistents did note that after the decease of anie of their companie or depture out of the towne, there shoulde bee a newe election made for succession wthin a time limited w{ch} was not accomplished, and therefore they desired that their nomber might bee full filled; And it appearinge that there were two wantinge George Jhonson glover, and Anthonie Paule butcher were assigned in their roomes, whose oathe was respighted untill some fittinge time. After that this writer willed them to remember what great losse the borough had sustenied by a wrongfull detention by the space of manie yeares of the annuall rent of ciij{s} iiij{d} due for the late dispked grounds out of Wedgenocke requestinge that howsoever some in private respecte had beene heretofore remisse, yet nowe they woulde

[a] From the handwriting the writer appears to have been M{r} William Spicer.

have a generall care of the comon welfare whereunto they were in conscience by oathe bounde and hee shewinge unto them a noate signed wth the hande of the Register of the Diocesse of worcester, wherein an absolute composicion was made what distincte rate everie severall grounde shoulde paie they thought meete to continue that wch former recorde woulde wth most ease warrante: But because throughe reason of longe discontinuance the memorie of those tenants and the rather throughe divission of the grounds was worne out it was resolved that M^r holbache one of the auncietest of the principall and Jhon weale one of the eldest of the assistant Burgesses shoulde associate this writer to take survey of the grounds y^t notice had of the p^{r}sent tenants a speadie course might bee resolved for recoverie of a due right. Then this writer acknowledginge himself thankfull to Mr Bailiue and all the rest for a leace to their owne benefitt by increase of rente and his good wthout demaunde of fine they had sealed unto him of the rectorie of Budbrook signified that he did finde by some records that the psonage shoulde bee possessed of more lande and manie other rights and proffitts then nowe it inioyed, wherewith it was his duetie to acquainte them leavinge anie farther pceedinge therein to theire owne discretion, yet insinuatinge that althoughe hee was noe waie contentious yet uppon good grounde to mainteine the right hee woulde not suffer the boroughe to the good estate whereof hee was sworne to indure anie manifest and apparant wronge. And therefore requested that the evidence concerninge the said rectorie remaininge in the comon cheste might be veiwed y^t beinge truelie informed hee might deale as conscience shoulde directe. To the wch they willingelie consented appointinge that uppon the first daie of marche then next followinge by seaven of the clocke in the morninge they woulde be readie to make searche for suche writings as shoulde bee thought requisite. These things thus determined Mr Bailiue informed them that hee had one matter more to move at the request of an honest gentleman their neighbor well knowen to them all M^r combe whose desire was to surrender upp a lease wch hee had of the tithes of muiton feilde ioynetlie wth the tithes of cotton and hardwicke feilds togither wth the privie tithes of St Nicholas and onelie to take a lease of cotton and hardwicke feilds wth the privie tithes not doubtainge but he shoulde obteine that favor to have y{t} lease renewed for the terme of xxj yeares wherein hee had xj yeares to come yf hee soe longe lived. This mocon was somewhat distastefull yet it semed savorie ptlie for affection ptelie for feare the tounge not utteringe what the harte conceaved made the minde muche distracted and the speaches differente, some comendinge the gentleman, some respectinge the profitte of the towne desired forberaunce of grauntinge leases in reversion, some pleaded the power of the gentleman to doe good, some approved his will, all consented to yeld a kindness, but manie doubted of the meanes and manner how. A iust scruple was made that the surrender woulde rather impeache the profitt then augment the estate of the boroughe, for that nowe there was yearlie to bee paide xl{li} for the rent reserved uppon the lease, w{ch} yf hee shoulde yelde upp then shoulde hee have a lease of cotton and hardwick tithes togither w{th} the privie tithes, and paie onelie the rente of xx{tie} marks yearlie, nowe the moitie of muiton tithes whereof M{r} combe was onelie possessed (althoughe uppon the acceptance of the lease hee assured himselfe of the whole coulde not be worthe xl{tie} marks yearlie soe that the rente by this meanes shoulde bee extenuated w{ch} reason and providence coulde not admitt. while muche debate was made and noe conclusion coulde bee had this writer who because hee had noe voyce in graunte thought silence best to beeseeme him yet wishinge an issue in the cause desired libertie to speake fewe words on the matter soe muche controverted. Affirminge that the time was a time of consultation wherein neither favor nor feare ought to bee respected, the place a place of counsel wherein as deliberation was used, soe he hoped secrecie woulde be observed. hee had noe purpose to speake against the gentleman to whome hee wished all aquall kindnes or service of love or duetie; but hee was resolved to speake for the boroughe whereof hee was bounde to have an especiall regarde. And because hee was the instrumente of the first grant pticalerlie interesstd w{th} the whole proceedinge hee iudged it his pte to relate that his memoirie reteaineth therein. After that one Richarde Brooke (a man of whome I make noe farther mention for that manie leafes of this booke are spotted w{th} the infamie of his name and yet doe not conteine all his reproache) had longe iniuriouslie deteined the moietie of the tithes of muiton by force wthout coulor of righte, and the other pte by p'tence of a lease supposte avoydable this writer for the settinge of a peace and increase of profitt privatelie conferred wth M^r combe to bee certified by him whither yf Mr Bailiue and others the Burgesses woulde graunte him a lease of all the tithes of Muiton the moietie whereof they in that yeare had gotten in to their possession, and the other moietie might bee by lawe recovered for the yearlie rente of xl^{tie} marks hee woulde accept of the same and soe ioynctlie take a lease of those tithes whereof hee had a former estate, and these yf soe they woulde tender them for the yearlie rent of xl^{li} hee then wished the writer to feele the disposition of Mr Bailiue and the rest therein, whereof when the writer did certifie him hee shoulde receave his directe answere The then Mr Bailiue beinge a faithfull welwiller, and others moved wth their owne quietnes and better gaine at the instance of this writer sett downe an order in these words insuinge. This is the effect and true meaninge of o^r intente and purpose. In consideracon of the counsell wch Mr Willm Combe hathe heretofore given and hereafter shall giue, and the paines wch hee hathe alreadie taken, and hereafter from time to time and at all times as often as occasion requirethe shall take and imploye to and for the use of this boroughe wee willingelie condiscende to demise unto him all the tithes of miton and coton fields whin the pishe of St Nicholas in Warwicke for the terme of xxj yeares from the feast of the blessed virgin St Marie last paste yf hee soe longe liue for and under the yearlie rente of xltie pounds to bee paide qterlie at foure usuall feasts or wthin fourteene daies after the saide feasts, and for defalte of paicmente wthin the time limited, o^r intente is that the estate and demise shall forthwith determine and surcease. And yf it shall happen that Mr Combe shall depte this life before the ende of eleven yeares next insuinge the date hereof, yet o^r true intente is that his Executors shall holde and inioye the saide tithes for and under the rente above remembred in suche sorte to bee paide for three yeares next and imediatelie insuinge the recited eleven yeares; soe y^t these covenants bee in the saide demise inserted y^t Mr Combe shall from time to time and at all times hereafter save harmeles us and o^r successors from all trobles, suites, expencs, and chardgs (folio 270) wch by reason and meanes of suche demise maie arise. And alsoe shall not assigne nor sett over the saide tithes nor anie pte thereof at anie time unlesse hee demise the same to us or o^r successors. In witnes whereof wee whose names are subscribed doe hereunto giue o^r consent. the xxxth daie of maie 1594. Raphe Townsend bailiue Thomas powell Jhon Greene Roger Hurlebutt, Jhon Townsende, Willm harmer. Willm Spicer, Barnabee Holbache, Thomas Camell Robt West Thomas Lathburie Willm hopkins. This order beeinge brought to London by the writer and delivered to Mr Combe in his chamber at the middle temple, wth thanks to the messinger hee entered into consideration of the cause and takinge into his studie the writer revolved manie bookes and findinge manie cases resolved accordinge to his desire yet doubtfull of the evente requested one weeks libtie for answer wch the messinger willingelie attendinge in duetie to the boroughe, in love to him, after conferance had and counsell receaved wth and from severall Justices of either benches as alsoe diverse srieants at the lawe wth others his freinds, he was determined to imbrace the offer and requestinge the writer to imploye his paines therein hee omitted no covenience for fartheraunce of y^t busines ; wch was wth kinde offer, and like acceptance pformed. Thus havinge delivered a true reporte of the pcedent circumstances and sheawinge the specified order signed under the hands of Mr Bailiue and some others then p^{r}sent hee desired them to remember the motiue wch induced them to grante wch was two folde counsell and paines, both past and future wch included the terme duringe life and therefore consonant wth their former love to yelde estate for terme of life likewise to consider thereafter wch induced his acceptance, wch was simply hope of gaine, whereof hee beeinge made frustrate, it was reputed inconveniente that the boroughe should loose a certenientie of p^{r}sente rente to hasarde the doubtefull losse ; hee utterlie disproved abatemente of rente, as wronge to the boroughe, hee disallowed the increase of rente p^{r}sentlie, as iniurie to the gentleman wished the continuance of his lease duringe his life wch hee did trust shoulde bee kindlie imbraced. After that a mocon was made by one that seeinge Mr Combe was verie familiarlie acquainted wth Mr Wagstaffe who had an estate in the other moietie of muiton tithes, that request shoulde bee made to Mr Combe to procure uppon fittinge consideration the surrender of the estate of y^t moietie from Mr Wagstaffe that beinge possessed of the whole they might more bee inabled to shewe favor to Mr Combe pfessinge this kindnes that duringe his life hee shoulde obteine his desire, wch receaved a generall applause and consente. Then there was speache hadde of a lease to be demised to Willm Shardley of the howse wherein hee nowe dwellethe in northgate streete wherein by reason of his great chardges hee had disbursed for reparacons of the same some favor was requested either for an easie fine or longe terme the first was thought reasonable the other intollerable improvinge anie p^rsident by grauntinge an estate above the terme of xxj yeares to deprive the righte of succeedinge posteritie. whereuppon it was concluded y^t hee should have a lease for xxj yeares for the fine of xx^{tie} marks, a doublinge the auncient rente wch now hee paide.

(folio 272) Eleccon of Burgesses for the Parlement in december Anno xviij^o Regis Jacobi 1620

Sherriffs warraunt   Memorand, that the Tenth of December Anno xviij^o of the Kinge above

Mr Richard Yardley then Baylif receaued a Warraunt from Sr Thomas Temple Knight then highe Sheriefe of the Countie of Warr. for eleccion of twoo Burgesses to be at the Parlement to beginne the xvjth of January then next followinge wch pcept conteyned the wrytt of Comons verbatim directed to the Sherief in forme before Entred

Elleccon   By vertue of wch warraunt uppon the xxvith of december then next following the said Mr Richard Yardley baylief Mr John Townsend Mr Rayfe Townsend Mr John Rigeley Mr Alexander Rogers Mr Edward Saunders, Mr Richard Lee Mr Thomas Shakespere, Mr Alexander dungan. Mr Willm Hopkins, Mr Michaell Harryott and Mr Thomas Chanders xi of the principall Burgesses, and Michael Moore Anthony Pall, Humfrey Jenkes, George Johnson, Thamas cowper, John corpson, Thomas Kempe John Jewce, Robt watts, John collyns Thomas Higgins & George weale the xii assistant Burgesses assembled at the court house at the Sheere hall who beinge there together in their court house had notice of divers ffreeholders & inhabitants assembled together in the yard of the sheer hall, wheruppon it was advised that Mr Baylive & Mr Norton Townclerke should goo downe & know the cause of their assembly & require them to depte At whose coming downe they found there Thomas Holbach, Humfry Kirbie Willm Pall & others to the nomber of thirtie psons & more who being demaundid by Mr Baylive the cause of their assemblye Thomas Holbach and Humfrey Kirbie answered they came to geeve their voyces in the Eleccon of Burgesses for the parlement if they had any Mr Baylive tould them they had noo voyces in that eleccion els they should have bene called and therfore required them to depte but they replyed if wee have any voyces wee choose S^r clement Throckmton & Sr Bartholimew Hales & soe cryed altogether wheruppon Mr Baylive & Mr Norton (folio 273) did againe advise them to bewarde how they indangered themselves by disturbinge the Kinges service and soe Mr Baylive & Mr Norton left them & went up to the company. Shortlye after Sr Bartholmew Hales came into the Councell house & tolde Mr Baylive & the rest that divers of his neighbo^{rs} had complayned unto him that they were denyed to geeve their voyces in the said eleccion & that they were by Mr Norton threatned wth the Starrchamber and then he wished they might receaue satisfaccon & see the charter wherunto it was answered that if they had come wthout tumult to Mr Baylief and desyred to be satisfied they should have binne satisfied Neverthelesse for his satisfaccon he should see the charter, and soe it was presently shewed him and while he was in readinge it the ffreeholders & others cryed out at the doore of the councell house some S^r clement Throckmton some Sr Barth. Hales & some Sr Grevill Verney wherat Sr Barth. Hales seemid to be offendid and blamed them and then tould them he had seen the charter and that he considered the interest of Eleccon was in the Baylive & Burgesses & not in them And after some other speeches concerning his owne sufficencie to be one he was

S{r} Ba: Hales his accusation of M{r} Norton falsified — about to depte but M{r} Norton intreated he would lett M{r} Baylive know who had informed him that the ffreeholders were threatened by M{r} Norton w{th} the Starrchamber he presently named Thomas Holbach and Humfrey Kirbie who being both present were callid & denyed that they heard any such woords from M{r} Norton or any other, And afterwards S{r} Barth. Hales named George Tonge to be his informer but he likewise being exam{d} denyed that he heard any such speeches After S{r} B. Hales depture M{r} Baylive and his bretheren w{th} the assistant Burgesses before named

Eleccon made of S{r} G. Verney M{r} Coke — pceeded to the Eleccon and by the Maior voyce S{r} Grevill Verney & M{r} John Cooke were Elected and then all the hole number assembled consented and agreed to that eleccon and soe the said S{r} Grevill Verney & M{r} Cooke were retorned by Indenture between the Baylive & Burgesses and S{r} Thomas Temple dated the xxvij{th} of december aforesaid and sealed w{th} the comon Seale of the Baylive & Burgesses accordinge to the forme

Retorne by the Sheriefe — of the Indenture before Entred w{ch} retorne made by the Sherief was receaved & the Burgesses admitted in parlement w{thout} opposition or question.

Copy of an Indenture dated 23rd of January, 1623, being an Indenture of the election of Edward Conwey, jun., and Francis Lucy to Parliament. Sir Thomas Puckering was High Sheriff.

Warwicke, Borough — (folio 274) At the Shire hall upon Monday the tenth day of July in the yeare of o{r} Lo{r}d God 1654 by vertue of a warrant from John Danvers Esq. high Sheriffe of the County of Warr. to William Harmar gent. Bailiffe of the Borough of Warwick directed for eleccon of one Burgesse to serue for this Borough at the Parliam{t} to be held at Westm{r} on the 3{rd} day of Septemb. next cominge, Richard Lucy Esq{r} then p{r}sent was with a unanimous voice & consent freely chosen Burgesse for this Borough to serve as aforesaid.

Copy of High Sheriff's warrant commencing "Whereas I have rec'd a writt from Oliver Lord Protector of the Comon wealth of England Scotland & Ireland & the dominions thereto belonging" &c.

Upon the receipt of this precept Mr Harmar Bailiffe caused publique proclamacion to be made by George Wincott Sergeant at Mace in all the severall words of this Borough as followeth

Proclamacon for the election

Whereas Mr Bailiffe of this Burrough hath rec'd a warrant fro. John Danvers Esq high Sheriffe of ye County of Warr. for the eleccon of one fitt & discreet pson to serue as Burgesse for this Burrough at the parliamt to be held at Westm^r upon the third day of September next coming: Theise are therfore to give notice to all Inhabitants of this Burrough that Mr Bailieffe doth intend to proceed to the said eleccon upon Monday next being the Tenth day of this instant July by 9 of the clock in the morning of the same day at the shire hall within this Burrough at wch tyme and place all ye said Inhabitants who are qualified to give votes in the said eleccon are required to make their apparance for the ppse.

Copy Indenture for election dated 10th of July, 1654.

Copy of Indenture dated 12th December, 1654, for the election of Clement Throckmorton in place of Richard Lucy, he having been elected and chosen to serve as Knight of the Shire. Edward Peyto, Esq. was High Sheriff.

(folio 275) Fulke Lucy and Thomas Archer, Esqrs., were elected to parliament on 5th January, 1658. Sir Robert Holt, Bart., High Sheriff.

Clement Throckmorton, jun., elected on 26th August, 1656. Thomas Willoughby, Esq., High Sheriff.

<small>The Originall of Mr Eyfler.</small> (folio 276) Nicholas Ifler[a] borne at Ozenbrigge in the Province of Westphalia in Germany under the obedience of the Duke of Saxony came into England & by letters patents dated 29th Marcii 4th Eliz. was made a free Denizen and placed himselfe at Warwicke & beinge a Glasier by pfession & skilfull in that mistery by his honest labour & endeavo^r attayned to some estate & came to be one of the principall Burgesses of this Borough but dyed soone after to witt on the 14th of January, 1591 34 Eliz. Yet before his <small>He founded a Hos-</small> death out of a charitable intention gaue order for the founding <small>pitall</small> of a hospitall, wch after his decease was substancially erected according to his mind by Robert West & Thomas Camell two of the principall Burgesses of this Borough & the Executors of his last Will & Testam^t upon a garden which he had purchased for that purpose without the East gate on the back hills over against the Vineyard.[b]

They beganne the building of the said Hospitall after the decease of the wife of the said Mr Eyffler, vizt on the last day of June 1597. & finisht it the 28th of October following: The charges of the building amounted to 72^l 5^s 2^d Mr Eyffler willed that there should be 8 poore women placed in the Hospitall whereof 4 should be poore old maydens that had spent their youthfull yeares in honest service & should be past service & past child bearinge: the other foure should be poore old widowes, past child-bearing & of honest life and conversation:

The first 8 poore women were placed in the said Hospitall on St Mathias day 1597 & had every one of them a new frize gowne & xij^d in money given them by the executors at their Entrance.

(a) The portraits of this Warwick worthy and of his wife are in the Court House.
(b) Eyflers almshouses are still on the Back Hills, now called Castle Hill, and are opposite to Vineyard Lane, now called Castle Lane.

And for the maintenance of the Hospitall the said Mr Ifler did by his last will & testamt devise a house in Jewry Street on the South side nere the high crosse in Warwicke And a rent charge of Tenne shillings p. Ann. issuing out of Meakin's close lying beyond the West Street, And a barne & garden at the back hills aforesaid to his exec^ts Robert West & Thomas Camell their heires & assignes to be by them settled on certen ffeoffees for the use aforesaid: who did settle the same accordingly as by their feoffm^t hereafter following may appeare.

Copy of patent of Denizenship to Nicholas Eyfler. Date 29th March, 1562.

(folio 277 to 306) Copies of Eyfler's will, and deeds of feofment: & copies of wills & deeds of other donors of charities.

A° Dni 1681 (folio 306) An Addresse made by the Corporacion to King Charles the Second upon his ma^ties Declaracion concerning the Dissolueing the Parliam^t

To the Kings most excellent ma^tie

The humble Adresse of yor ma^ties truely Loyall and most obedient Subjects the Mayor Ald^rmen & Assistant Burgesses of yor ma^ties auntient Burrough of Warwick in behalfe of themselves and ye rest of ye Inhabitants of ye sayd Burrough,

Humbly Sheweth

That wee are highly sensible of our happinesse as well under yor ma^ties good and gentle government as by yor ma^ties gratious expressions in yor late Declaracon. In yor ma^ties readinesse to satisfie ye Desires of yor good Subjects and to secure them ag^t theire feares, In the p^rservacon of theire Relligion, liberties, and pperties, In yor Maties care to prevent the returne of those miseries wee lately felt in a most unaturall warr and governm^t by a Standing Armey, In yor ma^ties great wisdome iudging Parliam^ts the best method for healeing the distempers of the kingdomes, and the onely meanes to p^rserve the monarchy in its due credit & respects both at home and abroad in your Maties steady resolucon of haueing frequent Parliam^ts and both in and out of them to use yor utmost endeavour to extirpate Popery to redresse all the greivances of yor good Subjects and in all things to governe according to Law: That as with due gratitude wee accnowledg these great blessings soe with all humilitie wee tender the Duty of our Allegiance Loyaltie and best affeccons to your Maties service and are unanimously ready wth our Lives and fortunes to stand by and assist yor ma^tie And hope wee shall approue our Duty in the choyce of such members to serue in Parliam^t (when in yor princely wisdome you see fitt to call one) as will concur with yor Matie in giveing such supplies as may Enable yor ma^tie to secure your owne Dominions and yor Allyes ag^t the power of any that shall oppose yor Maties iust designs praying god to preserue yor Maties sacred pson in a long and psperouse Raigne.

A^o Dni 1682   (folio 307) The like Addresse made to his Matie upon a Treasona^ble paper of Asociacion found in ye Closset of ye Earle of Shaftsbury.

To the King's most excellent Matie The humble Addresse of yor Maties truely Loyall subjects the Mayor Ald^rmen and Assistant Burgesses of yor Maties antient Burrough of Warwick

Haueing seene a papir pduced at the old Bayly in November last and since published by yor Maties comand and considred the termes of an Association therein conteyned: wee conceiue our selues as well as all other yor Maties subjects by our Duty to god and your Sacred Matie to endeavour the vindicacion of our Relligion from ye Scandall and of our loyallty from ye imputacion of the least connivaunce of ye treasonable and seditious matters therein expressed.

Hereupon wee humbly pray your Sacred Maties favour in giueing us leaue to pfesse our iust abhorrancy of w^t wee finde therein destructiue of your Sacred Maties undoubted right Of the knowne Lawes of the Land Of the liberties and properties of your Subjects and wch must indvitably place us under the vtmost Slavery of an Arbitrary power in our fellow Subjects.

Wee cannot butt Declare to your Matie and before ye whole world that nothing lesse than this can be the meaneing of any who as that papir imports shall take vpon them in contradiccion to x^rtienitie it selfe w^thout any and ag^t all authoritie to engage themselues & other Subjects by voluntary oathes to forsneare theire Allegiance; To assume a power of takeing Armes themselues and opposeing all others to destruccion who upon any title (how iust Soever) shall opose them; To subject themselues and force others to receiue a Law from private psons as all Members of Parliam^t are after a Dissolucion And lastly to determine by force of Armes who shall or who shall not succeed to the Crowne of England though legally placed by indubitable right of Inheritance where from our hearts wee pray the God of heaven continue it in all succeeding Generacons.

We are our selues by the Royall Charters of yor Ma^t^es Roy^ll Ancestors A legall Association a Body vnited in Deed name and thing and that Body animated wth a Soul of loyalty and from our Soules pfesse our selues ready with our lives and fortunes as wee are in Duty bound to stand by yor Matie in defence of all yor iust rights the establisshid Lawes the true Relligion of wch as God hath made you here The Defender soe wee beseech him still to p^rserue your Roy^ll pson from all force & treachery by whome soevr designed ag^t you howsoer carryed on by this or any other traitrous & seditious combinacions. In wittnesse whereof wee haue hereunto vnanimously affixed our Comon Seale.

(folio 308) THE VICAR AND THE MAYOR.

The true Coppye of severall Leters sent by Mr Willm Edes Vicar of St Mary to Mr Edward Heath Mayo^r

Sir

I desier you will consider what money hath been kept back from me wch was my Right & I doe by this demand it viz. After ye rate of a hundred a yeare from ye day of Mr Preston Death.^(a)

It. The Easter book & ye full pay since Midsomer for I have had no Curate by my apointment neither shall any preach in my pulpitt that you shall appoint : pick what sense yor malice will permit you out of this & I doe expect to be paid it forthwth

William Edes

this let^r was sent by ye sarjent to Mr Edward Heath Mayo^r upon the 8th day of October 1687

The Mayo^r & Aldermens Leter to Mr Brewitt

Sir

Knowing you to be a person of so great worth & Honor^r Remembring yor kind promis to Assist o^r Corporation freely as alsoe that if Mr Edes should not behave himself civilly towards us we should hope a frend of you Wee are encouraged to Inform you that one Saturday last wee Tendered him his full Mick. quarters stipend according to o^r Charter by o^r Serjents w^h he refused & returned this Answer in writing.

(Here is a copy of the letter of Mr. Edes.)

(a) The Stipend of the Vicar of St. Mary is now paid by Henry VIIIth Trustees.

Wee suppose he intends an immediate Application to yor selfe wee leave it to you to judg of his civil & prudent carrige & dont doubt but you will deale wth me & him According to yor owne justice & wisdom wee take leave wth all due respects as   Sir yor most humble servants

Edward Heath Mayo^r

John Hadley
John Townsend
Aaron Rogers
Stephen Nicholls
Willm Turner
Joseph Blissett
Saml Biddell

a note of Mr Edes demand from ye Corporation dated ye 15 oct^r 87

	£	s.	d.
I doe demand of the Corporation of Warwick being due to me from Mr Prestons death to Lady Day last past	6	10	0
I Demand for a sequestration	0	15	6
I Demand ye Easter book w^h was	7	10	0
I Demand from Lady Day to Midsom^r being behind & unpaid	12	0	0
& I Demand from Midsom^r day to Michaelmas	25	0	0
the whole is	51	15	6

Warwick Octo^r 24th 87

(folio 310)
Worthy Sir

2^d Let^r sent to Mr Prewitt

Since wee Gave you y^t trouble wth o^r last I thought fitt to acquaint you wth what hath happned Mr Willm Edes hath a Brother in Warwick that is a wild Debauched young man & Lately listed into one of ye Troopes of Majo^r Genl Wordens Regem^t now quarterd in Warwick the Saturday after his Broth^r went for London he was at a Barbers shopp in Warwick railing agaynst the Corporacion in Generall & perticulerly against myself as Mayo^r swearing God dam him if he did not kill me Wheresoever he mett me or whenever he saw me & repeated it over severall times by oathes wch thing I was made acquainted with being indisposed & not able to goe abroade & convinced it might be the effect of too much drinke I tooke no manner of notice of it But one Saturday last in the evening he came into the coffee-house in Warwick & not very ful of Drink & a Gentleman was asking how I did hearing I had been ill, he Brooke out into a violent passion against me as Mayor repeating the God-damming himself many times over if he did not kill me when ever he saw me if he were sure to be hanged ye next hour Though I had all ye officers in Towne to assist me These words were spoke by him before p'sons of good worth who made me acquinted of it what Dainger I should be in when I went abroad. one friday last I did complayne to his officer who hath confined him. I wish his Brother o^r Vicar be not an incourager of him in it, for he brought him to my house wth his sword by his side twice the day before he went for London but I was soe ill that I did not see neither of them, nor to my knowledge did ever see him that Threatens me I have the more reason to judg hardly of him because when I sent him the £5 given by Charter & sent him word I had noe money of the Corporations but was a great deale out of pockett he sent me that Leter wch I sent you the coppy of And alltho he Administrd the sacremt ye next day yet he was so out of Charity wth the Corporation that he left them out of his prayers. Sir I have Great Confidence in yor wisdom & Justice that you will not encourage any in such actions, is all at p^rsent begging pardon for this Trouble

from yor most humble servant

Edward Heath Mayo^{r (a)}

(a) During the year of office of Stephen Nicholls, who was elected Mayor in 1687, application was made for a new Charter. Warwick had shared the fate meted out to many other Boroughs by James II., when he was endeavouring to get all Corporations under his thumb, and its Charter had been annulled, and for a time the town seems to have been governed without a Charter. Some Boroughs were refactory, and had soldiers quartered on them. Warwick may have been one of the refactory, and, if so, this would account for the presence of a regiment in 1687. A Corporation minute dated the 15th September, 1689, is as follows:—"That whereas the late King James by his order of Counsell did dissolue the Corporacon of Warwick And whereas since by Proclamacon the King did comand all Corporacons that were dissolved to act and be in the state they were in by the Charter in the yeare 1679 By which the said Corporacon had since acted and proceeded It is ordered and agreed that Mr Prescott and Mr Edward Willes shall be and are hereby desired to draw and obteyne a new Charter under King William and Queen Mary for the said Corporacon the best and speediest way they can for setling the same." The Charter of William and Mary bears date the 18th of March, 1694, and continued in operation until the passing of the Municipal Corporations Act of 1835.

London 3rd Novembr 1687

Sir

a 2nd Lettr from Mr Eads

I am ashamed to hear yr Repeated evidences of yor Malice & unkindness, there needs noe other Circumstances to prove what I hinted at in that letter wch I wrote to you before then yor sending of it to Mr Brewitt & yor begging of his wthdrawing all kindness Towards me & yor backing of that by yor 2nd tho grounded only upon supposition; if you had either the feire of God or ye shame of doing evill you would never have given what you have undr yor hands in wrighting supposing my Brother had as you say when he was Drunk Threatend to stabb you & Mr Jematt. I dare pawne my life for yor he would never have offred any such thing when he was sober, you say in your last Leter that you sent me 5lb & told me you had no more money left wch is false, for you sent me an Aquittance to signe in full of all that was my due, & you could pay my Curatt his full pay, & Mr Jematt his; but doe not mistake, you false, for altho you were pleased to call me boy, & what not yet you will find me more in ye dealings you have wth me it was a very evident token of Malice to leave you out of my prayers when I was to Administr ye sacremt & it was as evident a token that I had combined with my Brother to stab you because I brought anothr along with me to be a witness against us if we had don any such thing nor these unjust complaints will never meet wth ye repect you think they will I have just Ground to make my complaints and should not I Act upon more honest principles than you have hitherto don, I might perhaps bring soe much mischief one ye Corporation, as never was knowen since it was a Corporation: you have don enough to make a stone speak & were I ye Thousand pt soe bad as I have been represented, I would never have my face so much brazened as to contest with you, but since I have honesty & justice one my side I will dye a beggar before I will flinch one jot, it would have been never ye wish, if Mr Prescott had kept his Tongue wth his Teeth & not told my Ld Chancellor I could not read Latin, he is better satisfyed concerning me, & it is probable yor dessigns may prove to my advantage It was never my principle nor my practise to doe ill to any one & you might be as safe in my Company as in yor wifes bosome: my Actions hitherto since I have come to London notwthstanding ye many provocations I have had to the contrary will sufficiently declare that I have been inclinable to make ye best construction of things & to endeavor all maner of ways to gett what was my Right w^thout any prejudice or dishono^r to the Corporation & this I am sure Mr Brewitt will testify. I do & will tell you that I would comply wth you upon any Reasonable Terms that I might liue Comfortably amongst you but if peace & quietness canot be obtained w^thout my parting wth my livelihood I will never purchase it att soe dear a rate; I will say noe more than this you will finde it as much for yor comfort & interest, as it will be for mine, & I am sure if I am uneasie ye Towne in general will not be much att rest. I will endeavo^r to serve any of you to ye utmost of my power & I will submit this for for quietness sake That if you will pay 25^{lb} immediately upon my returne I will give an aquittance in full & things may goe quietly in their usual course: but if you will not doe it the Corporation must not expect that out of complem^t to them I should grind myself. I doe assure you I stand faire to advance myself more by my not Complying then by Complying in this & if you will not (folio 311) believe me you may leave it to the tryall: if you are of that Charitable temper that you p^rtend for let yor rediness to comply w^h me upon such easie Tearmes shew it & by yor soe doing you will manifest you are Xtians & in the meane time I remayne

           Yo^r very much injured &
If you think it worth yor while to write to me I   abused servant
am at Mr Edwd Rainsfords at ye corner shope in   William Edes
Smock Ally neare Spittle feild
 Sir. Tho. you are now out of yor office yet   This to Mr Edward
 I having hitherto had no dealing w^t any   Heath neare y^e
 one else of y^r corporation thought it most   Hospitall in
 convenient to write to you   Warwick

Warwick Nov. 7. 1687

a 3r¹ Leter sent to Mr Brewr

Sir

The repeated provocations we receive from Mr Edes make us repeat the trouble of anoth^r leter to yor selfe for by ye last post he sent a leter to Mr Heath o^r late Mayo^r wherein he doth anew Charge us w^h Malice dishonesty & falsity whereof we have sent you the coppy because wee cannot repeate it in soe bad words as his owne but if we would recriminate we should make him a much worse man than he makes us to be, but we are much more tender of that littell reputation he has than he himself is, though were he never soe civill to us he could not expect more than the wholl proffitts of ye vestry wch wee doe assure you doe not amount to a bear 40^{lbs} a yeare the Easter booke excepted at most improved rent, the rest of o^r revenue Lying in other places but his ffather who hath no more breading than he has given his son did yesterday report in publick that his son had gotten the better of the Corporation & that in a few days they would have a Messenger to fetch them up to London, wee must Confess we take that to be a new way to try a Title to property but we had rather und^{r}goe any test than be further troubled wth his impertinances though o^r greatest trouble is you are hereby exposed to the unwilling sollicitations of

Sir, yor most humble servants

	Stephen Nicholls Mayo^r
Edward Heath	Tho. Stratford
Saml Biddell	Edmund Makepeace
Joseph Blissett	John Townsend
	John Hadley
	Tho. Jibbes
	Aaron Rogers
	Willm Turner

(This matter is not again referred to in the Black Book, so we are in ignorance as to the result of all this correspondence.)

The Submission of Charles Smith of the Borough of Warwick Barber upon his defameing the Corporacion by scandelous words.

I Charles Smith upon the 25th day of November last past did falsly and malitiously charge the Corporacion of Warwick by schandelouse words in saying that the Mayor & Aldermen were a pack of Knaves & Rogues And by speakeing to Mr Deverreux Whadcock one of the said Aldermen who was then and there p'sent and saying to him that he was one of them All which hath been proved by the said Mr Whadcock And William Crow of the said Borough Taylor And I doe believe that I spoke the said words Now I the said Charles Smith Doe hereby acknowledge and declare the said words (soe by me to be spoken) to be false schandalous and Malitious Tending very much to the defamation of the said Corporation of Warwick and Goverm't of the same And am heartily sorry that I did speake the said words And doe humbly begg the Corporation pardon prmissing that I will for the future neither say nor doe any thing that may disparage the said Corporacion or Goverm't thereof or any member of the same. In witness whereof I have hereunto set my hand the 31st day of January in the Third yeare of the reigne of our Soveraign Lady Anne Queen of England &c Annoq Doni 1704

Charles Smith

(folio 312 to 355) Mostly blank: an occasional memorandum.

(folio 356) The names of the Bailiffes of the Borough of Warwick in the Countie of Warr sithens the Charter granntid by King Phillippe and Quene Marye, And the tymes of their offyces

1. Humfrey Heath the first, creatid by the chr began his office wth the date of the patent being the xij^th day of Novembr 1554 being in the second yere of Quene Marye, And did contynewe untill the first daie of Novembr Ao iij^mo marie.[a]
2. John Butler   1555
3. Rycharde ffisher   1556
4. Thomas Oken   1557
5. Richarde Townesend 1558
6. John Whood   1559
7. 8. Richard Oughton entrid that office the first day of Novembr 1560 and contynued in the same but one moneth, ffor the xxix^th daie of the same moneth he departid this Lief and (   )[b] entrid into the same Office & continued untill the first day of Novembr Anno iij^em Eliz.
9. William huddisdon   1561
10. William Edmondes   1562

(a) Although Humphrey Heath is described as the first Bailiff under the Charter of Philip and Mary, Warwick had its Mayors and Bailiffs before that time. In the old minute book referred to on p. 224, there is a report of an address by Mr. Raynsford, Deputy-Recorder of Warwick, to Robert Lord Brook, on his being sworn in as Recorder, which event took place shortly before the death of the latter, in 1642. In his speech the Deputy remarked as follows: "we see at this day greater and lesser corporacions from the metropolisse and chieffe Citty of the Kingdome unto other cityes & townes of lesse noate & quality and amongst others this corporatn is not to be reputed the lesse ancient or ho^ble for it is recorded that in ye time of K: E: ye first that this towne was first a city and y^t one Tho. Payne was ye Maior therof wch is also ye more apparant for y^t Holingstid in his cronick reporteth that there weare 9 Parish Churches in Warwick wch manifesteth that the place was of great extent and very numerouse in people &c." And Mr. J. W. Ryland in his valuable work "Records of Rowington," records a grant of land at Shrewley, in 1483, to the execution of which deed Degor Haynes Bailiff of Warwick was one of the witnesses. The Deed was dated at Warwick, Saturday after the Feast of St. Mark the Evangelist 1 Edw. V. And in the accounts of the Churchwardens of St Nicholas for the 5th year of King Edward VI., a reference is made to "Jhon Ray, baly off the towne of Warwyke."

(b) The Bailiff, whose name should have filled up this blank, was evidently Daniel Haylye, whose dinner account was questioned; as to which see p. 4.

11.	Rycharde Roo	1563
12.	John ffisher	1564
13.	Rycharde Brooke	1565
14.	Richarde ffisher	1566
15.	Symon Yong	1567
16.	William ffrekulton	1568
17.	Thomas Powell	1569
18.	Thomas Burges	1570
19.	Robarte Phillippes	1571
20.	Thomas hankinson otherwise Jenkes	1572
21.	Humfrey Crane	1573
22.	Richarde ffisher	1574
23.	John Rigeley	1575
24.	John Grene	1576
25.	Richarde Townesend	1577
26.	Rycharde ffisher	1578
27.	Richarde Roo	1579

And continued untill the first day of Novembr following and from that first day untill the third day of the same Novembr[a]

(a) For the reason of this see page 380. This is also related more fully in the Book of John Fisher. On the first and three following pages there is an account of his election in the following words: "It is to be remembrid that John ffysher gentleman being on the feast day of S' Michaell tharkangel ellectid Bailief of the borough of Warwik for the yere to come and to begyn at the feast of all saintes than next following, refused to take the same office uppon him for divers resonable causes by him alledged, which notw'stonding the principall Burgesses & their assistants together w'th Richard Roo then bailief, woold not allowe, and therfore restid uppon their first ellection And they all comyng into the Shire Hall (being the place where the balief hathe bene accustomed to take his othe), uppon the feast daye of all saintes as aforesaid. The said John ffysher there showing agayne his resonable causes of let That is to say, his infirmitie of disseas, his Inhabilitie for lack of substance being in great debt, and withall remembring unto the then Balief burgesses & coraltie his duetie being to serve for the towne elswheare at the Parliament being then by prorogacion to begyn w'hin foure dayes after and more than that his other duetie & attendance for the towne

(folio 357)

28.	John ffisher	1580
29.	Thomas Powell	1581
30.	Humfrey Crane	1582
31.	Richarde ffisher	1583
32.	Robarte Sheldon	1584
33.	Roger Hurlebutt	1585
34.	Rychard ffisher	1586
35.	William Woster	1587
36.	John Hyckes	1588
37.	Jhon Townsende	1589
38.	Willm Harmar	1590
39.	Christopher Knight	1591
40.	Willm Spicer	1592
41.	Ralph Townsend	1593
42.	Barnabe Holbache	1594
43.	Robert West	1595

being Steward therof and towne clerk there and so deputie recorder and therby bound to their sruice otherwise, all which things indifferently considered of he took to be sufficient & resonable causes for his discharge, and therfore agayne utterly refusid to take the office of balief uppon him, And yet bicause he woold not seame to break Lawes & good order wherof him self had bene a maker and deviser. submyttid himself to pay such fyne as by former order agreid uppon should be ymposed on those that wilfully woold refuze to take the same office, But all this notwthstanding the former bailief principall burgesses & assistants in no wise woold alter their ellection but restid uppon the said ffisher to tak his othe alledging that for his sufficiency they both knewe & allowed And asfor his duetie & sruice at the parliament yf that should hold yt woold be but for a short tyme. and for that tyme he might apoint one of his bretherne of the principall burgesses to be his deputie. And towching his office of Stewardship or Towneclerk he might either use it or appoint such one to be his deputie therin as should best like him to exercise it for that yere and so to resume it at pleasure. And therfore no cause alledgid, by them was thought reasonable. wheruppon the said John ffisher stood w^t them untill by very earnest perswacion and frendly requests of them all or the most but namely of Richard ffisher his brother the said John ffisher yeldid to their desires w^t condicion that the old balif then present should kepe the same office but one week longer and that the said John might be spared for that tyme wch Mr Roo being bailief fearing further contynuance in that office woold not yeld unto. So as in thend it was agreid that on the thursday after Jo. ffisher should take uppon him that office And so on the said Thursday being the third day Novembr 1580 The said ffisher came into the said Shire Hall and their before the late Balief and principall Burgesses & others present was sworne and so investid into the offyce of baliwik.

	44.	Thomas Camell	1596
	45.	Jhon Ridgeley	1597
	46.	Alexander Rogers	1598
	47.	Thomas Saunders	1599
	48.	Robt Walforde	1600
	49.	Willm Roo	1601
	50.	Thomas Heath als Meeds	1602
	51.	Jhon Townsende	1603
	52.	Willm Harmar	1604
	53.	Rafe Townsende	1605
	54.	Barnabee Holbache	1606
	55.	Edwarde Saunders	1607
	56.	Richarde Lee	1608
	57.	Humfrey Kerbey	1609
	58.	John Rydgeley	1610
	59.	John Weale	1611
(folio 358)	60.	Thomas Shakespeare	1612
	61.	Alexander Dongan	1613
	62.	Alexander Rogers	1614
	63.	William Hopkins	1615
	64.	Michaell Harryott	1616
	65.	Richarde Lee	1617
	66.	Edwarde Saunders	1618
	67.	Thomas Chanders	1619
	68.	Richard Yardeley	1620
	69.	John Townesend	1621
	70.	Thomas Cowper	1622
	71.	Alexander Dongan	1623
	72.	John Corbison	1624
	73.	Thomas Kempe	1625
	74.	Thomas Shaxpere	1626

75.	Thomas Higgines	1627
76.	Wilim Hopkins	1628

and continued in office untill the Eighteenth daye of Aprill and then died

77. Edward Sanders finished the year.

(This is the bottom of the page; the last line is illegible having been cut through.)

(folio 359) The manner howe the Balieffes of the borough of Warr have bene electid.

Even from the begynnyng of thelleccions by vertue of the charter the manner was that the Balif for the tyme being and the Twelve principall Burgesses or the greater nombr of them did goo from the Church on Michilmas day yerely ymediately after nine of the clok to their hall, which for a tyme was a hall in the house nowe the hospitall, wch hall was then callid the Burges hall, and thither followid such psones as were of the second company wch sometymes were in nombr xxiiij^{ty} sometymes xx^{ty} and sometymes fewer, but about xvth yere of Quene Elizabeth reduced to a certen nombr of xij wch were callid Assistants to the Balif & Burgesses. Then the Bailief and principall Burgesses being come into the hall, and the others standing w^{t}out in an other Roome The Balif and principall Burgesses fell to the namyng of twoo psones to stand in ellection to be balif and that was doone in this maner the yongest or last callid principall Burges began & named twoo of the same company, then the second named twoo then the third named twoo and so fourth thorough the whole company of principall Burgesses & balief present one after an other in wch namyng often tymes they varied in their choise for one chose some twoo, an other other twoo or one of the first named & an other, but all of the principall Burgesses. And so when every one had named twoo & their names put in writing they were pused.

and those twoo that had the most voyces were appointid to stand for th[e]llection. Wherunto evry one of them present agreid although they were not the same as they pticulerly had named.

Then the twoo names being agreed uppon the second company or so many as were attending for the purpose, were callid in before the Balif & principall Burgesses, And then the Steward or Townclerk let them understand that according to the charter they were nowe togither to make eleccion of a newe Balief for the yere to come Therefore Mr Balif present & the principall Burgesses had considered of the choise and had resolued uppon twoo names to be given unto them to thend that they present representing the body of the Burrough might & should choose one of those twoo to be balif for the yere to come. Therfore desired them to goo togither and make choise of one of those twoo wch they woold have to be balif and being agreid uppon their choice to present & signifye the name to the said now Balif & his bretherne.

Wheruppon so many of the second company as were psent went togither into an other Rome, & comoned of the matter And when they were agreid came agayne before the balif and principall Burgesses, and most comonly usid thes woords or the like utterid by one of the company (viz) Wee have considered of the twoo men whose names you signified unto us, and wee think them both mete for the place, but for divers consideracions us at this moving, we have thought good to choose such a man & name him, if you like of it and him wee choose to be balif for the yere to come To wch woords most comonly is annswerid you have doon well and wee allowe of yor choise and agree wth you god give him ioy & well to exercise his office. And then all aswell the Bailief & principall Burgesses as the others goo away agayne most comonly to the church and from thence when sruice is doone euery man to his owne house. The man so electid most comonly prepareth himself to take the office uppon him on Alhollouday wch day The olde or present Balif & principall Burgesses or so many of them as be at home & hable, doo first goo to the church & here sruice And soone after ix of the clok the said Balif & principall Burgesses doo goo from the church unto their comon hall w^{ch}

sometyme was the burges hall before remebrid, but since to the court house at the crosse, and sithens into the great hall callid the Shire hall, And thither followe all psones that will come men women childerne boyes wenches of all sortes sexes & state, where the Bailief of old & the principall Burgesses doo sitt doone euery man in degree of antiquytie or auctority. Then the Steward or towneclerk speakith unto the people. I trust youe resolue of yor choise made of the Balif for the yere to come, And then yt is annswerid yea. yea and no cont^rdixion hath bene at any tyme made, Yf the pty electid bee p^rsent & will take thoffice uppon him, Then is offred to the elected Balief one obligacion wherin he becometh bound for such mony and other things as shall come to his hands during his office for the use of the borough and to make due accompt of the same. An obligacion of late usid for the redeliuery of c^rten playte then deliured to his custody & use wch bonds thellectid Balif sealith & deliuerith as his dede. Then is he callid to sweare. And first is tendered unto him the othe of Recognicion for his subiection to the Quenes ma^{ty} & her heires & Lawfull successors wch othe he speakith after the Steward or towneclerk woord by woord, wch he swerith &c after that is red unto him an othe towching the true & due execucion of his office of Balif and first to be a consruato^r of the peace & to mynister true & indifferent Justyce. Then to exercise the office of clerk of the market and lastly for the true annswer of such things as concerne his office & to make a true pfit & iust accompt. After thes othes taken all men or the most say god send you ioye, then the old bailief deliuereth to the newe sworn a white staf as signe of resignacion of his office, and deliuereth unto him the mace. and then taking a cup of wyne drinkith unto him. And so cakes & wyne being puided at the charge of the newe sworne balif are given & cast abrode in token of   and euery man drinkith of the wyne so farre as it will go. And this thing being doone they all come agayne to the church where most comonly they have a s^rmon

for example the election on Michelmas day 1579

John Dyche named	Richard Roo / John ffisher		
John Grene named	Ric Roo / Tho. Powell		
John Rigeley named	Ric Roo / Jo Dyche		
humfrey Crane named	Ric. Roo / Ric. Brookes		
Thomas Jenks named	Richard Roo / John Diche		
Robart Phillips named	Thomas Powell / John Diche		
Thomas Powell named	Richard Roo / Ric Brookes	So the ellection fell on	Richard Roo / Thoms Powell of them
Willm ffrekulton named	Richard Roo / Thoms. Powell		
Richard Brooks named	Ric Roo / Tho. Powell	Robert Sheldon / Oliver Brook / Roger hurlebut / henry Chaplen / John Bykar / Roger Weale / Thoms. chapman / John hickes / Leonard holmes / John Griffin / cristofer Knight	comoners assigne ch & name Ric Roo to be balif for the yere to come.
John ffisher named	Ric. Roo / Tho. Powell		
Richard Roo named	Thomas Jenks / Tho. Powell		
Richard Townesend named	Ric Roo / John ffisher		
Richard ffisher Balif named	Ric Roo / Jo ffisher		

(names of Bailifs continued)

(folio 360)
- 78. Cristopher Ainge — 1629
- 79. George Weale — 1630
- 80. Humphry Kirbye — 1631
- 81. Thomas Warner — 1632
- 82. Abraham Greene — 1633
- 83. John Corpson — 1634

84.	John Ridgeley	1635 [a]
85.	Alexander Dongan	1636
86.	Richard Boothe	1637
87.	Thomas Higgins	1638
88.	Thomas Griffyn	1639
89.	Cristofer Ainge	1640
90.	William Harmar	1641
91.	Richard Lacell	1642
92.	John Yardley	1643
93.	William Ley	1644
94.	Roger Eedes	1645
95.	Edward Raynsford the yonger	1646
96.	George Weale	1647
97.	Abraham Greene	1648
98.	Richard Boothe	1649
99.	Thomas Greene	1650
100.	John Cowper	1651 [b]
101.	Edmund Makepeace	1652
102.	William Harmar	1653

(a) During this Bailiff's year of office, King Charles I. visited Warwick in progress. I take this opportunity of mentioning this royal visit, as so far as I am aware, it has not been noticed in any history of Warwick. The visit is recorded in the old minute book referred to on p. 224. His Majesty came on August 20th, 1636, and was received by the Bailiff, principal burgesses, and assistants, and was presented with a grape cup and cover gilt weighing 65oz. odd, which had been purchased from Mr Thomas Viner, goldsmith of London for £21 7s. 5d. The King stayed at the Castle, and accompanied by the Bailiff and Corporation, attended service in the choir of St Mary's Church. The Corporation also paid in fees to the King's marshalls, ushers, yeomen, and other attendants the sum of £35, which included 10s. for the Jester.

(b) During this Bailiff's year, the great mace, now carried before the Mayor, was purchased at a cost of £40. Mr. W. H St. John Hope in his work on Corporation Insignia states that this mace is of the same pattern as the famous "bauble" of the House of Commons, and by the same maker, Thomas Maundy. It received alterations and additions at the Restoration.

103.	John Yardley	1654

(& continued till 21· May 1655 & then dyed and Abraham Greene supplied the office)

104.	Robert Heath	1655
105.	Robert Warner	1656
106.	Roger Edes	1657
107.	George Harrys	1658
108.	Thomas Stratford	1659

In whose Bailiwick viz 29 May King Charles y⁰ 2ᵈ was restored to his Kingdom.

109.	William Cooke als Cawdrey	1660
110.	Thomas Crane	1661

and continued till towards the end of August when he was ejected by the Commissioners appointed by the Act for regulating of Corporations and Mʳ Thomas Green one of the Senior Burgesses was chosen in his room & served out the residue of that yeare.⁽ᵃ⁾

(a) I find the reason for this expulsion on p. 231 of the old minute book, referred to on p. 224, and it is given in the following words :—

29 Augusti 14 Car. 2. 1662

By vertue of his Maᵗˢ comission under the great Seale of Engl. to James Earle of Northᵗᵒⁿ & divers others directed according to an Act of the present Parliamᵗ begun at Westmʳ 8 May 13 Caroli secundi 1661 Intituled An Act for the well governing & regulating Corporacons, six of the said comʳˢ vizᵗ Sʳ Robᵗ Holt, Sʳ Henry Puckering als Newton, Sʳ Edward Boughton Baronetts, Sʳ William Bromley Knᵗ of the Bath, Sʳ Willm Underhill Knt. & Tho. Temple Esqʳ mett at the great Swan in Warwick (the house of Moses Holloway). Where Tho: Crane, Mercer, then Bailife & the Principall & Assistant Burgesses appearing, the said comʳˢ tendred unto them the Oathes of Allegiance & Supremacy, And yᵉ Oath in the Act appointed vizᵗ

I A.B. doe declare & beleive That it is not lawfull upon any prᵗence whatsoever to take Armes against yᵉ King: And that I doe abhorre yᵗ traiterous position, of taking Armes by his authority agᵗ his person, or agᵗ those that are comissioned by him. So helpe me God. And also required them to subscribe the Declaracon by the said Act also appointed vizᵗ

I A.B. doe declare that I hold that there lies no obligacon upon me or any other person from the Oath comonly called The Solemn League & Covenant. And that the same was in it selfe an unlawfull Oath, and imposed upon the Subjects of this Realme, agᵗ the knowen Lawes & Liberties of the Kingdome. And first putting it to Mʳ Bailife, he refused, & so did Mʳ Robert Heath of the first & Richard Ainge of the 2ⁿᵈ Company: And upon their refusall the Comʳˢ declared their places & offices to be void.

111.	Wm Hind	1662
112.	John Kerby	1663

and continued till the latter end of October 1664 at
which time George Weale entered & tooke his oath of
Mayor the Corporation having then receued their

the 1^r Mayor
Mayors

113. Chre & being incorporated by the name of Mayor
Aldermen & burgesses. Mr Weale continued
(being nominated ye first Mayor)

114.	Edmund Makepeace	1665
115.	Wm Perkes	1666

and dyed the beginning of Dec following in whose
roome Thomas Stratford was electid and served the
residue of that yeare.

116.	Moses Holloway	1667
117.	John Townsend	1668
118.	Thomas Hickes	1669
119.	Edmund Makepeace	1670
120.	Edmund Wilson	1671
121.	John Welton	1672
122.	Wiliiam Hinde	1673
123.	Anthony Lane	1674
124.	John Warner	1675
125.	John Hadley	1676
126.	Edmond Makepeace	1677
127.	George Weale	1678
128.	Tho. Gibbs	1679
129.	Willm Rothwell	1680
130.	Moses Holloway	1681
131.	John Townesend	1682
132.	Aron Rogers	1683
133.	Wm Tarver	1684

134.	Jno. Hadley	1685
135.	Edw. Heath	1686
136.	Stephen Nicholes	1687

(This is the end of the list in the Black Book.)

(Eight pages further on the writer, having turned the book about, has made the following memoranda with regard to the accounts of the Bailiffs)

The note of such matters as I find unanswerid to the towne by any Acompt or matter sewed in writing 1571 viz.

In the Accompts of Walter haley and Thoms Roo sometymes Burgesses of this borough it appeareth That there were five obligacions made & delivered of trust to be kept by the said Burgesses wherin

1. Philippe Sheldon Walter hailie & oliver ffrancis stood bound in — viij^{li}

2. Thomas Oken John Rey & Walter hailie stood bound in — xx^{li}

3. Walter hailye humfrey heath & Thomas Oken stood bound in — xx^{marks}

4. Oliver ffrancis Lewes Smart & Philipp Sheldon stood bound in — xx^{li}

5. Thomas Brooks Thomas Barrett & Thoms Oken stood bound in — xx^{li}

} iiij^{xx} i^{li} vj^s viij^d

In the Accompt of William hill Burgeis

one Elme presed at vj^s viij^d chardgid upon Willm huddisdon } vj^s viij^d

monye delivered in prest to Roger Egeworth for the discharge of the charges of the charter } vj^li xiij^s iiij^d

The remayne of M^r hilles acompte   xv^li vij^s

} xxij^li vij^s

In the accompt of Thomas Eburhall Burges Twoo copes bought of Mr Robart Egeworth } xlvj^s viij^d

In the Accompt of Richerd Townesend burges Twoo vestiments of blewe velvet bought of Willm Tastell for } xvj^s

In thaccompt of Robart Philips & others burgers

The herbage of the pasture callid Combwell behind for three yeres endid at Michilmas in the xiij^th yere of the reigne of o^r souereign Lady quene Elizabeth p ann vj^s viij^d } xx^s paid to Richard ffisher a^o xvij^o Eliz.

The rent chardge going out of the lands somtyme mathewe ffairclifs & nowe Mr Thomas ffishers at xiij^s iiij^d p ann behind for three yeres endid at Michilmas a^o xiij^o Elizabethe } xl^s paid to Ric ffisher a^o xvij^o Eliz

The herbage of one of the Marshes due to be paid by Thoms Staunton at Michilmas anno x Eliz } vj^s viij^d

payment made to the somme of vj^s viij^d for the proxes due by the vikar of the Church of saint Maryes in Warwik at the Parliament holden in the xiij^th yere of quene Elizabeth. wherof no allowance to be given by the borough and therfore surchardgid uppon Jahn Tymes vicar there } vj^s viij^d

} lxxiij^s iiij^d

And at the Buriall of the Lord Marques of Northampton viz the (   ) daie of Decembr 1571 there was an offring by divers psones in the chauncell of the said church of saint Maryes emounting to xxi^s v^{d}, recevid by the said John Tymmes, being due to the bailief and Burgesses of this borough as psons of the same church and therfore the said Tymmes is chargid w^t the said monye by him recevid .xxi^s v^{d}

In thaccompts of divers Burgesses I finde the herbage of Wedgenok park for the part yet unparkid at iij^s iiij^d p ann to be unpaid for xij yeres endid at Michilmas anno xiij^o Regine Elizabeth .xl^s

In the Accompt of John Butler for the office of Bailiwik I find allowance for twoo bookes of Statutes wch bookes are to be callid for or their value xxxj^s

The rent of the wooll hall and shoppes under the same hall chargid uppon Richard Yardley for one yere endid at Michilmas in the third & fourth yere of Philip & Q Marye .xlviij^s

The remayne of thestreates not gathered for the tyme of Mr Butlers baliwik over & besides vij^{li} v^s iij^d paid by him .lxxix^s ix^d

vij^{li} xviij^s ix^d

In thaccompt of Thomas Oken Bailief I find a remayne of his Accompt xxiij^d ob

John Grene for the rent of the woll hall behind not answerid   xl^s

Richerd Towneshend of Warwik one hoggrell delivered to him by Mr Oken

In the Accompt of Richard Townsend I finde the remayne of his Acompt for his bailieswik to be besides all his allowances over & besides three silver spones } xv^{li} xiij^s xj^d

Also I find two somes allowed to him for the corporacion viz for the confirmacion of the corporacion x^{li} x^s viij^d
And for the corporacion besides viij^{li} x^s

In the Accompt of John Whood bailief made by Antony Richmond I find a remayne of estreats not levied amounting unto } liiij^s vj^d

In the Accompt of Willm huddisdon Bailief A remayn of streates not levied } lxxiiij^s v^d

In the hands of M^r huddisdon a remayne of certen household stuff wch sometyme was Willm Lathburyes viz twoo pounds of Russett wooll viij leys of Wikeyarn a litle Brasse pott a platter & a dish of Peawter }

In the handes of M^r hill remaned a mare being a Streave being yerd & dayd and therfore to be answerid to the towne. }

Item I finde the Remayne of a debt due by one ( ) Grene of London for divers yeres viz In the Accompt of humfrey heath xxiiij^s
In the Accompt of John Butler lx^s
In the Acompt of Thomas Oken lx^s
} vij^{li} iiij^s

(On the second page after these memoranda about accounts, and written in the book the right way up is the following list of names)

The names of xxiiij^{ty} comoners[a] chosen for to heare the Accompt of Mr Okens Rents &c the first tyme a yere after his death viz out of the

hiegh pavement	John Grene, Thomas Cawdrey, Roger hurlebutt		
castelstrete	John Nason, John hickes, John Balies		
Jury	henry Chaplin, henry Byrde, Baldwin Benford		
Market place	Robert Sheldon, Oliver Brook, Willm Shawe	The iiij^{or} Coll^{rs}	Robert Sheldon, John Grene, John Balyes, henry chaplin
Saltesford	John Bidwell, John Hopkins, Walter Balies		
West strete	John Reynoldes, Nicolas Smyth, Willm Lane		
Smyth strete	Nycolas Purslo, cristofer Knight, Thomas Allen		
Bridgend	John howe, Thomas howe, John hopkins		

(a) Thomas Oken by his deed of feoffment directed that three of the most honest and substantial of the commoners in each of the eight wards of the town should partake with the Bailiff and twelve principal burgesses of the feast which he ordered to be annually provided, and that they should assist in the distribution of the money which he left to the poor. At the present day the feoffees of Oken's Charity, after paying certain fixed charges, and any necessary repairs to the property, hand over the balance of the income to the twenty-four wardsmen, who distribute it weekly among a certain number of poor people.

xij August 1578 aⁿ xxⁿ Eliz.

The hiegh pavement	Thomas cawdrey
	Willm Loson
	Thomas Grene
The castelstrete	John hickes
	Ric heynes
	Richerd Alee
The Jury	Roger hurlebut
	henry Byrd
	henry chaplyn
The Mket place	Robart Sheldon
	Oliver Brook
	Philipp coo
Saltesford	John hopkins
	Walter Balies
	Richard Whood
West street	William Lane
	Nicolas Smyth
	John Reynoldes
Smith street	Nicolas purslowe
	xpofer Knight
	Thomas Alen
Bridge end	John howe
	Thoms howe
	John hopkins

(This is the last entry in the Black Book: after this there remain 164 pages unused.)

APPENDIX

APPENDIX A

Translation.

To all faithful Christians to whom this present writing may come the Bailiff and Burgesses of the Borough of Warwick in the County of Warwick send greeting. Whereas the most noble Lord Robert Earl of Leicester, Baron of Denbigh Knight of each order of St. George and St. Michael Master of the horse of our lady Elizabeth by the grace of God Queen of England &c and one of her privy council of his good will, charitable intention, and by his own free gift has determined to found and endow with all speed (God willing) a hospice or hospital within the Borough of Warwick aforesaid for the help and maintenance of poor people. Know therefore that we the aforesaid bailiff and burgesses &c by our unanimous assent and consent have given granted enfeoffed and confirmed and by these presents for ourselves and our successors do give grant and confirm unto the aforesaid Lord Robert Earl of Leicester his heirs and assigns for the object use and intent aforesaid all that our house or hall known by the name or names of the Burgers Hall or the Guild Hall in Warwick aforesaid together with our orchard or garden adjoining the same house and all other houses structures buildings and easements whatsoever situate and being below the entrance or outer gate of the same house or hall. And also all that our late Chapel known as the Chapel of St. James situate built and standing above a certain entrance or gate called the West gate of the borough aforesaid with all the appurtenances which aforesaid premises were formerly part of the possessions of the late Guild of the Holy Trinity and St. George in Warwick aforesaid and are now in the tenures or occupations of the aforesaid bailiff and burgesses and one John Fisher and Thomas Jenks or their assigns To have hold and enjoy the aforesaid house or hall orchard garden and chapel aforesaid with all & every the aforesaid buildings edifices and easements whatsoever unto the aforesaid lord Robert Earl of Leycester and his heirs to the use and intent aforesaid for ever holding of the chief Lords of that fee by the services therefor due and of right accustomed. And we the aforesaid Bailiff and Burgesses by these presents will warrant and for ever maintain the aforesaid house hall chapel and other premises to the aforesaid Lord Robert Earl of Leicester and his heirs to the use and intent aforesaid against us and our successors Know moreover that we the Bailiff and Burgesses have nominated ordered constituted and in our place appointed and by these presents nominate order constitute and in our place appoint our esteemed and faithful John Fisher gentleman our true and undisputed attorney giving and granting to our said attorney full and sufficient power right and authority to enter for us and in our name into the aforesaid house or hall orchard garden chapel and other premises or any part thereof and thenceforth to take seisin And after such seisin so taken and had to give over and by these presents to deliver full and peaceful possession and seisin of all and singular the aforesaid premises to the Lord Robert Earl of Leicester or to his Attorney or attornies for this purpose for us and in our name according to the tenor force, form and effect of this present gift or grant holding and ready to hold ratified and confirmed all and everything which our said attorney may do in this behalf. In witness whereof we have to this present writing caused to be affixed our common seal. Given 26th day of December in the 14th year of the reign of the aforesaid Lady Elizabeth by the Grace of God Queen of England France and Ireland defender of the faith &c.

APPENDIX B.

Translation.

To all faithful Christians to whom these present writings may come Ambrose Earl of Warwick Baron Lisle Knight of the most noble order of the garter Master of the ordinance of our Lady the Queen and one of her privy council. And Robert Earl of Leicester Baron Denbigh Knight of both the orders of the garter and St. Michael Master of the horse of the same Lady the Queen and Councillor of the same Lady the Queen send greeting in the Lord. Know that we the aforesaid Earls on account of the good will which we bear towards the commonwealth of the Borough of Warwick in the County of Warwick and of the youth of the same town that education in classical wholesome and doctrinal literature and learning and the better administration of the laws and statutes of this realm of England may be taught within the same borough have given granted and confirmed and by this present writing for ourselves and our heirs do give grant and confirm unto the Bailiff and Burgesses of the said borough of Warwick in the County of Warwick all that building or chapel lately called or known by the name of the chapel of St. Peter within the borough aforesaid established and situate above a certain gate called the East gate of the borough aforesaid and the wall adjoining the same chapel together with some waste ground lying and being between the aforesaid chapel and wall and a tenement now in the tenure of Margaret Haley widow. And all that hall or house lately known by the name of the Steward's Place and now called the Shire Hall in Warwick aforesaid together with the waste and garden to the same house or hall adjoining and belonging. And also all that messuage or tenement called or known by the name of the Cross tavern in Warwick aforesaid with all and singular their walls buildings structures cellars rooms easements and appurtenances whatsoever. To have hold and enjoy the aforesaid chapel wall waste and house or hall aforesaid called the Shire Hall or Steward's Place and the aforesaid waste and garden adjoining together with the messuage or tenement called the Cross tavern cellar room and other the premises with all and singular their appurtenances to the said Bailiff and Burgesses and their successors for the aforesaid use and purpose for ever. So nevertheless that the aforesaid Bailiff and Burgesses and their successors shall allow the Justices of the aforesaid lady the Queen her heirs and successors as well those appointed to keep the peace in the County of Warwick as also the Justices in Eyre and Justices of Assize and other the Justices of the aforesaid lady the Queen her heirs and successors from time to time whenever it may be necessary and appear fitting at their pleasure freely and quietly to enter and assemble in the same Hall or house called the Shire Hall and to hold their sessions as well to be taken at the Assizes as at the gaol delivery of prisoners therein being, as also their own sessions as well for the preservation of the peace as for the good regulation and government of the said county and all other their matters concerning the execution of the laws and statutes of this realm of England according to the tenor of their commission to be arranged and carried out in such and the same manner and form as before these times was in use and custom. Know moreover that we the aforesaid earls have nominated constituted and in our places put and by these presents nominate ordain and in our place put our well-beloved and trusty John Hubond Knight and William Edmondes gentleman our true and lawful Attornies and either of them our true and lawful Attorney giving and granting to our said Attornies and either of them jointly and severally power right and authority to enter jointly or severally for us and in our names into the aforesaid chapel Hall houses and other the premises or any part of them and thereof take seisin. And after seisin so in this manner taken and had to give full and peaceful possession and seisin of all and singular the premises to the aforesaid Bailiff and Burgesses or their Attornies or Attorney on their behalf and for us and in our names jointly or severally by these presents ratifying and confirming and ready to hold ratified and confirmed whatever our said Attornies or either of them does in the premises fully freely and wholly and in such ample manner and form as we ourselves should have done if we had been present. In witness whereof we have to this present writing set our seals this 8th day of April 1576 in the 18th year of the reign of our Lady Elizabeth by the grace of God Queen of England France and Ireland defender of the faith &c.

APPENDIX C.

Translation.

Elizabeth by the grace of God of England France and Ireland Queen Defender of the faith &c to the Bailiff of our town of Warwick greeting We command you that you take Richard brook and James Richerdson if they shall be alive in your bailiwick and them safely keep so that you may have their bodies before our Justices at the Assises at the gaol of our town of Warwick of the prisoners being therein deliberating and commissioned at the next general gaol delivery held in the County of Warwick viz on Friday the 27th day of July to answer us such things as may then be objected against them And have you there this writ Sir James Dyer at Northampton 23rd day of July in the 18th year of our reign

> To the Bailiff of our town of Warwick an attachment against Richard Brooks Tanner and James Richerdson to be before our Justices at the assises on the 27th day of July instant.

448   THE BLACK BOOK OF WARWICK.

CORRECTIONS AND ADDITIONS.

Page 2, line 11, for " defensq " read " defensor."
              for " Archducis " read " Archducu."
              for " Ducuni " read " Ducum."

Page 3, lines 10 and 24, for " pound " read " Toune."

Page 4, line 16, for " Byworth " read " Edgworth."

Page 17, line 25, for " othes " read " other."

Page 30, line 7, for " inst " read " iust."

Pages 92, 93. In the translation of the verses, the translation of the acrostic has been omitted; it is thus: " Thou Elizabeth being married to a man, shalt be a mother."

Page 165, line 11, for " than " read " that."

Page 173, line 7, between " as " and " might " read " one."

Page 192, line 16, for " Okn's " read " Oken's."

Page 206, line 25, for " decased " read " deceased."

Page 209, note a, after " impropriators " read " with liability for the maintenance and repair."

Page 314, note a, before " either lapsed " for " is " read " has."

Page 368, line 21, for " reuereud " read " reuerend."

Page 419, note a, lines 5 and 6, for " refactory " read " refractory."

Page 420, line 14, for " you false " read " yoʳ selfe."

INDEX.

A

	PAGE.
Account of Daniel Haylye, Bailiff, questioned	4
Address to King Charles II.	414, 415
Aglionby, Edward, chosen Burgess to Parliament in 1571	27, 28
,, ,, ,, Recorder	86
Alehouses	103
Appendix	441
Archer, Thomas, chosen Burgess to Parliament	411
Assistant Burgess, Thomas Saunders chosen	379
Assistant Burgesses, appointment of twenty-four	16
,, ,, rebel	56
,, ,, conference as to re-appointment of	105
,, ,, request of	108
,, ,, appointment of	115
Atkinson, Mr., a subtle sophister	333

B

Bailiff, note of election of the first	2
,, a difficulty in electing a	6
,, Burges, Thomas elected	15
,, Crane, Humphrey ,,	102, 381
,, Fisher, John ,, refuses	380

EE

		PAGE.
Bailiff, Fisher, Richard ,, second time		7
,, ,, ,, ,, third time		137
,, ,, ,, ,, fifth time		381
,, Grene, John ,,		206
,, Hylle, William ,,		6
,, Hudson, William ,,		379
,, Hurlebutt, Roger ,,		379, 382
,, Jenks, Thomas ,,		75
,, Philips, Robert ,,		35, 75
,, Powell, Thomas ,,		15
,, Ridgeley, John ,,		206
,, Roo, Richard ,,		4, 380
,, Sheldon, Robert ,,		382
,, Townsend, Richard ,,		128, 379
,, ,, ,, ,, refuses		130, 135
,, Woster, William ,,		382
,, The, rides to London		356
Bailiffs, manner and custom of choosing		428
,, accounts of		435
,, and Mayors, list of		424
Bakers, ordinance for		2
,, Book, The		77
Banbury, letters to the Bailiff of, about Thomas Oken's £40		148
,, the coming of the Bailiff of, to Warwick		153
,, Mr. Bentley of, and John Fisher		159
,, Mr. Knight of, comes to Warwick		159
,, the covenant sealed by the Bailiff of		164
,, the Mayor of, comes to Warwick and tenders the £40		165
Barkley, Lord		33, 52
Beoley		48

INDEX

	PAGE.
Beaumont, William	52
Beverley	49
Blount, Mr.	8
Bond of Edmund Gregory, Town-clerk	401
,, Ralph Hockenhull	361
Book, The Bakers	77
,, The Butchers	19
,, The Drapers and Tailors, 117, an addition to	206
,, The Mercers, Haberdashers, Grocers and Fishmongers	139
,, The Poyntmakers, Glovers and Skynners	66
,, The Walkers and Dyers	71
Boughton, Mr., at Warwick	331
Brooks, Richard, chosen a principal Burgess	7
,, ,, to have a barn and house	17
,, ,, expelled from the Corporation	367
,, ,, final allusion to	406
Bristowe (Bristol)	33
Burges, Thomas, elected Bailiff	15
,, ,, grant of a close at Woodcote to	15
Burghers Hall, grant to the Earl of Leycester of the	62
,, ,, copy of deed of grant of the	63
Burgesses, election of to Parliament	26, 411, 412, 413
Burghley, Lord	86
Budbrook tithes	209
,, Vicarage, presentation to	219
,, Rectory	305
Butchers Book, The	19
Butler, Mr.	55

C

	PAGE.
Catesbye, Sir William	222
Chaddesley, living of presented to Thomas Lawley	5
,, grant to Mr. Hubond of the Vicarage of	44
,, grant of advowson of	85
Chalices, the Corporation sell two	102
Chapel at the West Gate, lease of to John Fisher	5
Chaplen, Henry, chosen a principal burgess	379
Charlecote, Queen Elizabeth at	97
Charles I., visit of	432 note a
Charles II., address to	414, 415
Charter of Philip and Mary, examined	14, 341
,, ,, ,, Counsels opinion on	360
,, application for a new	419, note a
Charnel house at St. Mary's, grant to William Huddisdon of the	16, 18
Crane, Humphrey, refuses to serve as a principal burgess	7
,, ,, chosen principal burgess	75
,, ,, elected Bailiff	102, 181
,, ,, accounts of	220
Crane, Thomas, Bailiff, expelled	433
Combe, Mr. at the Middle Temple	408
Compton, Lord, Queen Elizabeth at the house of	97
Composition between the Dean of St. Mary's and the Vicar of Budbrook	367
Cooke, Mr. John, elected burgess to Parliament	411
Conway, Mr. Edward	411
Corrections and additions	448
Corporation The present Thomas Lawley to the living of Chaddesley	5
,, grant a lease of the dovehouse in the Guild Hall garden to Thomas Sheldon	5

	PAGE.

Corporation grant a lease of the chapel near their Guild Hall to John Fisher ... 5
,, stormy meeting of ... 8
,, suspicious words spoken about ... 130
,, come down to service ... 220
,, charged with misgovernment ... 313
,, submission of Charles Smith to ... 423
Coton and Herdwick, lease of tithes of to John Fisher ... 15, 18
Court leet ... 99, 288
Coventry ... 49
Covenant The solemn league and ... 433 note
Crofts, lease to of a close at Woodcote ... 19
Christmas Eve at St. Mary's in 1573 ... 115
Cristmas Robert ... 36
Crucifix, the Corporation sell a silver and gilt ... 102

D.

Danvers John, High Sheriff ... 411
Drapers Book, The, 117, an addition to ... 206
,, ,, letter from Earl of Warwick ... 208
Delenus Mr. Martin, Vicar preached ... 103
Dovehouse lease of to Thomas Sheldon ... 5
Dudley Lord ... 33
Dudley Thomas, elected Burgess to Parliament ... 85
,, ,, recommended by the Earl of Warwick ... 387, 398
Dyche John, chosen a principal burgess ... 75
Dyers Book, The ... 71
Dyer Mr. James, elected Recorder ... 382
,, ,, death of ... 383

E.

	PAGE.
Eastgate, deed of grant of to the Corporation	224
Election of first Bailiff, note of the	2
,, of Burgesses to Parliament	26, 411, 412, 413
,, proclamation for	412
,, a difficulty about a parliamentary	385
Elizabeth Queen, visit of in 1572	86
,, at Itchington	86
,, at Fordmill Hill received by the Bailiff	86
,, addresses the Recorder	92
,, receives verses	92
,, at the Priory	95
,, at Woodloes	95
,, at Kenilworth	95, 97
,, at Warwick Castle	94, 96
,, at Charlecote	97
,, at Lord Compton's	97
,, Recorders oration to	87
,, visit of in 1575	203
Eyffer Nicholas, a notice of	413
,, ,, patent of denizenship to	414
,, ,, will and deed of feoffment of	414

F.

Frekulton William put in ward for assault	204
,, ,, chosen a principal burgess	7
,, ,, grant of land at Myton to	16, 19

	PAGE.
Fisher John, interview of with the Earl of Leycester	44
,, ,, goes to Greenwich	44
,, ,, reversion of Myton tithes granted to	76
,, ,, elected Burgess to Parliament	27, 28, 85
,, ,, goes to Westminster	28
,, ,, patent of office to	16, 18, 102
,, ,, and John Grene at words	113
,, ,, ,, ,, forgive one another	116
,, ,, and Mr. Bentley of Banbury	159
,, ,, his quarrell with Phillips	199
,, ,, goes to Kenilworth	222
,, ,, sitting at the High cross	265
,, ,, dwelled at the sign of the Swan	312
,, ,, lease of tithes of Coton and Herdwick to	15, 18
,, ,, lease of chapel to	5
,, ,, lease of tithes of St. Mary's to	17
,, ,, surrender of ,, by	42
,, ,, elected Bailiff	380
,, ,, last speeches of	361
Fisher Edward	86
Fisher Richard, elected Bailiff second time	7
,, ,, ,, ,, third time	137
,, ,, ,, ,, fifth time	381
,, ,, bond for payment of money to	18
,, ,, lease of St. Lawrence tithe barn to	19
,, ,, wood sold to	75, 85
Fisher Mr. Thomas of the Priory	29, 100, 138
Fishmongers Book, The	139
Fortescue John	52, 55

G.

	PAGE.
Gaunt Agnes, punishment of	15
Green John, elected Bailiff	206
,, ,, and J. Fisher at words	113
Gregory Edmund, Town-clerk, bond of	401
Greville Sir Fulke	53, 222, 96
Griffin Raffe, the preacher	53
Glovers Book, The	66
Gower John, surrender of the vicarage of Stone by	15
,, ,, lease of vicarage of Stone to	15
George William	36, 53
Grocers Book, The	139

H.

	PAGE.
Haberdashers Book, The	139
Hales Bartholomew, conveyance of land at Snitterfield to	76
Haylye Daniel, account of questioned	4
Heath Humphrey, first Bailiff	2
Hertford the Earl of	33
Hickes John chosen a principal burgess	379, 385
High Cross, proclamation made at the	230
,, ,, J. Fisher sitting at the	265
,, ,, libels left at the	323
High Sheriff, Danvers John	411
,, Holt Sir Robert	412
,, Peyto Edward	412
,, Puckering Sir Thomas	411
,, Temple Sir Thomas	409
,, Willoughby Francis	26

	PAGE.
High Sheriff, Willoughby Thomas	413
,, precept to Henry Compton to elect two burgesses	85
Hockenhill Ralph, bond of	361
Howard of Effingham, Lord	86
Hubond Mr.	34
Hubond Sir John and John Fisher at Kenilworth	222
Huddisdon William, grant of charnel house to	16, 18
Hubond Mr., grant of vicarage of Chaddesley to	44
Hudson William, elected Bailiff, 379, absenteth himself	379
Huntingley Earl of	86
Hurlebutt Roger, elected Bailiff	379
Hylle William, elected Bailiff	6

I.

Itchington, Queen Elizabeth at	86
Interrogatories and depositions in Olney's case	385

J.

Jenks Thomas, chosen a principal burgess	75
,, ,, elected Bailiff	75

K.

Kenilworth, Queen Elizabeth at	95, 97
,, visit of the Queen to, in 1575	203
,, John Fisher goes to	222
,, the Bailiff goes to	270
Knightley Sir Richard	33, 53
Kynyat Mr.	8

L.

	PAGE.
Lane, Mr.	53
Lane, Sir Robert	53
Lawley Thomas, living of Chaddesley presented to	5
Lease of dovehouse to Thomas Sheldon	5
,, chapel to John Fisher	5
,, Vicarage of Stone to John Gower	15
,, of tithes of Coton and Herdwick to John Fisher	15, 18
,, of tithes of St. Mary's to John Fisher	17
,, of charnel house to W. Huddisdon	18
,, of St. Lawrance tithe barn to R. Fisher	19
,, of a close at Woodcote to Crofts	19
,, of a house in High Pavement to Thomas Powell	76
,, of a house in Northgate Street to J. Rey	126
,, of land at Ilmington	367
,, of land at Hatton	367
,, of land at Norton Lindsay	367
,, of churchyard of St. Mary's	399
,, of a shop under the school	399
Lee Sir Henry	33
Leet Court	99, 288
Leigh Mr. at Warwick	331
Leycester The Earl of, proposes to found a Hospital	28
,, ,, visit of, to Warwick	29
,, ,, a yoke of oxen for	30
,, ,, rides through the town	33
,, ,, offended at the Bailiff	33
,, ,, keeps the feast of St. Michael at St. Mary's Church	36
,, ,, views the Burghers Hall	39

	PAGE.
Leycester The Earl of, letter to from the Corporation offering their Hall for a Hospital	41
,, ,, visit of J. Fisher to	45
,, ,, grant of the Burghers Hall to	62
,, ,, copy deed of grant to	63
,, ,, newly dead	398
Leycester Hospital...	8
Libels on the Bailiff	323
Loan, request for a	127
Longbridge, Thomas Staunton of	362
Lucy Sir Thomas, and Oken's Executors	197
,, ,, at Warwick	331

M.

Mace, The great	432 note b
Map by J. Speed	126
Market, The wheat	2
,, The beef	2
,, The butter and cheese	2
,, The barley	2
,, Sessions	103
Mayor, The Vicar and the	417
,, threat by an officer of General Worden's regiment to kill the	418
Mercers Book, The	139
Middle Temple, Mr. Combe's chambers at the	408
Mousehold, Mr.	55
Myton, grant to Frekulton of land at	16, 19
,, tithes, reversion of granted to J. Fisher	76

	PAGE.
Myton Riots The	227
,, ,, Brooks proclaimed a Rebel at the High Cross	230
,, ,, The Bailiff goes to Myton	232
,, ,, Letters to Sir J. Hubond	235
,, ,, The Bailiff threatened	238
,, ,, Sir J. Hubond comes to Warwick	240
,, ,, The Bailiff goes to Kenilworth	270
,, ,, ,, is taken to the buttery	280
,, ,, ,, assembles the constables	288
,, ,, ,, at the barn	289
,, ,, ,, The assault on the barn	294
,, ,, ,, List of the wounded	295

N.

Northampton, Death and burial of the Marquis of	33
Norwich	33

O.

Oath of the principal burgesses	1
Oddel Mr.	55
Oken Thomas, speech by	42
,, ,, burial of	76
,, ,, plate of, delivered	103
,, ,, deeds as to £100 given to Warwick by	128
,, ,, conference regarding the £100 left to Warwick by	128, 314, 320, 338
,, ,, £40 left to Stratford and Banbury by	139, 146
,, ,, a feast at the Great Swan in memory of	166

	PAGE.
Oken Thomas, a note of the good deeds of	167
,, ,, a sketch of the life of	168
,, ,, extracts from the Will of	173
,, ,, last moments of	179
,, ,, proceedings by Executors of	184
,, ,, Executors of, and Sir T. Lucy	197
,, ,, wardsmen of	439
Olney Mr.	55
Ordinance for bakers	2
Oxen, a yoke of for the Earl of Leycester	30
Oxford Earl of	33, 86, 96

P.

Patent to J. Fisher of the offices of Steward, Auditor and Surveyor	16, 18, 102
Pembroke Earl of	52
Peyto Edward, High Sheriff	411
Philips Robart, chosen a principal burgess	15, 75
,, ,, infringes liberty of the borough	17
,, ,, elected Bailiff	35, 75
,, ,, advowson of Russhok granted to	75
Philip and Mary, Charter of	341
Plague, persons visited by the	404
Poor, removal of	401
Powell Thomas, advowson of Stone granted to	76
,, ,, lease of house in High Pavement to	76
,, ,, grant of land at Radford to	16, 19
,, ,, chosen a principal burgess	7
,, ,, elected Bailiff	15
Poyntmakers Book, The	66

	PAGE.
Principal Burgess, put in ward for an assault	204
Principal Burgesses, Oath of the	1
,, ,, displacing of	6
,, ,, election of	7
,, ,, expell Richard Brooks	367
Priory, Queen Elizabeth at the	95
Puckering Sir Thomas, High Sheriff	411
Puckering Serjeant, elected Recorder	384
Punishment of Agnes Gaunt	15
,, of Richard Wilkins	16

Q.

Queen, money taken out of the chest for the fee farm rent due to the	17

R.

Radford	32
,, grant to T. Powell of house and land at	16, 19
Recorder, Sir W. Wigston	14
,, Edward Aglionby chosen	86
,, oration of to Queen Elizabeth	87
,, Queen Elizabeth speaks to the	92
,, Mr. James Dyer elected	382
,, Serjeant Puckering elected	384
Rey John, lease of a house in Northgate Street to	126
Ridgeley John, chosen a principal burgess	76
,, ,, elected Bailiff	206

	PAGE
Roo Richard, elected Bailiff	4
Rowse Mr.	55
Russhok, advowson of granted to R. Philips	75, 85
Rutland Earl of	86

S.

Schoolmasters, complaint of Mr. Thomas Hall as to multiplicity of	399
Seal, The Borough	50
Sermon at St. Mary's	37
,, by Mr. Raffe Griffin	53
,, by Mr. Martin Delenus	103
Shandois Lord	33
Sheldon Thomas, lease of dovehouse to	5
Sheldon of Beoly	48
Sidney Sir Henry	33
Skinners Book, The	66
Snitterfield, conveyance to Bartholomew Hales of land at	76
Snobal Mr.	55
Speed J. map by	126
Spencer Sir John	33
St. Mary, lease to J. Fisher of tithes of	17
,, seats in the Church of	401
St. Nicholas, presentation of Hercules Marrell to the living of	399
St. Lawrence, lease to R. Fisher of tithe barn of	19
Staunton Thomas of Longbridge	362
,, ,, and Richard Fisher	201
Steward, resignation of	98
Stone, surrender of vicarage of by John Gower	15

	PAGE.
Stone, lease of vicarage of to John Gower	15
,, advowson of granted to T. Powell	76, 85
Stratford-on-Avon, visit of the Bailiff of to Warwick about Oken's £40	146
,, the Bailiff of tenders the £40	165
Sussex Earl of	86

T.

Tachebrok	86
Tailors Book, The	117
Temple Sir Thomas, High Sheriff	409
Throkmorton Sir R., came to Warwick	8
,, ,, pricks Richard Fisher to be Bailiff	8
,, Clement	53
,, Job takes the oath of a burgess of Warwick	396
,, Clement, a burgess to Parliament	411, 413
Townsend Richard elected Bailiff	128, 379
,, ,, refuses	130, 135
,, ,, fined	135, 136
Tresham Sir Thomas	222
Turvile Mr. George	270

V.

Vaux Lord	52
Verney Sir Grevill, burgess to Parliament	411
Verses to Queen Elizabeth	92
Vicar of St. Mary's, letter by as to stipend	417, 421
Vox clamantis	325

W.

	PAGE.
Wade Mr.	53
Walkers Book, The	71
Warwick Castle, Queen Elizabeth at	94, 96
,, Earl of, letter to the Bailiff about the election of burgesses	26
,, visit of the Earl of Leycester to	29
,, town and trade of	45
,, seal of the Borough of	50
Watts John	54
Wedgnock	42
Westminster, John Fisher goes to	28
Whateley's money	59, 104, 314, 319, 335
Wife, a promise to help Mr. Whateley to a good	336
,, want of a, to govern the house	6
Wilkins Richard, punishment of	16
Wigston Sir William, Recorder	14, 86
Willington's money	59, 104, 126, 314, 319, 335
Willoughby Francis, High Sheriff	26
Willoughby Thomas, ,,	413
Wood sold to Richard Fisher	75, 85
Woodloes, Queen Elizabeth at	95
Woodcote, grant to Burges of a close at	15
,, lease to Croft of a close at	19
Woolf George	53
Worcester, Bishop of	52
Woster William chosen a principal burgess	382
,, ,, elected Bailiff	382

Y.

Yong Simon, chosen a principal burgess	7

PHOTOGRAPHS.

FACING TITLE PAGE.

Photograph of the Black Book of Warwick.

PHOTOGRAPH 2, FACING PAGE 4.

Facsimile of folio 9a, which contains the protest against the cost of the Bailiff's two dinners.

PHOTOGRAPH 3, FACING PAGE 16.

Facsimile of folio 11b, which records the election of Richard Roo as Bailiff.

The signatures are Willm Edmonds balyffe, Richard ffisher, Richard townsend, Willm hyll, signū Johis Butler, Thome Barret, Johis dyche, Johis Mason, John ffissher, William ffrecvlton, Thomas staunton, John Rydgeley, homfre crane.

www.ingramcontent.com/pod-product-compliance
Ingram Content Group UK Ltd.
Pitfield, Milton Keynes, MK11 3LW, UK
UKHW050910070525
5796UKWH00026B/1141